"FREE ARTIST"

The Story of Anton and Nicholas Rubinstein

Nicholas and Anton Rubinstein in 1868

"FREE ARTIST"

THE STORY OF
ANTON AND NICHOLAS
RUBINSTEIN

BY CATHERINE DRINKER BOWEN

RANDOM HOUSE · NEW YORK

FIRST PRINTING

COPYRIGHT, 1939, BY CATHERINE DRINKER BOWEN

MANUFACTURED IN THE UNITED STATES OF AMERICA
BY THE HADDON CRAFTSMEN, INC.

To

FRANCES WOODWARD CURTIS

Dear Frances,

There comes a point in the making of every book when the writer, intoxicated by sight of the goal, believes he has actually said what he meant to say, and soars off in a half-filled balloon. It is you, severe editor and forgiving friend, who by neat insistent pinprick have so often deflated my balloon and brought me back to earth. Yourself a skilful story-teller, you constrain a writer to say what he means and get on with the job.

You have spent many hours on my manuscripts and when I tried to thank you, you would not listen. So I thank you now in print, where you cannot laugh me into silence.

C. D. B.

October, 1939.

ACKNOWLEDGMENT

To JOSEF HOFMANN, Anton Rubinstein's greatest pupil, the author makes grateful acknowledgment for his careful proofreading and highly spiced marginal comment. Nicolas Slonimsky, whose hawklike, lie-detecting eye brings terror to all writers upon musical subjects, consented to read the manuscript for errors and not only found them but added much interesting information of his own.

To Boris Kamensky in Paris I owe the liveliest accounts of Anton Rubinstein that I found in five countries, and to Alexander Siloti in New York the few really significant facts I was able to glean concerning Nicholas Rubinstein. Josef Lhevinne and Moritz Rosenthal talked to me about their friend Anton Gregorovitch, so did Madame Shimanovsky and Monsieur Stein and many others who knew him when they were young in Petersburg. Mr. Theodore Steinway directed me toward much material concerning Anton's American tour, and put at my disposal William Steinway's diary and the very interesting correspondence between William Steinway and Rubinstein.

I wish also to thank my kind friends in the Staatsbibliothek of Berlin.

In Leningrad, Maximilian Steinberg, Director of the Conservatory that Anton Rubinstein founded, showed cordial interest in explaining the present aims of the school. Monsieur Rukavishnikov, Curator of the Tchaikovsky Museum at Klin, and Monsieur Konchen, Curator of the Nicholas Rubinstein Museum at the Moscow Conservatory consented—at a time when all foreigners were under suspicion of spying or worse—to believe that an American woman was in Russia for no purpose but to write a book about the Rubinstein brothers, and opened the archives for her benefit.

To the late Mr. Müller, the New York iconographer, I owe thanks for the use of his splendid collection of pictures of musicians.

Barbara Von Meck, my collaborator in the writing of *Beloved Friend*, gave this manuscript the benefit of that training in scholarly research that is hers as daughter of a Russian house that knew intimately such historians as Kluchevsky and Platonov.

Dr. Otto E. Albrecht of the University of Pennsylvania rendered valuable assistance in preparing the Bibliography and Catalogue of Compositions. It was he who discovered the original programs of Anton Rubinstein's Historical Concerts.

To Virginia and Benny Dulaski at the American Embassy in Moscow, who showed true hospitality to a homesick stranger, I extend heartfelt thanks. And to Emily, my little Soviet guide, who, knowing neither music nor God, struggled with the translation of musical terms and Biblical quotations, I extend also my greeting—regretting that I could not, under her crusading tutelage, learn to marvel at the Moscow subway stations and the ball-bearing factory one-half so much as I marveled at the musty newspapers and faded hand-writing of a day that is past, at the cobblestones of Old Moscow and the tall malachite vases upon the staircase where Helena Pavlovna once stood to greet her friend, Anton Gregorovitch Rubinstein.

C. D. B.

Contents

1   The Rubinsteins experience complete submersion   3

2   The Rubinsteins use their Christian passports. Villoing
    and the Moscow début   11

3   1840-1842. The post road to Paris. Music under the
    Citizen King   25

4   1842-1844. Grand tournée   36

5   Nicholas Rubinstein. Adieu à Villoing   47

6   Palace interlude. Kaleria's two swans   57

7   1844. Mendelssohn and Siegfried Dehn. Kaleria faces
    disaster   60

8   1846-1848. Farewell Wunderkind. Revolution   70

9   Return to Saint Petersburg, as told by Anton Rubin-
    stein   79

10   Saint Petersburg under Nicholas I   85

11   1848-1850. Rubinstein begins his crusade   92

12   1850-1854. Helena Pavlovna   101

13   Franz Liszt and his princess. Zukunftmusik   113

14   1854-1856. The complete virtuoso   127

15   1856-1857. A new Tsar for Russia. Riviera sun. Young
    Saint-Saëns meets a hero   136

16   London and John Ella. Paradise Lost. Baden and
    the ladies   146

17   1858. The Russian Musical Society is founded   156

18   1862. The Petersburg Conservatory opens its doors   167

19   The opposition   180

20   Nicholas founds the Moscow Musical Society   189

21   Nicholas founds a Conservatory. Moscow's daughters.
    Anton marries a princess   200

ix

22 *1867. Anton Rubinstein resigns from his Conservatory. A little incident in Frankfort* 217

23 *The New World prepares for Anton Rubinstein* 226

24 *1872. The New World receives Anton Rubinstein* 234

25 *1873-1878. The villa at Peterhof. Death of Villoing* 251

26 *1878-1881. Alexander II is murdered. Death of Nicholas Rubinstein* 265

27 *1881-1887. Il Demonio. Artiste je suis. Hermann Wolff and the Historical Recitals* 280

28 *A Holy Procurator intervenes for a baptized Jew. Farewell London* 291

29 *1886-1888. The Conservatory once more. Anton becomes an Excellenz* 301

30 *1888-1889. Anton talks to his pupils about music and is very rude to his Tsar* 311

31 *The Jubilee* 321

32 *Petersburg. Anton as teacher. He leaves the Conservatory forever* 331

33 *1891-1894. Dresden. Rubinstein comes home* 347

34 *Death of Anton Rubinstein* 361

Appendix

   Catalogue of compositions by Anton Rubinstein 375

   Bibliography 391

   Index 403

List of Illustrations

Nicholas and Anton Rubinstein in 1868   Frontispiece

Map of Western Russia and the Jewish Pole   1

Anton Rubinstein at the age of 12   20

Program for Anton Rubinstein's Viennese concert of
January 9, 1842   36

Gregor Románovitch Rubinstein wearing the medal of
his Merchant Guild   52

Nicholas and Anton Rubinstein. From the portrait of
Sokolov   68

The Grand Duchess Helena Pavlovna   108

Franz Liszt as a young man   116

Anton Rubinstein in 1854   132

A letter to William Steinway   238

Alexandre Villoing   260

Nicholas Rubinstein. Photograph taken shortly before his
death   276

Il Demonio, Rubinstein-o   281

Anton Rubinstein in the late 1880's   308

Anton Rubinstein. From the portrait by Repin   324

FINLAND

OLONETZ

Gulf of Finland Kronstadt • St. Petersburg
Oranienbaum •   St. Petersburg
              Peterhof

NOVGOROD

ESTHONIA   ST. PETERSBURG

BALTIC SEA

Gulf of Riga

• Pskov

PSKOV

LIVONIA

YAROSLAV

TVER
• Oshtashkov
              • Tver

GREAT

RUSSIA

MOSCOW

Bogorodsk •

• Moscow

• Podolsk

COURLAND

VITEBSK

KOVNO

SMOLENSK

KALUGA • Kaluga

Niemen R.

VILNA

WEST

KÖNIGSBERG

Kozelsk •

TULA

Danzig

PRUSSIA   SUWALKI

MOGILEV

Bryansk •

OREL

PLOCK   LOMZHA

MINSK

Starodub •

RUSSIA

CHERNIGOV

Vistula R.

WARSAW GRODNO
KALISZ   SIEDICE
LODZ
RADOM   LUBLIN

Dnieper R.

Bug R.

RUSSIA

VOLHYNIA

KURSK

Nizhan •

• Nosovka

KIELCE

Kiev •

• Semipolki

Kharkov •

CARPATHIAN MOUNTAINS

HUNGARY

Berdichev •

KIEV

LITTLE

RUSSIA

KHARKOV

PODOLIA

PULTAVA

PODOLIA

Bug R.

Pultava •

SOUTH

RUMANIA

BESSARABIA

Dniester R.

Kamenka •
• Balka

KHERSON

RUSSIA

Jassy •

Vichvatinetz •

Kishinev • Odessa •

Sea of Azov

TAURIDA

Danube

Sevastopol •

CRIMEA

BLACK
(Chernoi More)

SEA

WESTERN RUSSIA
and the
JEWISH PALE
within shaded areas

▪▪▪▪▪▪▪ Indicates route followed
by the Rubinsteins
from Vichvatinetz to Moscow.

1

The Rubinsteins experience complete submersion

On a blazing July day of 1831, in the Jewish town of Berdichev, Southwest Russia, the priest of Saint Nicholas' Church closed heavy wooden doors against the sun, then hurried up the aisle to look after the baptismal linen. Sixty Jews were coming today to be baptized into the Christian faith—sixty Rubinsteins. Complete submersion, the Orthodox ceremony calls for. The baptismal linen was in a more than doubtful condition; family after family of Jews had been wrapped in it these last four years, since Tsar Nicholas' bitter ukase had come down from Petersburg: *Every Jewish male of twelve years, to the proportion of seven in every hundred of population, to be conscripted for the Imperial Army and to proceed immediately to cantonment school, to remain in the Imperial Army 25 years. . . .*

Even a Christian priest knew the meaning of this. Young boys, fed salted foods and denied water. Boys flogged, dying far from home with the insignia of a soldier on their collars. Children in cantonments weeping for their mothers, falling on the drill ground from fatigue. Only the strongest survived.

During the past year especially, Saint Nicholas' font had been crowded and the priest was under no illusion as to the reasons. On the heels of the army ukase, Tsar Nicholas had revived the Double Tax, compelling all Jews within the Pale to pay double for every tax a Christian paid. Moreover, every solvent Jew was liable for the taxes of his neighbor; those who did not pay were exiled, driven from their homes to wander starving on the plains.

There was one escape and one only: Christian baptism. Immersion in the holy water, repetition of a few magic words, and Israel was permitted to sign its name in the parish register. With that signature, boundaries of the Pale came crashing down. That signature

3

gave a man citizenship and a passport—a reprieve, a chance for life. With a passport, a man could cross the Jewish Pale, boundary between hell and heaven. With a passport a man could enter the university; he could send his sons to school. Moreover, all the professions closed their doors against a Jew: medicine, the law, teaching, even the army. All doors opened wide to the man with a Christian passport.

In the round dome above Saint Nicholas' Church the bell began to toll. The priest crossed himself and placed a fresh quill beside the parish register. No matter what the reason, be it expediency or dogma, sixty souls would today be saved for the Church, sixty *Christoprodavetz*—"those who have sold Christ"—would bow the knee before a Sign they had once held in scorn.

Silently, unobtrusively, sixty Rubinsteins picked their way through the dusty streets of Berdichev, guided by a tolling bell, by a cross that lifted above a round Greek dome. Bearded men in the long Jewish gabardine and round hat, women whose braided woolen wigs were covered with a kerchief. Young men in Russian smocks, clean-shaven, their wives and sisters carrying the children. At their head walked Román Rubinstein, their leader and patriarch who had brought them there. In his rabbinical cap and long gown he was the very picture of Israel, but under his arm was a bundle containing Christian garments; the formal casting-off of Jewish costume was an important part of the ritual they were all about to share.

Old Román's face was grim. It had been no easy task to assemble sixty Rubinsteins for what the Christians liked to call "conversion"; Román had traveled the countryside in his two-wheeled wagon, talking, cajoling, threatening. His own sons had murmured against him —Gregor, Emmanuel, Konstantin, Abraham, who lived across the river Dniester, within the Bessarabian border. Standing sturdily on their own land, Konstantin and Abraham, the farmers, their legs wrapped in birch-bark like any peasant, had declared against conversion as a senseless sacrifice. They would be spat upon by their own people; they would be *Vikresti*—apostates, traitors to the faith.

4

Emmanuel, the eldest, had been more reasonable. Emmanuel was educated; he could speak Latin and German and French and Russian. Emmanuel knew that a Tsar's heavy hand could reach across any border. Bessarabia was no longer free land, it belonged to the Tsar just as Berdichev did. Emmanuel had been reasonable. As for Gregor, father of two fine boys—Jacob and the baby Anton Rubinstein—Gregor had looked at his young wife before he spoke. . . .

Leading his tribe through the narrow streets of Berdichev, Román Rubinstein remembered the way Gregor had looked at his wife Kaleria, the tall German girl from over the border. . . . It was not fitting that a man should look to a woman for decisions, yet this blonde girl had more sense than all the Rubinstein sons put together, and old Román knew it. Kaleria had nodded quickly, her lips firm, her blue eyes blazing with decision, and Gregor, turning to his father, had said the word that would give passports to his sons.

Thank God, Kaleria was back there in the procession, thought Román Rubinstein now, with the Christian bell tolling ominously in his ears. Kaleria was only a woman, but if any Rubinstein endeavored to slip out of the procession, Kaleria would most certainly call him back. The girl was as fearless as she was sensible; an easygoing fellow like Gregor had been lucky to get such a wife.

Slowly, silently, the procession moved forward, avoiding the eyes of onlookers, fearing a word as yet unspoken, *Vikresti!* Traitor. . . . It was a breath, a sigh, a terrible curse. Spoken or unspoken, it was in the mind and heart of every member of the procession, reaching them from nowhere, from everywhere, swooping down through the air, through the walls of houses. Kaleria Rubinstein heard it and held her blonde head high. *Vikresti!* Was it, then, so much worse than those other words the Jews had borne for centuries? At least this word brought its reward, unlike the yellow badge her forefathers had worn, the yellow sign on their doorways that had branded them outcasts, unbelievers.

Baby Anton slept heavy on Kaleria's arm; the boy Jacob, walking beside her, dragged at her hand. Kaleria spoke sharply to Jacob in German, but even as she spoke, her blue eyes were kind. What, she

5

wondered, would her sons become, with their Christian passports in their pockets? Jacob was clever, and as for little Anton, he was a whirlwind of baby vigor and had been since the day he was born two years ago in Vichvatinetz. Kaleria remembered that blustery autumn night when, driving back to the farm after a visit with friends, she had known suddenly that her time was come. She had taken shelter at an inn, and there, on November 28, 1829, Anton Rubinstein was born.

He slept now in his mother's arms, limp and flushed, his blond curls falling over his forehead. The journey north to Berdichev had been long and arduous; the family had crossed the whole length of Podolia in the springless farm cart, some hundred and seventy miles, driving through black dust and white dust. They had crossed two rivers by ferry, and everywhere they had seen the wheat blazing golden under the sun, ripe and ready for the harvest. Down in Vichvatinetz the Rubinsteins' own wheat cried for the sickle; it was a serious matter, leaving the farm for two whole weeks at harvest time. . . .

How hot it was, here in town! Dust blew in stifling gusts through the crooked streets—thick dust, swirling down from Bald Mountain across the roofs of the Carmelite monastery, over the foul waters of the narrow stream called Rotten River. The doors and windows of the crowded houses were wide, letting in the flies, letting out the breath of garlic and the sweated stench of poverty. On each side of the way, stagnant water lay in a ditch; refuse floated on it. Kaleria Rubinstein wrinkled her nose.

Filth and flies and scummy water! Yet these ignorant citizens of Berdichev had the impudence to call their dirty town the Second Jerusalem. All kinds of stories circulated about it. People said an underground city lay beneath Berdichev, many times larger than the town itself. Miles of hidden corridors and halls contained all the treasure of the Jewish nation: bags of precious stones, all the golden sacramental objects that had disappeared from Christian altars throughout the centuries. In a great hall sat the white-bearded sages of Zion, conferring as to the government of the world, and round

6

the hall stood vases containing the blood of ritually murdered Christian infants. No Christian soul could find his way there, and if a Jew betrayed the secret, he would be killed with the Christian and their bodies would be hidden in the underground city.

Kaleria's lip curled. If she had been the sort to believe these tales, she would not now be traveling toward the baptismal font. In Prussian Silesia, where she was born, no such absurdities would be tolerated for a moment. There they had decent houses of brick and stone; windows let in the air.

Kaleria never forgot that she was German-born. Germans were educated; their domestic life possessed order and discipline; above all, they were clean. Kaleria spoke French and German well; she knew music and could play the piano. She came from the mountain districts of Silesia, between Poland and Bohemia; Clara (Kaleria is the Russian form) Levenstein, although a Prussian subject, was born far enough south to be more Slav than Teuton. Her features were decidedly Jewish-Slavic; only her education and bearing, the discipline of her character, showed her Western origin.

The Balkan borders have always been easily crossed, tides of migration flowing back and forth according to the changing political situation—which meant, as far as Jews were concerned, according to the disposition of whatever ruler occupied the Russian throne. Román Rubinstein had endured the caprice of four such rulers. He had been a man grown when Catherine the Great established the Jewish Pale, herding all Jews into the southwest corner of Russia; he had received with indifference the news of the murder of Catherine's son, Tsar Paul. Román had seen the soldiers of Catherine's grandson, Alexander I, enter Bessarabia with fire and sword; he had heard the crows call above the frozen corpses of Napoleon's legions and he had heard bells ring from every tower for the coronation of Nicholas I.

Kaleria Rubinstein, walking in slow procession behind Grandfather Román through the streets of Berdichev, had experienced none of these sights or sounds except the coronation bells. Born in 1803, she was, on this July day of the baptism, a young woman of

7

twenty-eight whose political bias was wholly practical, dictated by expediency. What was good for the family was good for Kaleria. She remembered Grandfather Román's words on that day he had visited them on the farm. "My family," he had said, "you are the descendants of centuries of Jews. The Tsar has issued a most unjust edict. It will exterminate us all. Take the advice of the head of your family. A live Christian is better than a dead Jew. A little holy water is an ordeal, but better a little holy water than death."

A live Christian is better than a dead Jew. . . . Kaleria looked down at the sleeping babe in her arms. The church was near, the bell very loud. Around her in the narrow streets people chattered in a dozen tongues—Ukrainian, Polish, Roumanian, gypsy dialects and above all, Yiddish. Suddenly a word was spoken, screamed, taken up by voice after voice: *Vikresti!*

Traitor, traitor to the faith! So the town knew, already. Word had been chalked up on some wall or doorway; Jews, reading it, had run to tell their neighbors. *Vikresti!* Kaleria did not turn her head but the child Anton woke in her arms and struggled to be put on his feet. Kaleria set him down and he trotted by her side, his face upturned to the sound of the church bells, his eyes wide with delight.

So the church bell could drown a curse. . . . Kaleria searched the walls for writing and saw instead above the doorways a sign she knew well, a small plate under which were inscribed the Ten Commandments of Moses. One touched that sign on entering every Jewish threshold, then kissed one's fingers, signifying, "I know and remember."

Kaleria's blue eyes narrowed. Blessing and curse alike pursued her on these streets. In a moment she would be in church with her family, accomplishing that for which they had come to town.

How dark the church was and how cool, after the blazing noon outside! Feet shuffled on the grimy floor: sixty Rubinsteins moving, young and old, toward the Cross. Uneasily the young men turned from one another, their serious, pale faces looking toward their leader, the patriarch, old Román, who had brought them there. Darkness, candle-light and the heavy breath of incense. . . . Candle-

8

light was not strange to these young men; candle-light and incense welcomed one also over the threshold of a synagogue. But that Sign above the altar—that was strange and more than strange. What had their forefathers not suffered under that Sign! And now they were about to embrace it, to kiss it with their lips.

Kaleria Rubinstein saw the young men falter, saw the women hang back, their faces drawn, tears wet upon their cheeks. Fools! Could they not see what it would mean to them when that priest had made the sign in holy oil on their baby's foreheads? Above the church the bell was tolling once more—a huge, strange sound. *Ad fugandos demones* . . . Emmanuel Rubinstein had told her the Christians inscribed those words upon their church bells. It was certainly a terrible sound, heard thus from within the church. No wonder devils fled from it! Small Anton tugged at his mother's skirts; this time he was not smiling.

Kaleria, looking down at her baby, shook her head. What was a Christian bell to scare a boy, compared to the terror that nightly had visited her and every Jewish mother these four years since the army ukase had been published? And if you tried to hide your boy, as Cousin Leah had done last winter, the *khapper* came and stole him from under your very roof. *Khappers*—not Christians at all, but men of one's own race and religion, Jewish agents, forced by the government to spy upon their own people in order to fill the town's conscription quota. . . .

Now God be thanked for Grandfather Román who had had the sense to get the family here to church! What would all the wisdom of the Talmud, all the sacred relics of the Ark, benefit sixty Rubinsteins dying in a ditch? God of the Jews—Jahveh, Jehovah—or God of the Christians who carried his cross on his back—what did it matter which God one worshiped? To live was the thing. And surely, one could live justly, even as a Christian! *"What doth the Lord require of thee, but to do justly, to love mercy, and to walk humbly with thy God?"* So had the prophet Micah taught Kaleria's fathers in the tents of Israel, and so Kaleria had taught her sons in the reed-thatched hut of her Bessarabian farm, the stately sentences

9

falling from her lips in cadence as slow, as rhythmic as the snow that sifted against the window. For baby Anton these had not been words but music, engraved upon his consciousness forever, as this bell of Saint Nicholas' Church was to be engraved upon it. . . .

Clinging to his mother's hand, the boy lifted his small face now to catch the vibrations of a bell that rang and rang, shouting through this dark place like something alive. . . . His mother picked him up and moved with him across the floor. Over to the left of the iconostas, Kaleria Rubinstein saw the priest hold up a dingy sheet. After immersion would come the ritual of the dressing, the discarding of Jewish wig and shawl. After that again, one signed the census book in the priest's presence. . . .

Taking up the pen, Kaleria Rubinstein wrote her name under her husband's and under that again, the names of her sons: Jacob Gregorovitch—*Anton Gregorovitch* . . .

Let the bell toll and the neighbors curse in the streets if they dared! Her boys were Christians now; they were citizens of Russia. They could dare anything, be anything. Henceforth their ambition would be limited only by their capacity, by their talents. And she, Kaleria Rubinstein, would see that these talents were trained, directed; she would not relax her vigilance. Let this Christian God be witness, she would teach German discipline to her sons! She would see to it also that the boys grew up in an environment worthy of their new status. Of what use these passports if they were all to remain in a reed-thatched Bessarabian hut, shoveling snow and tending cattle?

Kaleria bowed to the priest and with a son's hand in each of hers, turned to go. She crossed the church with a light step, her head high. At the door a blaze of sunlight met her.

2

*The Rubinsteins use their Christian passports. Villoing
and the Moscow début*

On the summit of the Sparrow Hills, the Rubinstein family sat in
their wooden wagon and watched the sun go down over Moscow.

Three years had passed since the baptism at Berdichev, years during which Kaleria Rubinstein—busy with the endless duties of a
farm woman, with the birth of a daughter and the care of two
growing boys—did not cease to remind her good-natured, easy-going
husband of the fact that he had a Christian passport in his pocket.
Was pretty Luba to grow up to marry a Bessarabian gypsy? Were
Anton and Jacob to be reared in this village of Vichvatinetz, ignorant as cattle, wild as the young deer that ran beyond the thorny
fences of their orchard? Had Gregor Románovitch married an educated wife in order to pen her up in a farmhouse with no neighbors
to talk to, and above all, no piano to play upon? Kaleria was an
excellent musician; she longed to teach music to her boys.

Her complaints were skilful and well-timed. Gregor Rubinstein,
born and reared as a town boy in Berdichev, was not a farmer by
nature; his father had bought this property and placed his sons upon
it. Year by year calamity seemed to visit them; in 1831 and '32 it
was locusts and in 1833 Gregor, always vague about the handling
of finance, wound himself up in a lawsuit that finally cost him most
of the farm. His land was gone, but not, his wife reminded him, his
money. For what purpose had she saved every rouble, every kopeck,
if not for this very emergency? They had enough to get them away
from here; they had enough, if the brothers pooled their resources,
to take them to Moscow and set up in some modest business. Had
not Gregor always wanted to be a manufacturer, Kaleria reminded
him tactfully, with a medal on his breast?

She persisted, and by dint of her persistence, early autumn of 1834 found the Rubinstein family—brothers, wives, children, servants, horses and baggage—on the summit of the Sparrow Hills, looking down upon Moscow. The shaggy Cossack horses hung their heads; the wooden wagon was caked with dirt; on the canvas cover dust lay deep. They had traveled eight hundred miles in the crowded cattle tracks, braving marsh fevers, bad water, dust storms, thievery and assault in the forests. Small Anton was nearly five. The long journey lay behind him like a dream, a never-ending confusion of strange new sights and sounds. He had heard the cataracts roar in Podolian ravines, had seen at night the campfires of the cattle-herders dotting the blackness of the sky above the great Southern plain. By day he had heard the strange, foreign shouts of Tartar cattlemen, driving their long-horned oxen northward to the markets of Moscow, had seen the dust rise beneath the feet of thousands upon thousands of driven sheep that jostled each other on the wide uncharted roads.

He had seen the Scythian tumuli ranged beneath Kiovian cliffs and had watched the little earth-hares scuttle before the sound of the approaching caravan. He had crossed great rivers and watched the water swirl about the ferry. Once, looking back across the widest of these waters, he had seen above high cliffs the pigeons circle around golden domes. Bells had flung their liquid voices across the river, their deep notes had followed the caravan beyond the last turning of the forest road. Kaleria Rubinstein had looked back. "Farewell, Mother Kiev," she had said.

Long after their vibrations ceased, the deep bell-notes beat in Anton's ears . . . All his life bells would sound for him, the deep-toned bells that every Russian loves and that every Russian musician from Glinka to Rachmaninov has reproduced in his music. A sound so traditional, so deeply significant that a future century, desiring to change the face of old Russia, would recognize the bells as dangerous and would mute their tongues in every tower.

Eight hundred miles of strange sights and stranger sounds, for it was the sounds that Anton Rubinstein's sensitive ears retained.

Wind in the trees of the great high forests of Chernigov, gloom of the forest trackway where far overhead the roof arched, dimly reminiscent of a vaulted place where bells had rung and a priest had touched one's forehead with cold fingers. . . . How loud in the forest stillness seemed the breathing of the horses, the creak of wagon wheels! At night when they camped in the forest, Anton kept very close to his father. Did not the one-eyed wood-demon lurk behind every white birch that glimmered in the moonlight, ready to pounce upon a child who strayed from its caravan? *Maman* said there were no wood-demons, but Ivan, the driver, knew better. . . .

And then the forest opening out, the long road once more, the caravans of other travelers, with the *yamshiks* cracking their whips, singing lusty endless songs or urging their weary horses. *"Poshla!* Go on! Climb up, my sweet pigeons! Run, my Cossack darlings! Go along, my angels. *Po-oshla-ah!"* Songs of the *yamshiks*, songs of the soldiers marching toward Moscow in their gray caps and suits. Sad songs, these last; *Maman* had clasped Anton suddenly in her arms and had said something he did not understand about children who were beaten to make soldiers of them. . . . The soldiers' songs had seemed as gray as their coats; their voices, saying the same phrase over and over, followed Anton all the way to Moscow. Once they had passed what looked like a small army, but it was not an army. Men and women chained together walked very slowly, not singing at all. Their chains dragged in the dust with quite a merry sound, but *Maman's* eyes, watching them, had not been merry. She had leaned out from the wagon and given bread and an apple to one of the women, and the woman had blessed her. A dusty Cossack had ridden up from behind the lines, a long pike resting in his stirrup, a heavy whip dangling from his wrist and had grinned at *Maman*, requesting an apple for himself. *Maman* had given him one, not very ripe, and afterward Father had said something sharp to her about Siberia where it snowed even harder than it did in Vichvatinetz. . . .

13

They had eaten rusks and wild honey and chicken roasted in the campfire at night. They had tasted plum-paste at Kaluga and lovely cookies all sweet with fruit, and they had ridden out of a town called Niezhin sucking each a sweet pickle from a wooden barrel *Maman* had bought from a peasant. And then, after a long time, after days of jogging and sleeping and waking and jogging again, the rooks had appeared, calling hoarsely across the treetops from their big brown nests. To Anton the sky seemed suddenly made of rooks, great gray-brown birds that cried and quarreled above the villages. Father, squinting up at them, said these were Moscow rooks and their journey was nearly ended.

It was sunset when the Rubinsteins reached the Sparrow Hills, a slow, easy climb. The summit gained, Kaleria drew long breaths and laid her hand on her husband's arm. Below her she saw the River Moskva and beyond it the Kremlin with its tessellated walls, the tower of Ivan Veliki where the great bells hung. A sinking sun struck fire from a hundred golden domes, spilling down along the chains that looped from spire to spire. East and west, the city was flanked with great fortress-like monasteries: Simonovski, with cannon mounted grimly at the corners, Donskoi, its ancient walls painted in broad streaks of red and white. Spires everywhere, and everywhere, bells ringing. It was September and already the fruit had been blessed, already—Kaleria remembered—the heretics had been cursed in the autumnal ceremony.

Let priests swing their censers and cry *anathema*! The curse could not reach Kaleria's sons, since that priest at Berdichev had put a sign upon their foreheads. . . . Down there among the myriad roofs of red and green lay the roof that was to shelter all the Rubinsteins. Gregor had already arranged their home. Kaleria was too tired to ask which was the Tsar's palace and which the house that Gregor had rented from Madame Pozniakov. Sitting in the wooden wagon with her baptized heretics, Kaleria Rubinstein had won her journey's end. She might well have murmured, paraphrasing the words of a famous convert of earlier days who had sacrificed a faith to gain a city: *Moscou vaut bien une messe!*

That winter of 1834-35 the three families Rubinstein lived together in a big house beyond the River Yaooza and were fairly free of money worries. But Gregor Románovitch remembered his wife's words about the medal he would one day wear around his neck. Working thus with his brothers was comfortable but it was not the way toward medals. Gregor decided to take his share from the Vichvatinetz stocking and set himself up as a manufacturer. Was not the government giving its august protection to new manufacturies every day? Did not every factory owner become a general sooner or later? It all looked very rosy.

Independently of his brothers, Gregor acquired machinery to make pins and pencils, and set up his machines in a brick building near the street called Grand Ordinka, in the Merchants' Quarter of town. Kaleria moved her two boys, Jacob and Anton, and her pretty blonde daughter Luba into comfortable rooms above the factory. Here in June, 1835, another pair of blue Rubinstein eyes opened upon the world. Nicholas was born, and it is significant that the first breath he drew was Moscow air—this true son of the town who was to be nurtured all his life by Mother Moscow.

For a while all went well and the factory flourished. Like all Russian manufacturers, Gregor Rubinstein prudently engaged a German foreman. This one, named Frey, extracted a maximum of labor from the seventy slipshod, illiterate factory hands, searched them every night when they left the place, finding everything in their blouses from pencil caps to bits of iron from the machinery. When they came to work drunk, Frey sent them to the nearest police station to be flogged; when they fell asleep at their posts, the German hand was prompt and heavy.

Gregor Rubinstein had a good time in Moscow. He was an attractive man, pleasant to look upon and extremely friendly; he and Kaleria soon had more visitors than they knew what to do with. Twenty to thirty sat down every Sunday at their table—small merchants, doctors, school teachers, respectable citizens of the new middle class that was just beginning to exist in Russia. The Rubinsteins lived in the Merchants' Quarter, but neither by inclination nor upbringing did they belong to the old-fashioned, intensely conservative merchant class which lived there in the ancient style—bearded, caftaned, guarding their women in Eastern seclusion. Compared with these, Gregor, in his frock coat and felt hat, looked like a foreigner. But he was no foreigner: Gregor Románovitch was Russian to the core; he had a Russian's love of card-playing and he drank cold *kvas* by the glassful like the oldest Moscow inhabitant. How the haughty Petersburgers loved to sneer at the Moscow *kvas* drinkers! *Kvas* belonged to Moscow as the Kremlin belonged to it and the Chinese Wall and the blue-sashed merchants sucking raw cucumbers in the bazaars on a summer's day.

Like the rest of Moscow, the Rubinsteins ate their Sunday dinner at five in the afternoon. Afterward Gregor had the factory horse harnessed to the small, springless carriage and took his handsome wife and four or five young people—his sons included—to the Big Theatre to hear the opera. Kaleria enjoyed all this; she was a brisk and cheerful hostess. But what chiefly occupied her was the education of her sons. Not in vain had she made that vow in the church at Berdichev. Kaleria did not send her boys to school in Moscow; she taught them herself and she did not spare the rod. Jacob, two years Anton's senior, was a clever, mischievous boy. Late one Sunday afternoon he committed some prank for which his mother promised him a whipping and then, busy with her guests, forgot it. That evening the family went to theatre and it was late when they got home to bed. Jacob smiled in secret glee over the forgotten punishment. At one in the morning, Kaleria Rubinstein woke and remembered. "One's word must be kept"—something Kaleria repeated very often to her sons. She rose, woke Jacob, thrashed him, kissed him, and the household slumbered once more while outside, stars looked down on a snowy courtyard and the watchman's stick, dragging behind him on the icy street, woke the dogs to barking.

In the long living room above the pencil factory the furniture was meager, but it contained one luxury that always moved with the family no matter what else was left behind—Kaleria's big square piano. No sooner were the Rubinsteins settled in Moscow than Kaleria began to teach Jacob to play. Jacob was a quick pupil but a slippery one; when his lesson was over he was gone instantly from the room and Kaleria, sitting alone, would play on. Soon she would hear a little sound behind her and know that curly-headed Tonia was standing there, his blue eyes fixed on her hands. "I watched my mother play at the piano, and I loved it." So wrote Anton Rubinstein when he had become famous.

Kaleria did not begin to teach Anton to play just yet; there had been nothing to indicate that he was in any way remarkable. True, he sang all day to himself, running about the house and yard in his belted white blouse, and his songs had tune and rhythm. One afternoon, hearing strange high scraping sounds, Kaleria ran into the music room and found the boy, his small face very serious, trying to play on a fiddle he had improvised from wood and elastic.

"So you want to make music, Tonia?" said Kaleria Rubinstein, and led her son to the piano.

Anton was five years old. All summer Kaleria taught him, tying him to the chair when she was too busy to sit in the room, placing on the scrolled music rack Czerny, Clementi, Hummel, Herz, Diabelli, Moscheles, Kalkbrenner. When his sixth birthday came in November, Anton had tasted them all and had composed a song of his own called *Meine Laura*. For two years Kaleria continued to teach him but as she afterward confessed, with no slightest notion of the dazzling career that lay ahead. She taught music to Anton as she taught it to Jacob, because she loved music. She was serious about it, but then so was she serious when she taught the boys German and French. She slapped their faces pink when they were stupid, which was not often; she hit their knuckles hard with the ferule when they stumbled over Clementi, while in the next room baby Nicholas lay and sucked his bottle to the rhythm of the scales and arpeggios he was himself to undertake in a year or two. . . .

And if Tonia composed a song when he was six, if he could play

17

Clementi's Sonatinas before he was seven, well—Kaleria Rubinstein expected things of her children! When they did badly they were punished, when they did well they had only done what was expected.

And then, when Anton was eight, appeared Alexandre Villoing, gray-eyed, sharp of tongue, sharper still of ear—the best music teacher in Moscow. Villoing had achieved local fame as the teacher of little Barbara Grünberg who at ten years of age had already astonished Moscow with her playing. A friend of Gregor Rubinstein's, one Rosenberg, a medical student at the University, was uncle to this prodigy. One Sunday, hearing Anton working away at the square piano, Rosenberg announced that he would bring his niece's teacher to the house. Kaleria shrugged her shoulders. She could not pay such a teacher. She had heard that Villoing was arbitrary about choosing his pupils and, like all Frenchmen, as quick-tempered as he was polite. Tonia was not headed for the concert stage, like little Barbara Grünberg. Why then should they all be exposed to this Villoing?

Villoing arrived in his neat gray suit, made his French bow, heard Anton play a Cramer *Etude* and, leaping from his chair, overwhelmed Kaleria with a torrent of French in which, excited though she was, Kaleria recognized an unmistakable Moscow accent. He wanted no money, said Alexandre Villoing. Not a kopeck, not a sou! In short, after the fashion of genuine teachers since the beginning of music, what Villoing desired was a chance to teach real talent.

Kaleria was very happy, especially when Villoing, after a long talk, agreed to let her supervise the boy's practice and to work along as supplementary coach. Almost daily now, Anton had his lesson with Villoing on Kaleria's square piano; during Villoing's occasional absences, Kaleria took over the lesson herself. Villoing was not a Frenchman-born, but the son of a Frenchman. His father had fled Paris during the Revolution of 1789 and had become cook in Moscow for Count Chernishev—an excellent and lucrative position. Alexandre, born in Moscow in 1804, was apprenticed at the age of twelve to a pharmacist at the Galitzin Hospital, but the boy hated it, and when he was seventeen, left the pharmacy to study music under Franz Goebel who had been a pupil of Abbé Vogler and Albrechtsberger in Vienna. For two years Villoing lived with Count Palen as musical instructor to his children; then he became an independent teacher around Moscow, keeping himself alive by showing young ladies how to play parlor waltzes.

Villoing was thirty-three when he met Anton Rubinstein. He was a thorough Russian; only his manners and his quick, lively wit betrayed the Frenchman in him. When teaching he played very little, preferring to instruct his pupils by pantomime or by that pungent, vivid metaphor heaven has bestowed on gifted music teachers. He was very strict with Anton but did not force him technically; rather, he took care to foster the boy's passion for music, meanwhile watching hand and tone that his pupil might not fall into bad habits.

As the boy grew old enough to find his way about Moscow alone, he visited Villoing's studio for his lessons. Here against the wall hung the fine Italian instruments that Villoing loved: violins and 'cellos picked up from musicians who had strayed into Russia and needed money to go home. Villoing himself played the violin quite well; on the piano his technique was excellent although he had a bad piano hand. Often young Anton found him tuning the piano. Like all first-rate musicians of his time and before it, Villoing was a clever craftsman. Had not Sebastian Bach, called in to supper by Magdalena, paused sometimes to replace a broken quill in his harpsichord? Anton listened while Villoing taught other pupils; in particular the playing of Barbara Grünberg stirred him. If a mere girl could run off Liszt's *Galop Chromatique*, then he, Anton Gregorovitch, could do it too. . . .

"In all my later life," wrote Anton, "I never met a better music teacher than Villoing. To him and no one else I owe a sound foundation in the art of music, a foundation so firm that I never slipped from it. Villoing took much pains in placing my hands correctly on the keys; he cared most of all about tone production—the notes must *sound*. He was wonderful, absolutely the best in his line. He required of me certain things, and it happened that these things were what I needed most in music. A patient man, yet severe in his requirements—a happy combination. Villoing and I quickly became friends and before long he was more to me than teacher; he was a friend, a second father. Nearly every day he came to our house in the Ordinka. He was indefatigable. In my lessons he probably found refreshment for himself, and pleasure. For me they were not lessons but true musical education, in spite of the knocks and slaps of the ruler that were then *à la mode*. At that time, both public and private education was carried on with a severity hard to describe to a later generation. It was a true discipline that trained the will to absolute obedience."

When Villoing had taught Anton Rubinstein a year and a half, the noise of his pupil's talent began to filter through the town. Being only human, Villoing desired to prove his pupil on the concert platform. But from Gregor Rubinstein, the teacher met unexpected opposition. Respectable Jewish families had a horror of thrusting children into the limelight, and all the holy water in Christendom could not erase the traditions of Gregor Rubinstein's upbringing. Even Kaleria had not yet foreseen her son's destiny; she would not permit the child to take money for making music.

Villoing, however, found a way round this. He called upon Count Bashilov, Marshal of the Nobility for Moscow, and the Count, eager to hear this *Wunderkind*, arranged a charity concert in the Petrovsky Park. The newspapers gave out that a prodigy was to be heard and that the prodigy's parents commendably would permit him to play only in the cause of charity.

On the eleventh of July, 1839, Anton Rubinstein made his début in the open air pavilion of Petrovsky Park. He began his program with the *Allegro* from Hummel's Concerto; an orchestra, led by Tepleff, accompanied him. Then the *Andante* from Thalberg's *Moses Fantasia*, two pieces by Field and Henselt, and finally, the fireworks of Liszt's *Galop Chromatique*. Dr. Rosenberg was there, sitting by Kaleria, and Rosenberg, who had brought Villoing first to the Rubinstein household, cried like a baby. Because the concert was a success. A roaring, handclapping audience applauded not only

Anton Rubinstein at the age of 12

the music but the player—this curly-headed, sturdy lad who played the piano as if it were fun, who laughed and ran off the stage as naturally as he had often laughed and left the merry-go-round next door to the pavilion. So great was the applause that Count Bashilov lifted the boy to a table where he could be better seen and let him take his bows from there.

Down in the audience, Kaleria Rubinstein sat with her hands in her lap. It needed no applause to prophesy for her this boy's destiny. How many times she had heard him play these same passages, over and over! But she had never before seen him set free, had never dreamed he possessed such sweep and mastery over his instrument. Why, Tonia played like a man grown! Not only did he possess the natural, heaven-sent technique of the virtuoso, but he really seemed to understand the music he was playing. Hummel and Thalberg and the Liszt *Galop* required nothing more than finger technique and brilliancy of execution, but Field and Henselt belonged to the new Romantic School that needed tone and feeling before their meaning was revealed. The *Nocturnes* of John Field could not be pattered off after the Hummel fashion, flat-wristed, with arched fingers darting up and down like so many hammers of precision. Anton's tones rang and lingered; they had a deep, long sustenance. The boy was only nine, but there were in him the seeds of a great and passionate musician.

There was no doubt now as to Anton's destiny. Driving home on that summer night, Anton's mother was more quiet than jubilant. The boy would be ten in November, and for a concert artist, ten is the beginning of maturity. Had not young Mozart, at eight, played for the King of France? Was not Felix Mendelssohn, at twelve, a full-fledged composer? Who in this Moscow village, this musical wilderness of 250,000 souls, could teach composition to her Anton? Villoing wrote music, but Villoing's music, although well known locally, was distinguished more for the beautiful precision of its calligraphy than for the sound of it. Villoing had not studied abroad and it was in Berlin or Paris that one learned to write fugues. Anton must go abroad.

Anton's father would have to be persuaded. Gregor Románovitch knew little about the technical side of music, but he was a Russian, and melody and rhythm were part of him. He adored music and was proud of his boy, but Gregor could be very stubborn where the welfare of his children was concerned. Better strike while the iron was hot, while the glow of this concert yet warmed the household. If the newspaper accounts proved favorable, it would help; men always set value on the printed word.

The newspapers were more than kind. They were positively flowery. Anton Rubinstein, said the critics, had very small fingers but where they failed, the child's artistic sympathy supplied the deficiency—something most unusual with *enfants prodiges*. The Moscow *Galatea* referred to Anton as "this wonderful talent, born and bred under the snow-laden skies of our white-walled Mother Moscow. Until now known only in the homes of friends where he has played, this boy is the nine-year-old son of the manufacturer Rubinstein, who to perfect the brilliant talent of his child-artist, uses the greater part of his modest income—an example deserving praise and encouragement."

Kaleria, watching her husband's face as he read, decided that the *Galatea* reporter could not have done better had he been employed as advocate. As a matter of fact, Anton's talents had not, so far, cost his father a rouble but that was not Gregor Rubinstein's fault. . . . "Music lovers," continued the *Galatea* columns, "have begged his parents to permit the sweet little artist to give at least one more concert, but the parents have declined this flattering request."

Directly after the concert, Count Bashilov had tried to arrange for another performance, but Gregor and Kaleria had been adamant. Gregor was deeply shocked to see his son, at nine, sitting on a stage like a monkey doing tricks; Kaleria, a trained musician, could see no harm in this. Her objection was professional—the boy was not ready for a career. He needed study, training in the harmonic principles of music, in form and theory. . . . "Though we regret," went on the *Galatea*, "that we shall have one less concert, yet we will not be so selfish as to object; the parents' reluctance is forgivable, and con-

22

structive, too, for the young artist. Let his talent develop in peace and quiet; the concert stage will always be open to him, late or early."

This, Kaleria knew, was the tone to take with Gregor. Anton was going abroad to study, not to perform in public—and indeed, such was Kaleria's own fervent wish. Villoing, of course, was concert-crazy; he would have Anton up on every platform in Europe if he had his way. Not to exploit the boy—there was no trace of greed in Monsieur Alexandre, but he was proud of his pupil. Moreover, the stage seemed somehow natural to Villoing. It would be a bit difficult to impress on Villoing that this trip, if it took place, would be for study, not for concert-getting.

When Kaleria broached the subject to her husband, she was surprised to find him as eager as she to give Tonia a Paris education. But where, asked Gregor Rubinstein sadly, would they find the money? During the past year, business had not been good; in fact, the pencil factory had been going rapidly to seed. There was no money to pay Villoing, let alone a stagecoach journey of two thousand miles.

But Villoing, called into conference, did not desire to be paid. He would look upon this journey as a speculation, investing in it what money he had saved. If Gregor Románovitch would consent to a few concerts, the boy could pay his own way. Looked at in this light, the platform appeared very different to Anton's father. The child was young but he was precocious; it would be good for him to take some responsibility for his own education. Moreover, it was reassuring that Villoing did not wish to start immediately; he said the boy would be better able to profit from the Paris Conservatoire after another year of study here at home.

All that winter and the summer following, Anton practiced in the big room over the pencil factory. Villoing and Kaleria drove the boy hard, but they did not over-drive him. There were plenty of good times; there was the week Tsar Nicholas came to town to lay the cornerstone of the great new cathedral under the west Kremlin wall. The streets were gay with bunting and paper lanterns; at every

23

corner curb, tallow flared in smoky basins after the ancient custom when Moscow entertained a Tsar. Merry-go-rounds, high swings, Punch-and-Judy shows, strolling peasants selling *kvas* by the glass— all the sights and sounds that Moscow loved. Friends had come to town for the show; one of them, Lokhvitsky, left an account of his visit to the Rubinsteins' big brick house with its spacious yard behind the Ordinka. After dinner, before the family went to the Park to see the fireworks, Gregor, who had to run downstairs to the factory, commanded young Anton to entertain his guests. The boy played a piece or two on the piano and then began with wild enthusiasm to describe Weber's *Freischütz* that he had heard last Sunday. To Lokhvitsky's amusement, the boy sang the huntsmen's song through with vigorous gestures. "Drink, drink, my friends!" sang Anton, whose succeeding years were to be as strictly temperate as his brother Nicholas' were to be convivial. . . .

There was the time, too, when Gregor took his sons to Borodino to witness the unveiling of a monument on the battlefield where Kutuzov and Napoleon had slaughtered or maimed some hundred thousand soldiers. The Tsar came down from Petersburg to dedicate the monument; a whole town had been built for the ceremony. . . . No, this prodigy Anton was not a slave like the young Haydn, the young Beethoven; neither poverty nor cruel parents oppressed his growth. Later, he was to suffer bitterly, but the time was not yet come.

So the months passed, until in December, 1840, Villoing declared his pupil ripe for travel.

3

1840-1842. The post road to Paris. Music under the Citizen King

KALERIA RUBINSTEIN bought her son knee-length felt boots to keep his feet from freezing on the sledge journey, wrapped him in a fur-collared sheepskin *shuba*, put mittens on his hands, a round, ear-muffed fur cap on his curly head and a neat plaid carpetbag in his hand. Late at night the family went down to the post station to bid the travelers Godspeed. Standing in the huge, gas-lighted barn beside the steel-runnered coach, Kaleria waited while the four horses, har-nessed abreast, stamped their feet and blew great clouds of frosted air toward the glass-domed roof. Kind-hearted, sentimental Gregor wept openly, embracing his boy again and again. But Kaleria smiled, holding the hand of her third son, Nicholas. She would have more time, now, to teach him music.

The postilion's horn roared through the cold barn, the *yamshiks*, pulling on the rope reins, shouted to their teams. The road to Peters-burg lay straight and smooth, 500 miles to the north. The freeze this year had been early and deep; they should make fast time if those rascal drivers at the other stations were sober and ready with fresh horses. Father Tsar had done well to open the new troop road to the public post, although now that the ice was solid they could have used the old roads; all roads were passable in winter. In summer the journey took seven days and a hundred horses, but by sledge they should do it in three days, if nothing broke down.

Out the Tverskaya Gate under the stars flew Anton and his tutor. Powdery snow lifted from beneath galloping hooves, dogs barked, bells jingled on the horses' collars. Past the Petrovsky Palace where Napoleon had retreated when Moscow began to burn—and where Anton had played his first concert two summers ago. To the left of

Petrovsky the race-tracks were a wide expanse of white, patched with great purple shadows. Northward, ever northward, with the coach windows frosted so thick young Anton could see neither shadow nor starlight. A cold so bitter it penetrated the straw stuffed in every crack. Smooth swinging of the sledge and a boy dozing against his teacher's shoulder until—whack!—the coach bumped crazily out of the deep sledge ruts, throwing the passengers against one another. Torches flaring beside the soldiers' huts, and every twenty miles a stop to change horses. . . .

Tver, Pozharsky, Ostashov—the stations seemed interminable. Villoing, who had made this journey many times, descended and drank his tea and smoked his cigar and dozed again in cold discomfort. But Anton knew when the sledge crossed a river; he heard the hollow sound of the bridge, and through a slit scratched in the frosted window, caught glimpses of golden eagles on granite parapets before the country opened out once more in monotonous whiteness. Sometimes as they approached the post stations, little disheveled horses could be seen galloping across the fields, dragging from the snowdrifts, *kibitkas* with country travelers for the post. Children and peasants ran barefoot in the snow; a mile away their village could be seen: log huts clustered among the bare birches.

Anton and Villoing were not the only musicians to make this journey. Louis Spohr had made it some thirty years earlier; Hector Berlioz was soon to travel this road. Spohr's account is cheerful, but Spohr was a German and a stoic; Spohr traveled all over Europe in a private coach with a wife, a harp, three children and an assortment of musical instruments, giving music lessons to the family on the way. Berlioz was French and fussy; shut up in his iron sledge he underwent, he said, tortures, shaken ceaselessly and violently like shot in a bottle.

But young Anton Rubinstein had no such complaint to make. Was he not out to see the world; was not this *adventure?* The frozen fields that surrounded Petersburg were fairy fields to Anton; the birches stood high and white, reminding him of home. He had no time to see Saint Petersburg itself, beyond the *Hotel des Postes* and a glimpse of the frozen Neva. In later years he was to know this city by heart, as his brother Nicholas was to know Moscow. The coach-house itself was exciting, bigger than the one at home and busy with generals in huge cocked hats. Anton heard the callers' cries as the teams prepared to start: *Coach for Kiev!—Coach for Kovno!—Coach for Viborg!*

"Antoine, viens!" cried Villoing, and the plaid carpetbag mounted yet another creaking step.

At Tilsit on the Prussian frontier, Anton cautiously addressed the postmaster in the German his mother had taught him so painstakingly. Herr Nernst replied with enthusiasm; he was a musician himself, he said, and liked nothing better than to welcome musical visitors to his post-house samovar. In Berlin they stopped only to change horses, but the rest of the journey was a delight. What hills and rolling vistas, what changing landscape, what beautiful neat large houses! Nobody wore furs; obviously, one's *shuba* and felt boots were curiosities. . . . If only brother Jacob were here to laugh and play pranks with, or little Nicholas, even! Villoing thought about nothing but music, and this delightful new world was filled with things other than music that needed exploration.

The Paris cobblestones were loud with traffic, the streets crooked like Moscow streets, but the houses here were high. One missed the dazzle of snow and the sound of bells. One's French seemed fluent enough, but it made the Parisian gentlemen laugh.

It did not make Monsieur Cherubini laugh, at the Conservatoire, and Cherubini was the man they had come so far to see. Paris was the focus of musical Europe; it had succeeded to the title as Vienna had once succeeded Florence. To make one's musical fortune one must give a Paris concert and to give it one must first know everybody, beginning with Cherubini, who was quite as important as God, and fully as old. He was a Florentine, trained in the old Italian contrapuntal style, who had found his way to France long ago and somehow survived the Terror in 1789.

It was 1840 when Alexandre Villoing arrived in Paris with his Russian pupil. Unfortunately, Monsieur Cherubini did not like

27

enfants prodiges. To Cherubini, music was a religion. Must it then be subject to the monkey tricks of children, performing at the crack of their masters' whips? Cherubini had turned away the young Liszt, giving for excuse the Conservatoire rule that forbade foreign pupils. He had refused young Jacques Offenbach when he arrived from Cologne with his father. But Offenbach, *père,* knew the meaning of persistence, and finally succeeded in obtaining an audition that gained his son admittance to this student Mecca.

Alexandre Villoing had with him an *enfant prodige* who could play Jacques Offenbach, young or old, off the piano stool, but where Cherubini was concerned, Villoing was beaten before ever he knocked at the Conservatoire gates.

Cherubini refused to see Monsieur Villoing, refused to hear his pupil play.

If this was defeat, Villoing did not recognize it. He made no outcry and no further attempt toward the Conservatoire but retreated with his pupil to a rented room that contained a piano, and settled down to teach the boy himself. Rubinstein's biographers have puzzled over Villoing's easy attitude in this matter, but Rubinstein himself said later that his teacher "looked upon me, quite simply, as his own creation and did not wish to be separated from me or to give over my musical education to anyone—even to the Paris Conservatoire."

After all, Villoing had "discovered" the boy; if other men refused to share his discovery, why, so much the worse for them! Not only did Villoing believe implicitly in Anton's genius, he believed quite as genuinely in his own capacity to direct that genius. All the winter of 1840-41, the teacher guarded his pupil jealously from everything that hinted of music teacher—and Paris was full of music teachers. Herr Kalkbrenner—gouty and pompous—was there and had a class so distinguished that even Chopin had attended it once or twice as a pupil. Cramer, too, old and erudite in the German tradition. The Conservatoire itself was not all Cherubini. Zimmerman was head of the pianoforte department; Auber, gentle soul who was too timid to go to performances of his own very successful operas, was soon to succeed Cherubini as Director.

Any of these men would have snapped up Anton and branded him as his own pupil, or so thought Monsieur Villoing. Nevertheless, they must hear the boy play. Anton's next step was a Paris début, and the inescapable preliminary to a musical début in Paris was to make the player known to important persons. Villoing went the rounds, bowing, leaving his card, introducing himself in careful French that bore unmistakable traces of Moscow—and before he left home he locked his pupil in their room with the piano. When it was time, he would produce his prodigy.

Villoing called first of all at the famous pianoforte houses: at Camille Pleyel's, in whose concert hall Chopin had made his Paris début, twenty years earlier. Villoing took his pupil to the Pleyel factory and let him try the new instruments, took him also to meet Pierre Erard, nephew of the famous Sebastian whose pianos were quite as wonderful as Monsieur Pleyel's.

Little by little, as the weeks wore on, the circle of acquaintances widened. Villoing had letters to the fashionable world, given him by such men as Count Bashilov and Prince Odoevsky in Moscow. In this bright and brittle Paris of Louis Phillipe, the salon reigned supreme—and music was the crown of the salon. Countess de Vaux vied with Princess Belgiojoso for the honor of displaying the most distinguished artists to her after-dinner guests. The great Polish nobles who had emigrated to Paris early in the 1830's, also had their "evenings." In them all, Liszt, the lion of lions, shook his glorious mane, and Chopin, pale, elegant, distinguished, played and was adored—and followed George Sand humbly to her carriage. . . .

These were marvelous times, these years from 1830 to '48, while the Citizen King staved off the coming cataclysm. Victor Hugo, George Sand, Dumas, Eugène Sue, Ary Scheffer, Delacroix, Halévy, Berlioz, Auber were in Paris. . . . In their boxes at the *Opéra*, the *gants jaunes* quarreled wittily over the burning question: Who had the more genius, Meyerbeer or Rossini? German visitors were outraged when their glorious *Freischütz* became, on Parisian

29

lips, *Robin des Bois,* impudently embellished by Berlioz with recitatives for reigning prima donnas.

This dazzling world did not, of course, open immediately to a pair of unknown visitors from a remote country that Paris considered the very heart of barbarism. Slowly, Villoing laid his plans and pulled his wires; meanwhile he took his pupil to hear music more wonderful than the Russian boy had ever dreamed. There were great singers at the *Opéra*; Signor Rubini, with his plump face, his melting Italian eyes and curly side-whiskers, walked out upon the stage and opened his mouth—and up in the gallery a boy's eyes were bright with tears. Anton could barely wait to get home and try to imitate upon the piano those lingering, heavenly notes. Rubini's tones were to haunt him for years.

Habeneck at the *Opéra* led his orchestra in the Paris fashion, standing up to face the players instead of leading from the first violinist's chair with bow and foot and shoulder. Villoing explained to his pupil that the modern orchestra was too large to be handled by concert master or soloist, especially since Hector Berlioz had introduced all this mad brass and woodwind into orchestration. It plainly required one man's attention—and a baton—to hold all these players together.

Slowly, unobtrusively—as became a foreigner—Villoing made his pupil known to Paris. At small gatherings in the Pleyel and Erard showrooms, musicians heard Anton play. Auber heard him and said the child played with understanding and "soul"—high praise from a Frenchman. Zimmerman heard him and called his performance a "musical revelation." But it was not until the end of 1841 that Villoing had his triumph. Anton was invited to play in the *Salle Erard* at an evening performance, an important occasion that was to include on the program such virtuosi as young Vieuxtemps, the brilliant violinist-composer who was to found a new school of violin playing. Other stars were on the programs; the fashion of one-man recitals was still new. Only lions like Liszt and Chopin dared ask the public to hazard the *ennui* of a whole evening with one player. But the gate receipts, to Villoing's considerable relief, were to be

Anton's alone. A year in Paris had eaten up every cent the two had brought from Moscow; tonight's gate would spell success or a rapid flight home on borrowed cash.

Peering out from the wings, that December evening, Villoing was not thinking of money. The company out front was too dazzling to permit any but the most exalted thoughts. Liszt himself was there—the brightest star of all the musical firmament, handsome as a young god, with the figure and grace of Apollo and a distinction of bearing that puzzled the aristocratic world, accustomed as it was to place musicians at the foot of the table. Chopin was there, elegant in light gloves and evening cape. Leopold Meyer, the pianist whom America was to call the "sledge-hammer artist," his powerful shoulders straining the seams of his black dress-coat. Herr Kalkbrenner was there, fastened up to the neck with gold buttons. Chopin wore his coat buttoned high too, but the buttons were elegantly black. Villoing caught sight of Meyerbeer's sensitive Jewish face, with the wide forehead and curling hair. Meyerbeer was writing operas nineteen hours of the day, but still could not satisfy the hungry Parisian appetite.

Liszt, Chopin, Meyerbeer! It was like playing at the gates of heaven. God grant that Anton would not be blinded by this dazzle of celestial coronets! But nothing seemed to bother Anton. Put a piano in front of him and the boy played; he never seemed flustered; he never forgot his notes. Moreover, he had the funniest little manner on the stage, especially charming because it was really no manner at all. Other *Wunderkinder* crept out from the wings looking like little victims, but Anton almost skipped to his instrument. When the audience laughed, he laughed too. When he came upon a difficult passage he made a face and shook his curly head, and the audience held its breath and helped him through it.

Anton played, and Liszt was enchanted. He lifted the boy in his arms, swung him onto a table and with characteristic theatricality pronounced: "On these shoulders my mantle will fall." Chopin too had words of praise and invited Villoing to bring the boy to his studio.

31

This, Villoing knew, was victory. Liszt and Chopin could open any doors; the future was assured. The purse was full, the great ones had saluted. Moscow would not see her wandering sons for many a moon.

Liszt's words had been extravagant, but like all of Liszt's extravagances, truth lay beneath. Voices would even arise to call Liszt's chosen heir the greater player of the two—though never the greater musician. As to theatricality, it was part and parcel of the times. Mannerism was expected of an artist; the matter-of-fact bearing of a Haydn, the cynical mask of a Mozart had been cracked by the storm of revolution. And in revolution's wake, romanticism flew its banners high. One wore one's heart on the sleeve *à la Rousseau* or one was suspected of having no heart. An Englishman, visiting Paris when Liszt was only twenty-three, went one evening to hear this perfectly healthy virtuoso play piano duets, and left an account of it. In the middle of the concert Liszt, with a "seraphic look on the face that Goethe has compared to the face of Our Saviour, fainted in the arms of a friend who was turning pages for him and was borne out in a strong fit of hysterics. Everyone sat breathless until they heard he had recovered. As I handed Madame de Circourt to her carriage, we both trembled like poplar leaves, and I tremble scarcely less as I write this."

This from John Bull, whom the artistic world had hitherto considered cold and unresponsive. Lord Byron had done his work well. . . . But Liszt's grandiose gestures were by no means unconstructive in the history of concert music. Not only was he the first to give a one-man recital but he was first to play a whole program from memory—a feat the public frowned upon as presumptuous. How could any one brain remember all those notes; surely, improvisation would fill in the gaps. When Clara Schumann adopted the so-called Parisian practice of playing from memory, the critics flayed her; the respected Frau Von Arnim called her the most insufferable artist she had ever come across, "who had the audacity to play the whole of her program by heart."

32

Previous to Liszt's time, pianists had presented either their faces or their backs to the audience. But Liszt, well aware of his handsome profile, boldly sat sidewise, and in the front rows ladies swooned. His theatricality was the more noteworthy in that it seemed truly part of him; it was the sincere affectation that is a quality of great actors. Leaving his green gloves and Hungarian pelisse on a chair in the audience, Liszt strode to the stage, stars and ribbons flashing from the lapels of his dress coat. The ladies turned dazzled eyes from his beautiful pale hands to the eyes that had been described as "incandescent grapes."

How the period loved this extravagant praise! One writer described Chopin's tones as "crystalline pearls falling on red-hot velvet."

And Villoing's Russian bear-cub, prancing healthily across Paris from out his Moscow snow-drifts—how was he affected by all this "red-hot velvet," these vapors and fainting fits of the great? Very little. He could never take home to *Maman* such manners as that! But he was precocious, nothing escaped him, and from the moment he met Franz Liszt, young Anton was a hero-worshiper. He himself has confessed that he copied Liszt's mannerisms, especially his trick of tossing back the hair and lifting the hands to dangerous heights above the keyboard. When first he heard Liszt play, here in Paris, Anton had a severe nervous seizure. Liszt took the boy in his arms, put him to bed and stayed several hours by his side until he was quiet and slept. This was no fashionable attack of the vapors; first and last, Anton Rubinstein was genuine. Beings with ears so sensitive respond to music all through the nervous system; young Mozart had fainted away at the sound of a trumpet.

And Liszt was a whole army of trumpets; he did not play as other men played. Not for him the dry, precise strokes of a Hummel, the dreamy poetry of a John Field. Liszt threw himself upon the piano; he made an orchestra of it. Young Rubinstein, hearing him, went out to do likewise.

Liszt, Rubini, Chopin—these three had enormous influence on the boy Anton, more influence indeed than all the adulation Paris

33

brought him after his December concert. "How many people I saw that year—and what wonderful people!" he wrote later. "Villoing was much gratified with my success, but as for me, I looked upon it all as fun—a play, a toy the world gave to me. And although my teacher was a severe man, I was a terribly mischievous child, a madcap. I made many acquaintances and was invited from one great house to another. I was too young to remember it in detail, yet I remember one thing clearly—my visit to Chopin."

In his quiet, candle-lighted room above the Chaussée d'Antin, Chopin sat at the piano with his pot of coffee and his manuscript paper on the little table beside him. Although he adored elegance and the drawing rooms of princesses, Chopin could not weather the fierce competition of a public musical career. "I am not fitted to give concerts," he told Liszt. "The crowd embarrasses me. I feel stifled by their hurried breathing, paralyzed by their curious glances, mute before these strange faces." To gain entrance to Chopin's privacy was difficult indeed. Young Anton, climbing the stairs to this especial heaven, bounded eagerly ahead of his teacher and knocked on the door before Villoing had fairly regained breath. The slim, pale young man who answered to his knock sat down promptly to the piano and played his own mazurkas, and to the listening boy it was as if a gate had opened, revealing splendors of whose existence neither Villoing nor Liszt nor *Maman* nor God had ever hinted. This music—so new, so strange, so passionately national—entered the boy's blood, never to leave it. Anton Rubinstein was to become one of the greatest interpreters of Chopin the world has known.

As for Alexandre Villoing, his cup was full. Everybody knew him, everybody sought him out. Paris called him "the happy teacher of the talented pupil," and urged him to abandon his Russian snowdrifts and remain in this better world, where such teachers receive their reward. It was all quite overwhelming; even at non-musical gatherings, the two were recognized. On that day when Napoleon's ashes were brought to the Invalides from St. Helena, the archbishop actually spoke to Anton and, while the crowd looked on, beckoned the boy to a front seat where he could see the ceremonies.

34

Liszt heard about it and frowned. "The child will be ruined!" he told Villoing. "Take your boy out of this nest of artist intrigues; take him off the platform and put him to work at counterpoint. Take him to Germany and have him taught to write a fugue!"

Privately, Villoing considered himself quite capable of finishing Anton's education alone, without help of German or devil. To a Russo-Frenchman like himself, piano-playing was piano-playing; it was not reams of paper covered with exercises in thorough-bass. But Liszt was king of music, and the king's word must be obeyed.

In the late spring of 1841, therefore, Villoing and his pupil stuffed the new Parisian nightshirts into Kaleria's plaid carpetbag, said a Russian farewell to their landlady and were off once more in the diligence for a long, long ride.

4

1842-1844. Grande tournée

Villoing set out for Germany to find the proper counterpoint factory and immure his pupil therein. It would be a dull life for them both, after Paris, but perhaps a dull life was better for young talent.

It would do no harm to stop in Amsterdam *en route*, where Anton had been invited to play at the Musical Society—a very advantageous offer and one they could not afford to miss. Royalty patronized the concerts of the Musical Society. The Queen of Holland, Anna Pavlovna, was a Russian, the sister of Tsar Nicholas himself. Anton played. The Queen heard him and was charmed. Promptly, she invited the boy to play at her palace. Under crystal chandeliers, in a circle of bediamonded ladies—satin crinolines, ostrich feathers—Anton sat down to the piano, and shaking his pretty mane in imitation of Liszt, lifted his hands high and plunged at the keyboard in a veritable fury of temperament.

Royalty was entranced. Anton made real friends that night. The Queen's nephew was there, young Grand Duke Konstantin, Tsar Nicholas' second son who was making the grand tour of Europe with his tutor. Konstantin at fourteen was a high-spirited lad who loved music far more than the Navy he was being groomed to command. A royal father who slept upon a pallet stuffed with straw and told his sons, "Live so that God will forgive you for being born Grand Dukes," was hardly the man to fill life with music and laughter. Konstantin was always running to his piano or 'cello; he played passably on both instruments. Small wonder he was instantly fascinated with his young compatriot who at one stroke could break the strings of a pianoforte. Konstantin wrote home

CONCERT
des jungen
Anton Rubinstein,
Schüler des Herrn A. Villoing,

Pianist aus Moskau,

Sonntag den 9. Jänner 1842,

Mittags um halb 1 Uhr,

im Saale der Gesellschaft der Musikfreunde.

Vorkommende Stücke:

1. **Fantaisie** über zwei russische Thema's, von Thalberg, vorgetragen von **Anton Rubinstein.**

2. **Zigeunermusik**, Gedicht von J. N. Vogl, für eine Singstimme mit Violin- und Pianoforte-Begleitung von E. Titl, gesungen von Herrn **Haimer**, die Violine vorgetragen von Herrn **A. Simon.**

3. **Fuge** aus der chromatischen Fantasie von S. Bach, und **Andante** aus der Lucia, von Liszt, vorgetragen von **Anton Rubinstein.**

4. **Lied** in österreichischer Mundart: Mai Suferl und J, Gedicht von A. Freiherrn v. Klesheim, für eine Singstimme mit Pianoforte-Begleitung von E. Titl, gesungen von Herrn **Haimer.**

5. **Zuruf aus der Ferne**, Gedicht von E. Weyden, in Musik gesetzt und seiner Mutter gewidmet von **Anton Rubinstein**, gesungen von Fräulein **Treffs**, Sängerin des k. k. Hof-Operntheaters.

6. **Lob der Thränen**, von Schubert, übertragen von Liszt, **Chromatischer Galop** von Liszt, vorgetragen von **Anton Rubinstein.**

Obgenannte Mitwirkende haben aus besonderer Gefälligkeit für den Concertgeber ihre Leistungen übernommen.

Eintrittskarten zu 1 fl. 20 kr. C. M. und Sperrsitze zu 2 fl. 30 kr. C. M.

sind in der k. k. Hof-Musikalienhandlung des Herrn Tobias Haslinger und am Tage des Concertes an der Cassa zu haben.

Program for Anton Rubinstein's Viennese concert of January 9, 1842

immediately, telling his Imperial parents to watch for the return to Petersburg of one Anton Rubinstein.

That evening at Court was more than a brilliant incident; it was something that Villoing, in a haze of delight, had not anticipated. In Paris, Anton had played his way into the confidence of the musical world; if he was to charm courts and queens as well, life would take on a very different aspect. Invitation after invitation poured in; Villoing and his pupil lived in garrets and ate their suppers with princes. All summer they stayed in Holland, and the counterpoint factory receded farther and farther into the background. Concert offers began to pour in from beyond the Dutch borders; it became obvious that if Villoing wished, the two could embark on a European concert tour.

It was too much for Alexandre Villoing. He was a good man and a conscientious teacher. He had no wish to exploit his pupil; but would Anton's parents, he wondered, wish him to refuse such offers? It meant a chance for the boy to see Europe, to acquire a poise that would be useful in after life—to acquire, also, money that might rehabilitate Gregor Románovitch's sick pencil factory.

Villoing made his decision. In the autumn of 1842, the plaid carpetbag was packed for a tour that was to last eighteen months.

That autumn, master and pupil traveled all over Germany—without pause for counterpoint. In Vienna, Anton walked out upon the platform and with one blow of his small Russian paw wrecked the strings of the Stein piano—a trick that was later to torture the nerves of concert managers from Moscow to New York City, making it necessary to provide, on every Rubinstein platform, two concert grands instead of one. At his second Viennese appearance Anton, aged twelve, played Villoing's own Concerto. The orchestra lost him completely, but Anton, like any veteran trouper, played calmly on until the violins found their way back. The redoubtable Dr. Becker pronounced the boy a "phenomenon" and the boy laughed and asked his teacher if such a description did not merit him a day's holiday.

Villoing shook his head. Nothing merited a holiday—nothing

37

except failure. Let Anton fail one evening in front of the *Herr Doktor* Beckers who wrote newspaper criticisms; he would soon find there were no further concerts to practice for! In Berlin Villoing bought a folding keyboard, one of those "dumb pianos" in use at the time. From now on the dumb piano clicked its muffled keys in stage-coach, post station, *pension* and palace. The teacher's vigilance never relaxed. Traveling down the Rhine by boat one summer's day, an English tourist came upon the boy below deck sitting alone with his dumb keyboard on a table. Touched by the sight of the youth shut up hour after hour while on deck the sun shone upon a scene unmatched in all Europe for beauty and historic romance, the Englishman approached and asked Anton if he would not stop work and come upstairs for a while.

Anton shook his head, looking down at his hands on the keyboard. "This won't wait," he said. "The other will."

The Englishman saw this boy whipped by his teacher on that Rhenish journey, and wasted much recorded indignation and sympathy. Anton Rubinstein loved his teacher, and in Anton's experience, those you love best whip you frequently and severely. The boy was sturdy and ambitious; he knew that he had entered a field crowded with competition. Europe at that time was overrun with musical *Wunderkinder*; in every city Anton saw their placards on the walls and turned eloquent eyes to Villoing, asking wordlessly if this boy depicted with his violin, this silly girl with hands on piano, was a better player than Anton Rubinstein. . . .

The two encountered many of these young rivals. There was Sophie Bohrer, the girl pianist who was a year younger than Anton. Daughter of the famous musical family founded by Grandfather Caspar, the Mannheim trumpeter, Sophie was to be the heroine of a romantic, tragic story and was to disappear from earth so mysteriously that forty years later, musicians would still be asking, "Where is Sophie Bohrer—does she no longer play the piano?" There were two boy-pianists who bore the uncompromising name of Fitch, and the English pianist, Palmer. There were the violin-playing sisters, Maria and Theresa Milanello, who appeared upon the stage in ruffled pantalettes and who were known from one end of Europe to the other as the *Mesdemoiselles Adagio* and *Staccato*. Truly brilliant performers, they were the daughters of an Italian carpenter. Theresa was the first woman ever admitted to the Paris Conservatoire—Cherubini was dead when she made her application.

The concert public has a fickle taste. In the 1840's, having refused for nearly a century to listen to child virtuosi, Europe suddenly demanded them again as eagerly as it had once welcomed the child Mozart. Hermann Wolff, the great impresario—later Rubinstein's manager—once said the demand for certain types of artists goes in cycles. One decade demands prodigies and nothing but prodigies, another decade will not listen to child players. There are periods when temperamental, spectacular artists are popular and periods when the public prefers impersonal musicians and pure music. Even the taste for instruments varies; the impresario must feel in his bones when to produce pianists from his bag, and when violinists.

Rubinstein himself attributed the contemporary demand of virtuoso players to Liszt, who had made the public impatient of any playing that did not possess extraordinary brilliance. This was true enough, provided one takes into account the factors that prepared the way for Liszt. The crazy wizardry of Paganini, playing encores on one string with the other three ostentatiously dangling, had given Europe an appetite for spectacular performance. Paganini impressed his fellow musicians as profoundly as he impressed his public; young Liszt, hearing him, determined to make the piano as facile under his hand as this mad Italian had made the violin.

Not an easy task. The instrument itself rebelled. If a human hand —Henri Herz' for instance—could strike the same note thirty times in a measure, that did not mean the note would respond mechanically. Messrs. Clementi, Erard, Pleyel and Broadwood sat up all night in their factories, working on fast repetitive hammer action. No sooner had they perfected it than devils like Liszt began to write pieces that demanded a quite new type of piano concerto:

sensational, colorful music, the score of which was black and dangerous, crying out for both virtuoso players and virtuoso instruments.

It was a circle of progress, rapid and dazzling; Anton Rubinstein grew up in the midst of it. In 1840 he was a child-wonder, and child-wonders have always served the concertgoing public as a kind of intellectual relief. One pays for one's ticket and sits down in the state of pleased anticipation one feels at the vaudeville. Will the wonder-child be spindly like the last boy pianist that came to town, with bushy hair and velvet jacket? Or will he be fat and handsome, obviously much older than the program says?

Alexandre Villoing's prodigy was neither spindly nor fat. He was twelve years old, but he was a musician. Those who heard him recognized it. On the platform he felt no fear; his musical memory was as reliable as it was extraordinary; he could learn a new program in a day and with Villoing as impresario, he had no worries whatever. "I was quite at the disposal of Villoing," he wrote later. "He planned all my programs and kept me under absolute discipline, yet I was a most playful and healthy child."

Vienna, Budapest, Cologne, Leipzig, Berlin, Hamburg—*pension, palace, platform*—crowds applauding, crowds fading as in a dream, the dumb piano clicking at the post stations. And now the Channel packet to England, with Villoing, suddenly nervous, making morose remarks about a cold British public that would require much coaxing before it was ready to put its hand in its pocket.

London was indeed a hard citadel to conquer. London distrusted musicians—long-haired, greasy fellows who came from abroad and took money at the gate, like acrobats. Signor Paganini, playing at the King's Theatre, had gone off with thousands of Her Majesty's good pounds sterling. Cruikshank had turned the thrust by caricaturing the violinist in *Punch*, with his great spidery arms and legs, his wild huge eyes and wilder hair. At evening parties in the great houses of London, foreign musicians were invited to play and then treated like the tailor who had strayed in to measure a coat. Louis Spohr, for instance, arriving from German courts where he had been entertained by princes trained in the *gemütlich* German tradi-

40

tion that made intimates or heroes of its musicians, was aghast when, in London, ducal footmen passed him by with trays of food as if he were not present at all. Spohr resolved, in the sacred name of art, to make a scene. Planting himself sturdily in the path of successive outraged footmen, he acquired a plate, and food, and sat down with the ladies to eat it. Thenceforth Louis Spohr was part of the company at every *salon* where he played his violin.

Lablache, young Queen Victoria's singing teacher, whose body was as huge as his voice—he was so fat he could not pick up a handkerchief when he was seated—was engaged to sing at a private party at Apsley House. As he walked to the piano he saw that a rope had been stretched to separate the artist from the guests—the goat from the sheep, as it were. Raising his heavy foot, Lablache kicked over the rope. It was never, he testified, replaced.

Little by little, London was learning its musical manners, but British snobbishness was more bitter to endure because it was offered quite unconsciously. England did not know how to enjoy musicians unless they were rich and respectable—a combination unusual with artists. Even Franz Liszt failed until quite late in life to blandish the Londoners. Two years before Anton Rubinstein's visit, Liszt had come over with his Madame d'Agoult, ready to take the city by storm as he had taken other cities, and found that only hostesses like Lady Blessington—bright but slightly tarnished—were ready to receive him. Even she had observed that it was a pity to put such a magnificent man at the piano.

London distrusted musicians unless they settled down, as Handel had, and made money and wrote good solid oratorios a man could sing without feeling embarrassed. They liked Mendelssohn too; Mendelssohn was a Jew but he was born rich and besides, his music had a tune to it. How clever of Mr. Mendelssohn to have written a *Scottish Symphony*! The winter that Anton Rubinstein came to London, Mendelssohn was in town to conduct the *première* of this symphony with the Philharmonic. Sigismund Thalberg was in London too. Here was another pianist the English could approve. Thalberg bowed like a colonel; worthy of a colonel also were

41

those neat side-whiskers, that rigid seat at the piano. Moreover, Thalberg was rich, and as the natural son of a prince, almost free from the taint of the professional musician. How was London to know that the man had trained himself to this stiff military bearing by smoking, while he practiced, a long Turkish pipe that would have spilled water if he swerved his body an inch?

Alexandre Villoing knew it. He did not attempt to conquer London by a quick public concert but went about the business as he had done in Paris, laying his underground wires, calling on important persons, presenting his letters, leaving his card—and locking his pupil in a room with a piano. His aim was to procure Anton an invitation to play with the London Philharmonic; in Berlin the boy had played with the Philharmonic and had been made an honorary member of that august organization. Ignaz Moscheles, the pianist, Beethoven's pupil, had conducted the London Philharmonic for many years now and was used to the town's manners. Time was, though, when Moscheles, visiting a nobleman's house to give piano lessons to the nobleman's daughter, had been instructed by a footman to ring the servants' bell.

Villoing saw to it that his pupil was introduced to both Moscheles and Mendelssohn. Anton played at private houses, splendid houses where great ladies made a fuss over the handsome boy, and powdered footmen turned up their noses at the foreign music-makers who spoke their excited crazy lingo. Before long, Anton's name was in the papers. Under the heading "A Musical Wonder," William Ayrton referred to him as "a Russian boy named Antoine Rubinstein, a native of Moldavia who has not yet completed his twelfth year and who has been for some weeks in London under the care of his teacher, M. Villoing, with a view to exhibit his extraordinary powers in this metropolis."

Villoing was particularly pleased when the review went on to say that at private parties the lad had played some of the pieces at which Thalberg excelled, difficult music that could only be performed—so London said—by an artist with two thumbs to each hand and steam power behind them. "We have heard," read Villoing, "Rubinstein play these pieces and can answer for the unimpeachable correctness of his performance; and, what is still more remarkable, for the force by which, through some unparalleled gift of nature, he is enabled to exercise a degree of muscular strength which his general conformation, and especially his arms and hands, would have induced us to suppose he could not possibly possess."

Villoing was well aware that nature had given his pupil a perfect hand—broad palm, padded fingertips. But every teacher knows that a hand without training—no matter how perfectly formed by nature —is no use upon the keyboard. *Control* was what the critic really meant. . . . Heartening, after all these years of conscientious work, to see one's teaching methods justified in print!

It was wonderful, went on the critic, to see this boy play from memory; he played fashionable music for the fashionable: the fantasias of Liszt, Thalberg and Herz. "But when exhibiting before real connoisseurs, he chooses for his purpose the elaborate compositions of the old German school—the learned and difficult fugues of Sebastian Bach and Handel, which he executes with ease. . . ."

So far, all was well; the campaign proceeded according to schedule. Anton was invited to play at the palace by Queen Victoria, whom he described as "young and pretty." Palaces, by now, were becoming part of young Anton's life; the evening at Buckingham Palace would be followed by other evenings quite as glittering and perhaps less dull. "I was amiably received by all the high society of London, I, a boy of twelve! And I was not intimidated among the stiff young English misses, the ladies and pompous lords; there was no timidity in me."

When spring came, Villoing decided the time was ripe to strike. Anton gave his first concert in Hanover Square in May, 1842. A fashionable audience included Moscheles; Mr. Mendelssohn himself led the boy to the piano. On the face of it, it was a success. Moscheles went home and wrote in his diary that here was "a rival to Thalberg, a Russian boy whose fingers are as light as feathers, and yet as strong as a man's."

But something was amiss, and Villoing felt it. Everyone had been most cordial—yet Moscheles, for all his spoken praise, did not invite Thalberg's rival to play with the London Philharmonic. For Villoing it was not enough that his pupil should be dubbed in the newspapers "Thalberg in embryo" and a "promising pianist *à la Liszt.*" Promising, indeed! Vienna had not called him "promising"; Berlin had not written him up in the papers as if he were a monkey, copying other musicians' tricks! These British did not know a musician when they saw one. In Paris, Franz Liszt had hinted it might be like this. The London visit had been next door to failure, and Villoing was glad to pack the carpetbag and set off to colder climes and warmer hearts. Fifteen years would pass before Rubinstein ventured again to these bleak musical shores.

Northward now, to Norway and Sweden, where all went merrily. Then back across the water to Lübeck, where Anton played Liszt, Schubert, four *Etudes* of Henselt and his own *Etude in D* which brought thunderous applause. Late summer found the travelers in Cologne and Vienna. It was becoming a routine, and the two were a trifle weary. At the turn of the year—1843—Anton played in Breslau and was so well received that Villoing stayed for several months, presenting his pupil in concert after concert. Breslau was the capital of Prussian Silesia—land of Kaleria Rubinstein's birth; Anton was very happy to be able to mail home a substantial money order. He played here his first published work, which Robert Schumann praised in the *Musik Zeitung*.

"*Ondine,* a Study for Pianoforte, Op. I, by Anton Rubinstein. The first work of a talented boy who has already made himself a great reputation as a pianist. Whether he also possesses a significant creative talent, one can neither affirm nor deny on the strength of this first effort. That in this little piece the melodic element is prevalent—without, however, forming a truly beautiful new melody—lets us hope that he is beginning to grasp the substance of music and will progress in this direction happily. The title of the *Etude* derives from the wave-like accompanying figure; anything more original and more completely successful we could not expect from one so young. But under no circumstances should such impure harmonies as the following be permitted to stand:

Any moderately skilful musician could have improved this place for him."

Did Villoing, reading this, blush for his own faulty pedagogy? One doubts it. Probably he dismissed Herr Schumann's strictures as mere German stuffiness. Anyway, *Ondine* remained as it was. (The manuscript, with its large neat childish script, can be seen, faulty harmonies and all, in the Berlin *Staatsbibliothek* today.)

The travelers were on their way home at last, and Anton was glad of it. After Breslau, the next concert platform was to be Warsaw— and Warsaw was within the boundaries of Russia. Warsaw, Petersburg, and then the coach for Moscow! How, he wondered impatiently, would *Maman* be? Was she well, was Nicholenka well, and Papa and Jacob and sister Luba? Letters from home had been infrequent; the two had traveled too fast for the Post to catch up with them. Anyway, Post letters were dreadfully expensive, and when they did arrive they were mostly accounts of how hard Nicholenka was working at his piano, exhortations to Villoing concerning procedure, or remarks about the bad condition of the pencil factory. There was going to be a new baby before long, *Maman* had written. Another mouth to feed! She was profoundly grateful for the money Villoing had sent from time to time, and very proud that her son had made this money by his talents. Through all Kaleria's letters, one note predominated: Was Tonia *learning*? How about the counterpoint and fugue he had gone abroad to master? The Queen of Holland had given him a diamond ring and the Queen of England had given him a diamond something else and the great Herr Liszt had bestowed upon him the heritage of his mantle. These were splendid things, said Kaleria, but they were not so splendid as the crown of learning, the laurels of true mastery over one's art.

Villoing, reading, said nothing at all, but he did some rather uncomfortable thinking. Someone had been talking to Kaleria Rubinstein. When they left home she had not been so specific about this infernal fugue. Kaleria was a German at heart, and Germans did not feel as Villoing felt concerning the high artistic value of virtuosity *per se*. Germans desired always to burrow deeper, to uncover the core of things, to take the very heart apart and analyze it.

Master and pupil had been abroad more than three years. Anton Rubinstein had composed music and had played it in public. Yet for all his triumphs, the boy could not, his teacher was well aware, take pen and paper and set one contrapuntal theme over against another.

5

Nicholas Rubinstein. Adieu à Villoing

Someone had indeed been talking to Kaleria Rubinstein. Liszt himself had been in Moscow—Liszt, the king of music whose command Alexandre Villoing had forgotten to obey. The great man came during the winter of 1842, not long after he had talked with Villoing in Paris. But Kaleria was not so concerned over what Liszt told her as Villoing had feared. By the time Herr Liszt arrived, Kaleria was already busy with another son than Anton; for two years now, she had spent upon her boy Nicholas every moment she could snatch from household and factory duties.

The big square piano above the pencil factory had been kept very busy. Nicholas was only four when he waved good-bye to his brother that cold night in the Petersburg coach, but Nicholas was old enough to play the piano. This time, Kaleria Rubinstein did not wait for her pupil to be five. She set him at the piano, and it was apparent immediately that the boy was as gifted as his brother. He was even more mischievous; his devices for squirming out of work were amazing; it required all a mother's ingenuity to circumvent them.

At six every morning, Kaleria routed her youngest son from bed, gave him a cup of milk and drove him to the piano where she made him practice for hours without stopping. Kaleria had heard of Frau Mendelssohn, who sat by the piano hour after hour while her son practiced. Kaleria did not sit by the piano, but she sat in the next room. There was a convenient little window in the wall through which, like the jailer in the Fortress of Peter and Paul, Kaleria could view her victim. In winter the room was dreadfully cold and, except for a round pool of light thrown by the oil lamp back of the piano stool, it was dark as night. Nicholas' eyes would begin to close, his yellow head to nod. Of all things in the world, sleep seemed most desirable, when—rap!—that thimble on the window. If it rapped once more, something worse would follow. Nicholas' back straightened, he sighed a long, childish sigh and in the factory room beneath, workmen, getting ready their machines, heard above their heads the rhythmic, tinkling climb of the C scale.

Gradus ad Parnassum, by M. Clementi—how many small fingers have labored up that steep and sacred slope! When Nicholas was five, Kaleria mercifully varied the monotony of Czerny and Clementi by little "pieces" that at first pleased the boy enormously. But *Maman* did not seem to care about what was pleasing. *Maman* made him play each piece over a stated number of times—ten times, twenty, fifty, a hundred—till it was perfect. Hummel's *Rondo Brilliant* was delightful, the first three times over, but by the fortieth repetition it had become an extreme irritant or else a dangerous soporific. Moreover, *Maman* sat just behind that window counting with a pack of cards. Twelve times the *Rondo*—*Maman* turned down a king. Thirteen times—she turned down the ace. . . .

Nicholas hit upon a superb escape. He had often experimented with modulation, inventing cadences quite as sizzling, in his opinion, as Hummel's or Diabelli's. Now he would make modulation his tool. Nicholenka's blue eyes sparkled; he stole a glance toward his jailer's window. Round and round went the *Rondo Brilliant,* back and back to the central theme. Long before the proper ending, Nicholas invented his cadence, coming down bravely on the tonic after a measure or two of nice embellishment.

It was dazzlingly successful. *Maman* did not even turn her head; the cards slapped down with cheerful rapidity. But one morning Nicholas became a little too fancy and cut a Bach fugue in half. The door opened suddenly; the child felt heavy hands on his shoulders; *Maman's* breath was on his cheek as she bent forward, peering at the music. . . . Thirty years afterward, Nicholas remembered that whipping and told his friend Kashkin about it. "For fraud and laziness," his mother had said.

One memorable day his mother whipped him three times! Nicholas did not always remember the cause, but Kaleria Rubinstein could not bear a lie any more than she could bear an unpaid debt of money. Her children, as they grew older, loved her for it and knew, somehow, that these traits set their mother apart from the easy-going, easily forgiving Russians around them. Their father, for instance, did not tell lies, but he smiled sometimes when Nicholenka was caught in flagrant fairy-telling, and he was always trying to beg off for the boy when Kaleria went for the birch. Afterward, Gregor would sneak into his son's room, pockets full of *pralines*.

After a year of study, Nicholas Rubinstein astonished everyone with his piano playing. Moscow declared him more remarkable even than his brother. After all, Anton Gregorovitch was lost to them now; he was in the West and would come home wearing a stiff collar, making foreign bows and speaking French. Moscow was provincial and loved its own; already the town sensed that Nicholas Gregorovitch would belong to it forever. At any rate, the boy learned with astonishing rapidity; at five Kaleria cast him definitely for the life role of concert artist. His mother loved to teach this boy. There was about him something enchanting. Anton was handsomer and had in him a force that made for respect, but Nicholenka was so very human! Nicholenka erred and was forgiven; he never bore malice; he was as good-natured as his father. And how he loved to laugh! He made friends instantly with young and old, with dogs and cats and everything that drew breath; the house and yard were always full of Nicholenka's friends, waiting for him to finish practicing and come out to play. Brother Jacob, dark-haired and dark-skinned, was in the *Realschule* now, preparing to enter the Surgical Academy and become a doctor like the good Rosenberg. Nicholas was seven and Luba was ten. Gregor Románovitch wore a medal around his neck at last and sat proudly at the meetings of the Merchants of the Second Guild.

Life would have been very pleasant indeed, if only the pencil factory had flourished. All the meetings and medals in Moscow could not cause those ledger sheets to balance. Kaleria spent hours at the big desk next the machine room, frowning and shaking her head. God be praised for two talented boys! If only they could manage to secure a thorough musical education, they would eventually take care of themselves and of their parents too. Only last week, when things at the factory had looked very black indeed and Gregor, returning from town, had said he could not persuade so much as a Blue Bill (five roubles) out of the bankers, a miracle had occurred that logically might prove the forerunner of other such miracles. A thousand roubles had arrived in a foreign envelope postmarked Berlin. Villoing wrote that Anton had earned it in two concerts. Gregor Románovitch, meeting a neighbor on the streets of Moscow, told about it with tears in his eyes. Kaleria did not say much; she looked at the money and then she rose and called Nicholas from the yard to practice, speaking to him sharply. "Nicholenka, you are seven. Shall your brother leave you behind in the race?"

Nicholenka did not care anything about races, but it was easier to do quickly what *Maman* wished, and anyway, it was so beautiful to see her smile when one had earned a smile. "Ho!" said Nicholenka. "Hear me play the Liszt *Galop, Maman!* Herr Liszt himself cannot run a faster chromatic scale."

Herr Liszt himself was soon to judge this question. When the great man came to town, Nicholas was seven—a small boy who played the piano from a high chair, squirming in vain to reach the pedal. Kaleria took him to hear the king of music play. Afterward Liszt asked to meet the brother of that Anton Rubinstein who had played so beautifully in Paris last year. Kaleria came forward, Nicholas' hand in hers. Liszt told her of Anton's triumphs in Paris, of how the boy had fallen ill after hearing his concert, how he had comforted the child and put him to sleep. Anton was destined for greatness, said Herr Liszt. And this little child, this Nicholenka—he also played the *fortepiano*?

The room where they were talking contained a piano; Kaleria looked anxiously about for a high chair. She hesitated—but Nicholenka did not hesitate. Quite cheerfully he went forward and played standing up, sliding his foot to the pedal, his whole body in motion, not a note missed. The king of music was pleased and said so, and then sat down and played himself for the Rubinsteins—a favor great musicians do not grant to tyros. So Chopin had sat and played for young Anton in Paris.

Liszt honored the family Rubinstein still further by coming over to the Ordinka to call on them. He talked seriously with Kaleria concerning the education of her sons. Had Monsieur Villoing taken Anton to Germany for study, as recommended? This boy also, this little Nicholenka, must go to Germany. Berlin was the best place now; Mendelssohn was there, and Siegfried Dehn the great counterpoint scholar. Would Madame Rubinstein like a letter to Herr Mendelssohn?

Kaleria accepted gratefully. Anton was still wandering in Europe. When he returned home she would judge for herself how much he had learned and how much he needed to learn. Meanwhile she would, said Kaleria, continue to teach Nicholas and to consider ways and means of getting the boys to Berlin.

The king of music looked with respect upon the handsome mother of two such sons; he kissed her hand in the best Lisztian manner and departed for Petersburg and triumphs unparalleled. Petersburg went wild over Franz Liszt; deputations stood on the steps of his hotel, waiting to crown him with flowers. A Polish princess, dark-eyed and fiery, heard him play and forgot her correct military husband and all the Podolian acres of the Witgenstein estates and became Liszt's inseparable companion for almost a lifetime. Not many years were to pass before Anton Rubinstein was to dine with this princess in Liszt's house at Weimar.

As for little Nicholas Rubinstein, he heard the king of music play, but he did not go into nervous attacks over it. He listened, and then played himself for Herr Liszt because *Maman* told him to. Then he went home and forgot about it.

In February, 1843, Anton and his teacher were due to arrive in Petersburg. Kaleria did not go north to meet them. She could not afford it and besides, she was too busy. Anton was to perform with the Petersburg Philharmonic and then take coach for Moscow.

Rocking his way in the sledge-coach from Warsaw with his

teacher, Anton Rubinstein was happy to be going home. Happy to give and receive Russian greetings, to see the huge samovar bubbling at the post stations, to wear the warm *shuba* and felt boots once more. In Warsaw he had played Villoing's C-minor Concerto very successfully; he hoped the Petersburg public would like it as well, but he was doubtful of the Petersburg orchestra. Villoing said they were an ill-assorted lot of players. Well, if they lost him as the Vienna orchestra had done in this same concerto, he would simply keep on till they found him. It was rather fun when something happened. Would the Tsar be at his concert?—Anton inquired of his teacher.

On March 20, 1843, Rubinstein played for the first time in Petersburg at a concert of the Philharmonic Society. Tsar Nicholas was indeed present, with his Tsarina who was instantly charmed by this fair-haired, spirited boy. Moreover, her son Konstantin had written about Anton from Amsterdam. She had been expecting him, said the Tsarina gaily; let him stand on a footstool then, so she could embrace him! The Tsar kissed him on both cheeks and asked jocularly, "How is Your Excellency?"

Everyone at court was an Excellency in those days—everyone, that is, but a Jew. This affable sovereign, relentless foe of Israel, who had driven sixty Rubinsteins to the altar, might have been surprised had he known that this little Jewish boy would some day be an Excellency in earnest.

The Emperor's embrace was a prelude to glory. Anton was summoned to the Palace and played again and again, coming away, he said, "heaped with gifts." Sometimes the gifts did not appear until next day, when they were sent to his lodgings by messenger. Villoing appraised them carefully; such valuables were all he had to take home to Kaleria Rubinstein; he had used up his last cash in travel. "I brought," wrote Anton, "many princely gifts from German courts, but certainly I had nowhere seen such generous and costly presents as the ones in Petersburg, especially as they were handed me on the spot in the Palace immediately after I played. The ones that came later through the office were not so valuable."

Gregor Románovitch Rubinstein wearing the medal
of his Merchant Guild

Early or late, Anton Rubinstein never questioned the rightness of Majesty. In the Rubinstein family, so intelligent, so ambitious, there existed, where Majesty was concerned, a curious paralysis of the critical faculty, a total disregard of the sequence of cause and effect. Tsar Nicholas was, from the beginning, personally kind to Anton Rubinstein; later on, the very existence of Nicholas Pavlovitch was to stand like a wall between Rubinstein and all he desired to achieve in the world of music. Yet Anton never raised the smallest voice in rebuke or rebellion—and Anton was not a patient man.

Truly there must have been in the person of this Emperor a very potent charm. Handsome, erect, he wore his epaulettes with more style than any general in Europe. Queen Victoria called him the handsomest sovereign she had ever seen. So convinced was Tsar Nicholas of the rightness of majesty that his presence carried something truly commanding. When he entered the room, men trembled—and his rare smile was correspondingly valued. "I remember with great gratitude," wrote Anton Rubinstein, "the kindness shown me as a child by the august family of Emperor Nicholas Pavlovitch. The family was very gracious to me. The Empress Alexandra Feodorovna loved music; the Emperor Nicholas was in his own way a musician and an artist. There was in him a true musical vein, a quick capacity to catch and remember a tune. I heard him one time at home sing right through a whole opera, and once I heard him whistle the entire music for the opera *Fenella*. He knew by heart the music for the ballet *Catherine, or the Brigand's Daughter*."

Villoing and Anton stayed longer in Petersburg than they had planned; it was June before they took coach for Moscow. News of the Petersburg triumphs had preceded them; Anton entered town a conquering hero. "Our Rubinstein is with us once more," said the Moscow *Galatea*. "Once more his sensitive fingers will flutter." His parents embraced him—Gregor with tears of joy, Kaleria with one eye upon Villoing, of whom, she said, she had many questions to ask. The plaid carpetbag was opened; out of it fell diamond stickpins, diamond brooches and all manner of royal gifts. Kaleria sent Gregor Románovitch to the best pawnshop in town. Gregor came home smiling and threw away the pawn tickets. Now they could invite all their friends to dinner.

Kaleria counted the money and went into conference with Villoing. There was no time for reproach; Kaleria understood well enough why her son had come home as innocent of counterpoint as when he set out for Europe three years ago. He was thirteen —not yet too old to learn musical theory. Money must be raised for an immediate journey to Berlin. There were two pupils now instead of one; Villoing had heard Nicholenka play. It was June. Could Villoing give Nicholas a few lessons, laying out his summer's work, and then take Anton on a concert tour of Russia to raise money for the Berlin journey? When the concert tour was ended, Villoing could spend the winter teaching the boys to play together; pianoforte duets were especially popular with the public just now. By the New Year, the boys should be ready to earn at least part of their way to Berlin. Kaleria would write to her cousins in Warsaw; she was sure they would advance her some money.

Villoing's response was immediate and wholehearted. He took Anton off to Nizhni-Novgorod where the boy played, he afterward told his mother, for exactly one deaf old man who had come to the concert to prove to the neighbors that he was not deaf and loved music. The tour was arduous. Dust and peasants and broken-down stagecoaches were not much fun after Paris and Vienna. But they brought home some money, and when the New Year came, Kaleria's program proceeded according to schedule. Anton was fourteen now; Nicholas was nine. A new baby sister had arrived during the summer. Kaleria intended to go herself to Berlin with the boys and to take their sister Luba with her, but she could not leave while the baby was still at her breast. She sent the boys up to Petersburg on a trial trip to see how the new duets would please the public. Anton declared himself quite competent to take care of his brother.

The boys found themselves in furnished rooms, quite alone, all their money gone but twenty kopecks. Most unexpectedly, appear-

54

ing at the door like a fairy messenger, arrived an equerry from Court. How splendid he looked in their shabby lodging, with his gold braid and shining boots! He took the boys in a beautiful sleigh to the Winter Palace, where they played and were kissed and petted and given, not diamond brooches but frilly bonbons. At nine in the evening they were returned to their lodgings, appetites only sharpened by Imperial delicacies. "I am a famous artist!" Anton told his brother. "I must not be seen in the bazaar with only twenty kopecks. Yet if we wait for the Tsar's messenger to bring presents, we shall starve. Run out, thou, and buy black bread and cucumbers."

Nicholas did as he was bid. Next morning rescue appeared in the welcome form of Gregor Románovitch who had come to fetch the boys home. With cries of delight, Nicholas threw himself upon his father, but Anton merely nodded to his parent as became an artist who had supped with his Tsar. This was too much for Gregor Románovitch. He fetched the great artist a cuff on the ear; they both broke into sobs and, recorded Nicholas, "it was a long time before either could calm himself."

After this the three left happily for Moscow by diligence.

In the spring of 1844 Kaleria was ready to leave Moscow. The plan was to go first to Petersburg and give a few concerts, then on to Berlin by way of Dorpat, Riga and Warsaw.

Kaleria advertised her departure three times in the newspaper, according to law. Then she took the newspapers under her arm to the College of Commerce and sat about in dingy ante-rooms waiting for her passport. Gregor had told her to be quick with her bribe, but Kaleria's hand, unlike her husband's, was slow toward the pocket. Kaleria waited and then gave five roubles to a man with dirty gold braid on his collar, and went back to the Ordinka carrying a passport on which were inscribed four names: Kaleria, Anton, Nicholas and Luba. Pretty Luba was twelve and the most agreeable companion imaginable. Anton was quite delirious with pleasure at the thought of showing his sister the sights of Europe.

The tenderest farewell, next to Gregor Rubinstein's, came from

Alexandre Villoing. There was no question of Villoing's accompanying them. All Moscow was clamoring to study with the master of so dazzling a success as Anton Gregorovitch. And Villoing needed money; the European tour had netted him nothing financially, beyond his living and traveling expenses. But as speculation toward the future it had been a complete success; the rest of Villoing's life would be built around it. Moreover, Villoing had no desire to sit idly in Berlin while his pupils attended a counterpoint factory.

But it was hard to say good-bye, hard to see Anton go from under his hand, and Nicholenka too. Villoing had become very fond of Nicholenka this past winter. He was an affectionate child, extraordinarily responsive and every bit as gifted as Anton, with the same broad hand and padded finger tips. The only difference was that Nicholas did not like platforms. He did not mind playing in public and he was a success wherever he appeared, but he did not regard the public seriously, as his brother did. "If we need money, I will play," said Nicholenka—and played and trundled off home to bed. Plainly, Nicholas looked upon his brother as the hero of the family and upon himself, quite contentedly, as a second number.

For their last evening together, Nicholas had composed a piece, *Adieu à Villoing*. He played it, squirming down for the pedal with his toe, and when he was done, ran from the piano and threw himself tearfully upon his teacher. Anton wept, Gregor wept, Kaleria and her son Jacob sat hand in hand, very silent.

At midnight in the big barn beside the coach and the stamping horses, Gregor Rubinstein embraced his wife. It was well that neither husband nor wife knew they would not meet again.

6

Palace interlude. Kaleria's two swans

ALL the way to Petersburg, Anton pointed out the sights to a small brother who by turns was wildly excited and nodding with sleep. But Kaleria's face, when she looked from the coach window, was more grave than smiling. More than once she opened her wallet to count roubles that she already knew by heart. Could the boys collect enough concert money in Petersburg to pay off the first part of the debt to her cousins in Warsaw? Kaleria Rubinstein was restless under debt; the boys must be made to understand that they earn their way—or return to Moscow.

Kaleria wrote about what happened in Petersburg. A German aunt happily decided this communication was history and preserved it:

Petersburg
May 23, 1844

"Until this minute I could not write you, as I have been too busy. But now, dear Aunt, I shall tell you many splendid things about my children. Unfortunately, I have not much to say about the concerts here as to profits, which were meager. But the first concert was attended by the Imperial family, who called the children to their box. They were kindly welcomed and talked to for a long time. The Grand Duchess Maria Nicholaevna kissed my Nicholenka! Her Majesty said to them, 'We are old acquaintances. We shall meet this summer in Berlin,' etc. All the Imperial family were delighted with the children.

"On April third the children were invited to Court, where they were wonderfully well received. Her Majesty commanded them to play. When Nicholenka played, the Grand Duchess Olga worked the pedal for him, and while Anton was playing the Empress told Nicholenka to sit by her on the footstool and petted him and talked with him, asking if he were tired, if he were hungry. . . . Just then the Emperor came in with the Grand Duke; they had been to the theatre. The children stood up, but His Majesty told them to be

57

seated. After supper the Emperor said, 'Clever lads, clever lads.' Pointing to Anton he said, 'That is Liszt, and this one' (pointing to Nicholenka), 'this is Number Two.'

"Then His Majesty said to Nicholenka, 'I have often been told that you play well and even compose. Is it true?' Then all the high society replied that it was quite unbelievably true; the boy could indeed play. The Emperor said, 'Play me Liszt's *Hungarian March* for four hands.' All the time they were playing, His Majesty applauded without stopping. Then His Majesty said, 'Play me something of your own compositions.' So Nicholenka played his *Nocturne*—which I am sending you, dear Aunt, and which pleased His Majesty extremely. The Grand Duchess Maria kissed him and asked him to copy the piece for her.

"When the children were ready to go home, the Emperor said to them, 'Study and learn. Do not be naughty. Then you will bring honor to Russia.' Three days later presents arrived from Court, to Anton a beautiful diamond pin, to Nicholenka a beautiful gold watch. On April sixteenth they were invited again, with Naumann [a violinist who was visiting Petersburg]. There was a big evening party at Court, and after he had played, Naumann was thanked and told adieu; he went home. The children wanted to go with him, but the Emperor said, 'The children must stay and have supper with us.' Imagine, what an honor! He talked with them a lot. The Grand Duchess Maria gave Nicholenka permission to dedicate his *Nocturne* to her and told him he must bring it to her himself.

"Some days later, each of the children received a beautiful diamond ring. Briefly, aside from money, things could not be better. You cannot imagine what honors have come to the children. Perhaps some day the money will come too.

"Now, dear Aunt, I have told you all that has happened. We go now to Warsaw, by Riga."

The letter ends with instructions to address her care of the Brothers Levenstein, in Warsaw. Before setting out, Kaleria took two diamond rings to the pawnshop. Selling these Imperial gifts was not at all like an ordinary visit to the pawnshop. One was bowed to the street by the entire staff, rubbing its hands and murmuring congratulations. Kaleria swept into the May morning, her purse heavy with gold. Plainly, two *Wunderkinder* could capture one more diamond than one *Wunderkind*.

She had not been wrong about the pianoforte duets, Kaleria reflected as the coach for Riga floundered through the spring mud outside of Petersburg. But then, Kaleria Rubinstein was seldom wrong about anything. She could not afford to be wrong.

7

1844. Mendelssohn and Siegfried Dehn.
Kaleria faces disaster

KALERIA RUBINSTEIN had not been three days in Berlin when she knew she was going to love this city. People here were serious and told the truth; a piece of work begun was a piece of work finished; one's daily routine was dictated not by the emotion of the moment, as in Moscow, but by the mind.

"Europe's stronghold of reason"—so a pupil of Chopin called Berlin in 1840. Dresden was "a charming butterfly-casket, where one finds everything—as in a surgeon's case—except caliber." Compared with Paris, where wit took the place of philosophy and a *bon mot* was treasured above wisdom, Berlin was indeed a stronghold of reason. A prison-house, most Parisians would have called it. "Those Lutherans!" wrote Berlioz to Hans Von Bülow, "people who never laugh, blond without gentleness."

Kaleria Rubinstein was blonde. She was forty-one when she brought her boys to Berlin; her sons could testify that, very often, she had not been gentle. In Berlin she was "Clara" again, as she had been in childhood. The German tongue clipped two soft syllables from her name. There was "caliber" enough in Berlin to satisfy even Clara Rubinstein. There was caliber in the University, which still shone with the aura of its great idealist philosophers: Fichte, Schelling, Hegel. At the famous Sundays in Leipzigerstrasse, Hegel was the only guest whom Abraham Mendelssohn had permitted to make up a game of cards while the music played.

Kaleria Rubinstein knew about Hegel, but she knew more about the Mendelssohn family that had entertained him. Abraham Mendelssohn was dead when the Rubinsteins came to Berlin, but Abraham's son Felix was the backbone, with Meyerbeer, of musical Berlin—and was that not caliber enough for any city? The new king of Prussia had not been on the throne a year when he summoned home the musical troops, Mendelssohn from Leipzig to direct the new Royal Academy of Music, Meyerbeer from Paris to manage the Royal Opera and the *Hoforchester*.

Meyerbeer was middle-aged now and very celebrated; Felix Mendelssohn was thirty-five; the old home on Leipzigerstrasse was broken up. Felix spent his Berlin months at his sister Fanny's but although he adored his sister, he declared himself oppressed by the nearness of the Court and the heavy air of officialdom; he preferred his Leipzig position. Mendelssohn was attracted to the new king, but he hated all ministers of state who meddled in musical affairs and he was constantly at odds with the authorities. Nevertheless, his influence pervaded all Berlin, and his influence was militantly on the side of pure music and sound scholarship.

The musical world of the 1840's was in need of such idealism as Mendelssohn's. The first quarter of the nineteenth century had nourished a craze for musical fireworks, for technique *per se*. Violinists chose one concerto, practiced it for years and practiced nothing else, then played it flawlessly. Technique was god; musicianship was not even the god's handmaiden. Louis Spohr, visiting Paris in the early twenties, had been shocked to discover that Parisians had no use for "an earnest, well-digested piece of music such as a quartet or quintet of our great masters." The Parisians had no use, either, for artistic feeling. If Spohr ventured to play a singing *cantabile* on his violin, Paris called it "too straightforward," and Spohr was forced to omit all adagios from his concerts. The great literature of classical music was unknown; Beethoven's sonatas were buried beneath heaps of *Concertstück* by Hummel, Herz and Kalkbrenner. "Here in Paris," complained one German student, "Beethoven is spelled J. N. Hummel."

Music needed crusaders—and crusaders were given to it. By the middle thirties, Liszt and Chopin had done much to educate Parisian taste, and down in Leipzig, Robert Schumann proclaimed passionately that music was more than technique. Music was poetry,

61

cried Schumann. Music was not bravura variations, *pièces de salon* and fantasias upon favorite operatic airs. A new spirit was abroad. "A rosy light," wrote Schumann, "is dawning in the sky. Whence it cometh I know not; but in any case, O youth, make for the light!"

Chopin, Schumann, Liszt—the great romanticists—were not only creaters but teachers of a new musical gospel, active crusaders for their belief. And with them marched Mendelssohn, the scholar, the classicist who knew that the immediate past held beauty as relevant to life and love as did the immediate future. It was Mendelssohn who revived Bach's *Matthew Passion* that had lain dusty on the shelf for a hundred years. Mendelssohn was only twenty when he dared this at the Berlin *Singakademie* one night against the sinister prophecy of all musical Berlin. A thousand persons were turned from the doors; the false prophets hung their heads and Felix Mendelssohn went out to resurrect cantatas for a public that hungered after the sustaining, long-forgotten music of the great cantor.

Mendelssohn was in Frankfurt when Kaleria Rubinstein brought her boys to Berlin; he was due at the Royal Academy the end of September. But Kaleria was not impatient. Herr Meyerbeer was in town; she had a letter to him and he was immediately kind and invited them all to his house every Sunday. Meyerbeer greeted Anton Rubinstein like an old friend, asked after Monsieur Villoing and promised Kaleria tickets for every Opera and *Hoforchester* concert all winter. And when Mendelssohn arrived, he too remembered Anton and wanted to know why the boy had left London so quickly after the concert in Hanover Square.

Felix and his sister Fanny were instantly drawn to these Russian boys whose musical temperament, so wild, so passionate, differed from their own deep German precision. They had another bond: were not all four—Mendelssohns and Rubinsteins—the baptized children of Jews? Did they speak of this together over the coffee and *Lebkuchen*? Did Kaleria and Fanny Mendelssohn mention that other converted Jew lying helpless on his mattress in Paris? "I am hated alike by Jew and Christian," Heinrich Heine had said. "When it became clear to me that Judaism was not a religion but a misfortune, I had myself baptized, and I regret it very deeply. I do not think I have been the better for it since."

Whatever the women talked about, all through it ran the sound of music, such music as Kaleria, on her Bessarabian farm, had longed for. Here with Mendelssohn the boys heard nothing of the *bravura* music that was the order of the day in Petersburg and Paris. The man who said, "I do not in the least concern myself as to what people wish or praise or pay for, but solely as to what I consider good,"—the man who confessed he could not understand "how anybody could get through twenty-four hours without playing some Sonata or Trio"—the man who said that what inspired his career was "to help the progress of art along the path that seemed to him the right one"—that man was Mendelssohn, and Kaleria's instinct had been sound when she brought her boys to him. Anton especially, with his stage-tricks and his quite calm acceptance of himself as a full-fledged success, needed to drink at this pure fountain.

Mendelssohn told Kaleria where to place her boys as students. Anton, he said, needed no further instruction on the pianoforte, but Nicholas should take lessons from Kullak. As for harmony, theory, counterpoint—Siegfried Dehn was the man. Kullak himself was student of Dehn's; so was Friedrich Kiel. Dehn was custodian of the music collection at the Royal Library; he knew all the music that ever was written and could take a five-part fugue apart and put it together again as easily as a watchmaker could repair the town chimes. Whoever emerged from Dehn's classroom, said Mendelssohn, carried his teacher's mark upon him—the ineradicable stamp of seriousness.

Kaleria Rubinstein looked at her sons and smiled. Seriousness, she said, was what they had come to Berlin to find.

Siegfried Dehn was, indeed, one of the most celebrated musical theorists of his century. Dehn had originally studied jurisprudence. The logic of counterpoint, the nice harmonic fitting of seam to seam, apparently pleases the legal mind. To master musical theory is to master the very essence of form. And how Siegfried Dehn loved to square the circle, loved to see the round completion of a musical phrase! With his silver-rimmed spectacles, high forehead, strong chin and careful, old-fashioned clothes, he looked, when the Rubinstein boys came to him, more like a gentleman barrister than a music teacher.

"Musical ideas without form," Herr Dehn proclaimed in his clipped, positive voice, "fail to possess an organic existence."

Strange nourishment this, for Russians, and hard to digest. The Rubinstein boys listened, but it was the younger one, Dehn soon found, who responded. This older boy, Anton, had *pianoforte* on the brain like a disease; he could not forget his fingers long enough to work properly on paper. He was always rushing to the instrument to try out his compositions. Compositions, indeed! Did he think he was Chopin, roared Dehn, composing thus on the keys? Except Chopin, nobody of the first rank had composed at the instrument. Sebastian Bach had called such keyboard composers "harpsichord knights" and laughed at them.

But Nicholas Rubinstein, though only ten, seized like lightning upon these problems of fitting and seaming with pen and paper. "In two years," Dehn told him, "you will be ready for counterpoint. Meanwhile you will work at thorough-bass, which Sebastian Bach has told us is the whole foundation of music." Did the boys know, asked the Herr Professor eagerly, what Bach himself had said concerning figured bass? Well, he would tell them and they could learn the words by heart. Played with both hands, said Bach, figured bass results in *"an agreeable harmony to the glory of God and the justifiable gratification of the senses; for the sole end and aim of general bass, like that of all music, should be nothing else than God's glory and pleasant recreation. Where this object is not kept in view . . ."* Here Dehn paused, looking over his glasses at Anton Rubinstein, *"Where this end is not kept in view there can be no true music, but an infernal scraping and bawling."*

Coming home in the cold north-German dusk to the furnished rooms they shared with their mother, the boys recited the words together. Nicholas was mischievous and, while he proclaimed the

64

rolling German sentences, pretended to look over his spectacles like the Herr Professor Dehn. But Kaleria was well pleased. A year or two of such teaching and her sons would be safe forever against the temptations of foolish music, against the flashy transcriptions and "arrangements" so much in vogue.

The boys had other lessons than music; Kaleria sent them to a priest of the Orthodox Russian Church—a Father Dormidont—to learn their catechism and some much-needed Russian grammar. As long as the money lasted the boys gave no public concerts, but Kaleria permitted them to play informally at private houses and musical clubs. The Empress Alexandra came over from Petersburg for her promised visit; the boys played for her and took home to their mother diamond-studded boxes enough to live upon for a year.

Kaleria Rubinstein had a lovely time here in Berlin. On Sundays at Fanny Mendelssohn Hensel's or at Herr Meyerbeer's, she and her boys met everyone musical that mattered. Nearly every night there was music somewhere—at the *Singakademie* or the Opera or some private *Musikabend*. The new Opera House was very splendid; Herr Mendelssohn told Kaleria privately that Meyerbeer's *Hoforchester* did not compare with his own orchestra in Leipzig; he blamed it on the Court, not on Herr Meyerbeer. The *Hoforchester* had had only one conductor before Meyerbeer; previously it had been, like all German orchestras, composed half of amateurs, some of them royalties and half-royalties—always an awkward situation for conductors. What could you do with a Grand Duke who played out of tune, when the Grand Duke had financed the concert and furnished the refreshments and bought shoes for all the woodwind and paid for the clarinetist's wife's last *accouchement*? Sometimes Royalty insisted not only upon playing in the orchestra but conducting the whole show, like the Grand Duke of Darmstadt who used to conduct the Sunday operas at his theatre, dressed in full uniform, star on breast. He could barely read music and would call out *"Piano! Forte!"* in the wrong places and cause dreadful confusion in the ranks. Grand Dukes were bad enough, but sometimes they were a better risk than other amateurs in the band, the fiddling shoe-makers, the barber-surgeons groaning on their double basses. After Beethoven appeared, these shoemakers and Grand Dukes had to retreat; Herr Beethoven's music was too black and dangerous for any Crown Prince to attempt.

It was no easy matter, Herr Mendelssohn told Kaleria Rubinstein, to assemble orchestras able to play modern scores. Every player must be thoroughly competent, a professional who spent his time at nothing but music. This meant a whole new scheme of financing; it meant tickets at the door and consequently, a performance that gave the ticket-buyers their money's worth.

And consequently—replied Kaleria gaily, the Rubinstein family was enjoying the *Hoforchester*! The question of how to finance musicians lay very close to her heart; she knew two musicians who were soon going to have to finance *her*. Meanwhile she would hear music and more music.

Kaleria drank in music, these two winters, as Gregor Rubinstein, back in Moscow, drank in *kvas*, and her conscientious German soul was intoxicated and forgot itself. But not, unfortunately, for long. Word came from Moscow that Gregor Rubinstein was ill—was very ill. Kaleria had barely time to pack her belongings for travel when she heard that her husband was dead.

For the Rubinstein family this meant more than grief; it meant calamity, a drawing-in of horizon, a closing of doors that had only just been opened. It meant poverty. Kaleria had known the pencil factory was failing; when she left home, she had adjured her husband to keep her posted. But Gregor Rubinstein's was not a nature to purvey bad news; he wrote his wife affectionately, saying that if she kept the Berlin end of the family afloat, she could leave the Moscow end to him.

Gregor kept his factory afloat—on loans from every friend he had in Moscow.

Kaleria did not learn the extent of this indebtedness immediately, but the letter informing her of Gregor's death said plainly there was no money left. Could Kaleria Christoforovna bring home enough to pay for a funeral befitting Gregor Románovitch's position as merchant?

With her bonnet on for travel, with three coach tickets in her pocket, Kaleria sent Nicholas and Luba into the bedroom of her Berlin lodging—bleak now, with all the belongings packed—and read this letter to Anton. She would have to take the younger children home. Anton must stay on in Berlin or wherever the concert business proved briskest; Europe certainly held more financial promise than Russia. There was no further question of lessons with Dehn or with anybody else. From now on he must play for his supper; God grant that she and Nicholenka in Moscow could successfully play for theirs.

Anton heard her with a mixture of sorrow and mounting pride. He was nearly sixteen: he was a man; his mother was looking to him as a man. He put his little family on the coach for Warsaw. "*Auf Wiedersehen,* Nicholenka," said Anton. "Practice your piano. Do not be lazy, and do not tell lies."

For Kaleria Rubinstein it was a sad parting and a sad homecoming. She found the pencil factory mortgaged to the hilt. She should never have left home, Kaleria told herself. Gregor had been unfit for business; he was too kind, business had killed him.

There was little time for regrets; debtors were no respecters of a widow's weeds. Kaleria put Luba in school and, to pay the tuition, herself took a position as governess in the same school. Her eldest son, Jacob, was in the Surgical Academy now; somehow she would keep him there. Determinedly Kaleria set herself to pay off every one of her husband's debts, giving music lessons, French lessons, German lessons from one end of Moscow to the other. Nicholas she sent off with Villoing on a concert tour of Russia. Villoing had come forward immediately; no one, in fact, had been kinder.

Nicholas was eleven; there was no question, this time, of sparing her son the rigors of the concert platform. It was play or starve. For two years, Nicholas and his teacher traveled around Russia,

67

making money and incidentally, making friends that were later to stand Nicholas Gregorovitch in good stead. Not only Moscow but all Russia began to know that the name Nicholas Gregorovitch meant music. To Russia as to the world, Anton was always to be, quite formally, *Anton Rubinstein,* but nobody in Russia ever thought of calling Nicholas by his last name. He was too close a friend, and belonged to Moscow—bearing only the familiar patronymic so comfortable to Russian tongues. Nicholas, first and last, was *Nicholas Gregorovitch.*

The boy was thirteen when he returned with Villoing from his long concert tour. He was playing, by now, such difficult pieces as Liszt's *Don Juan Fantasia.* Villoing told Kaleria Rubinstein he had taught the boy all he could teach anybody; from now on, Nicholenka must make his way alone.

The old home beyond the Ordinka was gone. Kaleria Rubinstein was living in a school where she could see her sons only by appointment; Nicholas Gregorovitch made his home with his uncles. Soberly the boy asked himself what lay ahead for him. He could play the piano and play it well, but a life of concert platforms loomed as a life of horror. Let Anton have the laurel wreaths and the diamond snuff boxes and the eternal traveling in foreign countries. Moscow was what Nicholas loved! But if he sat around Moscow playing the piano and giving lessons, he would presently and inevitably find himself, of all places, in the army. Now that there was no money to buy a substitute, he would be liable for Imperial service only a year or two hence. Even the concert platform would be preferable to that. A stiff collar and a bugle at dawn? Nicholas shuddered. Brother Jacob was exempt from conscription because he was a student at the University.

Here was the solution. He too would enter Moscow University and prepare for some kind—any kind—of a career. True enough, he knew almost nothing except music and languages. It would be necessary to go to school first and obtain a certificate. But there was no money for school. Very well, he would tutor, and pass an independent examination. But there was no money for tutoring. . . .

Nicholas and Anton Rubinstein. *From the portrait by Sokolov*

"Maman," said Nicholas Gregorovitch, his blue eyes sober, "I will teach myself these mathematics and this Latin they say I have to learn. And I will earn my board with Uncle Emmanuel, and my tuition for the University, by playing the piano. You and Tonia and Monsieur Alexandre are not the only ones who know how to teach rich little girls to play waltzes on the *fortepiano*."

8

1846-1848. Farewell Wunderkind. Revolution

O<small>N THAT</small> summer day of 1846 when Kaleria Rubinstein left her
son Anton alone in Berlin, the boy went home to his deserted lodgings and sat down to think over his position. For the first time in
his hard-working, triumphant life, he was alone. For sixteen years,
his days and his hours had been charted by *Maman* or by Villoing.
He had followed willingly. And always reward had come.

Now he must chart his own way. It was fortunate for Anton
Rubinstein that he did not realize how much alone he really was.
His youth had experienced triumphs and successes quite foreign to
the natural progress of boyhood; that Anton's head had not been
turned was due to the unremitting discipline of his teachers—Villoing and Dehn—and his mother's quiet, inexorable attitude of expecting from her children nothing but the best.

In that last brief conference in the Berlin bedroom, Kaleria
Rubinstein had said very little to her son. There had been no ora-
tory, no valedictory concerning the good life. Anton, remembering
now, was dimly grateful. His mother had counted over their joint
money, had placed on his bureau what she could spare, and looking
at him just once, a long look, had pressed his hand. There had
been tears in her eyes, and at this rare sight the boy had felt a sudden surge of emotion, a rising, roaring wave that threatened to engulf him if he spoke one answering word.

He felt it again, sitting in the empty room, remembering his
mother's face. But the feeling was not a sad one. It was a shout of
courage, urging him on. Oh, he would do great things! He would
write symphonies, operas, oratorios. Herr Dehn had said he was
not ready to write music, that if he was a man at the keyboard he
was only a babe at the writing table. Herr Dehn said a man should

be able to play every instrument in the orchestra before he tried to write a symphony, that it was dangerous to let one's manual technique outstrip one's intellectual equipment.

Dangerous! Ho, thought Anton Rubinstein, springing to his feet. Danger was a good word, a meaty, salty word. He would not stay a minute longer in Berlin, where Dehn and Mendelssohn and Meyerbeer invited him to dinner and gave him cautious, sober advice on how to become a musician. Vienna was the magic word! Vienna that had nourished Haydn, Mozart, Schubert, Beethoven, would surely nourish Anton Rubinstein. . . . Poverty? Poverty was boring; it meant bad food and dingy bedrooms, but given a piano and an audience, one could always, in an hour, play oneself out of poverty.

"In 1846," wrote Anton, "I started alone for Vienna, a youth of sixteen. I chose Vienna because it was one of the principal musical centers of Europe and the home of Liszt, Tsar of Music, upon whose help and protection I counted."

Franz Liszt was not sober and cautious like the Herren Mendelssohn and Dehn. Liszt was Hungarian. In him was something wild and dazzling that Anton had responded to as a little boy. Liszt would understand that Anton Rubinstein, at sixteen, desired not study, but a career and a quick one. Liszt would stretch out his hand and wave the magic wand; platforms would cry out for Anton Rubinstein, piano factories would lend him their instruments. The Paris triumphs would begin all over again and money would flow home to Moscow in a steady stream.

"I counted upon Liszt's help and protection. But these hopes were immediately dashed by the dry reserve of Liszt's welcome. He warned me that a talented person must attain his goal alone, by his own efforts, not leaning upon other men's help."

It was a hurt, bewildered boy who turned from Liszt's door that

71

day and faced the city of Vienna, a city gay and brilliant and more unkind to the stranger than the Sahara itself. Anton found himself a cheap bedroom and considered his next move.

"I had with me some ten or eleven letters of introduction from the Russian Ambassador in Berlin and his wife. I called and left the letters, then waited for the invitations that must follow. My only answer was silence. Silence answered the first letter, the second, third, fourth. What could be the matter? I was amazed. Well then, think I, let's look and see what they wrote about me in these letters of introduction. A big pile of them still remained on my table. I opened one; and what did I see? *'Dearest Countess So-and-so: To the title and position we hold as Ambassador and Ambassador's wife is attached the very tedious duty of presenting and introducing various of our countrymen, often at their own urgent request. Therefore we introduce to you the bearer of this letter, one Rubinstein . . .'*

"Well, that was one for me! It was clear now, why silence had followed all those letters. The rest vanished instantly into my stove."

Thus the iron entered into a soul that until now had been innocent. Villoing, Anton remembered, had delivered letters. In Paris, Vienna, Leipzig, London, Villoing had gone downstairs with a whole sheaf of envelopes in his pocket, telling Anton to practice until he came back. The letters had been answered by powdered footmen bearing invitations. In Berlin, *Maman* had called only once upon Herr Mendelssohn and gates had everywhere been flung wide open.

Anton did not know that before delivering his letters, Alexandre Villoing had laid a careful train of powder all the way from Petersburg to Paris. Moreover, the person, the bearing of Kaleria Rubinstein was something every musician respected upon sight, something earned by long years of courage, intelligence and pride. Kaleria and Villoing had introduced by their letters, not a serious youth bent upon money-making, but a *Wunderkind,* a pet, a toy for society to amuse itself with.

The soft pleasant wave that had surged upward within Anton

Rubinstein dwindled now to something small and hard and bright that he had never felt before, something that burned and prodded, following him through the streets, driving him, in default of a piano, to his attic writing table. . . . So they did not trust him, these kings of music, these Dearest Countess So-and-sos! He was an upstart, an unknown, he was "one Rubinstein." What was it his mother had said to Madame Mendelssohn-Hensel that Sunday afternoon in Berlin, about Henrich Heine, and Grandfather Román and old Abraham Mendelssohn? Fragments of conversation came back to Anton, words spoken beneath a low-roofed house in Bessarabia while snow drifted against the window-pane. . . .

He was a Jew. Anton Rubinstein wondered that he had not realized it sooner. And the world, for some crazy, bitter reason of its own, required of a Jew twice again what it required of a Christian. Well, thought Anton Rubinstein, he would give the world what it required. He would begin all over again, at the beginning.

"In Vienna I gave lessons, mostly for a *pfennig* a lesson. I lived at the top of a big house, almost in the attic. Often for two or three days at a time I had no money to pay for my dinner, and went without. My room was almost bare of furniture, but the floor was carpeted with my compositions to the very corners. What a quantity I wrote, and of what variety! Half-starving, the paper rolled from under my pen—oratorios, symphonies, operas, songs. If by chance I received a few gulden for certain of them, I thought myself lucky. I wrote not only music but literary pieces, critical articles, philosophic articles up there in my attic. I even wrote a newspaper for one reader—myself. And I was hungry, sometimes in dire need.

"For two months I did not go near Liszt. My long absence reminded him and suddenly he decided to pay me a visit. He came with his usual court—a prince, a count, an artist, a *savant*—his ardent admirers, following his beck and call. When they came in they all, especially the *maestro*, seemed much surprised to find me in such surroundings. It was a genuine surprise for Liszt, who had visited my family in Moscow and knew how we lived there. And here, suddenly, was I in the very dregs of poverty! In all justice, I must say that Liszt behaved with great tact and good humor. In the friendliest way he pressed me to come straight home with him for dinner, which was all the more to the point as I was extremely hungry."

Liszt offered more than dinner to the hungry boy; he offered a livelihood. He was, said Liszt, removing soon to Weimar as Court *Kapellmeister*. Would Anton care to take over such-and-such of his pupils? They would pay well. Anton shook his head; color rose darkly to his face. He did not need money, he told Herr Liszt gravely. He did not need help. . . .

Liszt went to Weimar with his princess; Anton Rubinstein returned to his attic and his music paper. He had made friends by now with young Heinrich Ehrlich, afterward famous as a pianist and music critic; the two shared a job playing in a café, receiving each thirty *pfennig* for their night's work.

Anton had been in Vienna a full year before he was able to arrange a concert at the *Bösendorfersaal*. He had practiced very little since leaving Berlin; it had been difficult to find a piano. When he walked onto the platform he knew he was ill prepared; it was the first time in his life that he had experienced such a sensation. He was not frightened but defiant; he had never failed an audience and it did not really occur to him that he could fail one now. As the concert progressed, Anton knew he was playing badly; before him rose the angry face of Villoing—Villoing who would have beaten him three years ago for such a display. And like a nightmare rose also the puzzled, reproachful face of *Maman* who did not know her son could play like that. . . . The worse he played, the more disagreeable Anton's manner became.

What a nonchalant youth! said the newspapers next day. "He treats the public rather too lightly for so young an artist. At this rate, he will destroy himself."

In the café next evening with Ehrlich and his new friend Heindle the flutist, Anton read the papers and decided there was nothing for it but to emigrate to America. He had failed. *Maman* in Moscow would eventually see these papers; when that day came Anton preferred to be somewhere in the New World, playing for settlers in

74

coonskin caps. Heindle said there was gold to be garnered over there; the Americans would listen to anything provided it was spectacular; in a place called Philadelphia, Henri Herz had put forty pianists on the stage at once and made money for all forty of them. . . .

Heindle and Rubinstein went off on a trial tour of Hungary and brought back to Vienna money enough to engage passage on the fast clipper leaving Hamburg for New York at the end of September, 1847. A certain Baron Fuhl was to go with them. Their route lay through Berlin, where Anton arrived in time to follow the mortal remains of Felix Mendelssohn to their last resting place in the family vault outside the *Hallethor*. Walking behind the bier of this pure, disinterested musician, Anton was assailed by confusion and a feeling he recognized dimly as shame. If Herr Mendelssohn had failed in his youth, would he have run away, would he have fled in a ship to where critics were ignorant and easy music could be traded for gold? What would Siegfried Dehn think of this American venture?

Anton decided on an immediate visit to Herr Dehn. Here was one person who would tell him the truth.

"America?" roared Siegfried Dehn, next morning.

"Jawohl!" said Anton. "I go to look for luck in the New World."

"Are you mad?" screamed the Herr Professor. "Can you find nothing in Europe to keep you busy? You are only a baby, yet here you push off for America, inviting disaster."

The trouble with Anton Rubinstein, said his teacher, suddenly calming and taking off his spectacles—the trouble with Anton was: he was suffering from growing pains. He had been a *Wunderkind*. He and that French piano teacher who didn't believe in counterpoint had traveled all over Europe giving concerts and being petted by princesses. And now of a sudden the *Wunderkind* had long legs and a deep voice. And the princesses lost interest and the piano makers shook their heads and told him he was not a good risk. Did Anton Rubinstein, then, imagine himself the only *Wunderkind* to experience this? It happened to all of them, which was why he,

Siegfried Dehn, did not like to teach *Wunderkinder*. Most of them, when the lightning struck, lay down and never got up again. The continent of Europe, said the Herr Professor, was carpeted with exhausted *Wunderkinder*. He had thought Anton Rubinstein was made of sterner stuff. So the Viennese did not like the way Anton Rubinstein played the pianoforte? The Viennese were pretty good judges. Had Anton practiced hard this year? Where was his dumb piano? What made him think the Americans were any greater fools than the Viennese? Even savages know when a man is not giving his best. And what, by the way, had Anton and this flutist played in Hungary to net them money for a ship's passage to New York?

Anton Rubinstein hung his head. "Never mind what we played, Herr Professor. I will not go to America."

Heindle and the Baron were naturally angry at such desertion. The Baron went off to America alone; young Heindle stayed in Berlin, and fared sadly indeed. 1848 arrived, a violent and bloody year. Revolution, that had been simmering so long beneath the surface, burst into sudden flame. Young Heindle would have been safer among the red Indians of Dehn's New York. Hurrying out one day in Berlin to call upon his *fiancée*, he tried to cross the barricades and was fatally wounded by a sharpshooter.

All over Europe, artists dodged bullets. Musicians in any century seem to be born immune to mass movements; this time, there had been voices to warn them—if they had cared to listen. Heine had warned them. Through the trickling of interest into the lap of capital, through the subdued sounds of poverty, he heard "something resembling the noise made by a knife whetted on a stone."

The knife was unsheathed now and flourished madly, to the confusion of art and artists. Europe had scarcely recovered from the Napoleonic wars. Only two decades had passed since Louis Spohr, strolling through the fields around Gotha, picked up the ramrod from a Prussian gun and sounding it against his ear with a piece of iron, took it home to use as a tuning fork for his wife's harp. . . .

And now the guns were roaring anew, and musicians, bewildered, asked themselves why a world that only yesterday had applauded the sound of music, today hurried eagerly toward the sound of destruction. Over in Raab, young Goldmark was mistaken for a well-known radical, and promptly led out to be shot. Fortunately, a friend appeared to swear the boy was only a harmless fiddler who did not even understand why the world was fighting. A disgusted war lord dismissed him alive.

In Paris, soldiers bivouacked in the streets, eating and drinking. Young Moscheles, son of that Ignaz who in London had acclaimed Anton Rubinstein, walked into a Parisian restaurant and was surprised to be addressed as *Citoyen*. From Russia and Switzerland, anarchists like Bakunin who for years had been waiting the carnage, wings outspread, hurried joyfully to Paris. Young César Franck, who loved God and the law, went out in Paris to get married. To reach the church the wedding party had to climb a barricade; delighted soldiers helped the bride across. The Massenet family, going in to luncheon on Jules' sixth birthday, were disturbed by the waitress rushing into the dining room, screaming, *"Aux armes, citoyens!"*

Rossini was caught in Italy in the very thick of it—poor Rossini who hated "modernism" and fainted the first time he rode in the steam-cars. "This art of music," wrote Rossini mournfully, "this art which is based solely on sentiment and ideals, cannot escape the influence of the times we live in, and the sentiment and ideals of the present day are wholly concerned with steam, rapine and barricades."

Hector Berlioz fled Paris for England, whence he wrote mournfully, "Republicanism is at this moment passing like a vast roller over the face of the Continent. Musical art, which has long been dying, is now dead, and will soon be buried, or thrown on the dustheap. England has become the center for streams of terrified artists, arriving from all points of the compass, like frightened sea birds before a storm."

Eastward in Saint Petersburg, Tsar Nicholas felt his throne tremble beneath him. The republican rabble was pressing nearer; neither Danube nor Dnieper seemed wide enough. Thrones were falling like ninepins; it was high time to recall all loyal Russians home from the contaminating air of republicanism. Henri Wieniawski, studying in Paris on a royal pension, received a command that sent him scurrying back to Petersburg with his violin.

As for Anton Rubinstein in Berlin, he fared as did the others.

"I found myself," he wrote, "in the very vanguard of revolution. Excitement was in the air; everything and everyone was strained, tense. I had many acquaintances among literary people, journalists, newspaper men, artists and persons of free profession. They were all agitated, excited as if ridden by fever. They awaited the signal. It came from Vienna, and like lightning Berlin obeyed. Revolution burst like a bomb. I wanted to be in the streets; I was only nineteen and did not realize the folly of meddling in what was not my business. The aims of the revolutionists were quite foreign to me and my nature. My kind landladies watched over me and would not let me leave the house. On the day of the hottest fighting they simply locked me, the artist, in my room! I had to be content to watch from my window the building of the barricades. But next day, when the people began carrying the dead bodies of their friends to the palace, I was in the crowd on the square, and after that I witnessed all these scenes of the people's revolution.

"I saw Dehn, my professor, an elderly man and famous contrapuntist, gun in hand, marching as a common soldier, pacing up and down as guard before one of the public buildings.

"I did not realize the great significance of what I was witnessing, the tremendous cleavage this Revolution of 1848 would make, not only in the policies of states and nations, but in art as well. It brought to music a quite new spirit; the world demanded from musicians not technique alone, but the very substance of art. It demanded this and it got—the devil take it!—Wagner. As for me, the Revolution divided my life into two distinct epochs, and for this reason, perhaps, gives my story a significance for historians. Certainly, from the moment revolution broke out, nobody had time for music. Lessons ceased, nobody gave concerts; musicians were on the shelf.

"There remained for me nothing but retreat. So retreat I did, turning my face once more toward Petersburg."

9

Return to Saint Petersburg, as told by Anton Rubinstein

"I packed my modest luggage and filled a big trunk with manuscript—the bulk of my as yet unpublished compositions. With all
the simplicity and guilelessness of youth, I set out for Russia."

So wrote Anton Rubinstein years afterward, when bitter experience had taught him that a bureaucracy is the last country to enter,
armed with nothing more than innocence. Imperial Russia was a
mass of corruption, plot, cliques within cliques; to its very borders it
was operated by paper, signed and countersigned. Permits were required for everything but acts of God, and nothing less than bribery
could expedite a permit. Eager and trusting, young Anton crossed
the border and stepping from the coach, felt his native earth beneath
his feet. The account continues:

" 'Passports, please,' says my compatriot.

" 'What passports?' I ask.

" 'How, what passports? What are you talking about? Is it possible you are not aware that everyone who re-enters Russia must
have a passport?'

"I had quite forgotten; in truth I did not even know the
regulations. When my mother took me to Berlin I was quite a
child; my sister and brother and I traveled on my mother's passport.
Then, when my mother returned to Moscow, I stayed in Vienna
without a passport and nobody asked me for one during the entire
three years, either in Berlin, Vienna or any other German town. But
no sooner do I set foot on my native heath than I am bombarded
with the demand for a passport, a passport—please, a passport! I
try to explain, and my innocence is convincing.

" 'Well, then, your luggage. What is in that trunk?' 'Notes?'
'What kind of notes? Oh, musical notes. We must seal it up until
it can be investigated. We shall find out about these musical notes!
Here is a paper, a receipt. Show it in Warsaw and your trunk will
be returned to you.'

"Somehow, they let me go. But in Warsaw they would not give me my trunk; they told me to look out for one Frevil when I reached home. . . . At last, after six years' absence, I found myself once more in Petersburg. I had left the city a pampered child. Now I returned a simple-minded youth, quite innocent of the customs of my country. Well, I can tell you that during those first days I suffered greatly from these customs. I was forced to drink a bitter cup.

"Listen: I went to a hotel; I could not even remember the names of my friends. I was alone as if in a desert, a twenty-year-old boy. Early next morning the police came to my room.

" 'Passport, please.'

" 'What passport? I have no passport.'

" 'No passport? Then we cannot permit you to stay.'

"What a state of things! I remembered a childhood acquaintance, one Carl Levy, an amateur musician, a meager little man. I rush out to look for him and find him somewhere in the Grafsky Pereulok. I tell him they will not let me stay in the hotel; they keep asking for my passport. He invites me to spend the night with him, and in the morning comes the porter.

" 'Passport, please.'

"They are all possessed by the devil in the shape of that passport. I go with the police to General Galakhov. I tell the clerk in the receiving room that I am just come from abroad and know nothing about passports. The clerk looks at me with greatest astonishment, and goes to tell Galakhov that somebody called Rubinstein has come from abroad without a passport.

" 'How? What? What is this?' raves Galakhov, shouting at me and the clerk. 'Where does he live, where does he belong? What impudence! How can he dare such things, etc. etc.'

"Finally I recollected that many people knew me in Petersburg—Prince Lvov, Count Strogonov, Count Vielgorsky. I hurried to Count Vielgorsky and told my story. His face was grave—after all, this was 1849.

" 'This is very serious,' he said. 'Let me write to Galakhov. Meanwhile, write your mother for your passport.'

"I wrote my mother, who in turn wrote to Berdichev for a special permit. While I awaited her answer, I went again to Galakhov and gave him Count Vielgorsky's letter.

" 'This is absolutely worthless!' he screamed. 'It means nothing and nothing and nothing. How dare you show your face here without a passport! Go and get one within two weeks, do you hear?'

"Yes, I hear! I hear and I think to myself, 'Why so hot, little one, there are generals higher than you.' So I betake myself to the Governor-general, Shulgin. I had hardly opened my mouth to state my case when he shouted, 'I will put you in irons! I will send you to Siberia on foot.'

"I was stupefied. A young man of twenty, straight from European centers of civilization, from the world of art and science, to return to my native country and find such conditions!

"I cannot remember how I got away from Shulgin or why he did not fulfil his threat. He had full power to do so. I remember only that my heart was very heavy. The days passed, and no passport arrived. I stayed with friends, here one day, there one night. Everywhere, I told my story. Meanwhile, a ball took place at the Court, or a concert or some kind of gathering. All the gentlemen to whom I had told my story were indignant with Shulgin and Galakhov.

"'What are you doing to Rubinstein?' they said. 'We all know him; he has been received at Court and has played for the Imperial family. What do you mean by treating him this way?'

"Next day I went again to Galakhov. For three hours I waited in the anteroom, standing all that time with the other petitioners, as was the custom. Indeed, those were strange times. At last I was summoned to the *sanctum*.

"'Well, brother, in the palace we have heard things about you. They say you are a musician, but we don't believe it. Our chief clerk, Chesnokov, understands music. So go and play something for him and we shall soon know if you are a musician.'

"All this was said in the most offensive tone. I was taken to Chesnokov and sat down at a shabby piano. All the hate, all the fury of resentment in my heart poured itself out upon the keys of that miserable instrument. I banged, I thundered, the piano fairly danced under my blows and threatened to fall into a dozen pieces. It was a paltry instrument anyway, and there was no limit to my madness. Chesnokov listened patiently and then returned with me to the Chief of Police.

"'Excellency, this Rubinstein is indeed a musician. He can play the piano.'

"'Then give him three weeks' grace,' roared Galakhov, and I went out with my reprieve.

"Yes, I repeat, those were crazy times. At last came a communication from Berdichev, and I found myself a man with a passport. This was my first adventure in my native country; the second was no less strange. I went to find my trunkful of manuscripts, the fruit of my three years' work in Berlin and Vienna. They would not give it to me.

" 'It is true your manuscript is in notation,' said they, 'but we are well aware that anarchists and revolutionists write their communications in cipher that looks like musical notation. Perhaps this is some of it. Wait five or six months and you shall have your music.'

"What could I do? I tried to rewrite from memory what I had lost. Some years later, I happened into Bernard's music shop, where I was told, 'Three days ago we bought some musical manuscript of yours.'

" 'Where did you buy it?'

" 'Oh, at an auction. It was sold as waste paper, a whole heap of it.'

"I instructed them to send out and buy it up for me, but it was too late. Probably the customs house had advertised in the *Police News* for the owner of the trunk and when no one replied, they simply sold the contents by weight. Some years later, when I applied at the office for a passport for abroad, the clerk boasted that he too had bought at auction some manuscript of mine from this same unlucky trunk.

"1849 was altogether an ill-starred year for me. Sophie Bohrer came to Petersburg, the pianist who had been so successful as a *Wunderkind.* As she was an old acquaintance, I went to call on her, and at my first visit I met a gentleman in student's uniform. Let him be nameless—perhaps he is still alive and a general by this time, like everybody else. He hastened to make my acquaintance and continued very attentive, coming to my apartment and insisting upon a friendship. 'Here you are,' said he, 'arrived from the most cultured countries of Europe, and you find, even among the intelligentsia of your own land, nothing congenial to you. From a country of action and progress you come straight to a desert. Yet say the word and I can lead you to a circle where your soul may take wing in the kind of conversation it needs.'

"Quite unsuspecting, I replied that I should be very happy to meet these educated persons. 'Splendid!' said he. 'Let us go there on Saturday.'

"At the appointed time he arrived and took me somewhere at the end of the Bolshaya Sadovaya behind the Pokrovsky Church. In an apartment I found a large assembly of men, young and old, military and civilian. Among the military I recognized Palin, but I could not seem to see my host. 'Wait!' they told me. At last a bell rang, a door opened and we went into a big room with a platform at one end and chairs arranged in rows as though for a concert. A handsome, bearded man walked onto the stage and began to read aloud something about socialism and anarchy. I was amazed and did not hide my feeling from my neighbor. In Russia I had not expected to find such goings-on. I could understand how such principles and ideas could be expressed abroad, where political and economic conditions invited it, but in our Russia there was no place for all this; it was quite unsuitable. I said so immediately to anyone who would listen. The man on the platform was Michael Petrashevsky. This was actually his house! Only now can one conceive of what that meant! Petrashevsky actually came to see me on the Bolshaya Morskaya and brought me all kinds of liberal books in foreign languages. We discussed constitutional government and so forth.

"Soon afterward I went to Moscow, where my mother asked if I had heard what was happening in Petersburg. 'Somebody named Petrashevsky has been arrested, and many persons who have visited him. They were all implicated in a plot and have been imprisoned in the Fortress.' You can imagine how this shook me. It was not without fear that I returned to Petersburg, every moment expecting arrest. On the Nevsky I met my acquaintance, the student who had taken me to Petrashevsky. He at any rate had not been arrested; he was as attentive as ever, but I was wary. It appeared that my frankly expressed opinions that night had saved me from the terrible Third Department—a name possessing frightful significance at that time in Russia."

So ends Rubinstein's record of his homecoming. It was lucky indeed for young Anton that he had been so outspoken among the anarchists. Petrashevsky was one of the most notorious of the earlier revolutionaries; young Dostoyevsky, quite as innocent as Rubinstein, was caught at one of these meetings and paid for it on the long, cold road to Siberia. These early Russian revolutionists were impractical and visionary to the last degree. Ready to die for the cause, they would have been hard put to it to define—to a Westerner at least —what the cause was. *Preux chevaliers* of the bomb and the hidden dagger, they were generous with their gift of life and determined to die with a flourish.

Anton Rubinstein at twenty, fiery, intelligent, artistic, and fresh from revolutionary Berlin, must have seemed to Petrashevsky's henchmen very ripe for conversion. No wonder they stopped the young artist on the Nevsky Prospekt; no wonder they came to his rooms with "all kinds of liberal books in foreign languages." But Petrashevsky did not know with whom he had to deal. There was in this son of Kaleria Rubinstein a strong practicality that revolted against the everlasting vagueness of the revolutionary intelligentsia. These were not men like the Herr Professor Dehn in Berlin, who when the time was ripe had shouldered his musket and marched with his pupils. These Russian plotters lacked the quality of sturdiness; to Anton they seemed actors, amateurs, poets *manqués*. They had all the egotism of the artist with none of the professional artist's practicality.

As for young Anton Rubinstein, he had a plan, and artist-like, it concerned no one but himself. Anton did not want to talk all night and throw bombs in the morning; he wanted to play the piano, and he wanted an audience to hear him. In Paris, London, Berlin, Vienna, he knew the ropes. But here in his own country, he was a very babe for innocence. Already on two counts he had barely missed deportation and exile; more than once he had been mistaken for a foreigner. It might be well to look about a little and examine this town of Petersburg before one undertook to conquer it musically; perhaps audience should be studied as well as instrument! Having tumbled into his country as it were head over heels, passportless, landing in a nest of plotters, Anton, son of Kaleria, drew back, bewildered, to study the place and the people that would make up his public.

10

Saint Petersburg under Nicholas I

SAINT PETERSBURG in 1848 was compounded of two essential things: the character of Nicholas I and the climate. Both were extreme, both were interesting, and both gave the inhabitants almost unremittent trouble. Father Tsar, reaching out from his crazy rococo palace on the Neva, touched to an extraordinary degree the personal, daily lives of his subjects. Annoyed one morning at being handed an illegible petition written in a sloping backhand, Tsar Nicholas issued a ukase commanding Russian subjects henceforth to slope their letters from right to left.

Tsar Nicholas liked to walk alone in the city; he was often to be seen striding along the Nevsky Prospekt in his long gray military coat like an ordinary citizen. It was against the law to smoke on the Petersburg streets—Petersburg was a wooden town and suffered from frequent fires. If the Tsar met a smoker he would stop the man and rebuke him. And on the other hand, if the post coach was delayed by mud, if the frozen meat spoiled in the winter markets, the peasants blamed it loudly upon Father Tsar, and Father Tsar accepted the charge and tried hard to give better roads, better food, better laws to his hundred million children.

The truth was that Nicholas Pavlovitch was born too late for the paternal role he considered himself destined to play. These were bitter times; during the thirty years of his reign (1825-1855) Tsar Nicholas saw European thrones collapsing to right and left. His grandfather had been murdered in the Castle of Ropsha; his father was strangled in the St. Michael Palace; he himself had taken the imperial oath under the hostile guns of his own nobles. When Nicholas Pavlovitch traveled the highways of this country he so truly loved, bonfires flared to keep away menacing revolutionaries. More-

85

over, Nicholas Pavlovitch was a third son; he had not been educated for the tsarship. He called himself a soldier and believed a young man's education complete when he had been taught to square his shoulders, turn right-about and give the military salute. He distrusted all intellectuality, loathing a word currently fashionable—the word "ideas." Had not *ideas* been responsible for the French Revolution of 1789? Philosophy and rebellion were sisters: *ergo,* ideas must be suppressed.

The most rigorous censorship was instituted upon education and the printing press; the universities of Russia were a mockery. And the world of art was as shackled, as bewildered as the world of education. In the realm of letters, the 1840's were a between-time for Russia; the language was yet in process of rebirth. Karamzin, the great poet-historian, was dead and so was Pushkin, whose poetry had touched the very roots of his native language as Chaucer's had once touched the Anglo-Saxon. Krylov, the fable-writer, who had gone bravely to the people for inspiration, died in the early '40's. When Anton Rubinstein returned to Russia, Glinka was only forty-four, but Glinka belonged in spirit to the Slavophiles and to the generation of his friend Pushkin; European influence had failed to make an eclectic of him. Like Rubinstein, Glinka had been a pupil of Dehn, but unlike Rubinstein, Glinka was bound, musically, to the soil of Russia and the Russian language.

Glinka's great patriotic opera, *A Life for the Tsar,* was produced in 1836. For an important artist—moreover, an aristocrat—to write an opera in Russian around a wholly Russian theme, was a tremendous departure. Russian was considered the language of peasants, not of art. Catherine the Great had discovered that what was cultural was French; her grandson Nicholas believed that what was military and important—was German.

It is difficult for a later century to understand how deeply this Western culture, these Western languages had become the fashion in upper-class nineteenth-century Russia. Tsar Nicholas' generals were Germans, his wife was German, his statesmen were Germans. The Court itself spoke French, as did the gentry on parade. The native tongue, so comfortable and so tender, was reserved for *negligée* occasions when, forgetting the vexing, stiff-collared West, one wore one's ancient dressing-gown to supper as one's Tartar ancestors had done. One spoke Russian to children and servants, but one was careful to have Western tutors in the house. Many an aristocratic Petersburg child learned to write French before he could write his native language.

As for music, Tsar Nicholas liked it well enough so long as it was kept in its place. To Petersburg, opera had always meant Italian prima donnas trilling high notes in recitative that possessed no possible relationship to life and therefore no danger to the state. But this Russian opera of Glinka's was focused in what imperialism considered the right direction: a tenor singer laying down his life for the Tsar would be a salutary sight for eyes deceived by anarchistic leaflets. Nicholas Pavlovitch gave the opera his open patronage and attended the dress rehearsal. But something bothered His Majesty. It was permissible for a sovereign to be represented on the stage in drama; the classic tradition placed kings upon the theatre stage. But a tsar, singing? A tsar, throwing out his chest in high C? It would never do. Nicholas Pavlovitch issued a ukase forbidding the operatic representation of any member of the House of Romanov.

Music must be kept in its place. Tsar Nicholas adored the Russian Church—and held Church music in chains by forbidding any music other than the watery compositions of Bortniansky. The ancient ritual melodies were permitted only in the adaptations of General Lvov. At the Petersburg *première* of Meyerbeer's *Prophète,* Nicholas Pavlovitch mounted the stage to compliment Mario on his performance. As they were talking, the Tsar asked Mario for his crown and the singer took it off and handed it to His Majesty. With no pause in the conversation, Nicholas Pavlovitch broke off the cross and returned the crown to a chastened tenor who wondered uncomfortably if he had been guilty of sacrilege or *lèse majesté*.

Art must be kept in its place. Music must have no message, no propaganda, no "ideas." It was a situation where one must adore Majesty or be cast into outer darkness. The sovereign who so graciously complimented one's singing in the evening, might next morning send the singer to Siberia. Yet in the world of art and letters were many who preferred the bitter apple of knowledge to the treacherous paradise of court favor. When Anton Rubinstein returned to Petersburg in 1848, Turgenev was thirty and his stories about serfdom were soon to involve him in serious trouble. Herzen had already gone abroad to fight his battle against Slavophilism on the Western front. In the world of science, the war between ape and angel had not begun. The germ theory being yet unknown, Petersburg midwives used incantation to guard young mothers against childbed fever. Continual fog and heavy rain robbed Petersburg streets of the disinfectant sun; typhus stalked the town. Scarlet fever was fatal in those days, fatal also was typhoid and what the Petersburgers called "local cholera."

Cholera raged that autumn when Rubinstein returned to Russia—cholera and the usual mud. Only the Nevsky Prospekt and the streets around the Admiralty were paved; the rest of the city was a mass of mud and in spring after the thaw it would be worse. One of Empress Alexandra's ladies-in-waiting looked out of the palace window one day at the citizens slipping and swearing and falling on their faces and remarked that had the Russians been Greeks, they would have set up an altar to Mud and made a god of it.

From Spohr to Tchaikovsky, many a musician, burning his lamp at mid-day or picking his way along unlighted streets by night, wondered irritably why Tsar Peter, in other things so wise, had chosen this foggy swamp to build a city upon. Merely because of the white nights in June, must Petersburg dispense with street lamps all the rest of the year, when night extended almost round the clock? And because the streets were a beautiful smooth sheet of ice from December to April and one's sledge runners traveled upon glass—did that excuse the city fathers from laying paving blocks all the rest of the year? Moscow knew no paving either, but Moscow made no pretensions to modernity. Here in the Emperor's city, where Western ways were aped, surely a little science might be practiced in the interests of comfort!

What with the climate and officialdom, only the hardiest souls could live happily in the Petersburg of the Romanovs. Anton Rubinstein was tough as any weed and Anton knew that he was going to like Petersburg. Imperial society was simple: you were at the top or you were at the bottom. There was no doubt at which end a Rubinstein belonged, but in his bones young Anton knew that he would some day break bread with princesses. Here was a public at once wildly ignorant and pleasantly sophisticated—a public worthy to spend one's talent upon.

Indeed, since the time of Mozart, musicians had been attracted by the glitter of the Russian Court. From Italy, Germany and France they came, braving the rigors of sledge travel to play in the Russian Lenten season when opera and theatres were closed. Rumor had it that Potemkin invited Mozart himself to Petersburg, and only death cut short the journey. From London came Muzio Clementi, bringing with him his young Irish pupil, John Field. The two were dazzlingly successful; Clementi sold pianos to Grand Duchesses while Field sat in the warehouse and played his lovely Nocturnes, causing the piano to sing with a tone that made customers forget to laugh at this melancholy young man with wrists projecting beyond shabby outgrown sleeves.

Louis Spohr came from Germany and found the city enveloped in ice and his concert cancelled lest coachmen freeze to death waiting outside for their masters. At the Citizens' Club, Spohr met the musicians from the Imperial Orchestra and was surprised to find them nearly all Germans, Swedes and Frenchmen. At the Club of the Nobility, tenors and Italian sopranos sang valiantly but in vain against the conversation of the social *élite*, who walked about and chatted all during the music. The princely courts of Germany would never have permitted such behavior, but, on the other hand, what German princeling could boast forty horn-players like the Tsar's? Each player had but one note to blow and timed it so perfectly the effect outdid the most splendid organ. The red and gold uniforms of the fifty male court singers entranced Louis Spohr, and as to the New Year Masquerade at the Winter Palace, he thought he must have dreamed it. White walls that mirrored the dazzle of twenty thousand wax tapers, marble pillars tinted in fairy colors, gigantic vases of malachite and lapis lazuli. Gold and silver dishes to eat from, flowers everywhere, and near the throne room a wall of gigantic grenadiers in high bear-skin hats to guard Majesty as it danced. In the wide square before the Winter Palace, a great fire burned; bearded coachmen and footmen in furred coats and enormous cocked hats threw shadows on the snow.

A barbaric country certainly, but where had civilization a show to compare with it?

Anton Rubinstein, coming home to Petersburg in 1848, confronted a city that was little changed since Spohr's day. The Court was as glittering, as madly extravagant; the bearded coachmen swore the same oaths and roared the same lusty songs. As for the musical scene, it had changed only in the names of the musicians. Adolf Henselt was the central figure now. He had come over from Germany twelve years ago and his first big concert had so charmed Majesty that he was made court pianist and given the post of Inspector-General of Music.

Henselt was a scholarly musician of the Brahms type, completely devoted to his art. It was Henselt who introduced to Russia the free, lyric, romantic style of piano playing, in contrast to the swift-fingered, dry performance that had been the fashion. Henselt's music urged his listeners to genuine emotion rather than to amazement at technical skill. Nobody said, How can his fingers fly so fast? They said instead, How happy this music makes us! Or, How sad!

This was something new for Petersburg, since John Field had left the scene. Henselt's own music was extremely popular in his day; Rubinstein, on that first concert tour with Villoing, had played the *Etudes* with much success. Henselt adored Bach and used to practice the fugues on a piano muffled with quills; listeners said it sounded like the dry bones of a skeleton rattled by the wind. It is something more than coincidence that the Romantics—those men whose music woke instant emotion in their hearers—were one and all practicers of the dryest, most bone-rattling keyboard exercises. Young Rubinstein with his dumb piano below-decks on the Rhine, Henselt, Chopin—what rounded vision of ultimate perfection lay behind those hours of gruelling toil, urging the haunted artist on?

Clementi, Field, Mayer, Henselt—these were the men who preceded Rubinstein as pianoforte teachers in Petersburg. Their work was done privately or in imperial educational institutions. They were one and all foreigners, missionaries who reaped good Russian gold for their labors. Their work bore little fruit. They played, they taught their pupils, but after they were gone, musical taste slid back to its state of unregenerate innocence. Nicholas Pavlovitch still hummed his favorite light operas and smiled indulgently when splendid young guards of his crack regiments flocked to the Italian Opera to pelt their favorite prima donnas with bouquets in which were hidden diamond bracelets. Music was not music, it was acting; a visiting virtuoso with a good stage personality could make more money in Petersburg in a night than he could wrest from Paris in a year. Rubini sang himself into 54,000 francs at his first Petersburg concert; moreover, he made Nicholas Pavlovitch shed tears, an occurrence so unusual as to call for special award. In a burst of imperial gratitude the monarch made the singer a colonel in the Imperial Army; plump Rubini woke to find himself heir to epaulettes.

Rubini in a colonel's hat, John Field selling Clementi's pianos, Henselt with his Bach and his Bible on the piano rack—Franz Liszt whirling through town like a meteor, the *Salle de la Noblesse* blazing with light, the Neva sullen with ice, the streets dark with disease and poverty and over all Tsar Nicholas in his Winter Palace, serious, conscientious—at once a patriot and a stumbling block to his country: such was Saint Petersburg in the year 1848 when Anton Rubinstein came to town.

11

1848-1850. Rubinstein begins his crusade

Anton Rubinstein did not enter Petersburg as a crusader, although a crusader he was soon to be. Not for him the anonymity so blissful to a Henselt; Anton desired to be seen and heard and known; the three verbs were synonymous to a youthful confidence that even the late Viennese defeat had not sapped. Rubinstein thirsted for the concert stage as a lamb for milk, and he had not long to wait for satisfaction. Vieuxtemps arrived. Anton considered himself fortunate when he was invited to "assist" this artist he had assisted in Paris seven years before. Petersburg knew Vieuxtemps and liked him.

They played in the hall of the Peter-Paul School, Vieuxtemps tall and elegant with his Parisian side-whiskers, Anton a fiery young whirlwind, all temperament and eagerness. But the two made the bad mistake of playing down to their audience, a mistake that one of them at least would not repeat. Their program announced a Bach Sonata for violin and piano—severe fare for a public accustomed to firework concerti or variations on favorite operatic themes. At the last moment the two lost courage. Plucking the most attractive movements from several Bach sonatas, they played them as one piece—an act of musical piracy that would have wrung screams of outrage from Siegfried Dehn back in Berlin.

In the audience was a sturdy little critic named Damske who was disgusted and said so next day in his paper. Rubinstein read the criticism in his rooms on the Vosnesensky Prospekt, and it gave him pause. Outside, November snow drove against his windows; the coachmen's hats were powdered with it, the Neva was freezing and the pontoon bridge just north of the apartment house had been removed. Anton had thought of going down to Moscow directly after this concert, but suppose *Maman* should see this *critique*?

What would she think of a son who tore Bach sonatas to pieces to please the public? Better stay here and procure some more concerts to show what he could really do with a piano, and not go home to *Maman* until reputation as well as roubles lay in his pocket.

Anton practiced hard that winter. Cruelly hard, hour after hour, until his face, his body, were wet and limp. This was a man not given to overstatement, yet he later confessed that he had striven "with labor and tears, bitter as death." Within him was a vision, a perfection of ordered sound; night and day he was pursued by the artist's desperate, relentless desire to make manifest this vision through his fingers. The tone that Anton heard in his head was not a percussion tone, dry, brief, brilliant; it was the long tone of the human voice, melting note into note, and behind this tone was the round cherubic face of Rubini, singing as he had sung in the Paris Opéra so long ago. Stubbornly, Anton at 20 set himself to do what he had longed to do ever since he heard that voice: to wring from a short-breathed percussion instrument the lingering tones of bird or human. A seemingly impossible demand from strings whose vibrations cease so soon after the hammer is raised. But not quite impossible. Anton was perfecting a technique which he was to master to an astonishing degree, so that in later years people flocked to the stage to examine Rubinstein's piano, confident that hidden pipes had been responsible for these prolonged singing tones.

When December came, Rubinstein was ready to face Petersburg in a musical *matinée*, his first in this cold city since his triumphant *Wunderkind* days. He played his own first *Concerto in F major*, never published, afterward lost and forgotten even by the composer himself. The afternoon was a success but not a furor. Damske gave the concerto high praise, and in February of the same winter Rubinstein played it again—this time with even more success. Petersburg liked its musicians better after long acquaintance; Anton could not rid himself of the feeling that he was known here, that people connected this young man with the curly-haired boy they had fêted years ago. How mistaken he was, he learned fully after this February concert. Sitting in a café with Dr. Rosenberg, that

Moscow friend who had introduced Villoing to Kaleria Rubinstein, Anton opened a Petersburg newspaper and saw himself described as a talented *foreigner*! More shocked than he cared to show, he tossed the paper across to Rosenberg. "So you thought the world was kind to artists?" said his mother's friend, softly. "Tonia, with every concert the artist must win his public anew."

Walking home through the dead quiet of the winter night, Anton knew his old friend was right. The streets were dark save where a lighted window threw a yellow spear across his feet, but the snow itself was luminous. Ice glimmered in the gutters and where Anton set his foot the hard snow muttered and snarled against his tread. The night was windless; Anton's ears caught weird tones from the frozen air—a continuous whisper as though snow were falling—"*Foreigner!*" So that was what they called him, here in his own country. Well, he would stay to fight and to conquer—until this city, that called him stranger, would doff its hat when he passed along the street.

In March, Rubinstein and Vieuxtemps played again together, and toward the end of Lent, Anton with three other pianists—one of them was Damske the critic—played Moscheles' *Contrast* for eight hands. Four other pianists joined them in a piece for sixteen hands written by the Grand Duchess Alexandra. This was an era when audiences liked to see a half dozen artists on the stage at once; four-hand and eight-hand concerts made the public confident they were having their money's worth.

In May the concert season closed and Anton was free to go down to Moscow. He longed for the meeting with his mother, yet dreaded it too, dreaded to miss the old home with its wide hospitality, his father's kindly greeting. More than three years had passed since the farewell in Berlin, and how much of defeat the family had met since then! He himself was young and so was brother Nicholas. Youth can bear defeat. But *Maman* was not young (she was only forty-six, but Kaleria's generation counted forty-six as time for lace cap and eternal serenity). It was hard to imagine *Maman* as governess in a school, her vigorous nature shaped to the domination of a mistress

94

upon whose bounty she depended for bread. Would her face show defeat? Would that straight carriage, that lift of the head, have disappeared forever? Jolting southward in the post coach through the spring mud, Anton frowned, feeling beneath his great-coat for his wallet, wishing it were fatter, wishing he had more money to bring to *Maman*.

But he need not have worried. As soon as he caught sight of his mother, Anton knew her spirit was unbroken. Her clothes were a little shabby and she was serious, coming straight to the point. What immediate prospects had Anton? The father's debts remained. Could Nicholenka continue to finance his schooling himself as he had miraculously done so far, up to seventeen years of age? Anton was used to seriousness from Kaleria Rubinstein, used also to thinking of piano playing in flat terms of money—concerts, pupils. He was surprised to find how many friends Nicholas had made; the boy seemed to know everybody in Moscow. When they walked the streets together, Nicholas bowed right and left like the Governor-general. Anton was a little skeptical of so much amiability. Was it not a dangerous waste of time? Nicholas shook his head. Friends were the pleasantest part of life, he said. And besides, were not friends more useful sometimes than gold itself? Anton, glancing at his brother, felt a swift satisfaction. Obviously, the boy had not been wasting his time.

But Anton could not linger long in Moscow; money was too needful. He played for *Maman*, for Villoing and Nicholas. All three seemed satisfied, although Villoing, as ever, had plenty of criticism ready. Then Anton took coach for the provinces and a concert tour that lasted all summer.

He was glad when autumn brought him back to Petersburg and his four rooms on the Vosnesensky Prospekt. No doubt but that Petersburg was his home; Moscow was too provincial; the Petersburgers were right when they called Moscow a big village. Moscow said there were too many uniforms on the Petersburg streets. Walking down the Nevsky Prospekt, Anton looked at the huge cocked hats and the generals, and smiled sardonically. Every artist knows that war is silly and dress parades a toy of the mighty—but in this case the presence of generals spelled the presence of the Court, and the Court was a patron of art. The Russian Court, it was true, had strange taste in music; it was opera-mad and so was the city. Anton himself caught the fever and later confessed that he had wept with the rest when Madame Grisi and her Mario sang their melting duets.

Anton Rubinstein was far from friendless in Petersburg. Carl Levy, who had rescued him from the passport devils that first night in Petersburg, was there; Carl Schubert and Fitztum who conducted the University concerts; Henri Wieniawski the violinist who, like Anton, had been forced home by the Revolution of 1848. On Saturdays when pupils had paid him, Anton kept open house. Dr. Rosenberg reported the gatherings as very gay, with much playing and singing and a supper of roast beef and beer.

At the height of the winter season, a gala concert took place in the Hall of the Nobility. Rubinstein was invited to share the program with such celebrities as Madame Salamon, Tamburlick, Tamburini, and his old colleague, Vieuxtemps. This was Anton's real Russian début; it was a brilliant occasion, with the Court in attendance. The *Salle de la Noblesse* was one of the most beautiful rooms in Europe—"the finest ballroom in the world," travelers used to call it. It was a stately glitter of white and gold and magnificent crystal chandeliers; around it marched a splendid colonnade of pillars.

After his appearance that night, Rubinstein's position in Petersburg was assured—which meant, in effect, that pupils were easier to acquire. Some of them paid one rouble and some paid twenty-five. Anton no longer lived a hazardous life of alternate feasting and starving; his income was steady; he had time to sit down once more and write music. He had time also to play music for its own sake and to look about him, more and more troubled by the sporadic, foundationless state of musical art in this his own country. There was native talent in abundance; Russia teemed with it. But it was talent uneducated and unorganized. Petersburg society, for all its sophistication, was almost entirely ignorant of symphonic music.

The only classical programs the city heard were given three or four times a year by the court a cappella choir—excellent singers led by General Lvov, attracting a group of intelligent amateurs, civilian and military. "Even Grand Dukes were included," wrote Rubinstein.

But this was too fashionable an affair for serious music lovers. Solo singers and Russian generals did not conduce to the spirit Anton Rubinstein had known in Germany and longed for here at home. Across the Neva the students of Petersburg University, humble and eager, formed an orchestra led by Carl Schubert the 'cellist. Anton joined it and conducted in Schubert's absence. Every Sunday they played in the Assembly Hall of the University, charging an entrance fee of a rouble. "The public," wrote Anton, "fought to get in. They came in amazing numbers, crossing the frozen Neva on foot by the narrow plank walk. Without a single rehearsal, the thing somehow carried itself every time. What love and energy those amateurs put into their work!"

Rare praise! Anton hated amateurs. In Russia the word had a bad connotation: Russian amateurs were apt to be rich, lazy and superficial. Yet without amateurs—*rich* amateurs—Rubinstein would later have been powerless to begin his crusade for the establishment of professional musicianship in Russia. The Grand Duke Konstantin, Count Solugub, the Princes Odoevsky and Viazemsky, the Counts Vielgorsky gave money, they gave splendid palace rooms in which to hold concerts—but they gave even more. They understood music and they deeply admired real musicians. It was Count Michael Vielgorsky who had organized the Court a cappella choir; when Robert Schumann came to Petersburg he pronounced Count Michael the pleasantest dilettante he had ever encountered, stayed as guest in his palace and conducted one of his symphonies there.

The Vielgorskys were perfect types of an exclusively Russian product. Artistically fastidious, genuinely discerning, fabulously rich, on intimate terms with the Court, they walked the earth with enthusiasm. Art was as necessary to them as wine—and they were wholly uncreative. They collected music and fine instruments, they

97

wrote little songs and even little operas. But something within them—perhaps the result of luxurious living, perhaps the eighteenth-century spirit that said a gentleman did not write music but paid less fortunate men to write it for him—branded them with that vague helplessness that has been called *l'improductivité slave.*

Count Matthew Vielgorsky came often to Anton's Saturday gatherings on the Vosnesensky Prospekt, no doubt frequently preceded by his footman bearing provisions for the party. Anton liked Count Matthew and confided to him his impatience with the estate of the musician here in Petersburg. It carried no dignity, no position at all. For himself Anton did not mind, but such a state of things was insulting to the name of music. Moreover, was he to spend a lifetime teaching young ladies to play insipid pieces on the pianoforte? One could charge high fees and make a very comfortable living—but one might better be buried at once or turn dancing master.

As concert player, Anton was succeeding in Petersburg; slowly he watched his reputation rise. A few more years and he would possess an enviable enough position as virtuoso. But what a goal for a true musician—to collect laurel wreaths from a servile public that would rather applaud an Offenbach waltz than a Beethoven symphony!

Rubinstein became more and more impatient. And then something happened to bring home to him with full force the anomalous position of the musician in Russian society.

Every Russian citizen was required once a year to go to confession in the Greek Orthodox Church. In accordance with this regulation Rubinstein walked one afternoon to the Kazan Cathedral in Petersburg. Crossing the wide square he mounted the long steps that led between the double line of pillars and entered the huge cold sanctuary. After confession he approached the table to inscribe his name in the census book. The deacon demanded his family name, grade and quality. Was he, in short, merchant, and of what guild? Was he student, independent nobleman, peasant, soldier, or manufacturer?

"Rubinstein, artist," was the reply.

"Ah, you serve in the theatre?"

"No."

Reporting this conversation, Rubinstein's autobiography falls dramatically into the present tense:

"The deacon is astonished, I am astonished. We both remain silent. . . . 'Yes,' I reply. 'I am an artist-musician.'

" 'Of course! I understand. You are in the government service.'

" 'I tell you again, no, I am not in the service.'

" 'But who are you then? How shall I inscribe you?'

"The questioning went on for several minutes. I do not know how it would have ended if the deacon had not been inspired with an idea. 'Permit me to ask,' said he, 'who your parents are. Who is your father?'

" 'A Merchant of the Second Guild.'

" 'Ah,' says Father Deacon, much relieved. 'Now we know who you are. You are the son of a Merchant of the Second Guild, and as such I shall inscribe you.'

"This sharp examination and final listing of my social position made a deep and lasting impression upon me. It was clear that in Russia the artist-musician, the professional musician, did not exist. Musical art was not recognized as a profession by which a man could support himself and his family. Architects existed, actors, painters, sculptors with the bureaucratic grade of 'artist,' but there were no artist-musicians. Who, after all, was Glinka? A clerk in the Post-Office Department. Every one of those who occupied themselves with music, even the creative musicians, were either noblemen or clerks serving in the government theatre, teachers in private or government schools."

"Was it impossible in Russia for the musician to have an independent position, a position worthy of an educated man? It was the Deacon of the Kazan Cathedral who first compelled me to ask myself this question."

All the prejudice of imperial despotism, all the red tape of Petersburg bureaucracy, stood between Rubinstein and the answer to his question. To rectify the matter would require, first of all, imperial sanction, and from Nicholas Pavlovitch that sanction could never be obtained. An artist belongs to the middle class; Emperor Nicholas, looking out over Europe torn with a revolution that had been inspired by middle-class intelligentsia, desired no extension of middle-class privileges at home. Rubinstein was helpless and knew it. In Russia, "progress" came all from above. The Court set the tone and the tone was far from high. Emperor Nicholas was a patriot and—aside from the customary Romanov excursions beyond the marital bed—a good family man. But his Court was the stiffest in Europe. Etiquette was cruel; the nearer one was placed to Majesty, the more unhappy one's life became. Sick or well, ladies-in-waiting must stand for hours in their heavy court dress; the Empress did not approve of ailing ladies, and said so. One's head must be held high and the smile assumed for approaching Majesty froze upon the face and remained frozen until death or disgrace released the courtier forever.

No room here for art or intellectuality—most certainly, no room for "progress" and the granting of independence to any one class of men. The gracious Imperial manners that Anton praised did not extend beyond the mere act of graciousness—a smile granted, a bauble given as to a child. This was a cold, a terrible city. Said Count Solugub, "How can one exist in a town where the streets are damp but the hearts dry?"

Was there none among these great ones, Anton Rubinstein asked himself, walking slowly down the long Cathedral steps after the Deacon's interrogation—was there none who would help him to give musicians an honorable place in Russia?

12

1850-1854. Helena Pavlovna

PALACE after palace lined the Neva; above tall doorways the Imperial eagle spread splendid stone wings. Coats-of-arms, carmine and black and gold, looked proudly down from the lintels, informing passers-by that the splendors within were reserved for princes. A bitter wind blew east past Kronstadt, sweeping over the naked spars of ships lying patiently in the ice; snow swirled and scudded around the Admiralty portico. Across the river the red walls of the University were hidden in a blanket of white. Palaces and princes— a city where the streets were damp and the hearts dry.

The Michael Palace was all of marble; from a dazzling hallway the staircase swept upward in wide arms; malachite vases, tall as a man, held flowers from Imperial hothouses. Second only to the Winter Palace, this was the most gorgeous house in town—and it sheltered the warmest heart, the keenest brain, the widest sympathy of Imperial Petersburg. Here lived Helena Pavlovna, sister-in-law to the Tsar, the woman who was to mean more to Anton Rubinstein than wife or mistress, the instrument that was to help him to his goal. Not yet. While Tsar Nicholas lived, Helena Pavlovna's hands were tied, but these years of the early 1850's rooted a friendship that would later bear rich fruit.

The Grand Duchess loved music passionately; if she could have had her way she would have been surrounded always with artists and persons of intellect, but she could not have her way against a Court that valued military prestige and palace etiquette beyond song and symphony. Helena Pavlovna was not a Russian at all, but a German. Born Princess Charlotte Mary of Würtemburg, she was brought up in Stuttgart. Her childhood was filled with music, not salon music in the Russian sense but *Hausmusik*: Haydn, Mozart,

Gluck—string quartets, minuets, charming, *gemütlich* music that was part of dinner and supper and part of the evening, heard through open drawing-room doors as one walked upstairs to bed clinging to the hand of one's nurse.

The young Princess' father was as unpleasant a parent as could be found; learning that Charlotte Mary was terrified of mice, he had a bag of them collected and threw them over her as a cure. Fortunately, the Prince was as bored with his daughters as he was with Stuttgart, and saw little of children and home. He took the girls to Paris and placed them in the celebrated *pension* of Madame Campan, where Charlotte made friends with the nieces of Cuvier, director of the *Jardin des Plantes*. On Sundays Monsieur Cuvier invited the young princesses to his house and, strolling with them through the gardens, taught young Charlotte a world beyond the boundaries of palaces and *pensions*.

Charlotte Mary was happy in Paris; she loved to study; learning was a passion with her. It was hard when at twelve she had to return to Stuttgart. She was only fifteen when the Empress of Russia selected her as a wife for her youngest son, Michael Pavlovitch. Immediately the girl began to prepare herself for the great role she was to play, studying Russian and learning all she could about the various personages she would meet. In September of 1823 she made the long journey to the foggy Finnish marsh that was to be her home—a pretty girl of sixteen with a little round fresh face and movements so quick the Russians smiled when they saw her and asked if at home also the little Princess ran so to greet her friends.

When at the border she stepped from the coach, the girl looked about her gravely. *"Je sens,"* said she, *"que j'entre dans une patrie."* This quick sympathy with all things Russian was never to leave her. Arrived at Court, the Princess amazed everyone by her knowledge of the country. When she told Karamzin, the historian, that she had read his work in the original Russian, she did not know that most Imperial ladies twice her age could digest nothing heavier than a French novel. At her marriage she became, of course, a member of the Orthodox Church; it was then she took the name of Helena Pavlovna.

Life at the Russian Court was far from easy for the little Grand Duchess. Every step was planned ahead by star-decked generals and stiff-backed ladies-in-waiting. The intellectual life she loved must be renounced lest a Grand Duchess be held up to ridicule. Had not intellectual ladies with *salons* helped to undermine the structure of French aristocracy only a generation ago? Aside from French novels and studies of the Orthodox catechism, Helena's reading was done in secret; all year she looked forward to Lent, when European musicians would come to town and she could hear serious music and speak a little with the musicians themselves. *"Elle est distinguée,"* these visitors remarked of the little Grand Duchess, *"mais elle a l'air de s'ennuyer."*

Her husband could do little to help her. The Grand Duke Michael was a clever man, but the circumstances of his birth chained him to all that was most rigid and superficial in Petersburg life. When Nicholas Pavlovitch ascended the throne, he gave his youngest brother a pair of diamond epaulettes and made him Grand Master of Artillery, a neat way of excluding a too-clever brother from all affairs of state. Michael became a straw general. His energy expended itself on the minutiae of military etiquette; when he reviewed his troops, the line trembled lest a missing coat button cause a flogging. Like his royal brother, Michael used to walk alone in the streets of Petersburg, wrapped in his military cloak. Persons who knew him avoided this tall figure with the heavy face, red moustache and sidewhiskers, who paced with head bent, hands clasped behind him. A good heart had been soured by the consciousness of powers utterly wasted; Michael's wit was bitter and quick. At the palace one evening in the midst of a crowd of order-bedecked adjutant-generals, the Grand Duke came upon the astronomer, Struve. "How do you feel," said Michael grimly, in his loud harsh voice, "when you see all these stars in the wrong places?"

His wife gave Michael Pavlovitch three daughters. Michael sighed —and taught the girls to play military signals on the fife and drum.

When one of his officers made a mistake in the signals, he would be dispatched to the palace and compelled ignominiously to learn from the girls. Like most Russian aristocrats, the Grand Duke was puzzled and a little bored by Glinka, who, although a gentleman and an aristocrat, insisted upon writing operas. This would have been forgivable, if the man had not stubbornly written in Russian and then been fearfully serious about it, as though Russian opera were a crusade! When Liszt came to town and professed great admiration for Glinka's genius, the Duke replied that for himself, he disciplined his officers by making them sit through Glinka's operas, a punishment far worse than the guardhouse. *"Est-ce que c'est une mauvaise plaisanterie à vous,"* asked the Grand Duke of Liszt, *"de trouver Glinka un genie?"*

Michael Pavlovitch was kind to his wife, but he was busy all day with army manoeuvres, and it was Helena Pavlovna's duty to remain alone or to visit the Empress. To choose her own friends would have been flagrant *lèse majesté*. Had she rebelled, she would have been crushed completely. She submitted, and slowly fate removed from her path those persons who were obstacles to her natural ambition. Helena Pavlovna did not see these persons as obstacles; she was aware of no ambition save the desire to read and learn and to have artists for her friends. She loved her husband, and when in 1849 he died, she grieved deeply.

Helena Pavlovna was widowed at forty-two. She could not know that the best of life was still before her, that a few years hence death would claim her husband's brother, Nicholas Pavlovitch, making her own life free to follow its star. Helena Pavlovna was handsome and warm-hearted, possessed of intelligence and wit. Anton Rubinstein had known her household casually for some months; it was impossible to be an artist in Saint Petersburg and not encounter the Grand Duchess Helena. Rubinstein had met her at Court, at the Grand Duke Konstantin's, at Vielgorsky's; he had accepted invitations to the Michael Palace.

For a year or two after her husband's death, Helena Pavlovna lived in seclusion with her daughter Catherine, married now to the

Duke of Mecklenburg-Strelitz. Then she returned to her huge and lonely Michael Palace.

Helena Pavlovna had lived in Russia nearly thirty years, and for thirty years she had been obedient to the will of her brother-in-law, Tsar Nicholas Pavlovitch. She had won the Tsar's confidence; he no longer feared either her intelligence or her education. Calling her the *savant* of the family, he was glad to deliver into her hands all visiting European notables who were not soldiers. It was a relief to know that one member of the Imperial family could talk to learned visitors on such subjects as Orthodox Church history or the origins of the Slavic tongue. There was palace gossip concerning Helena's too-artistic friends, but Tsar Nicholas dismissed it. If his sister-in-law desired to entertain Jewish musicians and wild-haired, talkative painters—well, Helena was well-bred and she was loyal. As long as she did not actually organize anything—music schools or clubs or "movements"—as long as she did not toy with "ideas," let Helena have her fun.

The Tsar knew that his sister-in-law loved Russia. And it was, indeed, through her love of things Russian that Helena Pavlovna first became deeply interested in Anton Rubinstein. In the Spring of 1852, Rubinstein's first opera, *Dmitri Donskoy,* was produced in Petersburg and the Grand Duchess heard it. The theme of the opera was Russian and so were the words; two acts of the libretto had been written by that Count Solugub who had described the Russian prima donna's voice as a *courant d'air*. Gedeonov, director of the theatre, said plainly that he did not like Russian opera, but for some reason that Rubinstein himself never fathomed, *Dmitri Donskoy* was accepted and rehearsals began. Count Solugub's hoarse prima donna was only one of the trials that Rubinstein had to endure.

"How well I remember the first rehearsal!" he writes. "Gedeonov was consistently rude to all the artists in his theatre; he addressed us as *thou,* like servants. A most distinguished audience came to the performance; I was already known in Petersburg and all my friends were present. The singing was dreadful and the music pleased no one. The only success was the aria, very well sung by young Bulakov, who made his début that night. He was recalled and encored. The curtain fell; I hurried to the stage and after considerable searching found the young man in a corner behind the backdrop, trembling all over. 'The Director has been roaring at me in language one would not use to a drunken cabby,' he sobbed.

"I asked what was wrong, and Bulakov replied that when he took his bow, he had snatched off his dervish cap. 'Gedeonov says dervishes don't bow and the hat is new and I might have ruined it. He said, what did I mean anyway, daring to go out there and bow!'

"This was not the only time Gedeonov had shouted down a young artist. Disgraced thus at his début, Bulakov was completely broken. He took to drink and never rose above the rank of second-rate, but useful artist."

This was Anton Rubinstein's first experience with a species that was to give him endless trouble—the operatic singer. Perhaps no artist is so temperamental as the actor-singer; Anton was to find to his exasperation that concerning the sobbing Bulakovs of this world, the fault does not always lie with cruel directors. Nicholas Rubinstein was to manage these creatures better than his brother. Nicholas was born tactful—born wicked also, he himself would have said, and knowing temptation, could be patient with human weakness. Anton was not patient. With "second-rate, but useful artists," Anton was to prove a worse roarer than Gedeonov.

As to the opera, *Dmitri Donskoy,* in spite of terrified tenors it passed off better than its young composer imagined. It had one very significant result. The Grand Duchess Helena Pavlovna was in the audience, and after the curtain fell she sent for Anton Rubinstein. Glowing with enthusiasm not only for the music, but for the fact that its author had had courage to attempt an opera in Russian, the Grand Duchess inquired of the young composer his plans for the immediate future.

Rubinstein shook his head. He had no plans, he said, but to write music and play music. And meanwhile, persisted the Grand Duchess,

Monsieur Rubinstein was living comfortably, with plenty of time for composition? Plenty of *money?* she added impulsively.

Rubinstein bowed. There were always pupils, he replied gravely. He could wish, sometimes, that the pupils did not live so far apart; half his day was consumed in going from one house to another. He could wish also that the mammas desired their daughters to learn music, rather than parlor pieces, but—he shrugged—Her Imperial Majesty realized that this was, after all, not Berlin but Petersburg.

The Grand Duchess replied quickly that *some* Petersburg mammas really did desire music for their daughters. And for themselves, too. Would Monsieur Rubinstein consider a position as Master of Music in the Michael Palace? His duties would not be arduous; he would have time to write. Indeed, to write music would be his chief duty—Russian music, more operas like *Dmitri Donskoy* that would show the world the temper of the Russian people. He would be required to arrange music in the evenings, to accompany the court ladies when they sang. Did Monsieur Rubinstein know the Michael Palace had its own girls' chorus, composed of the ladies of the household? The Grand Duke Konstantin often brought his 'cello in the evenings when he was home from his battleship cruises; he was always asking for someone to play sonatas with him. And she herself, how she longed for music!

Anton did not hesitate. He went home to the Vosnesensky Prospekt and put his affairs in order, and in June, 1852. accompanied the Grand Duchess to her villa on Kammenoy Island in the Neva.

It was like living in fairyland, a civilized fairyland that Anton could understand. "The Island of Stone" was beautiful; the lawns before the villa sloped to the water's edge. From his chamber window Anton glimpsed warships lying at anchor by Kronstadt fortress, saw the bay widen to the Baltic roads. Yet he was aware of the city at hand—far enough away to lose the pervasive scent of cheese and herring, near enough for a possible walk to town. Here in this enchanted isle was no hint of poverty—no commerce, even. Summer villas, gay with flowers, lined the bright river, elegant carriages paraded the streets.

Anton was free most of the day, and the white nights were long. When his evening duties were done, there were enchanting hours before dawn brought color to a sky already luminous. Pale birches, delicate green of the brief northern foliage, bells of the city borne faintly to one's window in the summer dawn, the long summer twilight. . . . Rubinstein's music wrote itself. Here on the island he produced the series of "portraits" that included the famous *Kammenoy Ostrov*. The world smiles now at *Kammenoy Ostrov*, calling it dated, facile, Victorian. Yet the world continues to play this music; radio organ and orchestral triangle sound those far cathedral bells, and tired people in living room, picture palace and church feel once more the summer enchantment, the green peace of a northern island—and sigh with innocent, comfortable nostalgia. The *Melody in F* was also written on Kammenoy Island. Dedicated to Rubinstein's hostess, the *Melody in F* is more notorious even than the *Portraits*, but Rubinstein himself did not play the *Melody* as it is played today, with a slow sugary *rubato*. Moritz Rosenthal, who heard the composer play it many times, says Rubinstein took it quite fast.

When autumn came, the Grand Duchess' household moved back to the huge palace on Michaelovsky Square. With the onset of the winter social season, Rubinstein's duties became more arduous. He composed song after song, waltz after waltz, playing gloriously for the young princesses to dance. They whirled past him on the polished floor, their light skirts flying, their faces flushed, throwing over their shoulders long glances at the handsome, terrifying young man who, Her Imperial Highness said, was a genius.

Anton called himself the "Palace Janitor for Music," considered himself lucky to have the job and worked hard for his salary, which was low. What money he could spare he sent to *Maman* in Moscow, and for his employer he felt the sincerest gratitude. Young Rubinstein was in a position occupied by scores of musicians in the century that preceded him, a position at which latter-day historians look askance, indignant at a patronage system that dressed musicians in livery and kept them at the foot of the table. Yet from the stand-

The Grand Duchess Helena Pavlovna

point of artistic production, the system worked amazingly well. Haydn, housed for thirty years with the Esterhazys, Bach and Weber grinding out cantata or opera for grand ducal church or theatre; the condition of writing to order has been responsible for some of the most inspired music ever written. Musicians are not easily discouraged; the one thing they cannot endure is to have their music lie too long unheard. As *Kapellmeister*—Janitor of Music— in a princely household, one was ensured an audience every day of the week. The music one wrote in the morning would sound that very evening to ears more eager than educated, but ears nevertheless.

Rubinstein did not write his best music during the winter and two summers he spent with the Grand Duchess Helena. But he wrote much. Some of it is forgotten; there have survived the *F Major Trio* for piano and strings, the *A Minor Violin Sonata* and the melodious, ever-popular *F Major 'cello Sonata*. The Grand Duchess begged him for a series of one-act operas that would present Russia's different nationalities from Siberia to the gypsy south, and Rubinstein seized gratefully upon the idea. Of the three operas he produced, the first was never performed in public, and only one, *The Siberian Hunters,* was to receive continental recognition. The second opera, *Tom the Fool,* reached the Petersburg stage in 1853, and was so badly sung that Anton fled the theatre in mid-performance and next day roared into the manager's office and demanded the return of his score.

Meanwhile, the Michael Palace played host to characters far saltier than waltzing young ladies. "To the Palace," wrote Anton, "came everyone that mattered. Often among the guests would appear the majestic figure of the Emperor, Nicholas Pavlovitch. The Imperial family loved the Emperor deeply but they were all afraid of him, especially when he happened to be in a bad humor. How well I remember two of these evenings! Some *tableaux vivants* were to be rehearsed at the Grand Duchess Maria Nicholaevna's. The Empress was indisposed and lay on a couch; the Grand Duchess, the princesses and ladies of the Court were having a splendid time.

All was noise, laughter and confusion. I sat at the piano playing while the ladies rehearsed their tableaux.

"Suddenly the threshold was darkened with the marble figure of a giant! It was Nicholas Pavlovitch. Everything froze; silence prevailed. The Emperor was obviously worried and upset; it was the first year of the Crimean War. Without warning, Nicholas Pavlovitch furiously attacked the scenic artist who was directing the tableaux, heaping execrations upon him for the bad taste of his sets. The fury and thunder stupefied us; we looked for Roller to dwindle to a wisp of straw. Imagine for yourself the position of the young pianist! But the angry Emperor did not deign to notice me.

"Next day, frightened and apprehensive, the actors met again. I sat very quiet, dreading the Emperor's arrival. He appeared, and in place of yesterday's explosion, was so amiable and kind, even to Roller, that he charmed the whole company into the most genuine gaiety. All evening the Emperor sat behind me at the piano, joking, and in the intermissions asked me if I remembered such-and-such a tune, and then whistled it through."

The Tsar was all grandeur and graciousness, the Tsarina all smiles. Indeed, she vowed openly that when Anton Rubinstein played the piano, she was "ready to fall on her knees before those divine fingers." The Tsar's daughters were handsome; his son Konstantin truly loved music; the ladies of Helena Pavlovna's court were young and enchanting. Most certainly, it was a pleasant company, and one seldom achieved by penniless young men of obscure birth. Anton fell in and out of love every fortnight; the legends are many and brief. He himself was surprisingly vocal about it—but not until long afterward, when the princesses were scattered or were dust. He acquired, however, in these early days, an ineradicable taste for princesses; nothing less could satisfy him. Yet of them all, one only captured his true, his lifelong devotion—the Grand Duchess Helena herself.

"She was wonderful, that woman!" Rubinstein wrote. "She looked every inch a Grand Duchess, dignified and gracious, yet she could enter completely into the mind and heart of all who approached her; an extraordinary sympathy enabled her to put herself into the most humble person's place. Scholar, statesman, artist, military man, writer, poet—upon each she made the most agreeable impression. The Emperor Nicholas Pavlovitch had for her the sincerest friendly feeling; he valued and respected her deeply. Yes, she was a highly intelligent and unusual person. I have never known her equal. History tells us the Empress Augusta was a highly educated person, but our Grand Duchess outdid her in brains and culture. Sometimes I would mention her name in Europe—to Auerbach or some other distinguished European; invariably I had the most enthusiastic response. When she went abroad, she would invite these notables to visit her in Petersburg; they came and stayed a week, a month—following the Grand Duchess about all day, quite charmed by her wonderful brain and wide education, her tact and friendliness."

For two winters and as many summers, Anton Rubinstein enjoyed the idyll of the Grand Duchess' court. He had no time for public performance; the Petersburg concert stage saw him seldom. But in the spring of 1854, as the ice broke in the Neva and the Lenten season brought musicians from abroad, restlessness arose in Anton Rubinstein. What was he doing, dreaming in palaces—he, a professional musician? The big box in his room was filled to overflowing with manuscript music. When was the world to judge if Anton Rubinstein deserved the title of composer? The Grand Duchess was appreciative and stimulating, but it was another, sharper stimulus that Rubinstein craved. The hard bright lights of the concert hall, the merciless gamble of one man alone against rows of upturned, unfamiliar faces, the orchestral players ready with frank praise or the silence that meant disapproval.

In April, 1854, he arranged an important Petersburg concert, with orchestra. He played a concerto of his own that was to become very popular and that a later century was to know through the composer's most famous pupil, Josef Hofmann—the *G Major Concerto, Number 3*. That night his *F Major Symphony* also was played, and

Petersburg liked it and next day accorded Anton Rubinstein full fame, establishing his title as composer-virtuoso.

This was the title he had longed for—but not in Petersburg alone. Anton was 24; before he was thirteen he had become a citizen of all Europe; he must re-establish that citizenship now in his maturity. Once again, his face turned to the West, toward musical pastures far greener than those on the foggy Neva. Paris, Vienna, Leipzig, London—cities that held no mercy, gave no quarter. Rubinstein did not desire mercy; he desired the judgment of the sophisticated world. Post-coach and railroad, impresario haggling over prices, the whirling, driving life of the concert stage beckoned to him and he obeyed.

The Grand Duchess was very sorry to part with her Janitor of Music. Twilight on Kammenoy Island would miss the silvery torrent of sound that had poured from those strong young fingers. But she did not oppose Rubinstein's departure; she knew it was right for him to go. In his place she appointed young Leschetizky, the Pole who had made his début two years ago at the Michael Theatre.

Rubinstein said farewell to the Grand Duchess and packed his music neatly into boxes. It was not a propitious year to choose for a European tour. The Crimean War was raging; as yet the walls of Sebastopol looked down unconquered over Malakhov Hill; the Continent united against a Tsar whose ambitions it had feared for two generations. Anton faced a West that hated Russia and all that stemmed from the East.

Grave, eager, conscious of a hostile world, but conscious also of his own superlative equipment to conquer that world, Anton Rubinstein took coach for the West. He would return, he told himself, with a name great enough to bear real authority in Petersburg. He would return to make a place for music, an honorable position for musicians who could not live in palaces.

13

Franz Liszt and his princess. Zukunftmusik

Embarking on a European concert tour that was to last four years,
Anton Rubinstein had much to think of besides music. No suave
manager traveled ahead to arrange publicity and to haggle for the
price of concert halls. This was in a day before concert-impresarios;
music publishers such as the fat and famous Haslinger acted as
partial business manager to artists, but years of wearisome business
detail lay ahead of Rubinstein before he would join forces with the
shrewd, small, bright-eyed and comfortable Hermann Wolff.

Rubinstein must win his way alone, and for such a venture he
possessed armor with which most musicians are not blessed—a sturdy,
healthy self-confidence. Anton Rubinstein was seldom beset by the
artist's demon—*folie de doute*—or if he was, he kept it robustly to
himself. Let his young rival, Hans Von Bülow, kneel weeping by
the bed at Frankfort in an agony of self-mistrust, let Peter Tchaikovsky faint dead away in railway carriages from sheer homesickness and terror—there was in Anton Rubinstein a brutal, elemental
strength that expended itself always outwardly. Distress visited him
and he received her in a fury of activity; he practiced ten hours on
end; he wrote sheet after sheet of music; he broke the strings, the
hammers of his instrument. He gave a huge party and spent all his
money so that more must be made immediately; he roared at his
pupils and sent them sobbing from the room. But he wrote no letters to sympathetic ladies, he kept no diary, he borrowed no money
and he did not confide in his friends. In a word, he was a lion, an
extrovert—a perfect virtuoso. Anton's approach to his public was
healthy, joyous, determined. The stage was his natural habitat, his
most familiar gestures the flipping back of dress-coat tails upon the

piano stool, the fierce stroking of hair before the heavy hands lifted high above the keys.

Like many an artist before and after, Anton Rubinstein preferred his lesser talent. Wagner valued himself as an epic poet; Rubinstein fancied himself seriously as a composer. And, he confesses in his autobiography, it was to push himself as a composer that he set out for Europe this spring of 1854. He had with him a whole trunkful of manuscript—music heard, to date, only in Russia. He desired first of all to play it on the concert stage, and secondly, to find a publisher for it.

Where, the traveler asked himself, was the logical place to begin? All Europe was arrayed against a Russia which for the past twenty years had been an object of uneasy suspicion. Tsar Nicholas had more men under arms than any sovereign alive, and no matter how often such a commander reiterates soothing phrases concerning an army created for peace, the world knows that armies are created for something quite different from peace. The *gendarme* of Europe flourished naked steel, ostensibly aiming at Turkey alone and tossing off brave phrases about the sick man of Europe and a holy defense of Cross against Crescent. But England, France and Austria could permit no tampering with the Balkans in the name of Crescent or Cross, and in the hot Crimean peninsula, British tommies lay gasping with dysentery while in Petersburg Helena Pavlovna organized the first Russian Red Cross and a Russian general, surveying his dazzlingly uniformed troops, remarked with a sigh, *"Je déteste la guerre, elle gâte les armées."*

Anton Rubinstein dared not attempt Paris, and the gates of England were barred to him. Moreover he hated England for patriotic reasons, as Tchaikovsky was to hate her later when Disraeli made a laughing-stock of Russia at the Congress of Berlin. Before he left home, Rubinstein had seen the British fleet swing anchor off Kronstadt; he desired no more of John Bull at present.

Germany was the logical place for music-making. Years later, looking back upon the Germany of the 1850's, Rubinstein described it with nostalgic pen. "Divided into some four dozens of courts,

Germany was a healthy place for the development of things intellectual. Each court rivaled its neighbor in the patronage of science and art; in the various German states the universities fought to possess the finest professors of science. The development of things intellectual stood incomparably higher in this divided Germany than afterward when Germany was united by iron bands into one great state. Divided Germany, with its magniloquent political dreams, stood amazingly high in the sphere of spiritual development. Intellectual and spiritual growth proceeds far more freely in small states. What was Italy before her unification—and what is she now? [1889.] The very factors that strengthened Germany politically and that drove her to unification, crushed like an iron hand the bounding growth of her intellectuality."

Anton Rubinstein, in 1854, had had enough of the iron hand at home in Russia. A too-strong central government with its inevitable militarism spells death to the arts; the crushing paternalism of Emperor Nicholas I made the little kingdoms of Germany, by comparison, very heavens of freedom.

Germany was the place to go, and now that Mendelssohn was dead, there was no doubt as to where lay the Mecca of music—Weimar, with Franz Liszt. Liszt had been established at Weimar some five years; he was only 43, but he had renounced all concert-giving for money and had begun the long life of musical service that was to earn him the gratitude of the world. In Weimar, *Lohengrin, Tannhäuser, The Flying Dutchman* were first performed; Weimar became the cradle of that school known as *"Zukunftmusik,"* the music of the future.

Here on his hill above the Grand Ducal park, Liszt, with his pupils and his beloved Princess Witgenstein, kept pure musical vigil in Schloss Altenburg. His sympathy with young musicians was rich and genuine; his natural theatricality, the aura that surrounded his name, never robbed Liszt of the sincerest humility. In Vienna eight years ago, he had spurned Anton Rubinstein because the young man seemed over-confident, a little conceited. And the Master had been right. Rubinstein knew it now; these years had taught him much. Already he suspected that early success had been dangerous, and was thankful for his escape. "Bad things, *Wunderkinder*," he told a friend. "I too was a *Wunderkind*—but I survived it." Now, in 1854, there lay behind him a record that justified the title of concert artist; his boxes strapped on the post-coach contained sufficient weight of written score to justify the title of serious composer. Rubinstein did not hesitate to go straight to Weimar, climb the hill and knock at the Master's door.

He received warm welcome. Like all hard workers, Liszt admired hard work in others, demanded it indeed as sign of artistic sincerity. "Do you know Rubinstein?" Liszt wrote to Von Bülow on June 7, 1854. "He is an exemplary worker, possessing a very unusual artistic individuality. In the past six years in Petersburg he has written several Russian operas, half a dozen symphonies and as many piano concerti, a mass of quartets, trios, sonatas, easy pieces, etc. . . . . He has been my guest in Altenburg for a week now, and although he expresses consistent prejudice against *Zukunftmusik*, I esteem him as a talent and as a person. He is 25 and possesses a genuine pianistic talent (although he has neglected it in the last few years). It would be unjust to measure him with the usual yardstick."

Liszt exaggerated Rubinstein's output of the past six years. Anton had brought with him to Weimar probably three piano concerti, the Kammenoy Ostrov cycle, the string quartet opus 17, a score of piano pieces, the first symphony in F (afterward lost, unknown today), and the Second Symphony, called *The Ocean*, that was to attain enormous popularity on two continents. He was working also upon the symphonic quartet, *Faust,* and upon his oratorio, *Paradise Lost,* based on Milton's poem. Liszt seized eagerly upon this mass of manuscript, read it, talked about it in the famous weekly classes when all the pupils gathered to play their own or others' music.

It was a stimulating company. These were not student-beginners, but young artists in the concert field who returned from time to time to drink fresh inspiration at the Master's fountain: Bronsart, Dionys Pruckner, William Mason the American who, with Theodore Thomas, was later to found the famous New York chamber-

Franz Liszt as a young man

music concerts. Peter Cornelius was there, and Carl Klindworth who later became a professor in the Moscow Conservatory. Joseph Joachim had left Weimar for his post at Hanover, but he had not yet repudiated the tenets of the New Music, and still visited Altenburg from time to time. Raff, whose seven symphonies were to enjoy a mad, brief popularity, was teaching now in Wiesbaden, but, like the others, appeared on Weimar hill from time to time.

Hans Von Bülow, Liszt's darling and Liszt's later grief, had been dispatched by the Master on his first concert tour of Germany. The extraordinary Tausig would not appear at Liszt's door until next year, but even without these two, Schloss Altenburg was enormously stimulating to a man just come from the musical barrens of St. Petersburg. Rubinstein did not arrive in Weimar as a pupil of Liszt. How could he, who had known applause for sixteen years? He came as a concert artist. But he came in all humility, with a trunkful of manuscript that cried for intelligent audience.

Like the young Michelangelo, who, standing before a masterpiece, exclaimed, *"I also am a painter,"* Rubinstein was inspired by the Master, but not overawed. He described Weimar as a "kingdom of literature, art and music, where Liszt reigned enthroned, attracting the homage of everything artistic." The Duke of Weimar— brother to the Empress Dowager of Prussia—was a pretentious kind of man, said Anton, and made himself slightly ridiculous by playing the role of great monarch from a provincial junker's throne. Nevertheless, the Duke's interest in art was sincere; especially he loved music, and desired to re-create around the person of Liszt the exalted Weimar atmosphere that had existed in Goethe's time, when the former Duke had not been ashamed of the town's good-natured jibe: "We, by the grace of Goethe, Duke So-and-so."

Much later, when comparison between Liszt and Rubinstein had become a public matter, Anton wrote that Liszt was a "virtuoso-god, a truly wonderful person. I always appreciated him as the greatest performer of us all—virtuoso-performer, mind you, not creator or composer, although for this opinion I risk being devoured alive."

But in this spring of 1854, friendship between the two was only beginning, and the favors were all on the Master's side. For initial encouragement, Liszt performed on his Weimar stage Anton's *Triumphal Overture* for orchestra, opus 43. This was toward the end of June; shortly afterward, Liszt sent Anton to Berlin to try his luck with the music publishers, while he himself went over to Rotterdam to take part in the Music Festival. Anton was to join him there.

The two musicians met again with mutual pleasure. Behold them ensconced in their hotel, driving out together in the gray sea air of Rotterdam. A striking pair—Liszt tall, slim, elegant with light kid gloves, his straight golden hair reaching to his shoulders, young Anton distinctly shabby, but conspicuous with his great lion head and dark thick mane of hair. A strange sight for quiet, provincial Rotterdam. Once, walking out together, the two were almost mobbed by a crowd of brawny fishwives who followed them noisily, plucking at their sleeves, inquiring their nationality and the reason for their long hair.

After the Festival at Rotterdam, Liszt and Rubinstein played in Brussels. There they met old Fétis, the musical scholar, who asked Anton for personal data to include in his *Biographie Universelle des Musiciens*. Afterward, Liszt returned to Schloss Altenburg but Rubinstein would not go with him, preferring to take himself off alone to Wiesbaden. The Master's invitations were seldom refused; artists of every capacity clamored for a glimpse of Schloss Altenburg. During the ensuing three years, Rubinstein was to return many times to the musical sanctuary on Weimar hill, yet always with a hesitation that must have been stimulating to the King of Music, accustomed as he was to a court, a crowd of adorers.

Rubinstein, most certainly, was used to courts, but courts of a very different nature from the one that surrounded Franz Liszt. About the air of Altenburg was something a trifle rarefied for Slavic taste. What caused this atmosphere was obvious. Upstairs in spacious apartments lived the Princess Witgenstein, *née* Ivanovska—that fiery lady who had heard Liszt play in Russia and had forthwith left husband, lands and position to follow this bright star. No marriage bonds would grace this union, no earthly circumstance prove strong enough to divorce it. The Princess was reckless, but she was also high-minded, formidable to a degree. Anton describes her as a "clever woman, not pretty, educated to the devil, to illness, with whom conversation was simply a torture." The fact that the Princess hailed from Podolia, home of Rubinstein's ancestors, land traversed by the family long ago in the covered wagon, did not make Rubinstein love her the more.

The trouble was that the Princess got in the way. She and her children lived upstairs; Liszt and Rubinstein occupied a delightful wing on the ground floor opening onto the garden. But at the evening dinner table the Princess presided, and afterward repaired with the rest of the company to the big music room where stood Liszt's beautiful Viennese concert piano and all his music. It seemed to Anton the men were never alone; the Princess was forever sailing in, plump, vital, commanding. And once her dark Polish eyes were turned upon Liszt, he knew no other presence.

Yet Rubinstein conceded that the Princess' influence upon Liszt was good. "It was she," wrote Anton, "who turned Liszt from a too-great emphasis upon virtuosity, from an absorption in the superficialities of art to a serious attitude that put virtuosity aside for the deeper sphere of composition. Together, immersing themselves in the very substance of art, they came to a conception of the music of the future—to Wagner. It was from Weimar that the music of the future was launched."

Liszt had written Von Bülow of Rubinstein's "consistent prejudice against *Zukunftmusik*." It was, indeed, more than prejudice. First and last, Anton hated the Music of the Future. The feeling was strong enough to appear almost instinctive, constitutional. Rubinstein went time and again to hear Wagner's operas, flinging himself at them as though his conscience bade him explore to the uttermost these sounds that half the world adored. And always he came away profoundly troubled, angry, disheartened. It was the only experience that could shake his belief in music. "If *Parsifal* is music," he cried out in real anguish of soul, "then why should music ever be written again?"

Anton Rubinstein was indeed one of those anomalies in the history of art—a pioneer who is at the same time deeply conservative. A wholehearted classicist, his pioneering was concerned with a revival of the past, a past immediate yet forgotten. Beethoven had been dead nearly thirty years but the world was not really familiar with his music. Years ago, Cherubini had said it sounded like a sneeze; Paris still preferred French or Italian music. Had it not been for Mendelssohn's courageous revivals, the world would already have forgotten the glorious cantatas of Sebastian Bach. Rubinstein's sympathies lay definitely with Mendelssohn rather than with the Liszt-Berlioz-Wagner school; Liszt, indeed, expressed regret that Rubinstein should try to "swim in Mendelssohnian waters." Mendelssohn had been dead only seven years, but already he belonged to a time past. The turgid, passionate stream of the "new music" had overwhelmed these clear classic waters, deflecting them into new courses, and those who lingered by deserted shores might find themselves alone.

Yet Rubinstein was not alone; others resented with him the domination of the new school. The musical world, at that time and for fifty years to come, was torn in twain, rent asunder by two factions. You were Wagnerite or anti-Wagnerite, and the controversy was no mere matter of intellect or conscious estheticism. It was a storm as elemental as an earthquake and, like an earthquake, threatened to engulf all that had gone before. Rubinstein bucked the storm, throwing himself against it with a force that would have been better employed elsewhere. His pupil, Tchaikovsky, was to pursue a wiser course; Tchaikovsky inherited his master's classicism and hated Wagner, but he admitted the man was a "master symphonist" and studied his scores to learn what he could of orchestration.

Anton Rubinstein had need to study orchestration. His gift was melody and he knew it and traded too much upon it. When Rubinstein composed a symphony he merely wrote a series of melodies—

often very good melodies—harmonized them and distributed the parts among the instruments as though he had counted the thing out on his fingers. Rubinstein professed high admiration of Berlioz because of the latter's extraordinary command of orchestration; he confessed also that Wagner was a master technician, but his own classicism revolted at what he called an excessive use of color at the expense of drawing. An uncommon man, this Wagner, said Anton. Highly interesting, very valuable to the world of music, but beautiful or great or deep or high—No! "This *motif* trick the world raves over—what is it? Where is its beauty? Can one call it art? Must a singer come on the boards with his photograph pinned on his breast in the shape of a *motif*? This man Wagner will send music to the devil. He and Berlioz and Liszt, all three are wanting in creation's chiefest charm—naïveté, that stamp and proof by which genius lets us know that it is, after all, the child of humanity."

Franz Liszt never tried to force young Rubinstein into the Wagnerian mold; he knew it was impossible. Moreover, it was part of Liszt's genius never to force anybody into anything. One of the greatest teachers the world has known, adored by scores of pupils who were proud to call themselves disciples, the essence of Liszt's teaching lay where Anton Rubinstein's was to lie—in the inspiration of his own passionate musical sincerity.

After pleasant weeks in Rotterdam and Brussels with Liszt, Rubinstein went down the Rhine alone and settled in Biebrich to work on the half-finished manuscript he had brought to Weimar. Liszt wrote almost daily, cautioning Anton against a tendency to "extreme productivity," urging him to perfect one piece before beginning on another. *"Il ne suffit pas de faire,"* the Master reminded this impetuous young man; *"il faut parfaire."*

Excellent advice which, unfortunately, the young man never obeyed. Impatient with those Russian dilettante composers who were forever beginning huge works they could not finish, Anton set a stubborn valuation upon the actual production of manuscript. Like the young Haydn who, gazing wearily upon his day's work of composition, cried out, "It must be good, there are so many notes upon the page!"—Anton valued quantity. Your true professional, said Anton, wrote music every day, by the clock; he did not sit drinking vodka while he waited for the Muse.

A salutary point of view, but very dangerous for a man impatient by nature. Liszt cautioned Anton about this, and cautioned him also on other, more intimate subjects. Biebrich was near to Baden and Mainz, towns gay with fashionable ladies who had come to play hostess to the distinguished colony that every summer arrived with its easels, pens and musical scores. Anton had always loved the ladies; it was quite impossible for him to live without women and he often confessed it to Liszt, who had found his Egeria and rejoiced to be led by her. Anton would never be led by a woman; he would be amused by women, he would love and suffer jealousy, but toward women he preserved the traditional patriarchal attitude. For Rubinstein, woman was born for no purpose but to comfort man. To share one's days with a woman like the Princess Witgenstein who wrote huge books and required her lover to read them, in Anton's eyes would have been torture worse even than the state of having no woman at all.

Somewhere in the neighborhood of Biebrich, Anton embroiled himself quite seriously with two ladies whom he referred to always as the Mesdames X and F. In midsummer Liszt wrote that Rubinstein's *Siberian Hunters* was to be staged in Weimar Court Theatre next September.

"Dear Van II," wrote Liszt, addressing his friend as usual by the flattering nickname that was a diminutive for Beethoven. "Come immediately and spend fifteen days in Weimar. I offer you rendezvous in Altenburg where your old quarters await you. Try to avoid too long farewells with the Lorelei of the Rhenish shores, and if Madame F is there, hide yourself, be secret so as to avoid ardent scenes. Get yourself to Weimar between September first and third as your score must be in the copyist's hands between the fifteenth and sixteenth.

"Yours wholly,
"Liszt."

Liszt was always extravagant in his expressions toward those he loved; it was not unnatural that he called Anton "Van II." Anton's face was strikingly like Beethoven's. So was his impetuous nature, his rugged strength. Moreover, Anton was a true Beethoven worshiper at a time when the musical world turned to music it considered more exciting and above all, more "modern" than Beethoven. Anton assured the Master he would be in Weimar within a few days. "I am so happy that I shall see you soon. Believe me, no Madame F can hold me when I desire to go to you. . . ."

Making his farewells to the mysterious and importunate Mesdames F and X, Rubinstein took coach for Weimar. Work went forward on the *Siberian Hunters*, which was performed on schedule with the half-success that all Rubinstein's operas—except the hugely popular *Demon*—were to have. A fatal preference for ponderous subjects beset Anton, overwhelming the very charming music he often wrote for them. Anton knew the *Siberian Hunters* had not pleased, and even though Liszt talked of immediate plans for the production of *Paradise Lost*, Anton felt a sadness that never reached him except through failure of his compositions. He had come to Europe, quite definitely, to further himself as a composer. How annoying, therefore, to discover daily, hourly, that what people wanted of him was to hear him play other men's pieces on the piano!

It was a comfort to know that the Master, for one, believed in his future as composer. "Rubinstein," wrote Liszt to his American pupil, William Mason, after one of Anton's visits to Weimar, "is conspicuously different from the opaque mass of self-styled *composer-pianists* who do not even know what it is to play the piano, still less with what fuel it is necessary to stoke oneself in order to compose, so that with what they lack in talent for composition, they fancy themselves pianists, and vice versa. Rubinstein will forthwith publish about fifty compositions—concertos, trios, symphonies, songs, light pieces, etc., which deserve notice."

Which deserve notice . . . Liszt believed in Van II, but he was not deceived into any overstatement. The music of this young Russian was uneven and hurried, faults that maturity would correct. The point was that to be a true virtuoso player, a man must be a composer as well—as all the great virtuosi to date had been. When people went to hear Mozart, they went to hear him play his own compositions. This idea of a man sitting up for two hours playing other men's music was something new and scandalous. Too many of the Altenburg pupils were mere keyboard technicians. Virtuosity implied that a man was first of all a musician, as Mozart, Bach, Beethoven, Chopin had been—the fingers merely an instrument through which creation took shape. How could a man interpret Beethoven if he himself had not the heart and the intellect to write music?

Rubinstein was, indeed, the very embodiment of the ideal virtuoso as defined by Liszt, who wrote: "The virtuoso is not a mason who, chisel in hand, faithfully and conscientiously cuts his stone after the design of the architect. He is not a passive tool that reproduces feeling and thought without adding *himself*. Musical works are in reality, for the virtuoso, only the tragic and touching *mise-en-scène* for feelings; he is called upon to let these speak, weep, sing, sigh— to render these to his own consciousness. He creates in this way like the composer himself, for he must embrace in himself those passions which he, in their complete brilliancy, has to bring to light. He breathes life into the lethargic body, infuses it with fire, and enlivens it with the pulse of gracefulness and charm."

In short, Liszt was asking for genius—and why should he ask for less? Years ago in Paris, Liszt had recognized in this Russian boy the quality he sought; let Rubinstein write his *Siberian Hunters* and his *Paradise Lost*; talent such as this might burn away reams of paper before it came to the white-hot kernel that lay at the core. Perhaps that core was not composition at all but sheer perfection of pianoforte playing. What did it matter? The world needed creative pianism.

Others than Liszt have given ample testimony to Rubinstein's possession of this rare quality of creative playing. Huneker pronounced Anton the greatest pianist in a long and varied list. "You felt," he wrote, "that the piece Rubinstein happened to be playing was heard by you for the first time—the creative element in his nature was so strong. The power and the passion of the man have never been equalled. He played many composers, but for me, he seemed to be playing the Book of Job, the Apocalypse and the Scarlet Sarafan."

How Liszt would have applauded this description of his stormy, elemental young Van II—Liszt the Abbé, the mystic to whom God and music and love were almost synonymous! All their lives these two remained friends although, as time passed, the two took very different directions. Liszt became more controlled, Rubinstein ever wilder and more passionate in his playing; on the stage Rubinstein's manner grew more brusque and rude, his clothes more defiantly slovenly. Sometimes he was suspicious of Liszt. "Demon of music!" he wrote of the Abbé, "inflaming, intoxicating by his fantastic style, bewitching by his grace—assuming and discarding all forms, at once ideal and earthy, knowing all, capable of all. . . ."

Critics have expended thousands of words comparing the playing of Liszt and Rubinstein. It is a fruitless exercise, like comparing sun with moon, Beethoven with Mozart or one hour with another. The difference between Rubinstein and Liszt lay first of all in their essential natures. A comparison of their faces, their hands, makes this instantly clear. Liszt's fingers were abnormally long, the tendons at the base set very deep, giving the fingers an extraordinary spread. Rubinstein called Liszt an incarnation of Satan; in his hand, as in the hand of Paganini, is something truly demonic.

Rubinstein's hand was not demonic. It contained neither spirit of hell nor spirit of heaven. It was earthbound, broad and heavy, the back tremendously powerful, the wrist massive. The owner of this hand was deeply religious—but deeply skeptical also; no one ever surprised Anton Rubinstein on his knees, lost in the ecstasy so natural to the Abbé Liszt. Anton's fingers were deeply cushioned at the ends, and these cushions were more than partially responsible for the velvet, sustained tone that was Anton's most remarkable technical achievement. "I have phenomenal fingers," he said once, "and I have cultivated strength and lightness in using them."

Josef Hofmann has made the most sensible comparison between the two men. After describing the dazzling qualities of Liszt's playing, he writes of Anton, his one-time teacher: "Rubinstein excelled by his sincerity, by his Heaven-storming power of great impassionedness, a quality which, with Liszt, had passed through the sieve of a superior education and gentlemanly elegance. Liszt was, in the highest sense of the word, a man of the world; Rubinstein was a world-stormer, with a sovereign disregard for conventionality and Mrs. Grundy."

Anton Rubinstein knew well enough that Liszt was his only serious rival, but he brusquely refused a word that implied envy of one he so sincerely admired. Time and again he bowed to Liszt's supremacy. "Put all the rest of us together," he told William Steinway in New York, "and we would not make one Liszt."

Wading through the petty jealousies that make up a large part of musical history, it is comforting to come upon natures so large as those of Liszt and Rubinstein. It is pleasant to know that young Anton, descending the hill below Altenburg Castle in January of 1855 to besiege the concert halls of Europe, took with him no envy but the sustaining consciousness that in Weimar he possessed a loyal friend who was also a very great musician.

14

1854-1856. The complete virtuoso

From city to city, season after season for three years, Anton Rubinstein traveled across Europe, playing with orchestras at evening concerts, playing with singers, sharing matinée programs, playing alone when he had the chance. Newspaper critics raved and stormed, praised and jeered. It is useless to quote what they said. To revive by the printed word the magic of musical performance is as difficult as to write convincingly about great acting or great dancing. Nijinsky leaps through a window as the *Spectre de la Rose*; Duse, as Camille, dies for a hundred nights—and a generation gives thanks. But not the next generation. . . . James Huneker has written a preface to the Schirmer edition of Chopin's *Nocturnes*. Of the *G Minor Nocturne*, Opus 15, he says, "In the seventeenth bar and during four succeeding bars there is a held note, F, and I once heard Anton Rubinstein keep this tone prolonged by some miraculous means. The *tempo* is very slow, and the tone is not in a position where the sustaining pedal can sensibly help it. Yet under Rubinstein's velvet fingers it swelled and diminished, and went on singing into the E as if the instrument were an organ. I suppose the inaudible changing of fingers on the note, with his artistic pedaling, achieved the wonderful effect."

Admiring Rubinstein greatly, Huneker tried time and again to express his sensations when hearing that magic singing tone. Yet he might as well not have spoken. Rubinstein played Chopin; thousands heard and the hearts of thousands were lifted; thousands, for a long moment, knew that life was good and sensed somehow the purpose that lay behind life. Yet even the vivid pen of a Huneker got no further than "I suppose the inaudible changing of fingers . . ."

Hopeless, to re-create the music Anton made upon that first tour in the 1850's. We can only describe the man himself, what he wore, how he looked, what he ate and drank, if he was tired, if he was gay. And somehow, the attempt justifies itself; it is not mere curiosity. A great man's life, said Froude, can claim no privacy, and upon the lives of remarkable men, said Goethe, pen and ink can least be spared. What causes the great to persist in their aim, what chemistry welds them always to their purpose, sobbing, bleeding, gasping, but returning ever to the business in hand? We long to discover the reason, we seek it in the laboratory; is it hereditary, is it functional, is it in the glands, the blood-stream, does it concern itself with the rhythm of the heart-beat? We seek and seek to the point of absurdity, yet somehow, the search is dignified in the end. In the end these victors, these giants are dust like the rest of us and, like us, these men know that they are dust. Yet they never permit life to lose its meaning; the prospect of that final humiliation spurs them desperately to action. It was Disraeli who said, "Life is too short for us not to try to make it great."

Anton Rubinstein at 24 was warm and alive—and very far from dissolution. He is described by contemporaries as a strikingly handsome man; the photograph taken on this concert tour in the 1850's is highly characteristic both of the player and the period. Observe the worn soft shoes, the unpressed trousers, the frock coat for *matinée* performance, the straggling tie and handsome mane of hair. The nostrils are spread in challenge; the wide, sensitive mouth is beautifully modeled and still curved with youth; later it will be the harsh straight line the world associates with a face that became rough-hewn, Beethovenesque. The lamp, the carven chair, the curtain trailing are nostalgic of a day when ladies rustled in crinoline and gentlemen knew how to bow from the waist. The ash tray on the piano indicates an inveterate habit. Weber's name sits boldly on the rack; in Anton's day the composer of *Der Freischütz* was considered a pioneer, a brave romantic who had defied the philistines of the piano. Anton thought highly of Weber and was an excellent interpreter of his works. Weber, moreover, had been an ardent Beethoven champion and Rubinstein loved him for it.

Storming through Europe with Beethoven and the Romantics, Rubinstein struck more wrong notes than any pianist in history—and knew it. But he knew also that the power within him could transcend wrong notes by the dozen. Once, in Berlin, he played Weber's *Polacca Brillante* with such irresistible rhythm that the audience began to stamp its feet, softly at first, then with an abandon extraordinary for academic Prussia. The theatre rocked. Anton did not notice but played on, his tie awry, buttons bursting from his vest.

Rubinstein knew his power. "I am not an amateur but an artist. I have voluntarily embarked upon a magnificent career. I believe that I shall succeed, yes, I believe it; it is not an occasion for modesty; to prove that I shall distinguish myself in music, everything points to it outwardly; and within me the voice of nature is stronger than the strictest objections of reason." These are not Rubinstein's words but Berlioz', written at the age of 22, yet they fit Anton Rubinstein perfectly. Moreover, Anton was so little given to self-confession that to understand him we are driven to the confessions of other musicians. What self-revelations he vouchsafed were expressed impersonally, and always in regard to work. He said that the best hours of his life were the hours of composition. "When a man is composing, he is happiest. Here he has his illusions and his dreams. But when this music is performed, the composer must be very strong-minded in order to surmount disappointment and turn again to work." And again: "Work is man's best friend, idleness his most dangerous enemy. The one gives you health, the other breaks you. Work makes life joyful, gives a man good spirits. Work is life, idleness is death."

These years of his late twenties held for Anton Rubinstein no idleness whatever. Going directly north from Weimar in January of 1855, he gave his first Berlin concert, playing his own Concerto in F. His *Ocean Symphony* received here its first performance, "by a third-class orchestra," the composer reported laconically to Liszt.

For musical history, this was an important event. Badly played or no, this was the first performance of a symphony by any Russian. Writing symphonies, until now, had been an accomplishment of the West. Anton went to Charlottenburg, next, and played for the King of Prussia—"not with orchestra, as I had desired, but simply *salon* pieces." In March he played in Vienna, redeeming forever the disaster of nine years ago. And when he had a few days' rest from traveling, Anton worked at his *Faust* quartet.

In April, Anton sat at his desk long enough to write a newspaper article that led him into endless trouble and unpleasantness. It was innocently conceived, purporting to be a presentation of present-day trends in Russian music, with a brief historical analysis as preface.

The article reads innocently enough today; Rubinstein suggested that although Russian folksong and dance existed authentically, the creation of a strictly Russian opera was impossible because love, jealousy, grief, loyalty are universal emotions and their musical expression cannot be strictly national. Between Eastern and Western music, said Rubinstein, exists a definite cleavage, born of differences in climate and blood. But Russia is too near the West to receive isolated treatment. Italian opera exists, certainly; so does German opera. But they possess only the superficial differentiation of language and native dance rhythms; they do not exist as a nationalist crusade.

Rubinstein was amazed at the storm that followed his article. Glinka himself was in Berlin when it appeared. Anton called on him and was received coldly and heaped with reproaches. Late that autumn, Glinka was still complaining. "The Jew Rubinstein," wrote Glinka to a friend, "has undertaken to acquaint Germany with our Russian music and has written an article in which he flings mud at us all, touching rather arrogantly my old lady, *A Life for the Tsar*. Apropos of this, the German newspaper in St. Petersburg has published a *feuilleton* in defense of my old lady, covering the impudent Jew with confusion. Barthold wrote it. He put sufficient chill into it, and the Jew suffered a thorough trouncing."

By this time, however, the "impudent Jew" had forgotten all

about the Glinka article, although Anton admitted it was a great indiscretion. "I am not in the habit," he wrote, "of regretting past indiscretions."

Anton Rubinstein was too healthy for repentance, too eager for the morrow to waste time regretting the past. In a bright aura of glory he continued his tour, playing, practicing, composing. Such Tartar fury was new to Europe; the persuasion of its passion was irresistible, city after city succumbed. In October Anton went down to Weimar for Liszt's birthday and found a marvelous new pupil installed—young Tausig who at fourteen had brought to the Master a superlative pianistic equipment. Peter Cornelius told Anton how the boy, at the first class lesson he attended, sat down at the piano and dashed into Chopin's *Polonaise in A flat*. "A very devil of a fellow," said Cornelius. "He knocked us clean over with the octaves."

Anton heard the boy and gave praise, and went forth again to post-coach, railroad and concert platform. All winter he traveled. Summer of 1856 found him in Stuttgart, ancestral home of Helena Pavlovna. Here Anton settled down to work on his opera, *Paradise Lost,* without, he wrote Liszt, much success. Always his letters to Liszt dwell upon composition; the actual concerts he records without much interest. "I played in Hamburg, Bremen, Bonn, Coblenz, Mainz, etc. Everywhere, successfully enough. In Brunswick they performed my overture from *Dmitri Donskoy*; it went very well. They plan to play it here in Stuttgart and I am much interested to see what impression it will make. . . . At Hanover I met Brahms and Grimm and Joachim, but the latter I have come to know better here."

It was a great trio that Rubinstein met in Hanover. They were still young, all under thirty. Joachim was 25 and had lately accepted the post of Court Director of Music at Hanover. Grimm, a pianist and teacher who was to command great respect in his century, was 29. The two were Leipzig-bred, educated under the beneficent shadow of Felix Mendelssohn. Brahms was the youngest of all; at 23 he had just returned from his first long concert tour with Remenyi, the wild Hungarian violinist. The world was yet innocent as to which of these three—Brahms, Grimm or Joachim—was to attain the greatest stature. Moreover, the musical alignments that history was to accept so definitely were as yet scarcely traced. Brahms was casting about for a livelihood, not for a "cause." He had no idea that his name was to represent anti-Wagnerism—although the alignment would never, basically, be quite so simple as that. Anton Rubinstein, for instance, remained bitterly anti-Wagner all his life, but he never became pro-Brahms. Slavic inheritance and a Mendelssohnian education made Rubinstein a melodist pure and simple, for whom Brahms' music proved turgid, over-rich harmonically. Rubinstein's pupil, Tchaikovsky, was to see eye-to-eye with him on this, complaining that every time Brahms started up a good melody, he hid it after two measures in a murky mass of harmonic construction.

For Rubinstein it was a great misfortune that Robert Schumann died that summer of 1856. As composer, this left Anton dangerously stranded; he could move forward neither with Wagner nor Brahms. Schumann alone might have saved him. Schumann possessed melody in abundance; he was the very apostle of that romanticism which was part of Anton Rubinstein, yet Schumann's music was neither murky nor thick. Twelve years ago, Schumann had noticed Rubinstein as a composer, prophesying that the boy who wrote the Etude called *Ondine* might go far. Had Schumann lived, Rubinstein's facility for composition might have taken a deeper, richer turn.

But when Anton Rubinstein came abroad in 1854, Schumann was already helpless within the walls of his asylum, bound to dreams as sterile as the torture of imagined discord that pressed unremittingly upon his ears. That very summer, when Rubinstein was enjoying the society of Schumann's greatest disciple, Brahms, Schumann died and his wife set bravely out to play her husband's music upon the concert platforms of Europe. Anton was to meet Clara Schumann in city after city. She was the greatest woman pianist who ever lived, but Anton Rubinstein confessed no woman as rival in the field of music. Madame Schumann was, moreover, a shade too in-

Anton Rubinstein in 1854

tellectual for the Rubinstein taste. Ambition, intellectuality, sat ill upon woman.

But it sat well upon man! Brahms was ambitious, so were Grimm and Joachim. Whatever he may have thought of their music, Rubinstein enjoyed the company of these men who looked upon their art with such deep seriousness. It is tempting to speculate on what might have happened to Rubinstein had he settled then and there in Germany, developing his gifts as a composer by the side of such musicians as Brahms and Joachim. These young men cared more for learning than for laurel wreaths; they were professional artists, but they were also perennial students. Brahms was busy destroying music as fast as he wrote it; he confessed later that a house could have been papered with the string quartets he threw away. But Anton Rubinstein was too impatient to throw away manuscripts. Anton must cover sheet after sheet with notes and then, instead of rewriting, must find a quick publisher for music that was watery with a diffusion which patient craftsmanship might have concentrated into a strong and lasting essence.

Brahms was by nature what Rubinstein longed to be—a composer-pianist. Rubinstein was a pianist-composer whose genius for interpretation, for sheer pianism, stood implacably in his way. Always he desired to write and always he played better than he wrote. As pianist, Brahms could not compare with Rubinstein; Brahms' performance was always more energetic than accurate; he played as a composer sings, not for the executional effect but for the purpose of sounding out the actual composition. Rubinstein was jealous of Brahms and said so now and again, roaring his distress quite frankly, like a child. And the world laughed indulgently, wondering why the giants descend to do battle instead of remaining each in his Valhalla to do his work—which is to feed with beauty the music-hungry children of men. . . .

With the completed score of *Paradise Lost* under his arm, Rubinstein left the pleasant company of Brahms and Joachim and followed his star to Berlin, seeking a publisher, a concert platform.

133

On the way north he stopped in Weimar, but Liszt was not there. Taciturn and gloomy, Anton wandered about the halls of Schloss Altenburg, ignoring the pupils, refusing to touch the piano for a lesser audience than the Master. When the Master failed to appear, Anton went on to Berlin where he planned to spend the winter.

Berlin was filled with a goodly musical company. Hans Von Bülow was there, teaching in the Conservatory of old Siegfried Dehn's colleagues, the Herren Stern and Marx. Rubinstein's junior by six weeks, Bülow had only just begun a concert career. Born a gentleman, he had studied jurisprudence in preparation for a gentleman's profession. But as diversion he had taken up counterpoint and piano playing—dangerous pastimes for the musically gifted. When he was twenty he heard *Lohengrin* in Weimar under Liszt's baton, and forgot the law forever. Liszt loved him and taught him, and in three years Bülow was ready for his first concert tour.

As pianist, Hans Von Bülow was a direct contrast to Rubinstein, being as passionately intellectual as Anton was passionately emotional. Every piece that Bülow played, every symphony he conducted was thought out, analyzed to the minutest detail. The effect was superb. As yet, Bülow, with only a year's concert experience, was a mere child upon the platform compared with a Rubinstein who had been playing since he was nine. But Anton sensed here a potential rival, and delighted in the prospect. "Fight, struggle, these are the salt and pepper of life," said Anton.

He would have enjoyed a winter in Berlin, with Bülow and his old teacher, Dehn. But it was not to be. Anton was, after all, a Russian; he held an important official position in Petersburg with the Grand Duchess Helena Pavlovna. Leschetizky was filling it now, but Leschetizky was only a stopgap. Anton was on leave of absence, a fact that he had forgotten completely, so absorbed had he been in Liszt and Weimar and *Paradise Lost* and the concert platforms of Europe. . . . When Tsar Nicholas had died in January of 1855, Rubinstein had felt real grief; he had sought out his Russian friends and talked of things past. But he had not gone home, the passing of his Tsar had not truly interrupted Anton's life.

And now in August of 1856, a new Tsar was to be crowned in Moscow. Nicholas Pavlovitch's son, tall Alexander of glorious destiny, was on his way from Petersburg to the Kremlin. Rubinstein received urgent summons home. Helena Pavlovna was to accompany the new Tsar to Moscow, and she needed her Janitor of Music. In September, Von Bülow wrote to a friend, "Rubinstein was here for two weeks, but suddenly was called to Moscow to help crown the Tsar."

Rubinstein left Germany for Moscow. Left Brahms, Joachim, Bülow and all the healthy, serious fraternity of young Germany for the glittering seduction of the Russian Court. Had Russia offered no more than this, perhaps Rubinstein would not have obeyed the call. But it offered much more. All Europe had heard rumors of the new Tsar's liberalism, of his intelligence and courage, his eagerness for reform. Rumors only, as yet, but very exciting to the patriot. And Rubinstein was more than a patriot; he was a crusader who had only been waiting the opportunity to do battle for the cause of music. Helena Pavlovna was the very core of Russian Imperial liberalism; in her salon were to be found representatives of every party, Slavophile and Western liberal scientist, poet and musician. Emancipation of the serfs had been her cause for fifteen years; she had worked actively in its behalf.

At last, Russia offered the kind of welcome Anton had longed for. The Grand Duchess had written nothing definite; to do so would have been, of course, the highest indiscretion. But Anton knew that Helena Pavlovna would not have summoned him home only to play music for coronation week, even though such playing might bring laurels and domestic acclaim. Something further was agitating her, something broader, more significant. The time had come to strike for the cause of musical education at home, or at least the time had come to talk about it. . . .

Lumbering across Prussia in the post-coach, glad impatience possessed Anton Rubinstein, a longing for the sight of his old friend, for the sound of her voice, the light, eager clasp of a hand that was always warm with welcome.

15

1856-1857. A new Tsar for Russia. Riviera sun.
Young Saint-Saëns meets a hero

Purposely, Anton arrived the day after the coronation. Moscow received him in a whirl of dust, heat, noise and excitement. The city was flag-hung and quite crazy with rejoicing. In every open square, children, riding the painted merry-go-rounds, screamed with joy; peasants danced hand in hand along the streets, their red boots twinkling, the bright ribbons from the girls' capes streaming in the sunlight. This new Father Tsar, it was rumored, would give the peasant serfs their freedom, which meant that a man could hold title to his field like a *barin*. There would be no more floggings; the hated German overseers would go home where they belonged. Everyone would get rich immediately; vodka would flow in a blessed, perpetual river. . . . "Oh, Moscow, Moscow, golden-haired Moscow!" sang Ivan happily in the warm streets, while overhead, sun glinted against the city's crown of gilded dome and minaret.

Anton made his way through the crowds to his mother's apartment. It was hopeless to try to see the Grand Duchess; this very ceremony that kept him from her would soon permit them a freer, more fruitful association than they had ever enjoyed under the breathless caution of Nicholas' régime. At his mother's he found the family: Kaleria, Nicholas, Jacob and the sisters, pretty Luba with her new husband from Odessa and faithful Sophie. They had watched the procession yesterday, they told Anton excitedly. They had seen the Tsar on horseback, tall and magnificent, his sons riding behind him. They had seen the frail Tsarina with her daughter in the golden coach, wearing the high *kokoshnik* on their heads, diamond-encrusted and splendid. The whole of fashionable Petersburg was in Moscow, said Nicholas with a grin. They had brought their own carriages and coachmen and kept getting lost and ringing people's doorbells to ask where they were. Official Petersburg had tried to rent the big houses over in the Merchant Quarter, offering huge sums, but old Moscow refused to be bought and many of the foreign embassies were forced to house themselves in quarters too modest for their taste.

Moscow had not celebrated a coronation in thirty years; her citizens were justly proud that her emperors came home to receive sacrament and crown from the mother city. The night of his arrival, Anton and his brothers went out to Hodinka Field for the People's Feast, mingling on foot with the singing, dancing peasants, watching the fireworks, listening to the music that floated down from the Tsar's pavilion. Nobody in Moscow had been sober for a week, Nicholas—aged 21—told his brother with satisfaction. He himself had not dined at home in a fortnight. There was something more to this rejoicing than the usual coronation excitement. There was a new spirit in the air. Had Anton, abroad, heard talk of Emancipation? All these millions of serfs! How in God's name could it be effected? Improvident, lazy, drunken creatures—it would be like turning crowds of children loose to fend for themselves.

But Ivan himself was not worrying. Why should anybody worry in coronation week? Ivan danced and drank and, happily insensible, rolled in the warm Moscow gutters. Through open windows in the Kremlin Palace the tall son of Nicholas Pavlovitch heard his city making merry—but he did not smile. Alexander, son of Nicholas, was a brave man; it was not fear of the assassin's bomb that kept his handsome face solemn. It was consciousness of an awful heritage. His father had willed him a kingdom of unnamed souls, humble, trusting, wildly ignorant. The time was past when a stroke of the Imperial pen spelled finality. Would his nobles work with him in this question of Emancipation? Would they rise to the personal sacrifice as, for instance, his Aunt Helena Pavlovna had risen?

Helena Pavlovna herself, housed grandly and uncomfortably in that part of the Kremlin called The Apartments, had no doubts as to the rightness of Emancipation. For years she had worked for it openly, as she had always worked for liberalism and reform. It had been Helena Pavlovna to whom Milioutin had presented his first plan for Emancipation, ten years ago when the very word was still taboo. Already she had freed the slaves on her own vast Poltavian estates and was experiencing endless difficulty. The peasants did not know how to work without a master; they drank up their crop money the day they received it and came to the steward's door, imploring bread.

But what immediately interested Helena Pavlovna this autumn of 1856 was not the freeing of slaves but the freeing of music. While Tsar Nicholas lived, her hands had been tied. Nicholas Pavlovitch had loved music, loved it, indeed, far more than his serious son Alexander. But to Nicholas Pavlovitch, music had been a toy and a pastime; to permit it to be more would have savored of ideas, of danger. Now all was different. Alexander Nicholaevitch was not musical, but he had given his aunt to understand that she could have a free hand in these matters. Waiting, amidst the long, exhausting coronation ceremonies, for an opportunity to see Rubinstein, Helena Pavlovna wondered if he knew why she had sent for him. No one else could carry out her purpose, no one else possessed both talent and a respect for royalty. Real genius was hard to handle when it came to court etiquette. Anton Rubinstein was a genius, but he possessed, happily, the manners of a man of the world. Moreover, he knew the necessity of planning slowly and cautiously; he knew that a soil made barren by the long censorship of Nicholas I must be prepared, as it were, plowed and sown anew.

The coronation robes were stiff with satin, heavy with pearls. Diadems pressed upon one's brow; curtseys put a stop to all but the most foolish, courtier-like conversation. Longing for the receptions to be ended, Helena Pavlovna was impatient to see if her one-time Janitor of Music had been changed by these three triumphant European years. Would he be, at twenty-six, the same eager, passionate artist she had known? When at last she was able to summon Anton to the palace, she was instantly reassured. Across the great room the two almost ran to meet each other; Anton's gesture as he bent over her hand left no doubt that he was still hers to command. Eagerly they plunged into talk of music. Had not Anton Rubinstein sensed already, asked the Grand Duchess, a great change at Court? Was not the atmosphere freer, less constrained? The cruel tension of the Crimean War was lifted; with peace at home and abroad it was an ideal time to set in motion the reforms, social, educational and artistic, that they all desired. Of course, added Helena Pavlovna, there were forces to combat. The old die-hards were very articulate; rigid conservatism ruled in many quarters. People said the peasants were too ignorant to be freed; people said education and art were dangerous.

Anton Rubinstein raised a cynical eyebrow. "Despots," he said, "never think the people ripe enough for freedom."

Rubinstein stayed three weeks in Moscow during that August and September of 1856. Several times he played at evening concerts in the Grand Duchess Helena's apartments. "The Emperor Alexander came," wrote Anton, "but he did not seem attracted by music." Even while he felt progress in the air, and freedom and a lightening of the dreaded censorship, Rubinstein could not but miss that other Emperor who had been called despot, but whose personal charm had conquered the most stubborn hearts, that Nicholas Pavlovitch who had loved music and followed its sound through the gorgeous impersonal rooms of his palace, whistling, humming, pleased to sit all evening behind the piano bench, beating time with a gleaming boot.

The son of Nicholas Pavlovitch was too conscientious to waste time in such frivolities. The courts of reformers are never so gay, so extravagant as the courts of despots. When Rubinstein played at evening parties in the palace, the Emperor sat in the next room playing cards, then rose and walked through the music room as a signal that the evening was ended. On rare occasions he stopped to compliment Anton or to give formal praise to a singer or actor. "One must remember," wrote Anton, "that the Emperor was harassed by questions of great importance for the good of our beloved country; he had no time for music. Yet even concerning music his reign was brilliant because he evoked a spirit of liberalism; he inspired Russian society not only to free the serfs but to untie many cords that had bound our country down. All this reacted to the good of music, making the reign of Alexander II glorious even in the sphere of musical art."

So far, the reign of Alexander II had only begun. More and more heavily, the ceremonies that marked its beginning palled upon Alexander's Aunt Helena. How endless these jeweled palace evenings, how hot this dusty city of Moscow! Helena Pavlovna longed for the sea and for freedom to think and talk and plan. The Empress Dowager, tired and lonely, suggested they go abroad for the winter —to the Riviera where there was sun and no etiquette. Helena Pavlovna could take her own suite; would she like to invite some musicians to come along?

Joyfully, the Grand Dutchess summoned her Janitor of Music, and the two imperial suites set out for Nice, traveling in state, setting themselves up in truly Russian magnificence. Freed from palace etiquette, released from the sullen breath of the Neva, these northerners opened like plants put out to air. The blue sky was a miracle, the sun a benediction. Like children, the bearded Grand Dukes romped in the sun and the Dowager Empress laughed, forgetting death and war and palace precedent. Visitors from Russia came in a steady stream. The Grand Duke Konstantin spent a week, so did the Grand Dukes Nicholas and Michael. Count Michael Vielgorsky was there, Apraksin in his gorgeous uniform. It was their business to divert the Dowager Empress and they went at it in true Russian style, with hearty pranks and practical jokes, huge laughter, huge eating and drinking. One night they serenaded poor Empress Alexandra with a masked orchestra, each member of which played an instrument strange to him. Michael Vielgorsky staggered in under a double bass fiddle, Anton with a kettle-drum, the Grand Dukes with flutes and fifes borrowed from the army. When they burst into her apartment the Empress was frightened, but soon she laughed.

Victor Emmanuel came across the border to visit. He was King of Sardinia then; in the Crimean war he had been Russia's deadly enemy; now he did what he could, wrote Rubinstein, to make things pleasant for his Imperial guests. Cavour came with his King. Anton talked with him and was stirred by what Cavour said about a united Italy. The Grand Duchess Helena bought a villa to house the overflow. "We played and sang and played again," wrote Anton. "There was music enough to satisfy everybody. We often discussed the state of music in our country. Count Vielgorsky and I led the talk and it went on for hours. The Grand Duchess was instantly responsive. We confessed that in Russia musical art was in a sad condition. We must do something about it. Of us all, the Grand Duchess was the most impatient for action. She would move forward, she said, the moment we returned to Petersburg.

"It was in Nice, therefore, under the beautiful southern sky, that the seeds were sown which later bore fruit in the foundation of the Russian Musical Society."

Anton Rubinstein was as susceptible as anybody to the "beautiful southern sky." Under it he played music and talked music, and the world was an enchanted place. Some say the Grand Duchess fell in love, that winter, with her handsome Janitor of Music, and that if she could, she would have married him. Be it true or false it does not matter now; even a Grand Duchess may be permitted her dream. Rubinstein was loyal; no hint of this ever escaped him. Beyond doubt he was very happy; for a brief moment, life had removed its fangs; ambition ceased to ride upon the shoulders of music. Not once during the winter did Rubinstein mount the concert stage; when he sat down to the piano it was in the Villa Abigore or the Villa Bermin—one housed an Empress, the other a Grand Duchess.

It was an enchanted time, soon ended. In April of 1857 the Court prepared for its return to Russia, and Rubinstein packed his music in boxes labeled "Paris." The night before he left, he gave a farewell concert in the Grand Duchess' villa. More than two hundred gathered to hear him; no tickets were taken, no money changed hands. Rubinstein played for hours to an audience wild with enthusiasm, an audience that at the end stood on chairs, neighbor embracing neighbor with tears of joy.

It was fun to play for such "amateurs." Rubinstein himself often used the word in its original sense. But somehow, one dared not linger too long; in the perfumed air of dilettantism was something poisonous to the professional artist. *En route* to Paris next day, Rubinstein felt his forces gather, his muscles tense and harden for the coming ordeal. This would be his first Paris concert since his *Wunderkind* days, and there was no use pretending it was not an important, a crucial occasion. Paris was still the city of musical light, no matter what Leipzig, Berlin and Vienna liked to think. The old faces were gone: Chopin and Cherubini and the pompous Herr Kalkbrenner. Meyerbeer was in Berlin now; at the Paris Conservatoire, gentle Auber consented to receive foreign students. The Conservatoire concerts had become very famous indeed; to be invited to play at one of them was the making of any young virtuoso.

Rossini, at 65, had come back to Paris after many wanderings. He no longer wrote operas but he was a great power in the musical world. All Paris came to his door, carrying away with them the famous *mots* that Parisians love. *"Monsieur Wagner,"* said Rossini after the Paris *première* of Tannhäuser, *"Monsieur Wagner a de beaux moments mais de mauvais quarts d'heures aussi."*

It was no easy business to please Paris. Rubinstein, entering the city alone that April day of 1857, was well aware that in disdaining press notices and preliminary visits to celebrities, he was behaving in a risky and high-handed manner. One of the most ruthless critics he must face was Berlioz, who, although a marvelous musician, was opportunist enough to slash Beethoven's melodies when they soared too high for a favorite soprano's voice. Even now Berlioz and Madame Viardot were tinkering with *Fidelio* for a Paris *première*; Paris taste would find nothing but tedium in a tale of wifely loyalty. So *Fidelio* was replotted into a story of political intrigue, with music transposed down for Viardot's best range. Even so, the professional critics pronounced this music *"très ennuyeuse."* Rossini, shrugging, said this was what he had expected of Paris.

April, 1857. The Citizen King was gone forever. In his place reigned Louis Napoleon, Emperor of the French, beside him the young and beautiful Eugénie. Night after night the Tuileries blazed with gaiety, while underground the revolutionists laid their train of powder. At the Opéra-Comique, Ambroise Thomas prepared his *Carnaval de Venise*; Jacques Offenbach rehearsed the notorious *cancan* for his *Orphée aux Enfers*. *Les soupers de Jacques* were held after every operatic first night; the boulevards hummed with life and scandal.

April, 1857. A serious young man named César Franck turned his back on boulevard and *opéra bouffe* and sat writing music in his quiet organ loft. And a much younger man named Camille Saint-Saëns, who though only twenty-two had had two symphonies performed, watched the billboards for foreign visitors, wondering why a world that boasted so many wonderful fiddle players brought so few first-rate pianists to Paris.

One April day his search was rewarded, his curiosity aroused by a brand-new name. In his memoirs, Saint-Saëns has left his own account of this extraordinary meeting, prefacing it with a reminder that since Chopin's death eight years earlier, the world had known no great pianists. Thalberg had retired to grow grapes in Italy; Liszt had forsaken the concert stage for Weimar and his young disciples. Dohler, Ravina, Gottschalk were left in possession of the field— brilliant players but nothing more—"heroes of the pianoforte," wrote Saint-Saëns, "but no gods. Olympia was occupied by the violinists, and while none had been able to take up the bow laid down by the marvelous Paganini, still, Alard, Vieuxtemps and Sivori shone as stars of the first magnitude, each having his disciples and admirers.

"But as to the gods of the piano, the race seemed forever extinct when there appeared one fine day on the billboards of Paris small notices bearing this name: Antoine Rubinstein—of whom no one so far had heard a word because the great artist had the coquettish

143

temerity to disdain the help of the press. No advance notice—not one—had announced his appearance. His début, with orchestra, was made in the Salle Herz. Adorable room, so original and elegant—no longer, alas, available! Needless to say, not a single paying listener was in the audience. But next day the artist found himself famous and the ensuing concert was crammed to suffocation. I was there, and from the first note I was knocked flat, chained to the chariot of the conqueror!"

Someone offered to present young Saint-Saëns to his hero, but the younger man was terrified in spite of Rubinstein's reputation for kindness and what Saint-Saëns called "urbanity." The invitation was refused for a whole year. Next spring, on Anton's second visit to Paris, young Saint-Saëns took his courage in his hands and was introduced. Instantly the two became friends; Saint-Saëns read at sight the orchestral score of Rubinstein's *Ocean Symphony*—a performance that would melt the heart of any composer. "I played quite well in those days," records Saint-Saëns ingenuously.

Meeting often, the two played four-hand duets, endlessly, with loud crashings and long repetitions. "We made music with passion, because we wanted to make it, and we never had enough." At last an artist had appeared who was truly an artist, with no jealousy, no petty spites, no petty plots against fellow artists. "A rare thing to meet on the boulevards," wrote young Saint-Saëns grimly. Finally, Rubinstein invited Saint-Saëns to conduct the orchestra in a series of concerts at which Anton was to play the piano. "I hesitated to accept," wrote Saint-Saëns, "having conducted very little up to then. But finally I gave in, and those concerts were my education as a conductor. Rubinstein brought to rehearsal scores all scribbled with erasures, cuts and alterations of every kind. Never could I obtain the music ahead of time. Rubinstein said it was too amusing to see me extricate myself when we got into difficulty! Moreover, while playing, Rubinstein paid absolutely no attention to the orchestra; each player had to follow him by hazard, and sometimes such a storm of sound issued from the piano that I could hear nothing else, and had no guide beyond the sight of his hands on the keyboard.

"Liszt was an eagle, Rubinstein a lion. Those who saw his fierce velvet paws attack the instrument with puissant caress will never forget it."

Anton and young Saint-Saëns became, recorded the latter, "well-nigh inseparable." They were a familiar sight on the boulevards together, Rubinstein with his broad shoulders and heavy head, Saint-Saëns small, frail, delicate. When he gave his first concert in Paris as a full-grown, full-fledged virtuoso, Anton was twenty-six. He played and conquered—and boarded the Channel packet for Dover in the cold April sunshine, headed for shores far bleaker than those he left behind.

16

London and John Ella Paradise Lost.
Baden and the ladies

Aɴᴛoɴ Ruʙɪɴsᴛᴇɪɴ knew from experience that, for him, Paris was easier to conquer than London. Fourteen years had passed since Alexandre Villoing had read aloud faint praise from London's *Daily Examiner*. Now it was 1857, but London still distrusted musicians, especially those who permitted themselves to look like musicians, and in this respect Anton Rubinstein was blatantly guilty. It was not his thick wavy hair, his black felt hat and string tie that distinguished him so much as his wild defiance of bearing. He was very handsome; eyewitnesses have said that those who knew him only in later life will find it difficult to conceive how handsome Rubinstein was that spring of 1857. But he was not a graceful man like Liszt and Chopin; Anton shuffled out upon the stage, a lion stalking, head bent, eyes on the floor. Without a glance beyond the footlights he fell upon the keyboard, while below him the audience stirred and cleared its British throat, looking faintly alarmed.

Moreover, England was not well disposed toward Russians; the Crimean War was too recent. Presenting his credentials at the Embassy, Rubinstein received in due time an invitation to Court and went there expecting an informal evening of music with some playing to do. What was his dismay to find the entire royal family in full dress with medals, drawn up in a semicircle, standing with grave, frozen faces to receive him. Anton went from end to end of the line, bowing, speaking no word. Sighting a piano in the corner he rushed to it, sat down without invitation and commenced to play. Instant relief of the circle, smiles, whispers. The royal family, it seems, had been informed that this was a Russian agent creeping into England under guise of a musician. But no mere spy could play like that. The Princess Royal offered her hand; to her consternation Rubinstein raised it to his lips. She withdrew it hastily, informing him that in England it was not the custom to kiss the hand of royalty.

Rubinstein bowed, raising his eyebrows. "With us, Madame," he said, "it is the law."

On May 18th, Anton made his début with the London Philharmonic in the famous Hanover Square Rooms that John Christian Bach had caused to be built when George III was on the throne. Sterndale Bennett conducted the Philharmonic; he had been appointed last year to succeed Richard Wagner's short tenure. Bennett had learned music in Leipzig; his first act as director in London was to present Clara Schumann to his compatriots, and his compatriots disliked her greatly. She was too serious, with her huge programs played all from memory. Moreover, she insisted upon performing her dead husband's compositions—queer, disturbing music, not nearly so easy to listen to as the music of Mr. Mendelssohn.

Daily, Sterndale Bennett battled against the wall of British indifference. Daily, the lines between his eyes grew deeper and he withdrew more into himself, writing less of his fastidious, Mozart-like music. With his fringe of whiskers beneath the chin, his tall thin figure, he looked like an English barrister who taught school during off hours.

Anton Rubinstein, thick-haired, frowning, roared into the arched and mirrored rooms of Hanover Square, and Sterndale Bennett was glad to see him. Anton played his own *Concerto in G,* and nobody liked it except Bennett and the orchestra players and little Mr. John Ella, Director of the Musical Union, who shook Anton's hand warmly and invited him to return to London next spring and play a whole program by himself. Play anything he wanted, said Mr. Ella sturdily, tapping his silver-handled cane on the floor, and play it as Mr. Rubinstein himself saw fit, with *tempo rubato* as wide as the Channel at Portsmouth.

Anton smiled and said yes, he would come back next year. He liked John Ella, and if Ella said the London audiences merely needed education, then they must be given the benefit of the doubt. It seemed to Rubinstein that what London audiences needed was not education, but heart; they were monsters of rigidity and decorum. Even springtime did not melt them, and London just now was looking her prettiest. Anton was glad to be quickly gone, headed for Germany where a musician could feel at home. He went down to Baden and stayed all summer, practicing and composing. Rumor has it that after every European tour Anton gambled away all his earnings, that the Grand Duchess Helena used to send hurried money drafts to bring him home to Petersburg. But this is only rumor; Nicholas was the real gambler of the family. Anton adored cards but he played for small stakes, explaining that as a young man he had lost everything at cards one night, even to his clothes. Once was enough, he said. When concert money accumulated too fast, he gave it away to other musicians, great chunks of it, waving his hand, frowning when the recipient voiced his thanks.

These were the days when Rubinstein still practiced hours on end, memorizing new programs, working on dynamics. He was laying the foundation of a repertoire that later would carry itself. After sixteen years the silver voice of Rubini haunted his ear; patiently, Anton worked to reproduce this sound, spending an hour at a time pressing one finger upon the key, lifting it, pressing it again. And always listening, listening, his head bent, his eyes half-closed with a deep, painful concentration. These were crucial hours; Rubinstein's pianism was crystallizing; soon he would be too old to set new molds.

Late autumn of 1857 found him in Leipzig, where his *Ocean Symphony* had had its *première* two years before. Every artist liked to play with the *Gewandhaus* orchestra. Julius Rietz was conductor now, but David in the concert master's chair was the real leader— Ferdinand David, guiding spirit of the great Leipzig Conservatory. David had a terrible temper; Rubinstein himself was a little afraid of this man whom all Europe respected and who produced pupils of the caliber of Joseph Joachim.

But Anton never felt really at home in "the blessed Leipzigland,"

148

as he called the city ironically in a letter to Liszt. There was about the town something too German, a little heavy for Slavic taste. Vienna suited Anton better; he went there after Leipzig and played four concerts to a city that adored him. Budapest next, then Prague, where Edouard Hanslick had lately been appointed Professor of Ethics at the University—the great Hanslick whose criticism could make or break an artist. Hanslick never really liked Rubinstein's playing; it was too free for his taste, but now and again he wrote glowingly of Anton, speaking of his "incomparable youth and strength, his wonderful memory and use of melody. This strong pure music," said Hanslick, "brings health to the listener."

Long ago, Anton had visited these Danubian cities with Villoing, had mounted these same platforms, played for almost the same audiences. Fifteen years is not a generation; many in his audiences remembered Rubinstein as a curly-headed lad with a sensational technique and an irresistible stage manner.

"Art," wrote Anton, "is Eve who gives an apple to the artist. He who tastes, loses the paradise of his soul's quietness, and success is the guilty serpent." Anton Rubinstein had been suckled on the very juice of that apple—dangerous elixir that induces everlasting restlessness. Now, in his young manhood, he was drinking deep. Moreover, having just completed the huge score of his opera, *Paradise Lost*, he was trafficking freely with such terms as paradise and peace. Liszt had offered to stage the opera, and in February of 1858, Anton went to Weimar for rehearsals. The white tile stoves of Schloss Altenburg were warm to the touch; damp winds blew across the garden and snow tumbled stickily from the fir trees, melting as it reached the ground. On March first, the performance took place at the Court Theatre. Everyone was most kind and cordial; the Princess especially, professed herself pleased with the composer's treatment of this high and serious subject.

It was fortunate that Rubinstein could not know the judgment posterity would put upon his opera. He had written his music after Milton's poem, and Anton loved Milton as he loved the Bible. This Cromwell man had known what freedom meant and fought for it.

Milton died long before Beethoven was born, before Romanticism was a name, yet Milton wrote with all the grandeur and rebellion of Beethoven. Anton read, and the great lines rolled their cadence straight home to a heart that had learned the silent, fierce humility that was its birthright:

> "High on a throne of royal state . . .
> Satan exalted sat, by merit raised
> To that bad eminence; and, from despair
> Thus high uplifted beyond hope, aspires
> Beyond thus high, insatiate to pursue
> Vain war with heaven. . . ."

And from despair, thus high uplifted beyond hope. . . . How the words rushed at a man, no matter where he read them—by green Rhenish shores or in the cold post-coach, floundering across Prussia! *Uplifted beyond hope.* . . . How much more attractive was Satan than his royal Foe, how much nearer to the heart of man! Surely not Milton but he, Anton Rubinstein, had written these words from the inmost chamber of his being.

And now, April once more. This time Paris knew what to expect when it saw that modest placard among the flaring yellow posters. Anton's concert was crowded, his reception enthusiastic. It was a success great enough to float him confidently back to London for two appearances. The first, on May 11th, was for John Ella's Musical Union, established now in elegant new quarters in Saint James's Hall. The concerts, held in the morning, attracted a fashionable audience of ladies who arrived in dazzling spring costumes and whispered excitedly while Anton played Chopin. In the first row sat little John Ella, hands crossed on the handle of his cane, his shrewd face smiling ever so faintly. Anton felt that presence while he played, and was grateful for it.

Next day the London critics turned angrily against this Russian who played with such shocking *rubato*, who "took liberties," wrenching from his instrument the most disturbing sounds. Life should preserve always a decent reticence: what right had a wild-haired foreigner to come to Saint James's Hall and play Chopin in a way that made one suddenly doubt one's whole philosophy of life, made one question standards one had accepted since childhood? This was not art but license and anyway, the man hit wrong notes.

Rubinstein read the papers and grinned through half-closed eyelids. Nearly four weeks of London lay ahead before his June concert with the Philharmonic. Well, he could work. His mind was filled with *Paradise Lost*, with this mad, attractive Lucifer who labored against a Foe as remote, priggish and unconquerable as the Lord Mayor of London himself. There was a young Jew in town named Julius Rodenberg who loved the Bible as Anton loved it. The two met that May of 1858, discovering with excitement their mutual taste, spending long days together discussing the Old Testament and its possibilities as libretto material. Rodenberg had already put nearly all the Psalms into verse; he was amazed to find how well this Russian knew the Scriptures. "There was something touching," wrote Rodenberg, "in hearing Rubinstein, the youthful, applauded man of the world, speak of these sacred things. To him they had human and artistic value."

Rodenberg described Anton's rooms in Margaret Street; he says Rubinstein lived very well. "Thick carpets, a marble mantel, dark mahogany furniture. While we talked, Rubinstein played with an ivory-handled paper knife; upon the handle was his name in Hebrew letters. Rubinstein never concealed his Jewish origin; his greatest delight was to tell anecdotes of Polish Jews, very salty anecdotes. He would tell the same story ten, twenty times. And how Rubinstein could laugh!"

The two young men seized eagerly upon the idea of setting to music the Song of Solomon. They would make it into a full-length musical drama. Let Richard Wagner spin out his *Nibelungen* yarns, with Brünnhildas and Frickas striding the mountaintops. Surely the lovely Sulamith was more appealing and infinitely more human! It was in Margaret Street that the opera *Sulamith* was conceived, and *Feramors* too. Rodenberg does not remember if the ideas originated with himself or with Rubinstein, but work went forward immedi-

151

ately. It was a collaboration that was to last a lifetime; half a dozen huge Biblical operas followed on that London May of 1858. *The Tower of Babel, The Maccabees, Sulamith, Moses, Christus.* Rubinstein became possessed with the idea of Biblical drama, half opera, half oratorio, an unwieldy, unrealizable form that for the rest of his life would ride his shoulders like an incubus. Other collaborators than Rodenberg were to work with him; one of them, Mosenthal, says that the whole conception of Old Testament opera was somehow bound up with Rubinstein's anti-Wagnerism, which in turn was inspired by Wagner's pronounced anti-Semitism. Wagner's pamphlet, *Judaism in Music,* published in 1850, offended Rubinstein deeply; it was undoubtedly responsible for his first concentration upon Judaism as a subject for opera. Anton himself did not think of these operatic subjects as Judaism; by his own confession he loved the Old Testament deeply, all its language, its cadence, the grandeur and scope of its stories. *"Dans les arts,"* Liszt had told him long ago, *"il faut faire grand."* And what, after all, was *plus grand* than the story of Moses, of Solomon and the glorious Sulamith?

"I have put off my shoe," chanted Rubinstein, walking across Cavendish Square on June 7th to play with Sterndale Bennett's orchestra. "I have put off my shoe, I am in the clothing of the night." These lines must be altered for the libretto. How could the Sulamith set out on her flight in a night-dress? He must write Rodenberg about it; the two would not meet again for months.

Anton walked into Hanover Rooms, greeted the orchestra, nodded briefly to Sterndale Bennett at the conductor's stand and fell upon the piano. . . . Then he hurried down to Dover and boarded the Channel boat, pleased to breathe his last of British air. These English! Did such people really live? Did they know heat and cold, could they taste, smell, feel grief and ecstasy? Did they fall in love, these blue-eyed misses, these correct, side-whiskered young sirs, or did they merely settle down and propagate, like oysters? Dover cliffs receded behind a shouting cloud of gulls. The June water was blue and rough; Rubinstein went hurriedly below. He would be sick on this crossing; he was always sick and he dreaded every piece of open water around Europe. Better to cross the Volga on a raft, the Neva by the footplank all slippery with ice, than ride this tossing blueness.

Rubinstein went straight to Baden, where consolation awaited him that was not the consolation of the gaming tables. Anton's discretion concerning the names and identities of his sweethearts is tantalizing in the extreme; everywhere, one finds hints of a delicious Madame X or an irresistible Mademoiselle Z, but one finds little more. Carl Weber used to refer to his ladies by musical key: "*D minor* is quite dead to me, which causes me heartfelt regret. *F major* has disappeared altogether." Rubinstein did not permit himself even so much designation; his sweethearts supplanted one another with a rapidity difficult to follow. Of his successive ladies he could have remarked, like Goethe, *It is pleasant to see the moon rise while the sun is still faintly shining.* Anton fell in love with princesses, with countesses; their names drift down to us through the years, but not through Rubinstein's own confession. He was as reticent concerning his individual preferences as he was eloquent concerning womankind in general. Woman, said he, is adorable and completely unmoral. "Woman is a snake, a cat, a cow. She is the dramatic element in life. She has always been most attractive to me. God made woman; she still remains the most beautiful of His creations, but full of faults. She is lovely, but she should not try to be composer or player. Let her be sweetheart, wife, mother."

An admirable viewpoint in the traditionally virile manner, but a viewpoint sometimes inconvenient to its disciples. Woman, if she be spirited and intelligent, refuses in the most perverse way to remain in this neat feminine niche. And it was Rubinstein's misfortune never to be attracted by stupid women. He suffered therefore a continual turmoil of jealousy. For a time all was bliss, the world forgotten for love. But soon the lady would demand a kind of companionship that Rubinstein was not prepared to give. If she were an artist, she desired her lover to show interest in her art; like Liszt's Polish Princess, she offered to read her works aloud, to play her own compositions in the twilight.

This would not do at all! Woman was not equipped for comradeship on terms of equality. "Woman pulls us ever downward to earth," said Anton—and gave woman no chance to do otherwise. When the comradeship stage arrived, Rubinstein abandoned the lady, which would have been well enough had he not suffered a raging jealousy when the discarded one consoled herself with another man. Anton admitted his jealousy and laughed at himself, but suffered nonetheless. His jealousies took odd forms; he could not bear to see a girl lavish affection on a dog or kitten. "I suffer very much," he wrote, "when I see girls having a passion for any animals except birds."

Brother Nicholas would have laughed at this, Nicholas who took life and music and womankind as he found them. Anton declared again and again that if a man would understand art, he must first know woman. But Anton himself knew only one side of woman, the side she turned toward him. The one woman to whom he remained from first to last completely devoted was Helena Pavlovna and she, as an Imperial Highness, was not subject to the rules of the game. Helena Pavlovna possessed all the qualities that Rubinstein professed to abhor in woman: a shrewd, vigorous intelligence that delighted in the abstract thought so unbecoming to her sex. Moreover, she was a born organizer. Had she not, aided by no one but Dr. Pirogov, organized the first Russian Red Cross in the late Crimean War? Her nurses were on the field before Miss Nightingale appeared from England. Helena Pavlovna had only to enter the room where a meeting was held and the meeting sprang instantly to life; motions were passed, plans crystallized to action.

Very soon now, Rubinstein was to renew his long friendship with Helena Pavlovna. He was going home, this summer of 1858, as soon as he could tear himself from the sweets and tortures of Baden. His long concert tour was ended; he had accomplished what he had set out to do four years ago: he had won a brilliant, solid European reputation. Not the Crimean War, not the apathy and distrust of London had been able to halt this triumphal march. Rubinstein was taking home to Petersburg a bright new armor, the shield and buckler of authority. People would listen not only to what he played but to what he said. Together, he and Helena Pavlovna would revolutionize the Russian musical world, would open the gates and let the noble flood roll in.

In mid-July, Rubinstein went up from Baden to say his farewells at Weimar. Both Liszt and Rubinstein felt it would be a brief parting. Van II belonged to the world now; Russia could never claim him for long.

Anton embraced the Master, bowed over the plump, ink-stained hand of the Princess Witgenstein, placed his boxes on the coach step, his battered black felt hat upon his head, and turned his face once more to the east.

17

1858. The Russian Musical Society is founded

Rubinstein reached Petersburg in July and took out a domestic passport. He had work to do that required long, patient planning and much pulling of official strings. But before he could begin work he must establish a home for himself. Anton was not returning to Russia as anybody's Janitor of Music; he was returning as a man famous and rich. In Europe he had lived well, even luxuriously, renting a whole house wherever he happened to stay more than a fortnight, to protect himself, he said, from the eyes of the curious and from English ladies who played the pianoforte in hotel drawing rooms!

He intended to keep on living well; the life of disorder that seemed so natural to Russian artists was quite intolerable to Rubinstein. To lie late in bed, writing music in one's old dressing-gown—ashes in the blankets, empty vodka tumblers on the floor, days stretching ahead with no schedule, no boundaries of night and waking—the very contemplation of such a life roused in Rubinstein a fury of impatience. Not a priggish impatience; this was no moralist. But his philosophy of artistic professionalism caused him to regard disorder as the mark of the dilettante. Your professional, said Rubinstein, respects the clock; he respects contracts and engagements and lesson hours. Like Joseph Haydn, who dressed himself in laced coat and powdered wig to sit alone at his attic table and write symphonies, Anton Rubinstein was fortified without by orderliness within. Every man must establish around him his particular illusion of permanency; Tchaikovsky, moving to new lodgings, required each picture, chair and knickknack to be placed in approximately the position it had occupied in the last lodging.

Rubinstein desired a home, a place large, serene and orderly that a man could walk through to his piano, undisturbed and comfortable. Who better could establish such a home than Kaleria Rubinstein? Anton went promptly down to Moscow and carried his mother north with him, pouring into her lap more roubles than she had seen in years, telling her to spend it on their home, telling her with violence that he desired no accounting.

Kaleria arranged the household in modest comfort, put the remaining roubles under the mattress and settled quietly down with her son. She was in no way awed by his continental reputation and his social glory. The palace comings and goings, the talk concerning Grand Duchesses and Highnesses, Kaleria received in silence, eyebrows raised ever so slightly. She herself held no traffic with Grand Duchesses and desired none. For the next six years she was to live with Anton, watch over him, scold him, play piano duets with him, remind him bluntly at times that he was getting a little beyond himself, and make him very happy.

The first recorded news we have of Anton that autumn of 1858 comes from the diary of a court lady who had charge of one of the young Grand Duchesses:

"October, 1858. In the evening, having put the Grand Duchess to bed, I went to the Arsenal. There was music; Rubinstein played and a certain Mlle. Stube sang. She has a beautiful voice. The Grand Duchess Helena Pavlovna brought her from Germany as a member of her suite. Unfortunately the Empress Mother, who likes things to be lively, had arranged for the young people to play *gorelky*, a very noisy game that requires much running about. On one side the hall was *gorelky*, on the other side, music. It was a terrible hubbub and when I saw Rubinstein's face, I actually blushed. He is the first pianist of Europe; everywhere one listens to his playing with delight and reverence, and here he must play before two Russian Empresses amid the shouts and noise and laughter of young people."

Madame Aksakov wrote this, and Madame Aksakov was no fool. She represented the best of court life, yet even the best was far removed from any experience that could give it understanding of a Rubinstein. Against the lady's distress one sees, somehow, the face of Anton as he played, a face hard, sardonic, resigned. Playing the piano at court parties was his job and he was paid for it. Let them laugh and run about; it was no worse than the hisses he had endured that night in Vienna. . . . Julie Stube, waiting her vocal entrance, smiled and, leaning close to him, whispered something. Madame Aksakov moved uncomfortably in her chair, raising her fan. . . .

"I suffered," the diary continues, "as I always do in the Imperial chambers. How keenly I understand the susceptibility of these sensitive artistic natures! I know so well what they think and feel. Their talent alone sets them above all these titled nobodies who deem it a right, even a duty, to treat artists with patronizing kindness. There is something humiliating in the very courtesy and amiability one shows them. We must seem to them so ridiculous and odious. If one does not talk to them, if one leaves them alone, it is awkward both for them and for us. And if one goes up and addresses them it looks like condescension; one would not make this kind of effort with an equal. It is true of course that all artists are sensitive and apt to be unsocial. I never feel easy when one of them is in the room. It may be imagined therefore what I went through yesterday. I felt forced to go to Rubinstein and apologize. We had supper together. He is a very clever man, natural, not too haughty for an artist. He can converse on any subject and has the good manners of a thoroughly cultivated man, something rarely to be found in our Petersburg society."

Conversing skilfully with Madame Aksakov "on any subject," Anton's eye wandered to the girl who had sung to his accompaniment. She was tall and beautiful and very musical; she had confessed to Anton that this magnificent, barbaric Court left her a trifle lonely. She did not like conversing always in French; would Herr Rubinstein talk with her sometimes in German? Rumor has linked her name with Anton's. But if they loved, there was no tragedy to their love's ending; in these matters Anton never walked, as did his brother Nicholas, on the edge of disaster. Julie Stube married soon and well; as Madame Abaza, wife of the Russian Minister of

158

Finance, she remained throughout her long life one of Rubinstein's closest friends and supporters.

It was no easy task for Helena Pavlovna to establish in the Michael Palace the intimate atmosphere that alone could lure men of intellect and imagination to her parties. One of her most successful devices was the *Soirée Morganatique,* when one of her ladies acted as hostess and she herself appeared incognito, doing away with curtseys and enabling guests to sit down while Her Highness was in the room and to converse with whom they chose, not waiting to be addressed by someone of superior rank. It was positively horrifying to see what one curtsey could do to wreck a conversation. The Evenings Incognito were highly successful; at the Winter Palace, ladies of the old regime looked askance. Was Helena Pavlovna trying to break down the shining barriers of majesty? But gossip dared not speak openly; Helena Pavlovna was too much loved by the Tsar.

In all the Imperial household, there was, besides Helena Pavlovna, but one truly liberal mind. It belonged to an old friend of Rubinstein's: that sailor prince for whom young Anton had played in Holland long ago. The Grand Duke Konstantin Nicholaevitch still played his 'cello, still championed all that was best and broadest in Russian life, and still loved Anton Rubinstein. It was Konstantin who brought to Helena Pavlovna's *salon* such Western liberals as Golovnin and Von Reutern who sat late, discussing the nation with their patriot opponents—eager Slavophiles like Aksakov and Kavelin. Scientists came there too: Von Oettingen the great naturalist, Count Keyserling and the Academician, Von Baer. Anton met these men, listened to their talk, then sat down and played for them.

It was at one of these evenings, intimate and stimulating, that the Russian Musical Society, conceived in Nice, chose its first members: Anton Rubinstein, Kologrivov, Kanshin, Dmitri Stassov, the Grand Duchess Helena and Count Matthew Vielgorsky. Count Matthew invited the Society to hold its first meeting at his house and the society accepted eagerly. Everyone liked Count Matthew; his brother Michael was dead now, but Matthew carried on the tradition of music that belonged to his house. For two blooded horses and

$10,000 the Count had acquired from one of his friends a gorgeous Stradivarius 'cello upon which he played happily and badly, confessing he was not worthy of it and promising it to that 'cellist who should give the best performance of Romberg's *Swiss Concerto*.

Count Matthew, with his unmistakable air of the squire, aristocratic, jovial, worldly, was a type fast disappearing, a type Rubinstein loved. "If I have to choose between good breeding and education," said Anton once, "I prefer the former."

But although Count Matthew belonged in manner to the regime of Nicholas I, in spirit he was a modern. He knew that Russia could not develop its native musicality on such stuff as the sporadic visits of foreign virtuosi and the "musical" *soirées* of an unmusical Court. Again and again Petersburg had tried to found a serious symphonic society. The Musical Club, instituted in Catherine II's reign, had functioned for twenty years and then turned by easy stages into a society for giving balls. Playing music for Russians, it is always difficult to prevent them springing up and dancing. The Philharmonic Society, appearing in 1802, was tougher fibred; its programs were serious and included great names, all of them foreign. The 'cellist Rode played, and John Field the Irishman, and Adolf Henselt the musical purist who absentmindedly smoked a cigar throughout his performance, to the delight of Tsar Nicholas in the Imperial box. Berlioz conducted this Philharmonic in 1847. But it was nearly 1850 before Russian names appeared on the programs: Bortniansky, Glinka, the two Counts Vielgorsky, Anton Rubinstein, General Lvov. Lvov was the archetype of Russian amateur musician, destined soon to make much trouble for Rubinstein. Serious, talented and naively unconscious that writing symphonies meant hard study in the German sense, Lvov conducted the very good court a capella choir around which still another Concert Society had been built only to evaporate like the others.

It was January, 1859, when the members of the new Russian Musical Society held their first meeting in Count Matthew Vielgorsky's palace. The snow that winter was exceptional even for Petersburg; with difficulty Rubinstein made his way through drifts

160

that blew fiercely across the wide squares, piling against brittle hedge and palace wall, covering the equestrian statue of Peter the Great with absurd mantle and helmet, making friend and stranger alike unrecognizable.

The first question raised by the directors of the society was how to secure Imperial sanction. "We proceeded very carefully," wrote Rubinstein. "Familiar with the procrastination of ante-room and government office, we knew we could never obtain permission for a brand-new society with a brand-new code; the air was still too thick with the breath of the Nicholas regime. We recalled that in 1840 a circle of music lovers had been permitted to affiliate themselves with the court a cappella choir; in the old days they had developed a fairly good orchestra, led by old Louis Maurer, which gave symphonic concerts. For some years all activity had ceased in this society, and it occurred to us now to resurrect it for our use. All we asked was to be allowed to continue with something that had already been permitted; we said we wanted to come together for the purpose of playing and singing.

" 'Well then, if you want to play and sing, sing and play then! Permission for that has already been given you.' That was how they answered us and that was how the Russian Musical Society was built, as if upon old foundations, a mere renewal of an old circle of amateur symphonists."

It was the first of May before the new Society received official sanction with the Tsar's signature—too late in the season for concerts. The Grand Duchess went out to her island in the Neva; Rubinstein, longing to work once more at composition, went abroad. He desired a librettist. Julius Rodenberg was not available, but Dr. Von Mosenthal was in Dornbeck, near Vienna, and to Dornbeck Rubinstein repaired. All summer the two worked on a poem they had selected as good libretto material. The entire script has disappeared. Anton must have thrown away every note he wrote of this epic called *Janko*. He had a pleasant villa all to himself where he worked twelve hours a day, stopping only to eat the roots and herbs brought to him from the garden by his housekeeper.

Roots and herbs, plain living and high thinking. . . . Was Anton doing penance, cleansing his soul from the caviar upon which he had fed last winter? Mosenthal loved to work with Anton who was, he said, "childlike in his good nature, free from all assumptions."

Early that autumn Rubinstein returned to Petersburg, eager to resume plans for the Russian Musical Society. In November the Society gave its inaugural concert, with Rubinstein playing his own *G Major Concerto*. He was acclaimed, but he knew that his success had wider implications than the personal. It meant that the Russian Musical Society was recognized, accepted; it meant the time had come to branch out in wider directions than the mere giving of concerts. Classes were organized, meeting in Helena Pavlovna's palace.

"Enthusiasm swept over all who participated," wrote Rubinstein. "The incredible happened! A crowd of men and women of the most varied social positions quickly filled our classes, thirsty for music and for education in music. Orchestras and choruses sprang into being. The Grand Duchess' interest was vital. She visited the classes, gave the necessary money. In short, she proved her patronage not only by kindness and gracious attentions, but materially, substantially. And alas, in artistic matters, money and more money is the vital nerve of the whole body!

"Among our founders, Kologrivov especially, made himself indispensable. Extremely energetic, he was an ardent admirer of musical art and played acceptably on the violoncello. I had known him well since 1852, a landed gentleman from Tula who held for some time a post in the Imperial Theatre. He tried to make some reforms in the Russian Opera Company but Pavel Feodorov, the Director, insulted him one night in front of everybody, and with a wave of his hand, Kologrivov abandoned them altogether."

Kologrivov exemplified the unfortunate position occupied by musicians in the Russia of Nicholas I. Because he was a nobleman, he was forbidden to act in any professional musical capacity. In order to attain his post of Musical Inspector in the Imperial Theatre, he had surrendered his nobility rights. He could not wear a uniform or own serfs; at ceremonies he must stand with the crowd rather than with his peers; he could not send his children to the aristocratic boarding-schools or serve in the army higher than the ranks.

None of these things was, actually, a sacrifice to Kologrivov. Yet in principle, it was just such matters that Rubinstein desired to reform. Years ago, Catherine II had raised painters and architects to the rank of Free Artist, granting them substantial privileges of citizenship. Rubinstein desired to raise the musician to a like rank. Kologrivov had suffered demotion for music's sake and was the very man to head a crusade. Stalking the streets of Petersburg, he stopped stranger and friend with his appeal, buttonholing them, asking for money. His own fortune he gave freely for the cause, dying in the end a pauper. Anton could not say enough in his praise.

Little by little, the thing progressed. "We, the leaders and supporters," wrote Rubinstein, "visited various wealthy persons in Petersburg, asking their help, begging from door to door like priests at Easter who glorify Christ! We called upon Prince Yusupov, Bernardski, Gromov and others; some gave a hundred roubles, some 300 and even 500. Various ladies of high society worked for us. One day Sophie Ivanovna Verigina brought in 300 roubles. Julie Abaza, *née* Stube, was our treasurer and Princess Elisabeth Witgenstein, *née* Eiler, sometimes brought us a few roubles."

Before the first concert of the Russian Musical Society in November of 1859, ice had closed over the Neva and the bridges had been removed. Along the palace quay, sentries, wrapped in fur, paced quickly to and fro, not daring to halt lest their limbs stiffen. The blizzards of last winter did not repeat themselves, but the cold was bitter enough to go down in history. Neither wind nor fog came across from Finland; clear skies and serene weather were deceptive and cruel, striking a man down if he relaxed his vigilance for an instant. From every housetop, tall columns of vapor rose, shining in the clear air, tinted with fairy colors, violet, green and pink. Along the wide streets and all across the river, snow lay white and motionless, like baked sugar. Water froze at the pumps while it was being poured, the water-wagons were encrusted with ice and so were their drivers. At the city canals, washerwomen, striking holes with an axe, dipped their linens and returned through the streets carrying bundles all coated with glass. From every roof and monument fantastic icicles, huge as monsters, glimmered in the early twilight.

Anton Rubinstein put on his big fur *shuba* and lived in it, played the piano in it, ate in it, would have slept in it had his mother not protested. He hated the cold. In the streets he ran to his destination, slipping on the ice, cursing this crazy climate, longing for spring, for Easter and blue water once more in the Neva. He saw ice mountains erected on the streets in Mad Week just before Lent, heard the hammers of workmen setting scaffolds against the mountains, watched men, young and old, climb up the ladders with their little sledges and flash down the slide, shouting, overturning, colliding, filled with vodka, recklessness and joy. Once he saw a man killed at this sport; often he saw men carried away, their limbs broken. If his countrymen could throw away their lives so easily for a little fun, reflected Anton Rubinstein, then surely they might be induced to give a little of this spirit to undertakings less dangerous but, to the initiated, equally satisfying.

In February of 1860, Anton played at the Big Theatre in Petersburg, then went down to Moscow and gave two concerts, conducting his *Ocean Symphony* and his *Third Symphony in A*, returning to Petersburg on a railway that was still a novelty. Spring came at last, and with it the desire for creation awoke as always. Anton longed to have done with teaching and organization. As soon as classes ceased in the Michael Palace, he returned to the quiet villa near Vienna with the unfinished score of a new opera, *Children of the Steppes*.

Young Carl Goldmark the composer lived near by. One evening Anton offered to play over the new Goldmark trio for piano and strings. Anton was tired of modern music; the Russian Musical Society required by charter the performance of a Russian composition at every concert. Usually Rubinstein played his own concerti, but someone was always submitting manuscripts that to him were turgid and over-massive. Reading Goldmark's Trio, Anton frowned and said it was too modern for his taste. "Go home," he told the young composer, "and play as much Mozart as you can."

Goldmark listened eagerly; in him was none of the rebellion against form that raged in the Russian Nationalist school. When Rubinstein had played, the two went into the garden and ate a simple supper served by the gardener's wife. It was yet light when they had eaten and they sat talking of Beethoven, of the humor in his music. From beyond the garden wall, suddenly a familiar tune reached them. It was the last movement of Beethoven's Eighth Symphony, creaking from a hurdy-gurdy in three-four time, rollicking along like a waltz. The two men laughed and went indoors; sitting at his piano Rubinstein took up the waltz motif and began to improvise upon it. Inventing a theme in the bass, he developed it into a four-voiced fugue, then let it dwindle to a song. Goldmark listened entranced, until in a storm of sound, of cascading arpeggios in the right hand over the theme in the bass, Rubinstein brought the whole to an end and laughing, swung round to his young guest. All his life Goldmark remembered that evening, swearing he never again heard improvisation to equal it.

Anton loved these summers in the Austrian countryside, or down the Rhine into Bavaria. The seasonal routine he was establishing was both stimulating and necessary; Rubinstein was too much the Westerner to endure Russia for more than ten months at a time. There was truth in the accusation of "foreigner" that his countrymen brought against him. He himself confesses that his youth abroad had left its ineradicable mark. He was an eclectic who had tasted Western culture and all his life thereafter he longed for it, needed it as he needed sun and bread and the music of Schubert and Mendelssohn. It was a strange artistic nomadism. Always, Anton went where there was work to do but always, beyond the Russian border, a restlessness gnawed him. Now, in the autumn of 1859 he traveled eastward once more, lumbering across Prussia by coach to Petersburg.

Waiting on the border for the business of passport examination, swearing silently at pompous officials whose manner, the moment their eye fell upon the Jewish inscription, became insufferably rude, Anton looked down and knew Russian ground beneath his feet. He saw the wintry copse, the white birch trees, the poor log huts of his native land and in his eyes were the tears of gratitude that announce a true homecoming.

18

1862. The Petersburg Conservatory opens its doors

Anton carried home the finished score of his opera, *Children of the Steppes*. His mother was waiting for him; she had spent the summer in Moscow with Nicholas and her daughter Sophie, but she had come home in time to see that the house was swept and garnished, the samovar steaming for the returning traveler. Anton roared into the house filled with health, his blue eyes blazing from a face richly tanned by the Austrian sun. His mother embraced him, went to his room while he unpacked his bag, listening as he bragged a little of his summer's exploits. "Here is my new baby, *Maman,* my *Children of the Steppes.*"

He piled the score in her arms. Anton had not been in the house twenty minutes when mother and son were at the piano, the son, as always, playing the second part. Who was Anton Rubinstein, after all, to take precedence over his first teacher? Outside, fog blew slowly down from Kronstadt, wreathing in and out among the pillars of the Admiralty, veiling the figure of Tsar Peter on his great horse. And along the Fontanka the lamplighter dragged his ladder over wooden cobbles, turning his head, when his taper had reached the wick, to listen for a moment to the cascade of music pouring from behind a curtained window in Number 88.

It seemed to Anton that the winter flew by on wings. He had never been so busy in his life. The classes at the Michael Palace were mobbed. Organization was needed. The Grand Duchess agreed they should have a charter, a name. For this, official sanction must be had. Helena Pavlovna advised a public appeal to the government, and in January of 1861 Anton published a strong article in the Russian magazine, *Vek.* The reason Russia had no musical artists, said

167

Anton, was because the government would not permit them to make a living. Music was left entirely in the hands of amateurs. And amateurs, no matter how talented, are not driven with the desperate spur that alone causes creative artists to complete a work begun. Your professional artist is on trial before the world; he is forced to win the public's approval and to hold it when won; he can never retreat into privacy and the spurious consolation of friends.

"Found a Russian Conservatory!" cried Rubinstein, and half of Petersburg echoed his cry. But official ears remained deaf, concerned at the moment with the grave question of Emancipation. The Tsar's Manifesto was ready at last; years of work had gone into it. For months the Imperial hand had hovered and now, in February of 1861, the Manifesto was signed. In March it was proclaimed to the nation. Officialdom trembled, wondering what these millions would do with their freedom. But Helena Pavlovna did not tremble. She smiled, and summoning Anton to the Michael Palace, told him not to be put off by these great matters. They were no greater than the matter he had in hand. Emancipation was a contagious term; now was the time to strike for musical freedom. The Grand Duchess went to the Winter Palace, faced her Imperial nephew by herself and came away with a subsidy of 5000 roubles and a promise of official sanction for her Conservatory.

The Tsar kept his word. Next autumn, October, 1861, Alexander II authorized the Conservatory, with Anton Rubinstein as its Director. Helena Pavlovna promised a thousand roubles a year from her own purse. Actually, the thing was under way. Anton went home and read the new statutes to his mother. Some of the clauses were pure nonsense: for instance, the school could not be called *conservatoire*—a Western word, offensive to Slavic patriotism. It must call itself *Music School* and its professors must be called *instructors*; "professor" was also a Westernism. Kaleria laughed. What, after all, did mere words signify? The first class would be graduated in three years and—how sweet the taste of victory!—upon each diploma would be engraved the glorious title: *Free Artist*.

Facing the Neva on the corner of two streets stood a fine old house that had belonged to the Demidov family. Here the Conservatory took up its quarters, sharing space with the German Club which functioned in the evenings. Most of Petersburg lived in high, narrow apartment buildings, each the copy of its neighbor. The Demidov mansion had an air of its own, with its spacious yard fenced by a high iron grille. Moscow students said it reminded them of home. Young Herman Laroche, pushing open the gate in the mornings, looked absent-mindedly for the watchdog that guarded every Moscow courtyard. Laroche was a typical member of the first class to be graduated from the Conservatory, and Laroche had a brilliant talent. It was no accident that these early students were of remarkable caliber; Russia had waited long for a Conservatory and when it appeared, men and women of mature talent hurried eagerly to its doors.

In the big house behind the iron fence Anton Rubinstein spent his days, appearing punctually at nine, remaining until the clock struck five. It was no imprisonment; teachers as well as pupils were a stimulating group. Dreyschock in the piano department had studied in Prague with the great Tomaschek and for twenty years thereafter had toured Europe; he brought to Petersburg a whole trunkful of medals and decorations. So did Madame Nissen-Salomon the singer and young Wieniawski the fiery Polish violinist. Anton had known Wieniawski for years. It was pleasant to staff the school with his old friends. Leschetizky in the piano department was especially close to him; it was Leschetizky who had taken Anton's place as Court Musician when Anton went on tour.

Leschetizky was a born teacher; he taught with passion and with care and Anton loved him. The two were much alike; Anton was by far the greater player and both men recognized it, but Leschetizky was the greater teacher. The Conservatory hours were long. When five o'clock came, Anton went home and ate his dinner and sat down to write music. But when Leschetizky had dined, he lit another cigar and wandered out toward the streets where his pupils lived, walking beneath their windows, listening to discover if they were obeying his precepts. Sometimes he walked upstairs and surprised them. Once a girl pupil, emerging from her room, was shocked to find the master sitting calmly on the landing in a rocking-chair. "I have been here two hours," he said. "You will never play those triplets unless you take them more slowly."

It was a teaching staff that has gone down in history. Youngest of them all was Carl Davidov the 'cellist. Moscow-born, a graduate of the University, he came to the Conservatory from Leipzig, where Ferdinand David had made him professor in his famous school at the age of 23. Davidov had an extraordinary facility with the left hand; he ignored the bulk of his instrument as if it were a violin. "The more difficult a piece is," he told his pupils, "the easier you must make it sound. You say my *Russian Fantasia* is hard? Well, you should find it as easy to play that piece as to eat a piece of bread and butter."

Rubinstein copied his velvet tone from Rubini the singer: Davidov confessed he had developed his 'cello tone from listening to men play upon the violin. Having himself studied the viola da gamba, he understood the sympathy and transition between large 'cello and small violin, between baritone and soprano voice. He surprised Petersburg by using a 'cello pin instead of holding the instrument with his knees in the old rigid, confining attitude. Davidov was an agreeable creature, full of laughter and good-will. Everyone liked him. Count Matthew Vielgorsky had not fulfilled his promise of giving his famous Stradivarius 'cello to that player who could best perform Romberg's *Swiss Concerto*; Petersburg decided the Count was going to keep his Stradivarius for himself. One night Davidov went to a party at Count Matthew's to play trios with Rubinstein and Wieniawski. When Davidov walked out to play, Count Matthew signaled him to leave his 'cello where it was and himself came forward, carrying the Stradivarius.

"Today," said the Count, "I am seventy. So I celebrate my birthday in my own way, by presenting you, Carl Yulievitch, with my Stradivarius."

Davidov smiled, accepting the gesture as a momentary whimsy. But he took the instrument between his knees and played upon it gloriously. Tsar Alexander himself was at the party; he had not observed the little tableau between the 'cellist and his host. When the music was done, the Tsar inquired of Count Matthew if he still possessed his famous Stradivarius? The Count shook his head, "I used to have one, Your Imperial Majesty. But tonight I gave it to Carl Yulievitch."

Carl stood motionless, his heart hammering. "But I have not fulfilled the terms, Count Matthew!" he said breathlessly. "I have not played the *Swiss Concerto*."

"That is true," replied the Count. "But I cannot possibly imagine anyone playing it better than you, Carl Yulievitch, if you tried."

It was a time and a place that enjoyed the dramatic gesture, the grand manner of eighteenth-century patronage. Only the manner survived, however; musicians could count upon magnificent gestures from their patrons, but not on a solid, reliable living. Rubinstein recognized this before his colleagues did. He staffed his Conservatory with men in their twenties, fiery, eager, independently minded. Anton himself was only thirty-two. He sensed, however, that his venture needed one or two older men; it would not do to frighten Petersburg with firebrands and hotheads. Carl Schubert in the 'cello department belonged to an older generation; he was a good solid fellow, and so was Nicholas Zaremba whom Anton placed at the head of the Department of Theory.

Zaremba was forty when he came to the Conservatory, but he seemed a hundred. He was a Pole who, like Rubinstein's old counterpoint master, Siegfried Dehn, had been seduced from a lawyer's career by that musical argument called counterpoint— eternal discussion, nicer than any legal case, precise and perfect as any geometric theorem yet in its final proof akin to poetry. Rubinstein adored Zaremba, with his long beard, his pedantry and his religious mysticism. Lecturing to his classes, Zaremba called frequently upon God. "We shall now take the theme in the dominant," he would say gravely. "And with God's help we shall arrive, after 64 measures—including some use of harmonic suspension, anticipation, thematic augmentation and like devices—with God's help we shall return, in the 64th measure, to the tonic, A flat."

Such a man was a perfect foil for Anton, whose teaching was passionate, incoherent and frequently terrifying. Fortunately, the first students at the Conservatory were far from the coddling age. Some of them had reached thirty, the majority were sixteen or seventeen. They came from Georgia, from Dorpat, from Moscow and Smolensk. There was the son of a police official, there was a Customs House officer, a full-fledged lawyer—Tchaikovsky—and a lieutenant of the Semenovsky Guard, resplendent in striped trousers and golden epaulettes. There was a clerk from the Anglo-Russian steamship company, there was a convoy officer known vaguely as the Prince and there was a Mohammedan in a turban.

All of these cherished violent musical prejudices and fought for them. The one Wagnerian, Richard Metsdorf, roared his way about the halls looking for combat, and when Wagner himself came to Petersburg in 1862 and played excerpts from the Nibelungen Ring, fistfights were frequent in the Conservatory yard behind the iron grille. Rubinstein heard of them and grinned. Let the boys battle; it proved the school was alive to its core. One of these early students has borne witness to an atmosphere that was happy even to exaltation. Herman Laroche was only seventeen, but he was well read and extremely well informed musically. The halls of the old Demidov mansion, he wrote, were "bright with poetry"; Anton Rubinstein was the god upon the mountain.

One October morning, in 1862, young Laroche entered Herr Gerke's pianoforte class and sat down to await his turn. Someone slipped into the place beside him and Laroche recognized a student he had seen about the halls, a man of about 22, clean-shaven, carefully dressed—almost foppish. In spite of his worldly appearance, the young man seemed ill at ease and very shy with the teacher. After class he approached Laroche, asking timidly if the latter would consent to talk with him a few moments and explain some questions about composition.

"Your name?" asked Laroche. "Peter Ilyich Tchaikovsky," said the other with an anxious, nervous smile that went straight to Laroche's heart and stayed there—seed of a friendship that was to

172

last a lifetime. A few months later, when Laroche complimented Tchaikovsky on his energy and hard work, Peter Ilyich confessed that this was not nature but conversion, that on first entering Zaremba's classes he had been anything but zealous and had worked "in a very superficial way, like a typical amateur." This was a word in very bad odor at the Conservatory; above all things Anton Rubinstein desired to make professionals out of his students. Zaremba, it seems, had drawn Tchaikovsky aside one day after class and reproached him for wasting a rich talent. Deeply touched, Peter Ilyich went home and threw himself into work, discovering stores of energy he had not known he possessed, energy that never left him, except for rare moments of ill health or discouragement, until he died.

From 1861 to '62, Tchaikovsky studied harmony under Zaremba, then strict counterpoint and the church modes. In the autumn of 1862 he was ready for Rubinstein's class in instrumentation. A graduate of the Petersburg School of Laws, Peter Ilyich held at the time a clerk's position in governmental law offices. Tchaikovsky and Herman Laroche were graduated the same year, 1865; their accounts agree as to the largeness of Rubinstein's nature and the feeling he gave to the beholder that this was not a man within ordinary bounds of humanity. "No teacher was more considerate or kindly," writes Laroche. "But his forbidding appearance, his hot temper and roughness, added to the glamour of his European fame, impressed us profoundly. All Europe knew of his extraordinary generosity expressed in the grand manner, but not of the simple generosity of his heart."

Rubinstein's piano class was, for the pupils, a hazardous affair. Nevertheless, they begged to be admitted. The master's moods and methods were unpredictable. One morning, for instance, he made his students play Czerny's "Daily Studies" through in every key, keeping precisely the same fingering throughout, and the master's eye, like his ear, was hawk-like. Teaching theory, Rubinstein was as taciturn as Zaremba was eloquent. And when he did speak out, half the class looked dispairingly at the other half which could understand German or French. "Rubinstein spoke," wrote Laroche, "half a dozen languages, but none quite correctly. In Russian he often expressed himself fluently and appropriately, but his grammar was sometimes faulty, especially when he expounded a theoretical problem demanding logical sequence. Strangely enough, this deficiency in no way spoiled his lectures. With Zaremba, all was systematic, each word had its place. With Rubinstein a fascinating disorder reigned. Ten minutes before the lesson, he did not know what he was going to talk about and left all to the inspiration of the moment."

This was more than accident; Rubinstein pursued the same method on the concert stage. There he knew, of course, what his program was to be and had prepared each piece scrupulously as to technique, but nobody could prophesy what emotional interpretation he would give these works. He admitted it. "How can I play joyfully when I feel sad?" he would say. "Or sorrowfully when I am gay?"

But even Rubinstein's inconsistencies enchanted his students. A man of such erudition could afford paradox. "His extraordinary practical knowledge of his instrument, his breadth of view, his experience as a composer—almost incredible for a man of thirty—gave his words an authority we could not but accept," wrote Laroche. "Lacking all system, when Rubinstein saw he had failed to reach his pupils he cast eagerly about for some new way to communicate his ideas to the class."

One day he made Tchaikovsky orchestrate Beethoven's *D Minor Sonata* in four different ways. Poor Peter Ilyich, more zealous than cautious, let fly on one of the four, introducing the chromatic French horn and all manner of effects unknown to Beethoven's orchestra. Anton rebuked him severely. Rubinstein was forever rebuking Tchaikovsky or else ignoring him, and the more he was chastened, the more Peter Ilyich adored the Master. For years, Anton's was the only portrait that hung on the walls of Tchaikovsky's bedroom. "Rubinstein cast a magic spell over Tchaikovsky," records Laroche, "and in his student days this was of greatest value to Peter Ilyich. The harder he worked, the more tasks Rubinstein set him. Sometimes Tchaikovsky spent the whole night upon some score he wished to lay before his insatiable teacher next morning. It was an extraordinary industry. Tchaikovsky kept his independence of judgment throughout, and even made fun of his master's lack of logic and of his mass of colorless and insipid compositions. But nothing, nothing at all could undermine Tchaikovsky's regard for Rubinstein as a man."

It was a strange relationship. Laroche says the reason that Rubinstein never appreciated Tchaikovsky's genius as a composer was partly because Tchaikovsky's artistic growth was slow and normal, "lacking the sudden brilliancy that rejoices the astonished teacher," partly because Tchaikovsky was rebellious. Rubinstein disliked "modern" orchestration that savored of Wagner and the New Music; he recognized only the classic orchestra of Beethoven's day. There were to be no chromatic trumpets in Rubinstein's master-class. . . . But there was plenty of modern orchestration in the concerts that Rubinstein conducted at the Russian Musical Society, and the concerts were—thanks to the Grand Duchess—free to Conservatory students. Here they heard works by Meyerbeer, Berlioz, Liszt and even Wagner. How could a Peter Tchaikovsky be expected to remain untouched by such handling of the orchestra? Peter Ilyich disliked Wagner's music, especially *The Ring*, inquiring angrily why a composer chose a remote and heroic Brünnhilda for heroine instead of, say, a warm human like Tatiana. But he was much impressed by Wagner's command of the orchestra. So was Rubinstein, for that matter. He explained the full modern orchestra to his classes, hoping that, having learned its secrets, they would lay temptation aside forever. "Here," writes Laroche, "Rubinstein experienced a bitter disappointment in Tchaikovsky who never, for all his love of Mozart, even attempted to write for the classic orchestra. His medium of expression was the full modern orchestra which comes after Meyerbeer. He did not master it easily, but even in those early days his preference for it was established."

Rubinstein did not understand Peter Tchaikovsky; perhaps there were other pupils to whom Anton was fundamentally unsympathetic. But in order to inspire one's pupils, it is not always necessary to understand them. It was enough for Rubinstein to be there, to exist, to play like an angel and roar like a lion, believing fiercely in music, believing in life and love, treasuring the hours that moved inexorably around the clock. Visiting his classes, observing his methods, Helena Pavlovna smiled, well pleased not only with her friend but with her own judgment. She had chosen, most certainly, the right man for this work.

And if Rubinstein was arbitrary in his methods, he had the right to be. He insisted upon rigid examinations with no quarter given, yet when he desired, he pulled a pupil through without benefit of grading. Alexandre Villoing himself, having moved from Moscow to be near the Conservatory, turned up one day and asked to take the examination for Free Artist. Rubinstein was touched but he was also worried; Villoing was a far better teacher than performer. Anton advised his old master to go home and practice. On that May day when Villoing appeared in the examination room, Anton met him at the door and told him to keep away from the piano and say nothing.

The examiners sat in a row: Gerke, Dreyschock, Leschetizky. Anton introduced the candidate gravely, then sat down himself and played the most difficult pieces in the repertory of piano literature, played them as only Rubinstein could play. Rising from the instrument he faced the jury, inquiring if his performance merited the title of Free Artist? There was instant agreement and the master waved his hand solemnly toward Villoing who, near to tears with pride over his old pupil, sat fidgeting in a corner.

"This man," said Anton quietly, "is the only piano teacher, besides my mother, that I have ever had. What do the examiners think of his qualifications as a teacher?"

Villoing went home with a diploma in his pocket and promptly wrote a book on how to learn to play the piano. With his usual foresight he dedicated it to the Grand Duchess Helena and it met with instant response all over Europe, selling ten thousand copies. For

176

a while, Villoing taught at the Conservatory, but he was unused to working within an organization and made wild scenes, screaming at his pupils in French, rushing about the corridors with a great slamming of doors. Rubinstein smiled, but he was relieved when Villoing resigned. "Antoine," said Villoing one morning, bursting into the Director's room in a state of pleased excitement, "you remember my pupils, Maria and Nadejda, daughters of the widow Harsher? The greatest talents I have taught since you and Nicholenka! Their mother plans to take them from me. To Paris, on tour. To lose them would be unendurable! So I shall marry their mother. Tomorrow. There are four other Harsher children. But they are not musical. Can you come to the church with me? Will Kaleria Christoforovna come too?"

There are times when expediency is near to heroism. To keep a good pupil, Villoing would have married all three of Macbeth's witches, and Anton knew it. He smiled, but he was touched when with Kaleria he went, next day, to the wedding. Villoing was not the only musician Anton pulled through the examinations. Vasily Bessel was a viola player with a passion for string quartets and a huge knowledge of musical literature. The trouble was that he knew far more than his viola technique permitted him to articulate; he was one of your intelligent, eager amateur stutterers. But Anton believed in him and loved him and desired to give him a degree. At the examination, Bessel played Anton's own viola Sonata in F minor, to Anton's accompaniment on the piano. Short, entirely undistinguished-looking, Vasily Bessel sat with his big viola under his chin and played, and nobody heard a note. The piano thundered, roared, sang, wept. Never had the master played more gloriously, or more loudly.

"Well?" growled Rubinstein at last, swinging round from the piano stool. Startled eyes returned to Bessel, embarrassed examiners passed him without a murmur, not liking to admit they had forgotten he was there. Grinning, Anton stalked out of the room and awaited his friend in the corridor. Neither man knew that Bessel was soon to be one of the foremost music publishers in Europe, bringing out Tchaikovsky's first works and many of Rubinstein's.

If a man's finger technique was faulty and his musicianship sound, Rubinstein sometimes gave him a diploma. But let the candidate fail in musicianship, and the Director cut him ruthlessly down. There was abundant talent in those early classes; Rubinstein had rich material to work upon. As the candidates advanced in experience, they played on the platforms of Petersburg and the city heard them, with results unforeseen and very vexing to the Conservatory. The mammas of fashionable Petersburg besieged Anton's office, driving up in their carriages, gloved and furred, hoping to get something for nothing. Conservatory education was notoriously cheaper than Institute education. Moreover, Anton Rubinstein was associated with the most exalted Court circles. It would be a twofold benefit.

"On introducing her young daughter to me," records Rubinstein sourly, "some fashionable lady would remark in French, 'Monsieur Rubinstein, I have brought my daughter. I hope she will benefit by your musical instruction, and also keep in practice with languages.'

" 'But all our lessons are given in Russian.'

" 'What, music in Russian!' exclaims the astonished lady. 'That is an original idea!'

"And surely, it was surprising that the theory of music was to be taught for the first time in the Russian language in our Conservatory. Professor Zaremba was responsible for this."

Nicholas Zaremba must indeed have puzzled these fashionable mammas—Zaremba who "with God's help" mowed down the incompetent, both princess and peasant. Anton loved him for it, swearing the Conservatory could not function without him. But the mammas, unfortunately, were not discouraged. Nearly thirty years afterward, Rubinstein recalled these mammas with eloquent bitterness. "They thought our Conservatory especially adapted for weak-minded children. Presenting her half-witted boy, 'Monsieur Rubinstein,' some afflicted mamma would say, 'I was obliged to remove my son from such-and-such an establishment on account of ill-health.' (She really meant, for incapacity.) 'What shall I do with him? I thought if I placed him in your Conservatory, it might be easier for him. He could take up a few branches, and might possibly develop a talent for music.'

"What could I do with such ladies? It was hard to make them understand that our Conservatory accepted only capable students, healthy physically and mentally.

"As soon as we decided to teach science parallel with music, calculating parents saw a cheap way to have their children learn both subjects. Still later, when the Conservatory was granted the same privilege of military exemption that the Academy of Fine Arts received—a service of one year instead of four—young people who had absolutely no artistic vocation hurried under the hospitable shelter of the Conservatory's wings.

"Surely, the cause of music gained little from these persons!"

Not only was it difficult to handle all these pupils, good and bad, in one inadequate building, but the spectacular response of the city to the Conservatory and to the concerts of the Musical Society inspired dangerous envy from unexpected quarters. Anton had been prepared for opposition but he had not expected it to come from musical circles; the very men on whose support he had counted, were plotting a rival school. Compared with the enmity of Balakirev's circle, the importuning mammas had been a mere nothing. Perplexed, Anton watched the storm clouds gather, feeling, for the first time in his life, that his youth was against him. Someone older was needed to advise him, someone tempered with the salt of disillusionment.

"Put on your hat, Tonia," said Kaleria Rubinstein, "and go over to the Michael Palace. Of what use Grand Duchesses, if they be not wise in the ways of wickedness?"

19

The opposition

I<small>T WAS</small> no small complaint that Rubinstein took to Helena Pavlovna, no mere account of gentlemanly disagreement on esthetic grounds. It was a long list of furious, printed abuse. The Musical Society had scarcely held its first concert, the Conservatory its first classes, when enemies sprang up like mushrooms. "In every street of the city they rose in arms against us," wrote Anton. "They talked, shouted, wrote and printed, swooping upon everything we did. They even attacked our quarter of the city, demanding how we dared to call our society *Russian*."

General Lvov, for instance, threatened to dismiss any of his a capella choir singers who took part in the Lenten concerts of the Russian Musical Society. Mili Balakirev, ardent champion of Russian nationalism in music, ardent foe of formal musical instruction that stemmed from the West, proceeded to found a rival Free School that he said would reach *the people,* not the snobs to whom Rubinstein's concerts catered. At the Free School concerts, Russian music was to be played, Russian songs sung in Russian and no stench of court influence, no Grand Duchess Helena or Grand Duke Konstantin would poison the air by their presence. Young Gussakovsky wrote a *Fool's Scherzo*, designed, he said, to be played by the following string quartet:

"Violin I .... Rubinstein I
Violin II .... Rubinstein II
Alto .... Kologrivov
'Cello ....Carl Schubert."

The music was to have a program:
"1. Kologrivov's joy at meeting Rubinstein.
2. Conspiracy against True Music.

3. Actions of the conspiracy.
4. Rubinstein gets ahead of everybody.
5. All bow before him.
6. Their deaths (their musical career).
7. Scherzo da capo (memories of the past)."

This was mere fooling. But Balakirev's disciples did not stop at fooling. They were in deadly earnest; Balakirev himself was not half so inimical to Rubinstein as were his cohorts. Mili Balakirev was a Slav of Slavs, mystic, emotional, wilful and greatly gifted. With no formal musical education and apparently no system, he had absorbed enormous musical erudition and was convinced that others could learn by a like magic. Formal training was ruinous to growth. This had always been the Slavic inclination as opposed to the rigorous systematic education favored by Germany and the West. Just now, in the 1860's, Balakirev's philosophy appealed especially to Slavophilic and nationalist patriotism. Away with the West! Away with tradition! Let us learn technique through our own creative act, let us plunge and blunder and revise! Such was Balakirev's philosophy; it succeeded because fate gave to Balakirev the most brilliant group of musical disciples ever to be found in one place and one generation: The *Mogutchaya Kutchka,* variously translated as the Circle, the Handful, the Invincible Band, known also throughout the world as "The Five." Their Bible—they referred to it always as the *Gospel*—was Dargomizhky's opera, *The Stone Guest,* which had as libretto Pushkin's poem, unaltered.

The *Kutchka* was the flower of Russia's renascence, fruit of the great 1860's, when all Russia was undergoing change. Emancipation was the watchword; the young Tsar was so obviously sincere that even the old die-hards were constrained to trust him. But the road to progress was far from simple, the *isms* many and complicated. If, for instance, you were Slavophile politically, you resented bitterly any incursion of Western culture, believing that Russia should progress by her own path, the ancient, Slavic, pre-Peterine path. You wore a beard and Russian high boots and confessed yourself proudly as a patriot reactionary. But if you were Slavophile in art and music you were automatically dubbed progressive, almost revolutionary. Because in art, Slavophilism—*nationalism,* they called it—meant the creation of a "new" art that stemmed from the people, from folk-scene, folk-psychology, folk-song, folk-dance. To create such art required perfect sympathy with the common people and consequent scorn for urban, Western or court culture. There must be no trafficking with the great classic tradition. Bach, Mozart, Mendelssohn and the long list of Italian masters who had prepared the way for Germany must not be permitted to influence a student. What mattered was the Russian language and the creation of music that would fit the Russian language.

This was not as unreasonable as it sounds. In Petersburg and Moscow Italian opera had reigned supreme for years, degenerating into an amusement of the fashionable world. Parterre boxes passed from father to son and were occupied in jeweled splendor by persons who laughed and conversed throughout the music. Even such a lover of Western culture as Rubinstein rebelled against the Italian opera, knowing it had no relationship to the Russian people, no true affinity with their daily life.

Anton never denied the essential talent of Balakirev and his *Kutchka.* What Anton denied, and bitterly, was the repudiation of Western culture. That men of such parts as Balakirev and Borodin should refuse the value of academic musical training was to him not only foolhardiness but a crime against the Holy Ghost. These men were amateurs, dilettantes, forever beginning huge compositions that they could not finish. They called themselves progressives in art, but to Rubinstein their amateurism branded them as throwbacks to the vicious system of aristocratic dilettantism that had stifled Russian music for so many centuries. Not one among the *Kutchka* was a professional musician who dared make music his life. Cesar Cui wore the uniform of a lieutenant in the Engineering Corps, Moussorgsky belonged to the aristocratic Preobrazhensky Guard. Young Rimsky-Korsakov, member of a family high in the ranks of the Imperial Navy, was forever sailing away on a battleship. Borodin was a chemist, Instructor at the University, calling himself "Sunday musician" because Sunday was the only day that gave him time for music.

Not one of these men had produced a symphony. How dared they hold up Western symphonism to scorn? How dared they laugh openly at Mendelssohn, a craftsman in symphonic technique who could have shown cards and spades to any of them? It was true that the *Kutchka* produced rich music, music that was amazingly original, and Rubinstein often acknowledged it. But these were great times, and great times produce great art. Later, when the violent patriotism inspired by the reforms of Alexander II should die—what then? Like smoke these amateur talents would vanish, leaving nothing for future generations to build upon.

Anton Rubinstein did not truly care if music was written around Russian folk tunes, the Eastern scale or the old Church modes. *Trend* was not his interest so much as the establishment of a professional musicianship in Russia. Once established, let music take what path it chose.

How loud were the voices of Balakirev's disciples! Walking across Petersburg to call on Helena Pavlovna, bitter words rang in Anton's ears. "The Jewish Musical Association," Serov had called the Russian Musical Society in his newspaper—Serov, whose own grandfather had been a Jew. Theophil Tolstoi had published an article denouncing every person in the Society and the Conservatory. A parcel of Germans, he had written. "Not a Russian in the lot."

It was hard to shake off these voices, so bewildering in their injustice. Anton walked up the steps of the Michael Palace with a frown on his face, and making his way through huge echoing halls, he found a familiar room, heard quick footsteps, an eager, well-loved voice. "Imperial Highness," said Anton, "what is the matter with us and our School? Why, all of a sudden, are we Germans and pedants—you and I and Zaremba who thought ourselves Russians, working for Russia? Is not music *music*, here and everywhere? Can Russia learn nothing from the West? Bach, Mozart, Mendelssohn—are they to be thrown down, forgotten like so many dolls that have become outmoded? Our Society has dedicated itself openly, in its charter, to the music of all lands and all races. What is this thing called *patriotism* that rages so loud?"

The Grand Duchess laughed. "You are very young, Anton Gregorovitch. An organization is not an organization until it has acquired enemies. This is not patriotism but something of a different name. We must find positions in our Society for these envious ones; we must put them on committees and print their names in good black ink."

Rubinstein lifted his shoulders and sighed a long sigh, listening carefully as Helena Pavlovna examined the reasons for this printed abuse. Serov, for instance: Had not the Russian Musical Society chorus refused, last Christmas, to perform his new *Hymn*? Besides, everyone knew that Serov had expected to be made a Director of the Society and perhaps a professor in the Conservatory. He had been offered neither post. Anyway, he was a Wagnerite. As for Moussorgsky, had not a battle occurred between him and Rubinstein over the performance of Moussorgsky's chorus, *Edipus*?

Helena Pavlovna was very wise, thought Rubinstein, walking slowly home across the city. A little healthy cynicism was bracing to the soul. What had happened, latterly, to his good common sense? This Conservatory, his darling, the very ambition of his heart —it had blinded him to reality as love for woman can blind a man. When, before, had he permitted criticism to wound him, he who had suffered blows that would fell an ox? In Vienna long ago, when the audience hissed, in Cologne the time nobody came to his concert, in Weimar when he overheard Liszt's pupils laughing at his *Paradise Lost*. . . . Never had these things remained with him longer than a day, except as treasured ammunition for the future. Arrows of fortune—always, he had seized them in his hand and rent them bodily from his side to forge anew as bolts to hurl against the enemy.

This Free School of Balakirev's; surely it could not harm his Conservatory! The Free School had no money. Even if it had, its Directors possessed no talent for organization. They were too lazy to run a school. What pure Russian could rise at seven, be at his office at nine, leave at five and spend the evening working on plans for the morrow? They called Anton Rubinstein a German. Now God be praised, thought Anton, walking up the steps to his house, for a mother with a German birch switch in her hand.

The fact that Rubinstein's Conservatory was supported by the Court gave his enemies a beautiful point of vantage. One day the Free School and the Conservatory gave concerts on the same evening, and Borodin the nationalist wrote scornfully to a friend about it. How artificial, said Borodin, was the Conservatory atmosphere that night! Generals in epaulettes, ladies in décolleté sweeping around the Grand Duchess Helena Pavlovna, and a bevy of white-frocked girls from the aristocratic boarding schools of Petersburg chattering French like parrots. Whereas at the Free School concert, all was simple and sincere, collarless, unbrushed and glowing with "reality."

Moussorgsky, the most ferocious of Balakirev's followers, wrote to his chief on the occasion of the formal opening of the Free School:

"Greetings, and may the new-born school grow great and prosper! . . . In Petersburg we now have two music schools, side by side but completely opposite in character. One is nothing but a professorate, while the other is a free confederation of art's allies. In the first Zaremba and Tupinstein" (in Russian, *tupin* suggests the word *stupid*) "dressed in their professorial and quite unmusical togas, stuff all kinds of rubbish down the pupils' throats, so they are diseased from the outset. The unfortunate pupils look up, not to human beings but to a couple of pillar-posts, scribbled over with some kind of silly writing in the guise of musical rules. But Tupinstein is stupid, so he is merely doing his duty in maliciously stupefying the others. Not so Zaremba—a clever fellow, the very man to take measurements of art by inches. 'Doctor of Music!'—cobbler in an academic nightcap would be more like it. But he is too clever to found his ideas and his teachings on mere esthetic and musical logic. Not he! He has been taught the rules. And with this smallpox he inoculates all those who aspire to *learn* art. . . . On your knees to Mendel! That is Zaremba's slogan. And Mendel is Zaremba's god, for Zaremba is his prophet!

"As for Aunty Helen" [the Grand Duchess], "we can suppose she cannot live as long as Methusaleh; as a scourge she is but temporary. In the other school we have you and Gaschenka [Gabriel Lomakin]. Is there more to say? You are a genius, therefore all that is brave and free and strong is yours by nature. Mankind needs such men. All success, therefore, and a happy future to your splendid work. Again I say, 'Hail to the newly-born!' "

Rubinstein, once he had formulated a policy, met all this abuse with indifference, an attitude that infuriated the enemy. In truth, Anton was too busy to write pieces in the newspaper, and anyway he had no gift with a pen; his eloquence had forever but one outlet. Volumes have been written about the *Kutchka* and the nationalist movement in music; we are concerned with it only as it touched the brothers Rubinstein. These artistic wars, so real and burning to their generation, appear to history only as fuel that nourished the future. A wall to kick against is healthy for growing muscles; partisanship feeds lustily upon the strength of its own hatred. Thus the *Kutchka* fed, while its allies, the professional critics, roared abuse in their newspapers. Serov was the most viciously articulate of them all. Questioned by a foreigner as to his artistic credo, Serov admitted, *"Ma position? C'est l'opposition."* A position of frank negation was quite incomprehensible to Anton Rubinstein, constructive, objective, out-going. "An extraordinary man," he said of Serov, "quite eaten by a sick pride and ambition, under the yoke of which he writes God-alone-knows what about music, talking and talking. Sometimes he actually does not know which side to take. . . ."

On one side was ranged the *Kutchka*, on the other the Rubinstein brothers, with Tchaikovsky, Arensky and all the Moscow group we shall meet so soon. From time to time the alignments shifted: Rimsky-Korsakov's eventual defection from the *Kutchka*, his placing himself under the tutelage of Tchaikovsky, his long, courageous study of fugue—this is a story that needs no repeating. But if Rubinstein remained silent under fire, the Grand Duchess did not. She

186

drew up committees and placed the rebels importantly upon the list; when this failed, she employed methods more direct. One day she read a venomous newspaper article, unsigned, attacking the Conservatory, and after some trouble was able to trace it to young Cesar Cui. Had it been written by a mere artist without position, the Grand Duchess would not have been so outraged. But Cesar Cui was an officer of the Imperial Engineers; he wore the uniform of His Majesty's Service. The Grand Duchess ordered her carriage.

Newspaper in hand, she drove to the palace of General Totleben, head of the Army Engineering Corps and hero of Sebastopol. "Is it part of the duty of your lieutenants," she inquired coldly of the general, "to write scurrilous articles against my plans? Be pleased to correct this young man with such military discipline as you see fit. And tell him to hold his tongue in future."

The general bowed, watching Her Highness drive off with a flourish of liveried footmen, sleek horses and shining harness. Then he sent for Lieutenant Cui and inquired wearily what this was all about. A torrent answered him. If silence was the price of a career in the service, said a very hot young man—then he resigned his lieutenancy here, now, this moment! The general sighed, stroking his chin with a gloved hand. "Might I be permitted to make my very honorable young lieutenant the proposition of just a *little* silence? A temporary silence—say until next Tuesday? Would such a procedure ruin forever the cause of Russian musical art?"

In spite of abuse, in spite of enemies and misunderstanding, Rubinstein knew and Helena Pavlovna knew that their Conservatory was on solid ground. At last, Petersburg was receiving the musical education these two had longed to give it. But Petersburg was not Russia; it was merely the brain of Russia—and the brain is nourished by the whole body. Conservatories must be opened in every key town: Kharkov, Omsk, Odessa, Kiev, Saratov, Tiflis and, above all, Moscow. The Grand Duchess reminded Rubinstein of these things. Calling a meeting of the Russian Musical Society she announced it was high time to spread the gospel to the south. Who, she inquired, would go to Kiev?

Instantly, Kologrivov stepped forward—the nobleman who had sacrificed place and position for music, the citizen turned crusader. His sister, said Kologrivov, was a music teacher; the two of them would go to Kiev. What mattered it where a man lived, so long as he could work for music?

Anton looked at his old friend and felt tears suddenly hot in his eyes. The Grand Duchess was speaking. Good! she said. Kiev was important. But there was a city more important than Kiev. Moscow! Without Moscow, nothing permanent could be accomplished for music in Russia. A sprawling, enormous city, Moscow had musical talent in plenty, but no court and no court money.

Anton interrupted. "There is a lot of money in Moscow," he said. "Those fish-scented merchants in the *Zamoskvoretchie* could buy out the Sheremetiev family itself. I know because I have lived among them. They hide their money behind courtyard walls; it does not show."

The Grand Duchess nodded. "I have heard of this wealth. It is stuffed under mattresses and it shines in diamonds around the necks of bourgeois wives, and I am told it is very hard to get at. To enlist the aid of such persons will require a man of courage and enterprise. And more than enterprise. The man who founds our Moscow school will have to possess charm, personality, a knowledge of the world. He must know his way about. Moreover, he must be acquainted with every name and fortune in Moscow. It would be even better if the names and fortunes were acquainted with *him* before he attempts to pass the barking dogs of those courtyard gates."

Helena Pavlovna sighed. "I am asking for the impossible. Such a man does not exist."

Turning a troubled eye upon Rubinstein, she saw that he was smiling. "There will be no difficulty about Moscow," he said. "Has your Imperial Highness forgotten my brother Nicholas?"

20

Nicholas founds the Moscow Musical Society

ALONG the Nevsky Prospekt the generals of Petersburg paraded in their stiff collars; ladies, furred and feathered, bowed from their carriages. Four hundred miles to the south, sacred pigeons clattered from the golden dome of a dozen cathedrals, dogs barked within courtyard gates and bearded porters came grumbling to the knocker, lifting the brass padlock, giving Russian greetings to the guest.

Across twenty square miles sprawled Mother Moscow within her ancient, broken walls—Moscow with her bells chiming the quarters, her brown rooks calling in spring, her hot Eastern summers, her autumns when from the southern gate one glimpsed endless caravans trudging dustily up from Kherson: sheep by the thousand for the open market, silk from Baku, wine from Tiflis, wild honey, attar of roses. Moscow with her clear winter nights when a candle could be carried unblinking in the streets while overhead stars burned in a blue-black sky and travelers, setting out by sledge before dawn, heard snow crunch beneath steel runners. Children, turning in their sleep, were aware of the gallop of hooves, the tinkle of sleighbells— Moscow's gay citizens returning late from restaurants where wine had been drunk, gypsies had danced and sung.

Moscow, in this year of 1860, went her comfortable, old-fashioned way, painting her roofs green, painting her wooden houses pink and blue, laughing at her deep-rutted, unpaved streets, aware that she had the best food, the best wine—in short, the most fun in all Russia!

Nicholas Gregorovitch Rubinstein thrived in this atmosphere. All the glitter of a Court, all the honors in the Tsar's outstretched palm could not have tempted him from his own convivial town. Since that summer day of 1846 when, with his mother, Nicholas had returned from Berlin to walk behind his father's funeral—since that day, he had left Moscow very often. He had gone abroad, to Paris, London, Wiesbaden; he had played the piano from Odessa to Saratov. And always, return seemed sweeter, always the bells brought tears to his eyes, a smile to his lips. At the station the red-sashed, rascally cab-drivers seemed more his brothers, the crack of their whip a sign that Nicholas Gregorovitch was home where he longed to be.

It had not been easy, these years since his father died. Inordinately lazy toward all effort that was not musical, Nicholas, by dint of three years' extremely hard study—he could not afford tutor or school—at sixteen followed his brother Jacob into the medical department of the Moscow University. Jacob had one year left before graduation; both boys were, by petition of their mother, Free Students. Kaleria lived now in a Moscow Ladies Seminary, teaching music and languages in a stubborn, characteristic effort to pay off her dead husband's bankruptcy.

The physician's course was, at that time, a four-year undergraduate schedule. Nicholas had worked hard to achieve entrance; his aim, quite frankly, was to avoid army conscription. But when he found himself actually within those pink stucco walls, behind those high white columns, the boy looked at his medical books and asked himself what in God's name he was doing in this place. Were the bugles at dawn more awful than these thick books wherein one studied drawings of disease and injury? Walking Moscow's streets in his student uniform, bought second-hand, Nicholas reached miserable fingers inside his stiff serge collar, feeling with padded fingertips at the slightly tarnished insignia. Tomorrow was the examination in *materia medica*; the very words were awful to contemplate. He would not study tonight, the boy told himself. He would go to the Begichevs' and read piano duos with old Leo Honoré. Honoré had called Nicholas the best sight-reader in Moscow; perhaps Prince X would be at the Begichevs', and afterward they could go somewhere and play cards.

Prince X was also a Free Student at the University, and it would have been better for Nicholas if the two had never met. The Prince was as dissipated as he was charming. Much older than Nicholas, he lived with one servant in a big empty house that had belonged to one of his aristocratic uncles. He spoke beautiful old-fashioned Russian, pure Moscow without a foreign word in it, and he was crazy about music. Moreover, he was as poor as Nicholas and when he invited the boy, with other classmates, to share his roof-tree, they accepted and set up what they called a commune. When anyone had food he shared it and when anyone had drink—which happened all too often—he shared it also. Wine was beyond the budget; the commune drank vodka, neat, and at first Nicholas did not like it. The house was very cold; the boys broke the furniture and stuffed it in the big stove. When their credit at the stores was exhausted they lived on macaroni, boiled in the samovar and eaten with sticks, all forks having long since gone to the pawnshop. One cold and hungry day someone came home with a rouble's worth of rum; the boys poured it in the samovar and on empty stomachs drank the steaming liquor. Lucky that Kaleria Rubinstein in her Young Ladies Seminary could not see her son that night.

Hungry or filled, drunk or sober, Nicholas Gregorovitch did not cease to play the piano. He gave lessons, he performed in concerts, he went to dine at his friends' houses in his student's uniform, was greeted with shouts of joy and led at once to the piano. For a man so young, without money, obscurely born, his social success was extraordinary. Everyone who met him invited this short, blond young man to dinner. Kaleria surveyed her son's threadbare coat. "In our old warehouse," she said, "is a whole heap of pencils. Pencils are worth money." Nicholas found the pencils and took them to the open market and stood in the snow and sold them, grinning when his fashionable friends passed by.

In the spring of 1854 when he was almost twenty, with a year's study still before him, Nicholas met at a party a girl named Krusheva, and proposed marriage to her. He said afterward that he could not recall exactly how it all happened, but he was much pleased with the event and very much in love. Neither Kaleria

Rubinstein nor the girl's family shared these pleasant emotions. T. D. Krushev was an old-fashioned gentleman, owner of a large estate in the South, who had come to Moscow to educate his daughters. When his youngest announced her intentions, he was horrified. A Jew, a common musician? Music as a profession was proper enough for low-born fellows, but most certainly not for the husband of a Krushev! The prospective father-in-law commenced to inquire concerning this fellow and was surprised to find that everybody who was anybody seemed to know him. "Nicholas Gregorovitch? Oh, certainly. He dines with us often. Plays like an angel on the pianoforte and loses at cards like a gentleman."

Prince Odoevsky, distinguished patron of the arts, announced with satisfaction that he had persuaded Nicholas Gregorovitch to attend his Friday *soirées*. . . . *Persuaded,* from an Odoevsky? Krushev began to feel more than a little mollified. The Governor-General of Moscow, Touchkov, claimed enthusiastic acquaintance with this young fellow, as did Kiselev and Prince Yuri Obolensky. As to the Princess Obolensky, she actually glowed when she spoke the name of Nicholas Gregorovitch, saying that if Moscow were to be brought to life musically, this was the man to do it. Krushev cared not one whit for Moscow's musical progress, but he cared for the right names, and if his son-in-law's piano-playing gained *entrée* to palaces, why, his piano-playing could be tolerated! Krushev learned—but not from Nicholas—that the boy had actually dined intimately with Prince Dolgoroukov himself! This was the hardest door to pass in all Russia; this was the greatest noble of Moscow, direct descendant of the pre-Romanov Tsars. Petersburg called Dolgoroukov the *Satrap*, and looked askance at the Eastern magnificence in which he lived, whispering that he was trying to out-do Tsar Alexander himself.

Kaleria Rubinstein summoned her son to the Young Ladies Seminary, listened to his glowing descriptions of his fiancée, then, looking at him serenely, inquired what he would do with a *lady* in his house. Provided, of course, that he had a house. Reminding Nicholas that he was accustomed to playing for his supper, reminding him that less than a fortnight past he had sold pencils on the street to buy a suit of clothes, Kaleria demanded bluntly if her son expected to live upon the Krushev money.

Nicholas' blue eyes flashed. He replied hotly that he would not accept a kopeck from his wife's people. "As soon as I am graduated I can make more money than we need, with my music. Somebody will give me a government job on account of my medical certificate, and the rest will be quite simple."

Kaleria Rubinstein shrugged her shoulders and went to call upon the Krushevs, who received her coldly until they discovered she was as opposed to this marriage as they were. If the union could not be prevented—and both young people seemed unalterably determined—then they must tell Madame Rubinstein one thing. After the wedding, Nicholas Gregorovitch must give up music as a profession. He could take pupils privately; he could play the piano as an amateur. But no more concerts for money! A son-in-law of Krushev could not demean himself by appearing on platforms like any juggling mountebank.

Kaleria met this with silence. She left the house and went to find her son. "Nicholenka," she said gently, "can a man change his nature? Are there then no other girls in Moscow?"

Nicholas shook his head and kissed his mother on both cheeks. What, he demanded, were platforms to him? Let Anton have the laurel wreaths and the theatre on its feet shouting *bravo*. He himself desired domesticity, the warm hearth, the wifely welcome at the door.

A month later Nicholas went to his final examinations with a high heart—and very little knowledge. There were only 900 students in the Moscow University; examinations were notoriously lax. Alexander II had not yet assumed the throne. Education was yet in the stupor induced by the long reign, the long censorship of Nicholas I. But even with laxity, it was obvious that young Rubinstein did not deserve a degree. Nevertheless he received it because someone on the Board—his name is hidden—insisted this was a young man of parts, that if he never practiced medicine at all, there was that about him which would some day bring honor to the University. "By order of His Majesty," began the cherished document, dated January 1, 1855. Nicholas Gregorovitch Rubinstein, son of a Merchant of the Second Class and therefore himself a member of the Merchant Class, was promoted to membership in the Professional Class with all the rights and privileges thereunto joined.

What a joke to realize he was a class higher than brother Anton whose laurel wreaths and fame counted not one whit against the bureaucracy of government! Forever, now, Nicholas would remain in this class unless—unlikely eventuality—he were decorated by the Tsar and received honorary membership in the class next above, called hereditary nobility but actually a civic promotion.

With his diploma in one pocket, an empty purse in the other, Nicholas Gregorovitch went to meet his bride. The week after his marriage he was given a nominal position in the Governor-General's office—a frankly political sinecure requiring no work except the drawing of a monthly stipend—a situation in no way considered scandalous in those Moscow days. The appointment gave him the added title of "Clerk"—a title that Nicholas, ironically enough, was to bear, on passport and other official documents, until his death.

In a daze of happiness and good-will, Nicholas showed his credentials to his father-in-law, promising to renounce the concert stage forever. "I am an official," Nicholas told his wife, proudly. "Every month, money will be given me."

Krusheva raised her eyebrows. Thank God for Papa and his estates in the south; this husband's few weekly roubles would not keep her in gloves. Krusheva moved herself and her bridegroom into an elegant apartment and prepared to entertain her friends. These two had met at a party; all their intimacy was founded upon parties; a mutual talent for gaiety had brought them together. Krusheva looked ahead to a life purely social; she was dismayed when she began to discover that this charming Nicholas Gregorovitch, so popular with the right people, cared not one whit for a society career. Nicholas dined with princes because he liked princes and because princes could do things for music. Moscow, musically, was asleep, Nicholas told his wife very often. The city was brimming with talent that needed awakening. When Nicholas talked about Moscow there was an intensity in his voice that his wife found amusing, at first. He would rise from his chair, puffing furiously at his cigarette, his face grave, eager. Krusheva watched him, aware of his power, aware slowly that here was something she had not bargained for. Nicholas' charm was not the charm of a playboy. It was built upon something foreign to Krusheva, a pride in work, a whole world of poverty and struggle she had never known. His intensity first frightened, then bored her.

This difficult bridegroom was scarcely twenty. Always good-natured, he had seemed easy material for a woman to work upon, to turn toward the life she desired for herself. But now a difficulty arose. Nicholas refused to take money from the Krushevs. Not a rouble, not a kopeck. He was neither disagreeable nor high-minded about it, refusing to argue or to orate. Rising early, he taught music for eighteen hours a day, coming home exhausted to a house filled with guests or to find his wife gone out for the evening.

Nicholas Gregorovitch was good-natured, but he was no fool. He began to examine this promise he had made his father-in-law, concerning the concert platform. Shamefacedly, he spoke of it one day to his mother. Kaleria, her eyes narrowed, merely remarked that a promise was a promise and Nicholas had better look about for more pupils. . . . Day by day, Nicholas saw less of his wife; he was making seven thousand roubles a year at teaching alone, a very large sum for those days. In 1857 he resigned his secretarial job (the title remained), and resigned also from his marital estate. Without scandal and without bad feeling, Krusheva left a husband whom for two years she had seen, she said, only on Sundays. Nicholas took an apartment alone with his man-servant. Even a poor bachelor had a valet in those Moscow days; Agathon, stupid, gruff, warm-hearted, was soon known to all Moscow as the complete adorer of his master, Nicholas Gregorovitch.

In the summer of 1858 Anton Rubinstein, who had been four

years abroad playing in concerts, came down to Moscow to see his mother. The three Rubinsteins stayed out at Bogorodskoe, near Sokolniki. "Tonia," said Nicholas gravely, laying his hand on his brother's shoulder, "take my advice. Never marry, never drink, never play cards." Anton looked up, roaring with laughter and told his brother the devil was in him. But—now that Cupid was subdued—how about music? How about concerts; or did the Krushev oath still bind?

Nicholas' lazy blue eyes opened a little wider. "Wieniawski and I are going to London," he said. "Chappell has a contract ready."

His brother had not, replied Anton, lost much time getting back into harness. But why, of all places, London? Nicholas replied that Broadwood made as good pianos as anyone and besides, he understood there was money in London. Anton, remembering the beautiful and unmusical ladies of Saint James's Hall, smiled grimly. "You are right, Nicholenka. There is money in London. I left it there for you to pick up."

Nicholas, grinning evilly, remarked that it required a real pianist to carry money out of the British Isles, and to his surprise his brother replied humbly that it was true. "You are a better pianist than I, Nicholenka, if you would practice."

It was not the first time Anton Rubinstein said this of his brother, nor the last. "You think I play well?" he would ask his admirers after a concert. "Ah, but you should hear my brother Nicholas!"

As for London, John Ella would welcome another Rubinstein, Anton told his brother. Nicholas must play for the Musical Union. But he had not come to Moscow to discuss concerts, Anton went on gravely. He had come to discuss something for which concerts would be a contribution, not an end in themselves. In Petersburg, he was planning to found a Russian Musical Society to parallel the Philharmonic Society of Berlin or the Friends of Music in Vienna. He was going right back to Petersburg to start the ball rolling, with Helena Pavlovna's help. It might take months, it might take a year; when the articles were drawn up, he would send them to Nicholas. Moscow needed such a Society even more than Petersburg.

By Nicholas' own account, Moscow was a musical desert. What were the chances for founding such a society in Moscow?

Nicholas was enthusiastic. As soon as autumn repopulated the town, he would sound out the right people. But when autumn came, Nicholas did not have to sound out the right people. The right people came to him instead. Anton had not been gone a fortnight when Prince Yuri Obolensky appeared at Nicholas' door. Leo Tolstoi, it seems, had been talking about organizing a serious musical circle and had been told that if anyone desired to organize something serious in Moscow, it could not be done without Nicholas Gregorovitch.

The time, apparently, was ripe. That January (1859) Nicholas received from Anton the newly written constitution of the Russian Musical Society. A brief scrawl inquired if Nicholas had as yet done anything toward the founding of the Moscow branch, or would lack of Imperial funds make it impossible?

Imperial funds, indeed! This was a challenge to any son of Moscow. Was not old Prince Odoevsky in Moscow, and the Dolgoroukovs? What had Petersburg to show in the way of princely philanthropy that could equal these? Odoevsky was a scholar, a Gold Medal graduate of the Moscow University; he adored music. Every Friday evening the Prince held a musical *soirée* where fashionable Moscow squirmed and sighed its boredom while the old Prince at his blackboard, chalk in hand, expounded the physics of sound. To be received at the Odoevskys' was the *cachet* of social success; nobody dared to stay away. Nicholas himself had gone whenever he had time. Occasionally, taking pity on the guests, Nicholas had come forward and offered to illustrate the Prince's lecture at the piano. The company, sitting up eagerly, applauded in an ecstasy of relief and pleasure.

Odoevsky would help with the Moscow Musical Society; so would the Friday ladies whom Nicholas had rescued from boredom. Oh, it was a glorious idea, this Musical Society! Nicholas postponed the London contract indefinitely; European concerts were not half so interesting as what was going on here at home. The first step would

be to organize a chorus of amateurs to perform Russian compositions and encourage young talent. Musicians could be borrowed
from the Bolshoi Orchestra and a private opera and oratorio company formed which could make Moscow acquainted with the beloved names of Mozart, Bach and the older Italians who had been
snowed under by this infernal Moscow craze for cheap operatic
effects.

Odoevsky would help and so would the *Satrap* himself, Prince
Dolgoroukov who had lately been made Governor-General to succeed Touchkov. Nicholas adored the Prince, who was a most en-
gaging conversationalist—racy, original, fearing neither Tsar nor
devil yet staunch in his old-fashioned patriotism. Nothing was more
amusing than an evening at his extraordinary palace, in the center
of which the *Satrap* sat in his ancient Tartar dressing-gown, roaring commands to an army of slaves, peasant girls, stewards and,
after the fashion of a bygone century, dwarfs and jesters. . . .

Dolgoroukov, Kiselev, Odoevsky, Obolensky—Nicholas had dined
with them, played cards with them at the English Club, played the
piano in their great houses from dark to dawn, not for money but
for the pleasure of making music. And now Anton wrote from
Petersburg to ask if a Musical Society could be established in Moscow, or would lack of Imperial money make it impossible!

"Agathon!" called Nicholas loudly to his servant. "Are my boots
polished? I am going out."

Placidly, Agathon ambled in with the boots, streaked with Moscow mud as they had been last night when his master took them
off. Placidly, Agathon heard his master's customary roar, heard
himself dismissed from the house forever, as he had been dismissed
last week and the week before. "Why," asked Agathon, "should I
clean your boots, Nicholas Gregorovitch? So you can take all the
money in the till, and go out to lose at cards and forget to pay me
on Monday as usual?"

Nicholas laughed. He was not playing cards tonight, he said. He
was going calling. And he would bring home more money and more
promises of money than Agathon—wretched servant that he was—

had seen or heard of in all his worthless life. "But not for you and me, Agathon. For music."

Grumbling, Agathon produced another pair of boots. Putting on his long coat and wide gray felt hat, filling his pockets with strong Turkish cigarettes, Nicholas Gregorovitch, with a list of names in his pocket, went out into the early Moscow dusk.

21

Nicholas founds a conservatory. Moscow's daughters.
Anton marries a princess

Nicholas worked harder over this new idea than he had ever worked in his life. One year later, in the spring of 1860, he was able to report that the Moscow Musical Society had four hundred members and ten thousand roubles. The amateur chorus was in full swing; professional musicians from the theatre orchestras came to help out and from these a string quartet developed, and trios, piano quintets and much chamber music. Nicholas, of course, led choir and orchestra. He was a better conductor than his brother, less impatient, more friendly to the players. And he loved to conduct, loved especially to take the piano part in chamber music. In Lent, the new organization gave concerts, and Moscow flocked to see its cousins and brothers and husbands and sisters on the platform. Nicholas permitted no music but the best; neither coaxing nor bullying could make him change his programs. Leo Tolstoi was delighted. This was what Moscow needed: someone vigorous and uncompromising to lead it to music. Tolstoi had moved to his estates by this time, but he came to the Lenten concerts and applauded loudly, visiting the musicians afterward for congratulation and encouragement.

Nicholas' right-hand man on the Directors' Board was Prince Obolensky. All of his old friends supported Nicholas. Moscow, that had pursued this man for his charm and his piano playing, began to respect him for his energy, his sudden gift for organization. The more Moscow played and sang with Nicholas Gregorovitch, the more it desired to play and sing. Nicholas Gregorovitch could make even counterpoint interesting, and figured bass and the austere polyphonic compositions of the old Italian school. Classes were formed,

200

meeting in Nicholas' apartment, to the disgust of Agathon who grumbled openly at the heaps of muddy boots in the cloakroom, the dripping *shubas*, the eternally smudgy piano keys.

Petersburg began to hear of these classes and concerts. The *Kutchka* was annoyed. It was bad enough to have one Rubinstein lording it musically over Petersburg without another springing up in Moscow. Could one escape these Rubinsteins nowhere in Russia? Absurd, old-fashioned creatures, with their loyalty to Mozart, Mendelssohn and Chopin and worst of all, their complete indifference to the nationalist movement in music! Moussorgsky, visiting his mother's estates just south of Moscow, wrote to his chief, Balakirev, in Petersburg, "I have not been to the German Ministry of Music they have established here. Nicholas Rubinstein is a worthy relation of Anton; he lets his home-made Moscow pianists play Chopin—*piéces de salon*—the height of absurdity."

It was not absurd to Moscow. Moscow drank up what Nicholas Gregorovitch offered, just as Petersburg drank from the fountain that was Anton Rubinstein. Nicholas had, at first, much the same difficulties as his brother: the classes became annoyingly fashionable. If Anton was harassed by ambitious mammas, Nicholas was even more harassed by the daughters of mammas who found his person as well as his music irresistible. Nicholas was short and stocky; he was lowborn, and most certainly his face was not handsome. His breath was heavy with cigarette fumes; all his movements were languid, careless, his blue eyes half-closed. He spoke slowly, as if half-asleep. Moscow's daughters observed these things and Moscow's daughters fell in love with Nicholas Gregorovitch. They wrote about him in their diaries, they pleaded with aristocratic papas for permission to sing in the Rubinstein chorus. Dressed all in white, they sat, sixteen strong, and played upon four pianos, losing their places, bursting into tears while their chaperones, the Princesses Troubetskoy and Obolensky, smiled encouragement from the audience. As for Nicholas Gregorovitch, he only laughed and said it was a beginning, and beginnings could not mar the record. One night after he had played, Nicholas gave one of his laurel wreaths to a pupil—

young Olga Dahl, daughter of an aristocratic, distinguished, old scholar whose values did not include borrowed laurels. The girl carried her wreath home and next morning took it proudly to her father's study. Her own diary records the conversation:

"'Rubinstein presented this to me!' I said with pride.

"'Nicholas Gregorovitch? Whatever for?' asked my father, astonished.

"'What are laurel wreaths always presented for?' I inquired indignantly.

"Father said they were presented to artists as a token of esteem and admiration. 'This one,' I replied, 'was presented for the same reason.'

"'To *you*?' Father said.

"'No,' I said. 'To Nicholas Gregorovitch.'

"'Then what good is it to you?'

"All in one breath, I said I kept it in memory of the esteem and admiration that belonged to him whom we all admire, respect, love and appreciate, and that I prized it as a gift from *dear* Nicholas Gregorovitch.

"'You are a little fool,' my father said.

"That was all he said."

In droves, these girls came to Nicholas' door for lessons. Nicholas taught them; he was a natural-born teacher and he taught anyone who desired to learn. He was not yet thirty; he was separated from his wife but not divorced. When he fell in love with Olga Anenkova—spoiled, beautiful, extravagant—he seriously considered obtaining a divorce and marrying again. But Olga, who possessed a magnificent voice, suddenly took the convent veil. On Sundays she sang in the church choir and Moscow, gazing upon the lovely face in the nun's hood, wondered if Nicholas Gregorovitch were cruel, or if the lady herself, well known for her dramatic gestures, had cannily made the most effective gesture of all.

Nicholas Gregorovitch shrugged his shoulders and worked harder than ever, played cards harder than ever, too. On the whole, it was safer to lose both at cards and at love. A loser does not make enemies. Last spring, for instance, a terrible thing had happened. . . .

There had been a girl pupil, very talented and quite poor, a governess. Nicholas had given her tickets to his Lenten concerts. He had known of course that she loved him, but after all, she was young and it is right for the young to love. Brother Anton actually told his pupils they could not know music until they had known love, but then, Anton could afford such statements. His personality was too commanding for dangerous intimacies. Anyway, Anton was never in one place long enough to gather sweet insidious mosses. Nicholas remained always in Moscow, always available for the temptations of the evening and the retribution of the morrow. His loyalty to Moscow had a price and he learned it to his horror from the little governess who, finding her suit rejected, staged a dreadful tragedy, taking care, like the Anenkova, to enact her drama in full public eye.

She chose one of Nicholas' Lenten concerts as backdrop. Walking into the Hall of the Nobility, she placed herself in an adjoining room under the portrait of Catherine the Great and waited until the music was at its height. Then she shot herself. Nicholas heard the noise and confusion but, innocent, played on. After his number they led him to where the girl lay, quite dead, with his picture over her heart. Nicholas wept, and returning to the platform, played *Warum*, played it so beautifully there was no irony in what he did. It was a time and place that loved a Byronic gesture. Moscow, the Big Village, could be very naïve, but a sharp and worldly cynicism soon reasserted itself. Moreover, women who became hysterical at concerts were very frequent in Russia. Forcing their way into the artists' room backstage after the performance they made scenes that quite terrified visiting European virtuosi. *"Psychopatka,"* the Russians called them, and shrugged.

For a week, a month, Moscow was shaken by the tragedy of Nicholas' little pupil. Then Moscow began to smile. Dostoyevsky wrote his sister, whose daughter Mashenka was a Rubinstein pupil:

"For God's sake and without fail, tell Mashenka that I have finally learned to respect her Nicholas. I admit wholeheartedly that he has done a great deal for musical education. But why for his sake do Russian ladies shoot themselves with a half dozen of his portraits on their bosoms? I ask you, why? Cruel creature! Tyrant! But I repent the calumnies I have heaped upon him. Tell Mashenka that I adore him, seriously."

Nicholas had no sooner paid for the funeral of the little governess than tragedy stalked him once more. This time, Nicholas had made love to no one. He had merely been kind to a girl of extraordinary talent whose rich and miserly father would not pay for her lessons. She came to class shabbily dressed; the other girls snubbed her. Nicholas tried to comfort her, encouraged her musical ambition, told her she must become a good enough pianist to break away from her father and support herself. One day she came to her lesson quite distracted. She had had a quarrel with her father that had lasted all night. While she was telling it she became incoherent, then hysterical. She was taken home and treated kindly, but she never recovered her reason.

Nicholas was bewildered. These lovely Russian girls, with their temperament and their talent—what was wrong with them? They have no education, Kaleria Rubinstein told her son. A girl who has been taught nothing beyond French and sewing and how to curtsey in a ballroom—what weapons are these with which to meet life? Nicholas resolved to be more careful.

But the noise of scandal spread beyond the town. Up in Petersburg, Anton opened his Moscow paper one morning and found a cartoon that caused him grave concern. It showed a kitchen-garden filled with cabbages. Out of each cabbage peeped a woman's head, and walking in the garden was a goat whose face bore a pleased expression and an unmistakable likeness to Nicholas Gregorovitch.

Anton went down to Moscow, stern words on his lips. His brother listened silently, on his face an expression of gloom, humility and something else—something small-boy and unregenerate that Anton recognized with sudden helpless laughter. Just so had

Nicholenka looked years ago when *Maman* threatened him with the birch. "Why does everyone forgive thee, Nicholenka?" said Anton.

Moscow laughed too. "If our Nicholas Gregorovitch is fatal to the ladies," said Moscow indulgently, "then let the ladies beware. A musician's business is music."

Nicholas worked too hard to be seriously upset by the ladies of Moscow. He fell in love, time and again, and no doubt of it. But the moment love interfered with work he became uneasy, then indifferent to love. He had no money to squander on women; his salary as president of the Musical Society was only 3000 rubles a year. He lived modestly and in summer went on tour to make money not only for himself but for the Musical Society whose finances were anything but stable. John Ella wrote from England offering two concerts with the Musical Union, and in the spring of 1861, Nicholas went to London with Wieniawski. The concerts went very well and the two received many invitations to play at private houses. One of these engagements was at the house of what Nicholas afterward described as a cotton king. Piatti the 'cellist went along; their agent had arranged for each of the three to play a solo; then they were to appear in a trio, receiving fifty pounds apiece.

Arrived at the mansion, the three were ushered upstairs and deposited in a small room. Sounds of the party floated up from below stairs. After some time their host entered: Would the musicians care for wine, tea, refreshments? Wieniawski, always polite, bowed and refused for all of them. Nicholas, his eyes all but closed, puffed on his cigarette and thought of Anton.

Their host disappeared, to be followed shortly by a servant who had been sent, he said, to conduct the musicians to the drawing room. "Ah, the jailer!" said Nicholas and, with exaggerated politeness, bowed the startled footman through the door, assuring him they would follow in good order. Arrived in the drawing room, the three played and were instantly escorted back to their room, given money by their host and informed that as he could of course take no more of their time, perhaps the three would like to be going.

Nicholas, who for years had broken bread with Princes and for whose presence at their parties, Grand Duchesses quarreled, remarked that London was a wonderful city. "Henri," he said to Wieniawski, "people live here from choice, people who could live in Paris or even in Moscow. Do you believe it? Tomorrow we are to play at Lord F's and Tuesday at the Duchess of Y's. And on Wednesday I will match you at *Écarté* for every penny we have earned."

Wieniawski threw his arms around Nicholas and embracing him on both cheeks declared that he loved the brothers Rubinstein with all his heart. He would gladly travel forever with either of them.

Nicholas went home with enough stories to make Moscow laugh all winter—and enough money to finance quite a few evenings at the card table. When he won, he gave away his winnings to needy musicians; when he lost he was in debt, but never for long. The sons of Kaleria Rubinstein were restless under debt; neither ever forgot those years when their mother had struggled to pay off their father's bankruptcy to the last kopeck—and had succeeded. They had been only boys, but they had contributed to that honorable fund. Nicholas played cards because he loved to play; now and again he tried seriously to make money gambling. In the summer of 1865 Leopold Auer met him one night at the Casino in Wiesbaden with Henri Wieniawski. The two announced gleefully that they were making 500 francs a day; they had an infallible system. Nicholas did the playing because his nature was so calm, explained Wieniawski. They had put their every kopeck into the venture and planned to retire from professional life, devoting themselves to music in a purely amateur way. Six hours a day, said Nicholas gravely, he sat at that gaming table. It was hard work.

Carried away by these plans, Auer added all his savings to the pot. For nearly a week the system flourished, and then one night Nicholas came home from the Casino with step slower than ever, cigarette drooping from his lips. The system had broken down. All their money was gone.

Auer persuaded a publisher at near-by Mainz to buy some new violin compositions; Nicholas rescued Wieniawski by selling two Russian bonds he had in his suitcase. The three musicians parted. Nicholas went off to Baden where he had business of the utmost importance. . . .

With little noise and no fanfare, Anton had very recently got himself engaged to be married. Turning his back on the Madame X's and the Madame F's, he had made his final choice: a Princess Chekuanov, daughter of an impoverished widow of the Tsar's Guard. Nicholas had met her once in Petersburg, a handsome girl with a strikingly aristocratic bearing, but to Nicholas' mind, a very cold proposition. It had never occurred to him that Anton would marry her; everyone knew that Leschetizky was desperately in love with her. Described everywhere as a *"femme du monde parfaite,"* the Princess cared nothing for music beyond the fact, so Nicholas suspected, that music brought her fiancé some thousands of roubles every time he chose to play the piano in public. Anton had told Nicholas more than once that when it came to a choice, he preferred good breeding to education. Tonia would have a good chance to prove it now, thought Nicholas.

En route to Baden for the wedding, Nicholas asked himself fearfully why Tonia should desire to tie himself to a woman who would require him to wear a starched collar and tight gloves? One could not talk to Vera about music, yet neither did she possess those warm feminine attributes that more than make up for lack of musical appreciation. In brief, Vera Alexandrovna was formidable and cold-hearted.

Quite apart from Vera's character and personality, there was good reason to prophesy disaster from Anton's marriage. He simply was not the marrying kind. Why should a concert artist go out of his way to assume family cares? Others than Anton's brother looked upon these plans with foreboding. Von Bülow wrote from Munich to young Raff who had known Anton at Weimar. "Anton Rubinstein arrived here," wrote Bülow, "for the third performance of Tristan. But in the night he went off again straight to Baden, where—do not be alarmed—he is about to marry a young Russian (without benefit of poison). Just see the consequences of not finding a good opera libretto!" Apparently Anton had been searching in vain for a new opera libretto and like all composers had been gloomy about it. The reference to poison remains a mystery; evidently, somebody had lately poisoned a bride!

Nicholas Rubinstein arrived in Baden filled with misgiving. He did not like Vera. Suppose his antipathy showed upon his face? Anton would never forgive him. A wedding was a place for gaiety, and when had Nicholas Gregorovitch ever ruined a party by silence or sulking? The only remedy lay in wine. The wedding feast would be lavish; Anton would see to that. Perhaps it would be safer to begin right away with a drink before he so much as greeted the prospective bride.

Herman Laroche, who came from Russia for the occasion, records that Nicholas Gregorovitch was "so gay he nearly ruined the wedding."

That Anton forgave his brother goes without saying. What the Princess thought goes also without saying. As for Kaleria Rubinstein, she did not come to Baden at all but remained in Petersburg preparing the bridal apartments, sewing curtains, counting linen and silver. Kaleria's home had been with her son for years, but she had no intention of remaining there. "Where there is a married man," said she, "there must not be a mother-in-law." Upon the day the pair were to return, Kaleria prepared the evening meal herself. Anton and his bride found the samovar boiling, everything in perfect order —and nobody in the house. Anton was grateful. Had his mother ever, he asked himself, made the wrong gesture?

Nicholas Gregorovitch came home from his brother's wedding and fell furiously to work as if work were the cure for marriages, sick roulette systems and all the ills of life. His classes were more popular than ever. They overflowed his little apartment; they brought in money enough to rent a sizeable house that could be devoted to teaching. It was near the Rumiantsov Museum of which Prince Odoevsky was Curator. All day, fashionable carriages stood outside, fashionable young ladies, furred and chaperoned, tripped in and out the door, carrying their music cases.

In 1866 the classes received a charter and a name; the Moscow Conservatory was formally opened.

And now the fashionable young ladies received a shock. As teacher, Nicholas Gregorovitch had always been strict; the Rubinstein gallantry of manner that entranced at evening parties disappeared completely in the class room. Even so, with no examinations required, the girls had been able to remain Rubinstein's pupils. But now, suddenly, things were very different. Nicholas Rubinstein was Director of a Conservatory that he announced was on a par with any music school in Europe. Paris gowns, plumed bonnets bearing the label, *de Pétersburg,* could not help a pupil through examinations. Many fell by the wayside. Nicholas was not sorry to see them go.

The original nucleus of teachers came, quite naturally, from Moscow. Old Dubuc, John Field's pupil, had taught Villoing himself to play the piano. Moscow already knew Honoré and Langer and Dohr as piano teachers. As these grew older, Nicholas replaced them by men from other towns and other nationalities: Laub for violin, Cossmann for 'cello. A Petersburg man, none other than the bitter-tongued Serov, headed the Theory Department for a winter and then resigned. Nicholas wrote to Anton. Had he someone on hand who understood hard work and could teach composition without being too dry?

Anton replied promptly that he had the very man—a pianist who had been graduated this year with the Gold Medal. He was a gentleman, a product of the very snobbish School of Laws, but he was no mere amateur. Such was his passion for music that he had abandoned a government position to become a composer. All his former flippancy had disappeared; he was, wrote Anton, one of the steadiest workers to be found. He would be dispatched on the Monday night train for Moscow. He was very poor and very proud. Could Nicholas meet him at the station?

The young man's name, added Anton, was Peter Ilyich Tchaikovsky.

On Tuesday morning Nicholas met the Petersburg train and found a young man who was excessively nervous, excessively charming and excessively anxious to please. This dark-bearded, blue-eyed Tchaikovsky was only five years younger than Nicholas, but the latter saw at once that in the ways of the world, Peter Ilyich was a babe. Nicholas carried his new professor home, gave him a room, food and a dress coat. When Peter Ilyich demurred, Nicholas told him the Conservatory could not afford to have shabby-looking professors roaming its halls. He could soon work off the debt, said Nicholas a trifle grimly.

All day long Peter Ilyich taught his classes; in the evening, sitting in the little room next to Nicholas', he tried to write music. But his host was the most incurably sociable of men; laughter, conversation, card-playing went on all night. And what was more disturbing, piano-playing. Nicholas Gregorovitch played the piano hours on end for himself and for his friends, and when he played, one could not run away. A spell was cast. Peter Ilyich had thought no pianist lived who could equal Anton Rubinstein.

Now he had found one. Extraordinary, that these brothers, with the same thick fingers, the same technical methods, should be each so individual, so completely original in his playing! Nicholas' performance was as disciplined as Anton's was temperamental; Nicholas brought out the smallest details; one heard every note, every *nuance*. Nevertheless, Nicholas' playing possessed power as great as his brother's. Like Anton, Nicholas Gregorovitch could make the piano sound like an orchestra; reading over a concerto, when he reached the *tutti* places there was no need for him to tell his listeners, "This is the French horn," or "Here the 'cellos have it." You knew it was the horn; its brave golden notes soared upward, then retreated to the woody, resinous baritone that was unmistakably 'cello.

210

How easily these heavy hands spread to a tenth! Peter Ilyich, fascinated, watched the padded fingers flash across the keys and reaching between the black notes, delicately select a key as if they had been the slim fingers of a girl.

Listening to Nicholas Gregorovitch, Tchaikovsky was aware always of the structure of the piece that was being played. All the outer form, the melody, modulations and rhythmic changes, emerged as if cut in cameo. This was a performance profoundly analytic; to listen was to experience a great practical lesson in form and theory. Up in Petersburg when Anton Rubinstein played, Peter Ilyich had sat entranced, drowned in feeling. . . . But the music he heard now, while it possessed poetry in plenty, did not cause one to lose consciousness. And this, to a born craftsman like Peter Ilyich, was a grateful thing. To be conscious, measure by measure, of the structure, to sense, after the development, the slow return to the first theme, feeling it step by step. . . . Ah, but this Moscow Rubinstein was a musician's musician! Listening, Tchaikovsky was stirred by a restless, driving ambition to write music that Nicholas Gregorovitch could play.

Peter Ilyich went out and told Carl Albrecht of this ambition. Albrecht was a 'cellist who bore the official title of Inspector of the Conservatory; everybody called him "Carlusha" and everybody loved him. He had a wife and numerous children; in summer he was to be seen driving out of town with three or four of these and an assortment of butterfly nets, his dark fine beard moving in the breeze, his long hair ruffled. He was Nicholas' chief support; the Conservatory needed Albrecht's precision, his talent for book-keeping. Nicholas himself had little time for book-keeping; he taught longer hours than anybody except perhaps Tchaikovsky. Forgetting the names of his dozens of pupils, Nicholas never forgot the music they played; he knew by heart every piece in student repertory. His temper was short; when it was roused his voice, enormous for so small a man, could be heard all over the building. Like Anton, when Nicholas was angry he talked through his nose. *"Noch einmal!"* he would roar. Anton would have hurled the offender from the chair and played the piece himself, but Nicholas made the trembling pupil play it, and from that short angry figure there issued something that permitted the pupil to play better than he knew how, to understand suddenly the music before him and go away glowing with a humility that was nearer happiness than shame.

As the Conservatory prospered, Nicholas was able to engage teachers of European reputation. Klindworth came from Germany to teach piano and the glorious Sverev began to develop in Moscow his incomparable pupils. The names were many, the nationalities varied. More than one musical historian has recorded the growth of the Conservatory under its great Director. Through all their accounts runs the theme of Nicholas' devotion to Moscow. "Moscow repaid him," writes Laroche, "with a devotion truly extraordinary. Before he was thirty, this little man with the official rank of 'government clerk' was a local celebrity on terms of equality with the most important older people, invited to preside at celebrations as if he were a bishop. Yet in spite of having bound himself to a provincial town—and Moscow's size did not prevent it from being culturally provincial—N. G. never let his life slide into the commonplace. Strangely enough, his talent as a virtuoso developed and enriched; the beauty of his playing increased each year and could be compared only with the playing of his famous brother. And for healthiness, clarity and perfection of detail, many persons gave the palm to Nicholas even above Anton Gregorovitch."

Kashkin, who wrote so much about Tchaikovsky, desired also to write about Nicholas Gregorovitch, but complained that he could never see Nicholas except between seven and nine in the morning —after he returned from the Club where he had played cards all night and before he went off to the Conservatory where he stayed all day. "Consequently," wrote Kashkin, "when I saw the man he was always sleepy. He practically never went to sleep; as a worker he was inexhaustible. . . . In appearance he had not a single feature suggesting Jewish origin; he was of middle size, a thick-set blond, with curly hair, a pensive look, a face that expressed firm energy in spite of his mannerisms of a spoiled, lazy nobleman's son.

He was always ready with service or help to any artist—especially to a Russian, and in this he never considered his own means, but simply gave away what he had at the moment. In art he was a pure idealist, permitting no compromise with personal sympathies or prejudices."

"*A pure idealist, permitting no compromise.*" Through the paradox of this man's personality, these words give the key to his power over people. For twenty years Nicholas was to hold the title of Moscow's Tsar of Music—despotic, impatient, autocratic. His subjects murmured rebelliously. Two of them, Tchaikovsky and the widow Von Meck, exchanged sympathetic letters concerning the high-handedness of this sovereign whom they called the "thunder-hurler." Yet, like the rest of Moscow, these fantastic correspondents respected Nicholas Rubinstein to the core. He was the only man permitted within the guarded walls of the huge Von Meck establishment on the Rozhdestvensky Boulevard; the widow declared he played like a god and Peter Ilyich confessed that no earthly creature could play the music of Tchaikovsky as Nicholas Gregorovitch played it.

Nicholas Gregorovitch gambled; Nicholas drank too much and too often; Nicholas loved the ladies less wisely than well. But beyond all this, Nicholas Gregorovitch loved music and fought for music, never lowering his standards, never permitting on his programs what was cheap or easy. All his betrayal was against himself; he was to throw away his life in foolish, reckless dissipation like many of his talented countrymen before and after him. But with it all, Nicholas' character never softened, he never let down, never worked less hard, never was late for his classes at the Conservatory, never betrayed what Laroche called his pure idealism.

This was Kaleria Rubinstein's favorite son. Kaleria could not live with him now; these wild long hours of card-playing, this coming home at dawn with haggard eyes and step uncertain was something this mother could not condone. From now on, Kaleria saw little of Nicholas. She loved him as much as ever. But she went north to Petersburg and lived with Anton until his marriage, then down to

Odessa to spend her old age with the loyal spinster daughter, Sophie.

Nevertheless, behind these last years of Nicholas' life one sees, somehow, the features of his mother, strong, benign and faithful. One senses always the rock of that early training and one knows that without it Nicholas would not have accomplished what he did accomplish. He would have gone to pieces as a young student in the great empty house with Prince X, drinking rum from the samovar. He would have succumbed to the well-bred, comfortable life of the family into which he married. He would have given up professional musical life to become a charming, sought-after dilettante.

There was a rock in Nicholas Gregorovitch, and Moscow felt it and dared not presume too far with this Jewish son of a German mother. The concerts of the Musical Society, once they became established, were given in the Hall of the Nobility, a beautiful room surrounded with a colonnade of stately white pillars, lighted by crystal chandeliers, its ceiling copper-netted, perfect acoustically. Moscow, trained to nothing more serious than the Italian opera, was accustomed to converse pleasantly during musical performance, to enter late and stroll about. One night while Nicholas Gregorovitch was conducting in the Nobility Hall, an entire family arrived in the midst of the symphony and, with rustling of silk and shuffling of feet, made its way up the center aisle. These were the Alexeyevs, among them the little boy, silk-bloused, red-booted, who was to become Russia's greatest theatrical producer—Stanislavsky. When the procession reached the center of the hall, Rubinstein stopped the orchestra. Baton in hand, he turned and stared at the offenders. The audience, turning with him, waited, highly interested, until the family was seated—all but young Stanislavsky who, terrified, fled the hall and was found at the end of the evening hiding in a remote corner of the farthest room.

Kaleria Rubinstein had taught her sons to approach the Muse with reverence. Having founded a Conservatory, having persuaded all Moscow to his symphonic concerts, Nicholas saw before him an even harder task: he must make Moscow love serious music as he himself loved it. It was far from easy to turn Moscow's attention from performer to music, from the top notes of a favorite prima donna to the symphonic intricacies of Beethoven, the pure melodic line of Schubert. Rubinstein went about his task with persistence and diplomacy, teaching, conducting, playing in concerts. There was no time to practice the piano and no time to write new music. When friends inquired why Nicholas Gregorovitch neglected his gift for composition, he laughed and said his brother Anton wrote enough for three. To compose music required solitude, and solitude was abhorrent to Nicholas. When he walked the streets of Moscow it was a triumphal procession; hats were lifted, greetings called, friends crossed the street to join him.

Nicholas Rubinstein lived to the full the life he had chosen and enjoyed every minute of it. *La gaîté est près de la bonté.* Nicholas' gaiety was an essential part of him; it was a quality that somehow brought its owner very close to life. Artists know this quality. Said Leschetizky to a solemn young pupil who shut himself up all day and all night to practice the piano: "Young man, you will never be an artist. You must live; you must be lively; be gay, learn to dance."

No one had to tell this to Nicholas Gregorovitch. And if sometimes his gaiety was feverish and overstepped the mark, taking the guise of practical jokes that all but terrified poor Peter Tchaikovsky, yet this feverishness was part of Moscow like the card-playing, the long nights in gypsy restaurants outside the city, the long sledge drives homeward with the colored lantern swinging above the coachman's whip, the powdered snow tingling against one's flushed cheeks.

How easily the seasons rolled by! Moscow winters, with peasant carts rumbling to the Frozen Market outside the Chinese Wall. Spring, with the log rafts winding down the Moskva River. Standing on the bridge in the evening, Nicholas saw smoke rise from the rafts where the drivers were cooking their suppers, heard the high sound of a flute as the logs disappeared around the bend. . . . Summer, with thunderclouds piled high against golden church spires and the windows of the big houses white-washed. Strawberries in the market, all warm and sweet. . . . Autumn, with red-petticoated

215

nurses walking their charges in the park, and everyone's friends coming in from the country. Faithful, stupid Agathon grumbling over the boots, Peter Ilyich knocking humbly at the door, begging Nicholas Gregorovitch to play over his latest composition. Sverev and a new generation of pupils springing up. Taneiev, Siloti, Emil Sauer. Anton, arriving on one of his rare visits, the Conservatory halls hushed as if the gods themselves were treading past those glass doors. Prince Odoevsky with his blackboard, Prince Dolgoroukov with his slaves. Moscow streets filled with freed serfs from the country, begging their bread. . . .

Not so spectacular a life as Anton's, certainly. But a life happy and warm, filled with friendship, love and laughter. And always the ladies as beautiful, the wine as delicious, the cards as alluring. Always, work to do, music to play and to teach. Music, and more music, and more.

22

*1867. Anton Rubinstein resigns from his Conservatory.
A little incident in Frankfort*

THE years that witnessed Nicholas Rubinstein, busy and content,
entrench himself ever deeper into Moscow, saw his older brother up
in Petersburg growing more and more restless. Chains were good for
Nicholas, whose nature needed limitations imposed from without.
Anton, on the other hand, desired no boundaries. The Petersburg
Conservatory, after five years of existence, was prosperous and successful. No fewer than seven hundred names were on the roster.
The Director, scanning the list, shook his head, muttering darkly.
This spring of 1867, twelve Masters' diplomas would be given, bearing the title, *Free Artist*. Only seven were deserved; the other five
pupils knew their lessons by rote and could play their exhibition
concerti nicely, but not one among them was what Anton Rubinstein called *musician*. These five would go into the world and play.
They would go abroad. Bülow would hear them; Liszt would hear
them and know them as bunglers who carried a Rubinstein diploma
in their pockets.

It was not to be borne. Anton argued with his fellow directors
and his teachers but they would not yield; they would not sacrifice
their pupils. Rubinstein, said they, was asking for genius, and conservatories did not function for the benefit of genius. . . . Anton
went to see his mother. "I am going away," he told her. "I cannot
stay in this accursed city where they give an idiot a piece of paper
and call him musician."

Kaleria nodded gravely. "Go soon, then. Days are not given to be
wasted in anger. Surely you have music yet to write."

Rumor spread quickly around the city. One morning in March,
Anton found on his Conservatory desk two long letters, one signed

by the students, one by the teachers, pleading with him to remain as Director. Expressions of affection, of regret, but nowhere a yielding of the main point. Anton's lip curled; he put on his hat and went over to the theatre to rehearse his *Children of the Steppes* that was to be performed in April. Such was his temper that the orchestra players scarcely dared breathe and the singers choked desperately through their parts. When Anton Rubinstein became angry at rehearsals he behaved, wrote one of his victims, "like a dozen madmen let loose."

It might be as well, whispered Petersburg, to let Anton Gregorovitch go away for a while. Wieniawski, too, was restless, being passionately loyal to his chief and also a trifle nostalgic for the concert stage. Zaremba, the counterpoint man, agreed to take over the Director's tasks. Zaremba was one man who would not let standards be lowered, and Zaremba had time to spend at desks before rows of accounts and the figured bass worked out by cretins.

Together, Rubinstein and Wieniawski handed in their resignations in June of 1867. Zaremba became Director. Balakirev who, although he led the *Kutchka* and the Nationalists, had never been unfriendly to Anton, took over the conductorship of the Musical Society concerts. After five years of steady application to the needs of his Conservatory, five winters of clocklike regulation of his days, Anton Rubinstein found himself once more his own master, free to use his time as he saw fit.

Studying Anton's schedule for the next five years, one marvels that he found time to sleep, eat or breathe, much less to compose such quantities of music. From one end of Russia to the other, from one end of Europe to the other, he traveled. By train, by coach, on river boats with the paddle wheel churning outside his cabin, down the Volga and by dusty train to Odessa to see his mother settled in the home she had chosen. And everywhere the concert stage, with Rubinstein playing or conducting his own music, frankly eager to spread his fame as composer.

Over in Berlin his librettist, Jules Rodenburg, worked hard to have copy ready whenever Anton should make one of his sudden appearances. One spring morning Rubinstein appeared in Rodenburg's apartment at six-thirty, threw his hat on the table and without taking off his big Russian fur coat, sat down at the piano and sang through thirty pages of his latest operatic score to the words *Rats, mice, rats, mice.*

"If you are so slow producing a libretto," said Anton, "then I must make my own words."

The summer that Rubinstein and Rodenburg worked on his sacred opera, *The Tower of Babel,* Anton arrived in Thuringia with nothing whatever in his suitcase but his thick musical score, a plaid shawl and the Bible, which he had read all the way from Petersburg. The rapidity with which this torrential Russian produced new scores was the admiration and despair of publishers and conductors from one end of Europe to the other. The worst of it was that the composer desired his scores to be played without alteration, exactly as written. In Dresden, Julius Rietz tried to persuade him to alter parts of his opera *Feramors* for production, but Anton would not change a note. "I cannot go back," he said. "Not while new music is crowding my head."

In June of 1869, Rubinstein arrived in Liverpool in a state of shabbiness that appalled his host. Anton's clothes were unpressed, his hat looked as if he had sat on it, his hair nearly reached his shoulders. Rubinstein always traveled first class. But this time, he said gloomily, the guards had protested and tried to put him in the steerage. Firmly the English friend led him to the barber, who advised his client to have the hair shorn "unless he wished to pass for a German fiddler."

Anton laughed his great hearty laugh and went up to London with his hair long and sat down in Saint James's Hall with Leopold Auer and Piatti the 'cellist to play trios for John Ella's Musical Union. Auer was young; he had neither seen nor heard Rubinstein. Fiddle under his chin, bow poised, young Auer waited for the piano to announce the opening theme of Beethoven *B Flat Trio*. It came. "I was struck dumb," wrote Auer. "Never before had such a tremendous, noble, vibrant human tone fallen on my ears. Never since have I encountered his equal. This was the greatest master of piano tone that ever lived."

This, from a fiddle player, is praise indeed. Rubinstein must have returned the compliment, for shortly after the concert, Auer received an invitation to join the staff of the Petersburg Conservatory. He accepted, never dreaming that he would remain there into a new century, a new time when revolution itself would drive him westward.

On that spring morning of 1869 when Rubinstein announced a Beethoven theme, Leopold Auer heard it in rapture, but the London critics listened with feelings far removed from rapture. They were as obdurate as ever concerning this Russian. Joseph Bennett, who lived to eat his words, wrote next day that Anton Rubinstein was a poseur, one of those "high-action" pianists who throw their hands in the air. As to Rubinstein's own *D Minor Concerto* that he had played after the Beethoven *Trio*, Bennett called it "unintelligible, gloomy, wild, rhapsodical," and suggested darkly that its composer belonged to the "modern German school."

This meant, of course, the school of Richard Wagner. Rubinstein scowled. Must these English couple him with the name he hated above all names? Then he shrugged his shoulders and forgot about it. After all, abuse was part of public life. Sometimes, after a failure, Anton indulged in sardonic humor at his own expense. In Leipzig one season, David had conducted one of Brahms' *Serenades* to a house silent with disapproval. Directly after it, he performed Mozart's well-loved *G Minor Symphony*. A few concerts later, Rubinstein conducted his own *Ocean Symphony* which fell as flat as the Brahms' *Serenade*. Once more David mounted the stand and played Mozart's symphony. When the applause died away, Rubinstein walked up to David. "Is it required by law in Leipzig," asked Anton, "always to give the *G Minor Symphony* after any piece which is expected to fail?"

Back and forth from east to west traveled Anton Rubinstein, and felt the face of Europe changing. Paris especially wore its rue with a difference. Napoleon III, infirm, secretive, listened to the counsels of his Empress as the wily Bismarck tempted him to war. The labor party and Bakunin's revolutionaries bored from within. Politically and intellectually, Paris was torn in two. These were the days of the new scientific materialism. Darwin's theory of evolution had been grumblingly accepted, but at the *Académie*, Pouchet rose to his feet and declared that Monsieur Pasteur's germ theory was as absurd as his so-called cure for anthrax. Saint-Saëns reported all Paris taking sides; as for himself, on being asked which he believed in— Pouchet or Pasteur—he always replied, "I shall be for the one who is right."

Anton Rubinstein, playing at the Salle Herz in April of 1870, cared little who was right in these matters. His business was music and he went about it in spite of Iron Chancellor, revolutionists and Royal Academy. Making a flying visit to Petersburg, he was disturbed to find Zaremba ill and ready to resign as Director of the Conservatory. Anton took the problem to the Grand Duchess Helena, who at sixty-odd possessed a step as quick, an affection as warm as ever. Asantchevsky, said she, would be the proper successor for Zaremba. Asantchevsky was Moscow-born, but Paris-trained—a cultivated man.

Anton remained in Russia until late spring. His *Don Quixote* (Opus 87, Musical Portrait for Orchestra) was performed in Lent. For the last Lenten concert of the Russian Musical Society, Nicholas came up from Moscow and played second piano with Anton in the latter's *Sonata Duet*, Opus 89. Petersburg loved seeing the brothers on the stage together and received them with a deep affection that forgot all difference in schools and artistic isms.

In June Anton went, as usual, to Germany, pleased with a world that was so friendly, pleased with spring and the prospect of summer in a land that always received him hospitably. This time, however, he was to be disappointed. A new spirit was abroad in the Germany that Anton had always loved. Bismarck the nationalist had worked with a powerful yeast; the Franco-Prussian War was about to burst upon Europe; already Jews and Catholics were feeling the heavy hand of nationalistic patriotism. Anton went down to Frankfort, a city he loved. Until three years ago, Frankfort had been independent of Prussia, now it was part of the North German Union, and there lay upon it a heavy hand.

Innocent as always of politics, Anton Rubinstein arrived in Frankfort to give a concert and went as usual to the city library. He walked up the library steps, nodded to the custodian at the desk and wrote his name in the visitor's album. Peering at the inscription, the official shook his head. "Jews are not permitted in the building," he said.

Rubinstein went down the steps to the street, in his heart a strange, blind feeling that was not rage. What a fool is man, he thought, ever to call himself victor! At forty, Anton Rubinstein had conquered all of Europe. "The world requires of a Jew twice what it requires of a Christian." Whose words were these that came so familiarly to mind? Anton did not recognize them as his own words, spoken long years ago in Vienna when, a boy of sixteen, he had first realized he was a Jew. Bitterness mounted once more, the old, cold, implacable resolution.

Victor? Half the world remained as yet unconquered, that Western Hemisphere they called the New World, where men boasted of independence, of an equal opportunity not bounded by creed or color. America had more than once invited Rubinstein to its shores. If America asked once more, he would accept. He would brave that horrible ocean and find for himself if these things were true.

Meanwhile a flattering offer arrived from Vienna. *The Friends of Music* wished Rubinstein to conduct their concerts for the winter of 1871-72. This meant leading the Philharmonic and the Choral Society. Anton was pleased; he was sick of hearing himself praised as a virtuoso; he wanted to be known as composer and conductor. He went to Vienna and stayed all winter, enjoying himself hugely. His wife remained at home; she was not to be torn from Petersburg in the winter social season. Moreover, she had by now presented her husband with two children, a boy and a girl; it was easier to care for them at home. Anton loved his children sincerely, especially his little daughter. But the life of a concert artist makes domesticity spasmodic; Vera desired her household to be run smoothly. Conventionality was the core and center of her character, and the presence of Anton Rubinstein did not foster smoothness and conventionality in any household. It was as well the two were often separated. Anton sent home plenty of money, but he also spent princely sums upon himself. In Vienna that winter of 1871-72, he gave weekly supper parties which were the talk of the town. Vienna whispered that the caterer's bill amounted to four thousand florins, more than Rubinstein's entire salary as Director of the *Gesellschaft*.

Vienna loved parties and magnificence, and Vienna loved Rubinstein, the pianist. Once more the autocrat, Anton did as he pleased. A distinguished nobleman sent him a large sum of money, requesting that Rubinstein perform at an approaching *soirée* in his house. Anton returned the money with the message that Graf So-and-so could come to the forthcoming Rubinstein concert in such-and-such a hall for a twentieth part of the money. Even the English, observing Rubinstein in Vienna, were impressed. "I have seen a pianist here," Lady Eastbrook wrote home, "who did not inspire me with pity. It was Anton Rubinstein. They call him the Piano Emperor."

Dr. Mosenthal, one of Anton's librettists, was in Vienna that winter and went one night to a concert in which Anton accompanied Herr Walter—Vienna's idol—in a Schumann song. Walter, the great German tenor, was famous for liquid smoothness of phrasing, but that night, after he had sung a ravishing phrase, Rubinstein repeated it in the accompaniment, playing with such extraordinary imitative charm that Walter forgot to sing and stood listening while the audience smiled.

Vienna loved all this. Vienna never missed a Rubinstein concert, as long as Rubinstein played the piano. But Vienna refused to take to her heart Rubinstein the composer. *Feramors* was produced, and Anton wrote to his old friend and librettist Rodenburg:

"It was a failure. I am very sorry, for I love this opera dearly, in spite of everything. The Wagner clique set up hostile demonstrations; then professional criticism, with which I am everywhere on bad terms, made me feel the entire weight of its arm. In addition, the public is now so led astray by brochures on Opera, Drama, New Paths and the Future, that a harmless, purely lyrical, specifically musical composition—moreover a Russo-Jewish composition—must leave the people cold. But I live in the conviction that these things will pass sooner or later, and then my *Feramors* will win its way. If it is true that people can no longer enjoy simple melody, beautifully performed, then surely—woe to music, woe to the musician and woe, most of all, to me!"

Anton Rubinstein the composer followed no new paths, declaring frankly that he looked backward toward Mendelssohn and that what men called the artistic future held for him only chaos, discord and turgidity. Liszt and Brahms were often in Vienna that winter; Anton was personally very fond of them both, but their creative musical aims remained very wide of his. Liszt was an old man now, his hair nearly white, but he played the piano as gloriously as ever. Sometimes he came to Anton's supper parties and sat down with his host to play four-hand duets. Once, when Liszt, Brahms and Rubinstein were in the room together, a finger was pointed, a voice called, "The Triumvirate!" There was silence until, pointing at Liszt, Anton said aloud, "Caesar!" Then, pointing to himself, "Brutus!" and at Brahms, "Lepidus!"

When spring came (1872) Anton carried the huge score of his sacred opera, *The Tower of Babel,* to the Lower Rhine Festival where it was performed under his own baton and received with an enthusiasm which Rubinstein fortunately did not recognize as a *succès d'estime*. Young men flocked to the stage, begging a leaf from the composer's laurel wreath. For a brief but glorious moment Rubinstein, surounded by Old Testament characters with good tenor voices, saw himself elbowing Richard Wagner off the stage forever.

That summer Vera came over with the children and kept house for Anton at Ischl, near Salzburg. It was pleasant in the green south country, gay with music and many friends. A stream wandered through the town. On the fine Esplanade was the famed *Café Wal-*

ter, where early every afternoon, musicians met to drink their coffee in the open air. Brahms came and Ignaz Brüll, Carl Goldmark, David Popper and Leschetizky. Then they all went home to work. Brahms always refused to tell what he was composing at the moment; when challenged he would reply, "Oh, I am writing nothing at all, absolutely nothing."

During these few weeks of comparative calm, Anton wrote much music. He began his opera, *The Demon,* and composed songs from Goethe's *Wilhelm Meister.* In July Vera Rubinstein said a long farewell to her husband. This time he was going very far afield. To Berlin, Leipzig, Weimar, Paris, London, Liverpool—whence his itinerary took a great leap westward.

In September, 1872, Anton Rubinstein was scheduled to play in Steinway Hall, New York City.

23

The New World prepares for Anton Rubinstein

ON THE last day of August, 1872, Rubinstein boarded the steamship *Cuba* at Liverpool. Ten days of misery lay ahead, days of racking illness for a man who was not used to illness. Rubinstein was in his cabin before the ship left the docks and stayed there until the sheltering arm of Sandy Hook shut out the terrible blue rollers, the bang and slide and bump that destroyed a man's sight, hearing, soul and digestion. Worse even than the ship's motion was the throb of the screw, insistent, unremitting. Before Anton's head was safely on the pillow the engines announced their theme:

Amor, das verliebte Kind
Lud nur blind, lud nur blind . . .

Over and over the rhythm repeated itself, the same words, the same even, maddening four-four time. Moaning in his bunk, Anton told himself he would go crazy before the ship docked; and then what of his contract with Maurice Grau, what of William Steinway awaiting him in New York City?

He had braved this voyage for several reasons. First of all, he needed money. He had been married six years, he had two young children. Vera was extravagant; she lived the role of the lady, the *mondaine* who had sacrificed a worldly career to serve as wife to an artist. This was the front she presented to the world, and she chose to present it with a background of comfort. She ran up debts, big fat ones; on his return from a tour, Anton found bills that ate up every *thaler* he brought home. Vera could not live in Petersburg in summer, she said. Anton must buy her a villa in the country, at Kammenoy Island or Peterhof or some place where the fashionable world was found.

Anton needed money, and money was to be found in the New World. With Jacob Grau in Vienna he had signed a contract to appear 200 times in America for $200 a concert. William Steinway had advanced money, and Grau's nephew Maurice, who was only twenty-one and whose experience in managing artists had so far been limited to the management of the Aimée Comic Opera Troupe, was to plan the itinerary. Anton was not undertaking the tour alone. Henri Wieniawski was to share the platform; he came over on the *Cuba* too, vainly endeavoring to practice his violin against the pitching and plunging, vainly endeavoring to rally his old friend Anton with champagne brought from Paris.

Both artists were prepared for strange experiences in the New World. Although Petersburg knew better, the rest of Russia still was convinced that the tiger, the crocodile and the Red Indian infested the very doorways of American houses. Two Massachusetts Yankees wrote home from Moscow about the old Prince who refused pointblank to believe they were Americans. He took them to the theatre and pointed to one of the orchestra fiddlers, a coal-black Alabama darkie.

"*That* is an American!" said the Prince.

No Russian musician of eminence had as yet ventured to North America; the term "United States" was seldom used. Thalberg had been across in 1865, and his stories of the New World still circulated about Vienna. But old Henri Herz in Paris, owner of the Salle Herz, was the one from whom to learn about Americans. He had come over in 1845 and toured for six years, covering South and North America, ravishing both continents with his rapid-fire finger technique. The first necessity for such a tour, said Herz, was an American manager. Ullmann had directed every detail of the Herz tours, and Ullmann knew how to fill a theatre. In Philadelphia, for instance, he had advertised a concert hall illuminated by a thousand candles. When a member of the audience had protested that there were eight candles too few, Ullmann commanded Herz to send eight candles to the complainant. Barnum himself urged Herz to play upon a platform on which Jenny Lind was to appear suddenly, floating downstage as an angel from heaven. . . .

Anton Rubinstein had laughed at these tales, but somehow they had captured his sympathy. These Americans were only children, eager, unsophisticated. It was a shame to exploit them; they needed to be taught, to be treated with honesty, to have good music introduced to them simply, with no trickery. Surely, good music was its own advertisement! From the outset of his career, Rubinstein had scorned advertisement. In Paris, for instance, he had broken all the rules by announcing himself merely in small letters on the billboards. And he had succeeded; after one concert, the Parisians had flocked to hear him play.

Here in America, Anton told his manager, he would submit to no tricks; moreover, he would not play down to his audience. He would fulfill every term of the contract; sick or well he would be on hand for each of those two hundred performances. But he would make his own programs. He would play Beethoven and Mozart and Schumann and Liszt and he would play old composers from the eighteenth century that America had never heard of. Maurice Grau replied gloomily that except for New York and Boston, America had not heard of Liszt and Chopin, let alone Couperin and Friedemann Bach. What America really liked, Grau knew, was spectacles: monster concerts, with sixteen people playing eight pianos, monster choruses singing with two orchestras combined. America thought of music in connection with State Fairs, when a man brought his family in from the farm along with his prize cattle, and wandered from the building where giant cabbages were displayed to the hall where the foreign *artistes* were assembled.

Maurice Grau did not tell this to Anton Rubinstein. He was afraid to tell it. Seasick or no, Anton would have turned around and gone home on the same boat. Grau told neither his fears nor his hopes to this wild Russian genius he had captured to bring home to William Steinway. America had never seen or heard anything like Anton Rubinstein, and herein lay Grau's hopes. Anton could play like the Angel Gabriel. He took the abstraction out of classical music and made it into something a man could understand, something instantly familiar, that a man could possess. Anton Rubinstein made Beethoven sound like something any American had heard before he was born, music that had rocked him to sleep in the cradle, music to which he had marched to Appomattox and back again.

Rubinstein could play like that, and moreover he looked the part, looked like the common man's dream of a musician, with his mane of hair, his great, heavy shoulders, his falling-down socks and his wild string tie. . . .

The chances of success, Grau told himself, were a good seventy to thirty, yet Grau was nervous and with reason. In 1872 the United States was incredibly naïve concerning the arts. Only twenty-two years had passed since Jenny Lind, escorted from her ship by seven hundred red-shirted, trumpet-blowing firemen, had made her Castle Garden début under the illuminated inscription, "Welcome, Sweet Warbler." New York had enjoyed this whole-heartedly, but had been forced to pay for it by severe ribbings from across the water. A Monsieur Tajan-Rogét, filling Clinton Hall for two monster lectures on *Les Beaux-Arts*, told the citizens they had no taste. New York required its artists to be pretty and virtuous. America, that called itself a New World, was already ruined artistically by its love for *le soft*! Why had New York adored the Sweet Warbler? Merely because Barnum called her an angel and canonized her after instructing her to give away her surplus earnings to charity! How had the city received Rachel, the great tragedian, last winter? The public had refused to see her act, had called her immoral when her only fault was that she was old and wrinkled. . . .

What Monsieur Tajan-Rogét and his *confrères* who came to excoriate the Americans in lucrative lectures did not realize was the background that caused America to long for *le soft*. It was a background harsher than anything in the experience of the lecturing gentlemen. Foreign visitors, driving up New York's elegant street called Broadway, could not see the forest that lay west of the city gates. There was good reason for the ungodly reputation art bore in this New World. Outside the walls of one's house were a hundred enemies: rain and cold, drought and heat, trees to be felled—more trees and more. For hundreds of miles west of the Alleghenies, the forest was still an enemy to be conquered. What time had man or woman for those things called Art and Music? No wonder they were condemned as immoral, to be indulged in only by the lazy and the wicked.

What deceived foreigners was the amazing material luxury of New York. As early as the 1840's, Henri Herz had marveled at the *"consommation d'eau qui se fait en Amérique,"* where each house was provided with its bathroom and where, every Saturday, Philadelphia's servants washed the façades of the houses with pumps "as if they were afraid of fire." The combination of luxury and Puritanism puzzled Monsieur Herz, who was annoyed because a man could not smoke on the city streets and appalled at Philadelphia Sundays when certain thoroughfares were closed so as not to disturb church worshippers. He felicitated a country where the practice of tipping had not been introduced. His ship had not been tied to the dock when reporters from Mr. Greeley's and Mr. Bennett's newspapers rushed up and asked him how he liked New York.

"Attendez au moins que je débarque," said Monsieur Herz, antedating the reply of a whole century of visiting artists.

One-man concerts being as yet unheard of in America, Herz was supported, on the platform, by a whole bevy of assisting "artists." His farewell concert in Philadelphia was announced as a "Great Festival in Honor of the Declaration of Independence," and opened with a cantata entitled *"Hommage à Washington,"* performed by five orchestras and 1800 singers. Then came a lecture on "The American People and the Rights of Women," delivered by what was described as a well-known lady orator.

Women's rights, temperance, bloomerism, Fourierism—music had many competitors. No wonder Herz and his successors had recourse to ingenuity to fill their halls! Volovski, the Pole, advertised that he could play four hundred notes in one measure. Ole Bull came down from Norway with a bow arm as long as Paganini's and played miraculous double stops on a flattened fiddle bridge, charming

America to the very edge of the Oregon forests. Whole families drove into town by oxcart the day his concert was advertised. Leopold Meyer played the piano with his fists and his elbows, sometimes with his cane. He made the piano ring bells, he invented thunderclaps in the base, he waved at the ladies with his right hand while his left executed roulades. Then he went home to Europe— and returned to America ten years later to garner some more easy money. He was surprised to be received with coldness, even hisses.

"This is a marvelous player," wrote a New York critic, "if only he would play good music."

If only he would play good music. Ten years had worked wonders in the New World. Chicago was very far west in those days, yet as early as 1835, the town had its Old Settlers Harmonic Union, where men could sing songs to such instruments as its members brought in their pockets. Chicago, with its mud and its fierce lake winds and its cattle, had a Sacred Music Society in 1842, a Choral Union in '46, a Mozart Society in '49 and a *Männergesangverein* in '52. America, groping for music, had been rewarded with foreign pianists who played with their elbows. Disgusted, America began to make music for itself. Louis Gottschalk appeared upon the platform in 1852—the first native American pianist of real ability and education. In Russia, a Grand Duchess had asked him if Barnum were not one of America's greatest statesmen. Gottschalk toured all during the Civil War and his countrymen came to hear him, marveling that a man could speak American and wear his hair short and yet play the piano. One autumn day of 1865, traveling from Erie to Lockport, Gottschalk's train went off the tracks.

"The first time in six months," said the conductor proudly.

"For me, the forty-eighth time in three months," amended Gottschalk wearily in his diary.

Up in Boston, Lowell Mason told the city fathers that if America desired music, America must teach her children to sing. The fathers heard him, and from east to west public school children were taught to read music. Mason's son, William, went down to New York and began to work with Theodore Thomas, who had enterprise enough for ten ordinary men. Programs of serious chamber music were introduced with a daring brochure which declared that "the novel feature of the entertainment will be the presentation of music rarely heard even in Europe: the later quartets of Beethoven, the works of Schumann, Schubert, Franck, Volkmann, Brahms, Rubinstein and Bärmann."

The experiment succeeded and Thomas went further. Gathering together musicians enough for an orchestra, he began a series of symphonic concerts in Irving Hall, followed by summer concerts nightly in Central Park Garden. Greatly daring, Thomas interlarded the "serious" programs with Strauss waltzes and told his audience that good music need not always be dull. Rocking with joy to *The Blue Danube*, his audience watched the conductor beat the first note of every measure up instead of down "because," said Thomas, "you cannot put continuous motion into dance music if you knock the poor tune down at the beginning of every measure."

Until now, America had believed that pleasant-sounding music was either "low," in the class with black-face comedians, or dangerous, savoring of Latin decadence, of Paris gentlemen who wore gloves on their hands and lived upon the sweat of other men's brows. Folk music already had a place in America, but art music had no part in the republican movement—the movement against kings and titles and all that went on in palaces where dukes had kept musicians like slaves to do their bidding, and ladies made beauty and immorality synonymous terms. The notion that "classical music" could be not only pleasing but inspiring was foreign to any but a few eastern-seaboard cities.

The year before Rubinstein sailed for New York, a young man named Henry Finck, ambitious for an education at Harvard College, boarded the new east-bound train at San Francisco. "In our Oregon home," wrote this boy who was later to be one of America's greatest music critics, "Liszt was unknown; we did not have the right kind of piano or necessary technique for his pieces. What is stranger, we did not know Chopin." On the way east, whistles blew frantically to get the buffalo off the track; Indians crowded the stations, and one night young Henry was wakened by hands fumbling over his body, searching for his money belt. Arrived in Boston, he strolled into Ditson's Music Store and saw a collection of *Nocturnes* printed between bright red covers, signed by one F. Chopin. Finck carried the new red book into a basement room at college and played the *Nocturnes* to himself, weeping, trembling, wondering if god or devil had written this rich, wild music . . .

It was fortunate for America when Anton Rubinstein accepted Mr. Grau's offer in Vienna that winter of 1872. Already, New York knew his orchestral music; Theodore Thomas had seen to that. The Thomas Orchestra had played the *Faust* scenes, the overture to *Dmitri Donskoy* and the *Humoreske* from *Don Quixote*. As composer, the name of Rubinstein was classed with Brahms and Raff— music not quite so disagreeable as Brahms' and not quite so pleasing as Raff's. Nothing like this advent had happened to the New World; the Marios, Grisis, Jenny Linds, Ole Bulls were marvels, miracles. But Rubinstein was not a miracle. He was a tough-minded, cultivated musician of the first water, Director of a great Conservatory, a man on familiar terms with Tsars, Queens and operatic tenors.

At last, Europe had recognized America. At last, their front-rank men were leaving Paris, Leipzig, Petersburg—all the strange nostalgic names that had once been home to Americans. At last, art was coming to the New World. Not charlatanism, but the real thing.

Anton Rubinstein was its harbinger.

24

1872. The New World receives Anton Rubinstein

THE *Cuba* landed in New York on the morning of September 10th. Anton Rubinstein, morose, shabby, shattered by ten days of seasickness, was led from the docks by Wieniawski, fiddle case in hand. Wieniawski never looked shattered: he was as *soigné* as Anton was careless. With his dark moustache and imperial, his dark clothes and the ribbon in his buttonhole, Henri Wieniawski looked every inch the artist, but every inch also the man of the world. Among musicians, Wieniawski was almost as famous for his wit as for his violin-playing—and his wit was not always charitable. Under heavy, lazy eyelids his bold, prominent dark eyes flashed suddenly upon the conversational opponent who braced himself instantly for the sally that was sure to come.

In a haze of mid-September New York heat, the two drove to the Clarendon Hotel on Fourth Avenue at 17th Street and left their baggage, then went at noon to call upon their sponsor, William Steinway. Rubinstein professed himself much pleased with the new Steinway Hall and the instrument he was to use. Then the two went home to their hotel and began straightway to practice. The first concert was to be on September 23rd.

A day passed, two days, and in the evening, trying to practice with his windows open on the noisy street, hot gaslight pouring on his damp face, his coat off, his collar open, Rubinstein, pausing for a cigarette, heard below his window, against the roar of wheels and the sharp sound of horses' hooves, another sound. Music! Why, they were playing Meyerbeer's *Torch Dance*!

Rubinstein and Wieniawski, hurrying to their window, saw in the street below a whole orchestra playing away for dear life and playing very well, like a professional symphonic ensemble. It was Carl

Bergmann, leading the Philharmonic in a serenade. Only one other visiting artist had received this honor—the Sweet Warbler herself, Jenny Lind. The street was crowded with listeners almost to Union Square. They played the *Rienzi* Overture. How could America know that Rubinstein hated Wagner? Wieniawski grinned sardonically, then was silent as the orchestra swung softly into the Andante from Beethoven's Fifth Symphony.

Anton was touched. He wished to thank the musicians. After the serenade some of them came to his room. In default of words, Anton sat down to his piano and played the music he loved best—Chopin, Beethoven's March from the *Ruins of Athens*, Liszt's magnificent transcription of the *Erlking*. Young Maurice Grau, who was present, had never heard music like this. Moreover, he had never met a man like this.

"Rubinstein sat, genial yet grave. . . . I never saw anyone with such magnetism. He had a perfectly enchanting smile. When he was pleased his rugged Tartar face would become quite sunny and fascinating."

Monday evening, September 23rd, was as hot as New York can be in September. Steinway Hall was packed to the doors. People stood on the stairs, overflowed down the steps into the street. From all over the country, artists had come to hear Rubinstein and Wieniawski; Anna Mehlig, the pianist, had traveled all the way from California. Carl Bergmann conducted the Philharmonic Orchestra, and various singers were included on the program. When Rubinstein, raising his hands, crashed down upon the opening chords of his *D Minor Concerto*, the audience, according to eyewitnesses, went suddenly quite crazy. They stood up and began to shout. . . . And indeed, more than one tough-minded critic has borne witness to the amazing magic of Rubinstein's attack. If Leopold Auer and Sir George Grove were struck dumb by it, what of America that had known only Messieurs Herz, Thalberg, Jaell and Wallace?

That night, besides his own *D Minor Concerto*, Rubinstein played Handel, Beethoven, Mozart, Schumann, and for encore, his own *Melody in F, Valse Caprice,* and his enchanting *Barcarolle in G.*

But when, at the close, he was recalled again and again, Anton's bows were remote; he gazed stonily over the heads of a howling, frenzied audience. Obviously, this was not a man to cajole the groundlings. He had come to play the piano. He had played it, and now his evening, quite evidently, was finished. Flowers were presented, masses of roses; someone mounted the stage to offer a silver wreath on a white satin cushion. Anton looked at it and shook his head, unsmiling.

Maurice Grau, in the wings, knew what was the matter. So did William Steinway. In the very middle of the *D Minor Concerto*, while Rubinstein was trying to play *pianissimo*, a terrible howl had arisen from under the open windows on the east side of Steinway Hall, while on the west side was heard a fearful pounding. Anton had turned to the wings and thrown at Steinway a beseeching glance, and the latter had rushed out and bribed two colored gentlemen to cease their employment: one was splitting kindling, the other was training his dog to jump rope.

Next day Anton called upon Mr. Steinway, in his arms a large canvas bag filled with gold and silver. They had told him in Europe, explained Anton, that most Americans were rascals, their paper currency quite worthless since the War of the Rebellion. His contract had arranged, therefore, that he be paid semi-monthly, in advance—and all in specie.

"What," said Anton, helplessly, "shall I do with all this money?"

Gravely Mr. Steinway suggested that the Bank of the Metropolis would exchange these coins with no loss to the owner. Anton returned to Seventeenth Street much cheered.

Five times Rubinstein and Wieniawski played in New York, always with success, then prepared to go on tour. It was to be an ordeal and Rubinstein knew it. His contract called for no fewer than seven concerts a week. Daily, before his departure, Anton stopped at Steinway Hall, hoping for Russian mail, and the afternoon before he was to leave for Boston—October 10th—a bulky registered letter was handed to him. It contained letters from his wife and children and a batch of new photographs of the family. With tears in his eyes,

236

"Friend Steinway," said Anton, "I am so happy that I must play for you." The doors were closed; Anton sat at the piano until midnight.

"We were spellbound," wrote Steinway. "Such heavenly playing I had never heard before. At the risk of being called sentimental, I must say that on that memorable night, while Rubinstein played the *Erlking*, it appeared to us as if we heard the voice of the little child, the clattering of the horses' hooves, the wild entreaties of the Erlking, as plainly as if we had witnessed it all ourselves. As I went home that night, I thought truly that was a day that could never be repeated in all the course of my life."

And now the Rubinstein Troupe, as it was called, started off for Boston. There were the singers, Liebhart and Ormeny, and various instrumental players. One of these was Wulf Fries, the 'cellist, whose place in the Boston Theatre Orchestra was taken by young Henry Finck during the tour. Boston led America in what was frankly called "culture," and Boston had a right to lead. Longfellow, Emerson, Oliver Wendell Holmes flourished; William Dean Howells had just taken over the editorship of the *Atlantic Monthly*. The new president of Harvard College was a fiery young man called Charles Eliot, who actually believed in the arts as education and said so, hurling into the news such pronouncements as: "Music, rightly taught, is the best mind-trainer on the list. We should have more of the practical subjects like music and drawing and less grammar and arithmetic."

Rubinstein stayed at the Tremont House, practicing vigorously in his room, besieged with would-be pupils. He was extraordinarily generous with these. One girl especially he taught every day, pacing the room while she played, running his hands through his hair, often impatient, often angry. At such times his eyes darkened, changed color completely; he would push his pupil from the piano stool and sitting down, play himself, breathing heavily, his eyes half closed and always, when he rose, dissatisfied with his performance.

Boston gathered to watch "this Russian genius" come down the steps of the Tremont House; Boston wrote descriptions in the paper, mentioning his seedy clothes, his string tie hanging down over his

I

Boston den 14ten October
1872

Lieber Herr Steinway

Die waren so freundlich mir zu
versprechen sich mit meinen Geld-
angelegenheiten hier beschäftigen
zu wollen — ich schicke Ihnen hier
den check von Hoon ein, Ihnen
die einzucassiren wie Sie es für gut
befinden werden. —

Außerdem bitte ich Sie, sollte mir
hierzulande ein Unglück zustoßen
daß ich sterbe, oder dergleichen Unan-
nehmlichkeiten, das Geld welches ich
bei Ihnen zu Gute habe, meiner
Frau Wera Rubinstein geborene
von Tschikouanoff in St. Petersburg
schicken zu wollen.

Mit besten Grüßen, vielen Dank
und verfluscht viel Concerten

Ant. Rubinstein

coat, his untied shoelaces, his socks that fell over his shoes. Anton's impatience grew daily. "Damn many concerts!" he wrote William Steinway in German on October 14th, the day of his first Boston appearance.

After Boston, the tour began in earnest. Every night Rubinstein played in a different town, frequently boarding the train immediately after his concert—Buffalo, Toronto, Montreal, Detroit, Cleveland. In Chicago the drinking water was so muddy the citizens laughed and said it was nourishing as food. There was cholera in the States that year. "Slowly and steadily," said the *Boston Globe*, "the disease is moving along our great arteries of travel from South to North."

Asiatic cholera was no new thing to Anton Rubinstein. He feared it less than he feared the sheer weight of business that pressed upon him, the greedy, ever-present audience that waited, night after night, demanding his best, demanding music and more music. A kind of horror descended upon him.

"Each day I feel unhappier," he wrote William Steinway from Cincinnati. "I think often of breaking my contract. The tour makes no end and becomes daily more difficult, more unbearable. We play so often in the same town that now I even have reached the end of my repertoire and must study and memorize new pieces. I cannot give the public always the same. But we travel every day and I have no time to practice. . . ."

Anton Rubinstein, with the longest repertoire in Europe, learned new pieces for the citizens of Detroit, and Maurice Grau, his manager, watched and marveled.

"The moment he arrived in his hotel room," wrote Grau, "Rubinstein would begin to practice. He never slighted a single audience, no matter how small, by neglect or carelessness. He studied and worked, studied and worked continuously. How his constitution stood the immense strain is remarkable. Yet there was never a complaint. His was the most lovable disposition imaginable."

Over in Rome, Franz Liszt, hearing about the tour, called it a "steeplechase *de concerts*." But if Rubinstein did not complain to his manager of hard work, he complained of other things. He resented fiercely the personal publicity of an American tour, resented the sight of his photograph in shop windows and on wallboards, and was pacified only when in a western town he and Grau came upon the portrait of the Reverend Henry Ward Beecher plastered from end to end of the city. It was an awful portrait; it made Mr. Beecher look like a murderer.

"Is it a priest, then, who will lecture?" asked Anton in wonderment. "His face looks even more dreadful than mine. It must be that such portrait advertisement is not so insulting as I had thought."

Absurd things happened, wild things that could never have occurred in Europe. There was the evening—recounted afterward by Anton himself at a dinner party at Madame Clara Schumann's—when Rubinstein, resting in a little room backstage, looked up to see a head thrust in the door.

"Don't you think, Boss," said a good-natured voice, "that it's about time to have your face blacked for the show?"

Poor, bewildered Madame Schumann gasped when she heard this story. "And did you do it?" she asked. "Did you paint your face black?"

It was a far cry from Madame Schumann's dinner table to Memphis, Tennessee. Anton would bear anything so long as he heard occasionally from home.

"My mother in Odessa has written that she received the last money I sent her, but there is no letter from my wife. Who knows what goes on at home—sickness, accident? All kinds of thoughts go through my head." So wrote Anton to William Steinway as the troupe went southward. New Orleans seemed actually civilized; one spoke French there, gentlemen bowed when they were introduced, colored servants fetched one's hat, smiling, not addressing one by the friendly title of "Boss," "Pardner" or "Professor."

Baltimore, Philadelphia . . . Anton was tired. His musical memory began to fail. Once, playing his *D Minor Concerto* that he knew better than his name, he forgot in the middle; but shaking his locks, as the newspapers reported, "he wove appropriate harmonies and sequences with his great paws, and like a true lion, kept on to the end." Over and over, in city after city, Anton played his encores, played them in a kind of rage, as though the audience were his enemy and he must battle or perish. His own *Valse Caprice* was a favorite everywhere; when he flung his hands in air, the audience waited breathlessly to see if he would strike that high E flat. Frequently he missed it, but nobody minded. In Philadelphia's Academy of Music, when Anton finished playing the *Appassionata*, an habitually staid audience rose to its feet shouting *"Bravo, bravissimo!"*— strange foreign words that came suddenly from the heart, uncalled, like a child's cry of delight. Backstage, dripping with sweat, his shoulders sagging, Anton told his manager he would give no more encores that night. "I have played enough."

Maurice Grau shook his head. "These people have paid to hear you, Mr. Rubinstein." Anton "catapulted onto the stage," says a contemporary report, "as if shot from a cannon, and roared into the Chopin *Berceuse*, playing it very fast, beating the bass hand as in a wild barbaric dance. He was in a frenzy."

Anton was tired. He began to quarrel with Wieniawski. Rumor has it the two artists never spoke to each other except during rehearsal, although on the stage they played together divinely, as if cast in one mold. They played the *Kreutzer Sonata* without notes, and with a fire and a fury that electrified America. Wieniawski played many of his own compositions, the lovely *Legende*, the brilliant Polonaises in A and D, the *Concerto in D Minor*. He played Paganini's *Carnaval de Venise*, and always he played like the Slav he was, sliding and swooping, adding fireworks to every cadenza. Wieniawski was as impetuous, musically, as Rubinstein himself. And musically, Anton was outspokenly his champion, declaring that no violinist but Paganini had ever equaled him. This was high praise in a violinistic era that enjoyed such stars as Joachim, Ernst, Ole Bull, de Bériot, Spohr, Sivori, Lipinski, David, Léonard, Alard and Sarasate.

Rubinstein had known Wieniawski for years and had been, indeed, dubious about signing a contract with a man who notoriously broke his professional appointments whenever he felt indisposed to play. In America, however, Wieniawski appeared on the stage with clocklike punctuality, owing to a contract that forfeited a thousand francs for every non-appearance. Nevertheless, the contract itself made continued friendship between the two artists almost impossible; Anton received twice as much money for every concert as Wieniawski and usually, twice as much applause. By the time the western tour was ended and the two were back in New York, Wieniawski was complaining openly to the newspapers that he would never have come to America had he known he was to play second fiddle to Anton Gregorovitch.

Anton complained to no newspapers, but he was heard to mutter dark words on leaving rehearsal. As for professional critics, Anton could never have complained to them because he hated them. It was their fault, he said, that the American people looked too lightly upon the serious art of music. It was their fault that the Rubinstein Concerts were discussed in print under the heading of "Amusements"; it was they who had permitted the publication of letters demanding the inclusion of popular music in the Rubinstein programs. Openly, Rubinstein told the gentlemen of the press that he liked neither their tactics nor their ideas. The young people of America, quite obviously, considered music as a mere accomplishment or adornment, "as important as fine or fashionable dress," said Anton indignantly, "but not more important." It was the duty of musical critics to change such an attitude, not to foster it.

This was a musician who looked seriously upon his chosen profession. "Sturdy-minded," Maurice Grau called him, and above all men, Grau had reason to know. Manager and artist had frequent battles concerning program-making. It was nothing short of suicidal, said Grau, to play all-classical evenings. But, as the tour progressed, Grau noticed with surprise that the more severe Rubinstein made his program, the higher rose the gate receipts! Anton desired to give a *matinée* by himself, without orchestra, without singers, without Wieniawski's violin. A "recital," he called it; the word was yet new to America. For a long time Grau dissuaded him, declaring that America was not ripe for one-man concerts, that it would be too severe fare for New York to digest.

In January, 1873, two concerts were advertised to be held in New York's Academy of Music, on Irving Place.

The Great Combination
of the
Theodore Thomas
Concert Companies
and positively the last joint appearance of
Rubinstein   Wieniawski
and
Theodore Thomas
with his
Unrivalled Orchestra.

So far, so good. This was the kind of announcement America was used to; often it included the words *colossal, stupendous, magnificent*. But this time, underneath the first announcement appeared another.

Rubinstein's
Matinée d'Adieu
at Steinway Hall,
Monday afternoon, January 13, 1873,
at two o'clock.

Maurice Grau read the words and trembled.

The grand ensemble concerts went off very well, both in Brooklyn and New York. Grau had expected that. But what was Grau's amazement when the Monday *Matinée d'Adieu* gathered in the largest gate receipts of the entire tour to date—$3100. Rubinstein was jubilant. Now he could dispense with orchestras and singers, dispense with Wieniawski too, if that gentleman agreed. He could play Beethoven and Chopin and Liszt to his heart's content; he could cease amazing the public and begin to teach it. Suddenly pleased with the New World, Anton sat down and wrote a set of variations on *Yankee Doodle*, dedicating them to his American friend, William Mason.

Mason accepted the *Yankee Doodle Fantasia* gravely. He spent much time with Anton in New York, listening sympathetically to the bewildered questions of the Russian. Anton became very angry when people said to him, as they often did, "You, of course, do not need to practice, being a born genius who gets everything by nature."

"How can they say this to me," cried Anton, "after I have worked so hard?"

The dumb piano on a Rhenish steamer long ago, the big square piano at home in Moscow, with *Maman* standing, ruler in hand. . . . Pianos in hotel rooms in Paris, London, Amsterdam. Pianos begged from dealers in Vienna by a boy of sixteen: "Sir, may I use your instrument in the early mornings, before customers arrive at the shop?" Pianos in dingy boarding-houses, broken ivories, broken pedals, pianos out of tune and jangling. . . . Czerny, Diabelli, Clementi, scales, exercises, *Gradus ad Parnassum!* . . . Pianos in gas-lit American rooms, hot, steamy rooms filled with flies. A man's shoulders aching, eyes aching, a man wet with sweat from scalp to ankle. . . . "You, Mr. Rubinstein, of course do not need to practice."

"This is an ungracious man," said the American newspapers. "He will not accept social invitations; he refuses to show himself. Does he think he is royalty that he keeps so to himself?" Once at the door of Steinway Hall a girl handed William Mason paper and pencil. Would he please ask Mr. Rubinstein for an autograph? Rubinstein was upstairs; he opened the window and threw paper and pencil into the street. "Mason," he said, "I don't like your country. People pry too much into private affairs."

Anton was tired. January weather was bad that year, the streets heavy with melted snow; but all the world plowed through it to hear Rubinstein play. Hitherto, Boston had never given the Rubinstein Troupe a gate of over a thousand dollars, but when, after the New York *Matinée*, Rubinstein repeated the one-man program in Boston, he took in $2600. Never before had America so much as intimated that she would like to hear a one-man recital. Grau was amazed and said so, but Rubinstein shrugged his shoulders. "You have underestimated the power of good music," he told his manager.

In April, Anton conducted, in New York, his *Ocean Symphony* with Theodore Thomas' Orchestra. They played all six movements; the performance required a full hour, and the audience loved it, applauding wildly after each movement. That same night, Wieniawski played the Bach *Chaconne*, a severe piece, rough, rhythmic and austere. America was being educated—and America liked it, and said so with loud, heart-warming applause.

Up and down the eastern seaboard traveled Anton Rubinstein, playing, practicing, memorizing. In spite of all success it was, he declared, a nightmare existence. "God preserve the artist from falling into such slavery," he wrote, "and from being at the entire disposition of an impresario. It is all over with art then; only the shop remains. One becomes an automaton and the dignity of the artist is lost."

May arrived, and with it, sight of the end. Anton was to sail for home May 24th. Suddenly, new life poured into him. Before he left New York City, he would show America what real piano music meant! Calmly he informed Maurice Grau that he desired to give, not one farewell New York recital, but seven. He handed the programs to his manager, and his manager, blanching, ran his eye down the list and found not one relief. Not one Spanish dance with castanets clicking, not one rollicking folk tune! Bach, Handel, Scarlatti, Mozart, for the first recital. And for the second, nothing at all but Beethoven sonatas! Six of them in a row, with their *opus* numbers staring up. . . .

"Do they accept this kind of program in Europe?" Grau inquired desperately. Rubinstein replied that they were beginning to. Bülow played all-Beethoven recitals, Madame Schumann all-Schumann programs. For himself, he had only recently been converted to such programs but he believed in it from the historical-musical point of

245

view, and he felt sure it would do New York good to undertake such an afternoon.

"Undertake," thought Maurice Grau, was exactly the word. He began to feel slightly sick at his stomach, but there was no gainsaying a Rubinstein who had made up his mind. Subscribers received an advance brochure; in its proud superlatives is something touching. Evidently Grau burned the gaslight late the night he wrote this notice:

"Before giving the several programs of these seven recitals, it is impossible to refrain from calling attention to the vast knowledge, herculean power, and unmatched skill they require in their execution, and to hazard the doubt that any other executant than Anton Rubinstein would venture on their consecutive presentation."

On the afternoons of May 12th, 14th, 16th, 17th, 19th and 20th, Rubinstein played at Steinway Hall to an audience that grew daily more fervent and more respectful. Immediately after the sixth recital, Anton went up to Boston for his last appearance there. He played, bowed his adieux—and was swamped by a sudden rush to the platform. People tore at his clothes, desiring a handkerchief, a button for souvenir. Women embraced him, weeping, and the theatre rocked to shouts of "Come back soon, Rubinstein! Come back again to us!"

Dazed, but pleased in spite of himself, Anton took the night train for New York and next evening met for the last time his American public in a whole program of his own compositions, ending with the brand-new *Yankee Doodle* variations. Then he came down from the platform, wiped his brow with a large, torn handkerchief and told a lady reporter from the *Tribune* that he was through forever with being a pianist. He was going home to Petersburg to write sacred operas. Perhaps America would produce them, America that had no established religion to combat and no politico-religious censorship. Warming to his theme, Rubinstein told the lady reporter he would like his children to be American citizens. "America," said he, "is the land for those who love liberty."

But it was to William Steinway that the real valedictory was made. There was a farewell supper at the Café Brunswick. Toasts were drunk, and Rubinstein responded with a speech that surprised everybody.

"Mr. Steinway," said Anton, "I have found in America something I least expected to find. While I knew that first-class American pianos stand unexcelled by any in the world, I had no idea that such a country had an orchestra like Theodore Thomas'. Never in my life, although I have given concerts in St. Petersburg, Vienna, Berlin, Paris, London and other great centers, have I found an orchestra that was as perfect as the organization Theodore Thomas has created and built up. When he accompanies me with his orchestra, it is as though he could divine my thoughts, and then as though his orchestra could divine his. It is as perfect as the work of some gifted pianist accompanying a singer with whom he has often rehearsed. I know of but one orchestra that can compare with that of Theodore Thomas', and that is the orchestra of the Royal Academy of Paris, which was established by the first Napoleon in the year 1808, into which only artists, when young, are admitted; and they may have any number of rehearsals until they arrive at absolute perfection. It is that orchestra alone which is as perfect as Theodore Thomas', but, alas, they have no Theodore Thomas to conduct them!"

On May 24th, Rubinstein sailed for home, taking with him sixty thousand well-earned dollars and the good-will of a continent. Not only had this man played his best for thousands of people who did not know music, but he had talked eagerly with the leaders of music, urging them to organized efforts for the propagation of musical education. When Leopold Damrosch in New York said he longed for an orchestra to lead, Anton replied that this was no hopeless ambition. "Begin by founding an oratorio society. This will lead to other things." Immediately, Dr. Damrosch collected eighteen singers who called themselves the New York Oratorio Society, and as Anton had predicted, four years later the Symphonic Society came into being, with an orchestra worthy the powers of the father of Walter Damrosch.

Rubinstein sowed fertile seed in the New World. In Baltimore, he expressed himself amazed at the princely legacy George Peabody had left to music, and more amazed that it was not put to better practical use. A first-rate conservatory could be handled with this sum. "I have done it myself," said Anton sturdily. Every American musician whose orbit touched his went away disturbed, inspired. In Central Park Garden, Theodore Thomas soared off with his orchestra to programs no impresario would have dared before the Rubinstein concerts paved the way. As to the *Ocean Symphony*, New York cried for it. Every Thursday night, Thomas played it, raising the admission price to pay the extra players required for an orchestration so modern and elaborate. In spite of the higher price, Thursday audiences proved the largest of the week.

Somebody wrote a monologue called *How Ruby Played*, and from Boston to New Orleans, young lady elocutionists seized upon it as the perfect recitation for church socials. Old ladies may be found to this day who can "recite" it, word for word, and it may be purchased in a brisk, yellow-backed booklet entitled *One Hundred Choice Selections*. From Texas, Joe Brownin comes to New York, hears Rubinstein play and tells about it in the vernacular of his day.

The piece is valuable because it describes a quality of Rubinstein's playing that was peculiar to him and that affected not only simple persons of the Joe Brownin type, but listeners of the most worldly and intellectual kind. While Rubinstein played, Joe Brownin saw pictures; actual faces floated before him, the figures of men and angels. And so did William Steinway see pictures, and Sir George Grove saw them, and that hard-boiled critic, James Huneker. Moreover, in his description of Rubinstein's violent physical motions at the piano, his indifference to the audience, Brownin did not exaggerate one item.

"Well, sir," says Joe, "Rubin had the blamedest, biggest, cattycorneredest pianner you ever laid eyes on: somethin' like a distracted billiard table on three legs. The lid was hoisted, and mighty well it was. If it hadn't been he'd a' tore the entire insides clean out, and scattered 'em to the four winds of heaven. . . . When he first

248

sit down, Rubin 'peared to keer mighty little 'bout playin', and wisht he hadn't come. He tweedle-leeded a little on the treble, and twoodle-oodled some on the bass—just foolin' and boxin' the things' jaws for bein' in his way. I says to the man sittin' next to me, says I: 'What sort of fool playin' is that?' And he says, 'Heish!'

"I was just about to git up and go home, bein' tired of that kind of foolishness, when I heard a little bird waking up away off in the woods, and call sleepy-like to his mate, and I looked up and see that Rubin was beginning to take some interest in his business. It was the peep of day. The light came faint from the east, the breezes blowed gentle and fresh, some more birds waked up in the orchard. People begun to stir, and the gal opened the shutters. . . . Next thing it was broad day and the whole world as bright and happy as a king. Seemed to me like there was a good breakfast in every house in the land, and not a sick child or woman anywhere. It was a fine mornin'.

"And I says to my neighbor: 'That's music, that is.'

"Presently the wind turned; it began to thicken up, and a kind of gray mist came over things; I got low-spirited directly. Then a silver rain begun to fall. . . . The moonlight came, and splendid marble houses rose up, with fine ladies in the lit-up windows, and men that loved 'em, but could never get a-nigh 'em, who played on guitars under the trees, and made me that miserable I could have cried because I wanted to love somebody, I don't know who, better than the men with the guitars did. . . .

"All of a sudden, old Rubin changed his tune. He ripped out and he rared, he tipped and he tared, he pranced and he charged like the grand entry at a circus. 'Peared to me that all the gas in the house was turned on at once, things got so bright, and I hilt up my head, ready to look any man in the face, and not afraid of nothin'. He lit into them keys like a thousand of brick; he set every livin' joint in me a-goin', and not bein' able to stand it no longer, I jumped spang onto my seat, and jest hollered: *'Go it, my Rube!'*

"Then he changed his tune again. . . . I heard the church bells over the hills. The candles of heaven was lit, one by one. . . . I tell you the audience cheered. Rubin, he kinder bowed, like he wanted to say, 'Much obleeged, but I'd rather you wouldn' interrupt me.'

"He stopt a moment or two to ketch breath. Then he got mad. He run his fingers through his hair, he shoved up his sleeve, he opened his coattails a leetle further, he drug up his stool, he leaned over, and, sir, he just went for that old pianner. He slapped her face, he boxed her jaws, he pulled her nose. . . . He knockt her down and he stampt on her shameful. . . . She bellowed like a bull, she bleated like a calf, she howled like a hound. The house trembled, the lights danced, the walls shuk, the floor came up, the ceilin' come down, the sky split, the ground rokt. . . .

"Bang! He lifted himself bodily into the a'r and he come down with his knees, his ten fingers, his ten toes, his elbows, and his nose, striking every single solitary key on the pianner at the same time. The thing busted and went off into seventeen hundred and fifty-seven thousand five hundred and forty-two hemi-demi-semi-quivers, and I know'd no mo'."

Anton Rubinstein would have liked Joe Brownin; Nicholas would have adored him. Nicholas and Joe would have gone out together and got happily drunk; Anton would have wished to teach Joe to play the piano. Always serious about music, always the crusader, Rubinstein—the complete professional—knew what he was doing and did it. Whether he played Mendelssohn, Field, Moscheles, Scarlatti or Beethoven, the New World heard him and wakened to things it had dreamed of but had never known.

On the twenty-fourth of May, 1873, Anton Rubinstein sailed for Liverpool, leaving the New World forever.

25

1873-1878. The villa at Peterhof Death of Villoing

ANTON landed in Hamburg and made the journey to Petersburg overland. He felt tired, ill from ocean and from the cruel demands of his journey. Few indeed could withstand the rigors of that American tour. Von Bülow tried it a few winters later and fell ill after the first concerts. Madame Essipov went over too, leaving Petersburg with a high heart, but neither her beauty nor the excellence of her piano playing was able to capture American hearts. "America is a nightmare," wrote Wagner to Liszt. "If the New York people should ever make me an offer, I should be in the most awful quandary."

Anton had faced America and had come away victorious. He looked forward to his homecoming with a mixture of sadness and joy. Petersburg would be very different without Helena Pavlovna. Always upon arrival, he had reported himself to the Michael Palace. Now in the Michael Palace Helena's daughter, the Grand Duchess Catherine, held court. For six months, Anton had known of Helena Pavlovna's death. But in America, amid strange scenes, living a strange, unnatural life, he had not truly realized his loss. He had dreaded the moment when he would realize it. Now the moment was here; it would attack him with unbearable sharpness when he stepped upon the open square outside Petersburg station. Very soon, tomorrow morning if possible, he would go to the palace and talk with someone who had loved Helena Pavlovna—old friends like Julie Abaza or the Countess Bludov. He must find out if Helena Pavlovna had suffered, if that bright spirit had been dimmed before she died. Surely she had met death quickly, bravely, as she had met life always. . . .

In the swamps about Petersburg little blue flowers blazed; under the rushes the water was still high from the thaw, the birches not yet in full leaf. Did all the world hold a glory like the northern spring? Anton told himself he never wanted to see another theatre full of faces. He would stay in Russia, retire from the concert stage and spend the rest of his life writing music. In his mind another sacred opera was germinating; he must write Mosenthal immediately about the libretto. At the hotel in Hamburg a tune had presented itself, a full musical theme that would do well for the first movement of a symphony. Anton had jotted it down in D minor.

There was really nothing to prevent his devoting himself to composition. The American money should last for years, provided Vera's ideas had not grown with Herr Steinway's money orders. Already Vera had completed her plans for the country villa. The wooded acres lay ready at Peterhof; Vera was only waiting her husband's approval before setting the workmen to hammer the thing together. Anton smiled. Even if they sank every one of the American dollars in Peterhof, it would be worth the money to give Vera a toy for her spare time so he could write music in peace. Besides, Peterhof was beautiful; it would be splendid to bring up one's children within sight of the sea and the fortress of Kronstadt, with the battleships ranged in the roads, flying the Tsar's colors.

Eagerly, as the train approached Petersburg, Anton counted the familiar sights. Vera was at the station, dressed all in summer white and looking handsomer than he had remembered. Both children were with her, Alexander quite tall and slim at six, his baby plumpness gone. Little Anna trailed at her nurse's side, dancing, animated, her yellow hair and blue eyes enchanting. Droshkys waited in rows before the station, their bearded drivers standing up to shout the advantage of their equipage in language picturesque and hearty. How good to hear Russian spoken, to sit with one's family in the open landau and bowl along through the fresh, sharp June air! Compared with this, New York had been almost tropical. In the river, ships lay at anchor, along the quays sailors walked, the ribbons from their caps blowing against red, healthy cheeks. Passing under the gray bulk of Saint Isaac's Cathedral, Anton squinted up to where the sun struck fire from a golden dome. Down the Neva the slim spires of the Peter Paul Fortress cut sharp against a light-blue sky. The Winter Palace was even vaster than he had remembered; along its roof the statues stood sentinel, shabby after the long winter, losing themselves amidst myriad chimney pots. The yellow and white Admiralty building looked very handsome and Western, with its white-columned portico. Across the river the University stood bravely red.

How good to be home, where a man was his own master! Maurice Grau was thousands of miles away. So were the autograph hunters, the button-grabbers. . . . The carriage stopped before his door in the Troitskaya Ulitsa and Anton sprang out, holding up his arms for baby Anna, his face shining, his heart full. Now in this hour, even death could be forgotten and the loss of old, dear friends. Anton Rubinstein was home again. Life lay before him, and work, and more work.

"In France," wrote Anton in his little book, "I take my pleasure. In Italy, Spain and Switzerland, I marvel. In Germany, I think. In England, Holland and Belgium, I work. In America, I play a part, like an actor. Everywhere, I love. But in Russia, I *live*."

Anton took his family out to Peterhof and rented a small villa, amused to walk through the woods in the early afternoon and watch his new house go up. He had been round to see Julie Abaza who told him that the Grand Duchess Catherine, who was abroad, planned to give Anton Gregorovitch a portrait statue of her mother for the Peterhof villa. Helena Pavlovna had known that her end was approaching; it had not come swiftly. They had been torn, watching her fail, watching her strength ebb. But her courage had not ebbed. She had not been bedridden; to the last she had kept on her feet, walking slowly with a stick, speaking slowly, with difficulty. It was this slow step, Julie Abaza said, that seemed more unnatural even than death, when death came.

Anton knew he must not think of this. He was glad he had not seen Helena Pavlovna at the end, glad he could remember her as swift and eager, coming toward him through the palace rooms, hands outstretched, her voice warm and welcoming.

There was but one anodyne for death, and that was life and hard work. Here in Russia there would be no traveling and no business; Anton could write music and practice all day. He began immediately to work on his opera, *The Maccabees,* and his *Dramatic Symphony* that was to become so popular. He said often that the best hours of his life were the hours of composition. "When a man is composing, he is happiest. Here he has his illusions and his dreams."

When autumn came Anton found himself caught up in the affairs of the Musical Society, which since July had borne the proud title of Imperial Society, the Grand Duke Konstantin having persuaded the government to take the Society under its wing. As for the Conservatory, Zaremba had died while Anton was in Vienna, Azantchevsky was Director now and was forever bringing Conservatory problems to the Troitskaya Ulitsa, notably the problem of where to house brilliantly talented young Jewish students whose parents were not permitted to live within the city limits.

Looking at Azantchevsky, a kind man, always agreeable, Anton felt misgivings. This job of Director had killed Zaremba; Azantchevsky was becoming paler and thinner under one's very eyes. It was a good thing that Imperial support gave the school an annual stipend—a small one, to be sure, but very necessary now that Helena Pavlovna was gone. The Grand Duke's interest in the Conservatory was intense but spasmodic; invariably when most needed he went off on a battleship cruise. Anton did what he could for the school but was fearful of involving himself; he had not resigned his directorship six years ago in order to spend his days working for the Conservatory *sub rosa.*

At Easter Anton went down to Odessa for his annual visit to his mother. Kaleria, at seventy-one, was as spry as ever. She had taken to caps, prim starched ones that became her surprisingly. On weekdays she wore a black one, on Sundays it was gray, but at Christmas and Easter she appeared in a white cap with frills around the edge. From beneath this badge and panoply of femininity her strong face and clear eyes emerged invincible. She was intensely interested in all that concerned America and the tour, showing surprise at nothing except the fact that Anton had not remained longer where gold was to be garnered in such gratifying heaps. "But I was a slave in that country!" her son protested. "I was not an artist but an automaton." Kaleria's lips pursed skeptically. "Art is none the less art when there is a large reward," said Kaleria Rubinstein, and could not be budged from her conviction.

From Odessa, Anton went to Milan, where, to his great pleasure, *Feramors* was performed, and with success. He was fond of this opera, always displeased when impresarios desired to use, as they often did, the very tuneful ballet music and omit all the rest. After Milan, Rubinstein went up to Berlin to see about a future performance of *The Maccabees*—no easy matter to arrange. Theatre directors refused point blank to stage these huge Biblical dramas unless Rubinstein came over from Russia to conduct them himself. At first, Anton complied; he was slow to realize that the crowded houses were due to his personal popularity rather than to his compositions.

The villa at Peterhof was completed that summer and the family moved into it, Vera quite beside herself with pleasure. Before a week was up, Anton had learned to love the place as his wife and children loved it. In the entrance hall facing the door stood Helena Pavlovna's statue. Young, beautiful, gracious, she greeted him whenever he entered this house, which until the end of his life was to mean refuge to a restless man. No matter how many platforms Anton mounted, what hisses or applause he endured, this hallway and this portrait would receive him in summer; fresh ocean airs would blow in his study window, giving him new life, new hope.

The house itself was a wooden affair in the worst of late nineteenth-century bay-window rococo style. Monstrous with turret, colored glass and tessellated roof, the villa was extravagantly admired by Rubinstein's friends. Inlaid floors, painted ceilings, marble busts of musicians decorated the drawing rooms downstairs. In the library were Rubinstein's trophies, carefully arranged by Vera in glass cases: huge wreaths of gold and silver gilt, batons, albums, illuminated addresses, addresses carved on silver and silver gilt. "There is of course nothing baronial about the villa," wrote an English girl pupil, "nothing in the style that the master of Abbotsford would look for; but it is elegant, luxurious and refined, just what might be expected from Rubinstein."

Anton was the child of his time and place. Why should he not love what was "elegant, luxurious and refined"? As a matter of fact, it was Vera who arranged this luxurious interior; Anton was concerned only with his fruit trees and with his private study in the turret, which a few chosen friends were permitted to visit. Leaning from his high window, Anton saw beyond the forest, wild ducks winging high above the Baltic; from the road he heard the wheels of country dogcarts. Far to the right gleamed the golden dome of Saint Isaac's above city roofs, and in the evening, the east wind carried to him the sound of vesper bells.

The turret room itself was very plain, furnished only with a piano, a big desk, a few chairs and an old divan. Anton had the floor lined with sawdust to spare the ears of his family, who frankly did not like to hear him practice. Nicholas' picture was on the desk; the only ornament was a bronze bust of Mephistopheles scowling from a corner. Looking about for the usual portraits of Beethoven, Chopin, Mendelssohn, Anton's friends were puzzled. Was it possible that Rubinstein was not so tough as he seemed? He who seemed ruthless, strong and wise—did he, like other men, need armor against the world, need a reminder that to maintain one's position one must be more than a little wicked, and that art for art's sake could not always prevail against the forces of Mammon and the hypocrisy of the righteous? Ever since he began to write *Paradise Lost*, years ago, Anton had admired Lucifer, the shining rebel, Mephisto, the Demon. When his friends came to the turret room, Anton would wave his hand toward the dark figure in the corner. "My inspiration," he would say.

This year of 1875, Rubinstein had need of such inspiration. Three major works were to receive first performance, which meant battles with impresarios and theatre directors—the only kind of battle

256

Anton Rubinstein shrank from. In January the brand-new *Dramatic Symphony* was played in Petersburg under the composer's baton. This was his fourth symphony, in D minor. It was well received, but Anton was so taken up with rehearsals for his opera, *The Demon,* that he scarcely knew if the symphony or himself was applauded—question raised fearfully by every composer in his own town.

Anton was always more concerned over his operas than over anything he wrote or played, and this special opera had been lying unheard for five years. Senff in Leipzig had finally consented to publish it. Shortly after he wrote it, Anton had played it one night for the *Five*, the *Kutchka*, at Stassov's house in Petersburg. Tamara had stood on a chair to sing to her Demon lover. For Rubinstein it had been a nightmare evening such as Tchaikovsky endured when first he played his new *B Flat Minor Concerto* to Nicholas Rubinstein. "How disappointing, how unbearable when a man offers his friends a dish of his work, and the other sits and remains silent!" Tchaikovsky reported to his friend Nadejda Von Meck. "Well, say something. Scold, in a friendly way, but for God's sake, one sympathetic word, even if uncomplimentary!" Anton Rubinstein was of tougher fiber than Peter Tchaikovsky, yet even Anton was shaken that evening at Stassov's. After each number there was silence. Cold with apprehension, Anton sat waiting—and heard no word. He who was never ill went home literally sick with disappointment and took to his bed for three days.

And now in January of 1875, the opera was to be performed at the Maryinsky Theatre with the composer at the stand. The management prophesied ruin, so did Anton's friends. They were wrong. The theatre was packed, the audience loved not only the music but this highly impossible, highly romantic story of the Demon who desired a mortal.

Of all Rubinstein's operas, *The Demon* is the only one that has survived. It is part of the regular repertory today in every Russian opera company; Petersburg and Moscow know it almost as well as they know Tchaikovsky's *Onegin*. The Demon's aria, "Without oar,

257

without sail," his song to Tamara, "Do not weep, my child," are whistled along Moscow's streets. The opera has been played all over Europe and in London and New York as well. It is the only Rubinstein opera that ever reached the Paris stage. By 1890 it had been given a hundred times in Russia alone.

Musically, *The Demon* will not bear strict analysis. The orchestration is standardized: angels, devils, mysterious moonlit caves are introduced each by its musical figure (Rubinstein would have scorned to call them *motifs*). When Rubinstein sat down to write an opera, the devils of self-consciousness seemed to attack him, devils that were not present when he wrote songs and piano pieces. Critics have tried to explain Anton's bad music by the fact that he wrote too fast. But the reason lies deeper. In these big works something came between the composer and the music, obscuring Anton's passionate desire for musical sincerity, damming the clear stream of melody that was his birthright. Rubinstein's character was plainly extrovert; he was the virtuoso, the doer, the actor who moves easily in the world, fearing no personal contact, rejoicing in battle and adversity. Yet when he desired to express himself in original musical composition, this very outgoingness stood squarely in his way. Contrast him with Tchaikovsky who, terrified of crowds and of every single personal contact outside his family, was able to project himself in his writings with fullest, sincerest expression, constrained, indeed, to spread his most secret personality over every measure he wrote.

Rubinstein was frankly elated by the success of *The Demon* at its Petersburg *première* in January of 1875. He hurried over to Berlin and persuaded the management to accept his latest opera, the Biblical drama called *The Maccabees*, promising to conduct it himself. In April the performance took place, the audience responding warmly to Rubinstein's appearance with the baton, slightly puzzled by the heavy Old Testament personages but enduring them all in good part. During the next seven years, *The Maccabees* was repeated forty-one times in various European cities: Dresden, Vienna, Munich, Leipzig. Berensdorf the critic wrote highly of it, declaring it rich in fantasy and color.

Anton played in Paris and then went home in May and began forthwith to compose another huge opera, *Nero,* working on it all summer very happily out at Peterhof. Autumn saw him touring Europe once more, playing and conducting. Down in Moscow he played his *E Flat Concerto* with Nicholas' orchestra, Nicholas conducting. The gay, showy *finale* was much enjoyed by Nicholas' players who surpassed themselves racing after Anton Gregorovitch. Anton, notoriously, could play faster and louder than any collection of musicians on earth. Afterward the brothers played Anton's *Fantasia for Two Pianos,* and Moscow stood up to shout its delight. Coming down the aisle when they were done, the brothers were seen to be arguing. "Nicholas, Nicholas," Anton said, "you played like a shoemaker. In God's name, can you never practice before a concert?"

Nicholas shrugged, grinning evilly at his brother. "Practice?" he said. "It is not for the gods to labor and strive like cobblers."

Anton spent Christmas at home. He had the Russian's love of feast day and ceremony, and suffered much when forced to spend Christmas alone or in foreign countries. In June he went over to London and played five times to an audience that was stirred in spite of itself. London critics, who often complained of the good pounds sterling carried away by visiting virtuosi, were impressed by Rubinstein's generosity. "He has played for both Philharmonic Societies for nothing," wrote Wilkes in the *Spirit of the Times,* "and the proceeds of his first concert next year will be devoted to the support of the unfortunate widow of a familiar friend."

Rubinstein was surprised at this British acclaim of his generosity. For years he had played all over Europe in charity concerts; it was nothing to him to turn over to a city his huge gate receipts. He went home and the forests of Peterhof received him like a benediction. All summer the villa was gay with friends who drove out in the long Northern twilight to hear Rubinstein play, sitting on the terrace beside the open French windows, silent and enchanted.

Leopold Auer came often with his violin; bearded, handsome Carl Davidov with his 'cello. That autumn *Paradise Lost* was performed in Dresden and just before Christmas, again in Petersburg with Rubinstein conducting. George Henschel the great German tenor came over from Berlin to sing *Lucifer*. Anton was happy.

But his contentment was short-lived. *The Maccabees* was scheduled for Petersburg performance and the operatic management was doing its best, as usual, to stop the performance. The Imperial Theatres, both in Petersburg and Moscow, were controlled by a single director who had the monopoly of all theatrical and operatic performances and private concerts given in the winter season, which lasted from September until Lent. Every detail was under Count Adlerberg's control; even posters and program notices must be printed by the Imperial press. Only the Musical Society was outside this law; it could give concerts every Saturday all winter, the court theatres being closed on Saturday.

Adlerberg was a terror, hostile to the Conservatory, which he considered a hotbed of radicalism, hostile to all "foreigners"—he was himself a German—and hostile especially to Jews. From first to last, Rubinstein had trouble with these various Imperial Theatre directors. Had he not possessed powerful friends at Court, none of his operas would have reached the Petersburg stage. As it was, when Count Adlerberg finally consented to produce *The Maccabees*, he wrote in the order, "The opera may be given provided the Imperial Theatre spends nothing for costumes or decoration."

Furious, Anton planned to leave Petersburg for Europe the evening of the performance. But his old friend Bessel would not let him go. He stood beside Anton in the wings, joking with him, comforting him, promising whole magnums of champagne when the performance was over. The opera was a success; Anton did not regret the money he had spent to supplement the management's niggardly outlay.

George Henschel was in London to receive Rubinstein in April— Henschel and Anton's old friend John Ella who welcomed Anton to 9 Victoria Street with a warmth that most of London was not

Alexandre Villoing

yet ready to show. Ella had "discovered" Anton Rubinstein years ago, and neither of them ever forgot it. When Anton arrived from Russia he always went straight to Ella's house and rushed at the little man, hugging him, kissing him heartily on both cheeks in a manner that astonished the bystanders. Then Anton would go to the piano and play his very best. So intense was Anton's concentration even in a simple, quiet Chopin Nocturne that the sweat gathered on his brow and dropped to the keys; afterward he went downstairs and stayed alone for an hour, to recover.

Everybody came to John Ella's; Robert Browning was there one night and told Anton he had better give up his idea of Biblical opera as far as England was concerned. The British would never stand for any tampering with sacred subjects. This was the London of Charles Hallé, of Henry Broadwood and of Max Schlesinger's Friday *soirées*. It was the London of the Monday "Pops," when all the world sat stiffly upon green upholstered benches and George Eliot wrote a friend that she always went in her bonnet, sat in the center of the hall and "heard to perfection for a shilling." If the music was soft and a door happened to open, one could hear from Christy's Minstrel Rooms downstairs a distant jingle of tambourines. Here Rubinstein played Schumann to an audience that was shocked because he took it more freely than Madame Schumann, whom at last London had learned to love. Most certainly, there was in Anton a quality that maddened English professional critics. One of them wrote: "any intelligent student could play Mozart's *Rondo* as well as this Moldavian, and as for the *Sonata Opus 106*, if Beethoven had been alive and not deaf, he would have dragged Herr Rubinstein by main force from the platform." Nevertheless, people came in crowds to hear Herr Rubinstein play, paying high prices for their tickets; the critics explained it by saying the people came "from curiosity."

Rubinstein conducted his *Ocean Symphony* and then went out to Windsor with George Henschel to play for the Queen.

The two were received in a long drawing-room, empty of people except the Queen and two of her ladies. The ladies retired to the far end of the salon; the Queen seated herself very near the piano where she could watch Rubinstein's face as he played.

Anton began with a Chopin Nocturne, soft and tender. The Queen's eyes glowed with pleasure. Then he pulled the stool closer and hurled himself into Liszt's transcription of the Erlking, the noisiest piece in Anton's repertoire. The child screamed: *Mein Vater, mein Vater!* The horses thundered. The instrument shook, the floor shook. The Queen's eyes widened. Carefully, so as not to disturb the player, she began to move her chair backward, hitching it along until she had arrived at a safe distance from the strings and hammers that threatened to fly into a thousand pieces.

At last it was ended. With the final chord, relief and pleasure spread over the Queen's face; she rose to thank Herr Rubinstein who bowed gravely and mopping his face with a large handkerchief, innocently took his departure.

Rubinstein went home next day. He was due in Petersburg for a ceremony of promotion. In June of 1877 the records tell us there was "Granted, to the Free Artist Anton Rubinstein, the title of Russian nobleman."

Three times, now, Anton had moved up a rung in the slow social scale: in 1858 when he became Director of an Imperial Theatre orchestra and was called "Government Clerk" instead of merely "Son of a Merchant of the Second Grade." This gave him citizenship and rights to a pension. Later, when his own Conservatory made him a Free Artist he advanced, actually, no further but was called "Free Artist" instead of "Government Clerk." Now he was an "hereditary nobleman." The Grand Duke Konstantin must have been busy about this at Court, Anton knew. He received the honor with the mixture of cynicism and gratitude that characterized all his relations with the Russian Court. For a Rubinstein to be "hereditary nobleman" was certainly absurd; moreover, compared with what Europe gave him, Russia's conventional rewards, so far, had been very slim, yet far more deeply coveted by Anton than any French or Prussian decoration.

Anton's mother had something to say about this new honor. She was of course delighted, but she did not confess it to her son. Kaleria's tongue was sharper than ever. "Hereditary nobleman!" she said, and made a clucking sound with her tongue. "You will be too proud now, my son, to mount the stage for money . . . like Nicholenka after his marriage to Krusheva."

Anton winced, then grinned delightedly. Kaleria never failed to strike home, and her son loved her for it. Liszt, during the last half of his career, had made the grand gesture of refusing money for concerts. "I shall always play for money," Anton told his mother gravely. "But if ever the time comes when I can afford it, I shall give away every kopeck that music earns for me."

When autumn came, Anton opened the Petersburg musical season by playing in a huge concert for the benefit of needy artists, a gesture he began to repeat yearly, as though in acknowledgment of the honors his city had conferred upon him. This year he received in Paris from Marshal MacMahon the *Légion d'Honneur*, wearing it, like his other decorations, very seldom. Auer says that in their long association he only once saw Rubinstein in full splendor with all his stars and ribbons upon his breast.

All winter, Anton was abroad, playing in Vienna, Amsterdam, Brussels, Paris, Königsberg, Hanover, Berlin, London. It was nearly July when he got home to Peterhof. Late summer was clouded by an event more nostalgic perhaps than sorrowful. Villoing died in Petersburg, an old man full of years. To the end he had taught music, although financially he did not need pupils at all. His pleasure in his craft was visible. Even when he was angry—and in his last years the old man had been extremely irritable—anyone entering the room, felt the challenge of this teacher's eagerness and knew within his own veins an answering quickening of the blood.

Nicholas came up from Moscow for the funeral. The brothers followed the coffin out to Alexander Nevsky Cemetery, walking sadly among the graves, grieved to lose their old friend, grieved also at the passing of years, the severance of this strong tie with their youth. "Do you remember," said Nicholas, looking down at the freshly turned earth over his teacher's grave, "do you remember,

263

Tonia, how slowly he tuned his piano, and how perfectly? How he held his ear to the strings, tapping and listening, and how he screamed with rage if we interrupted? Do you remember the stick, and how he beat us when we were lazy? Do you remember how he longed to praise us when we had played well, and then when he began to speak his conscience would stop him short with his face all red, and he would take off his spectacles and wipe his forehead, trying not to let us see that he was weeping?"

"I remember," said Anton slowly. "Nicholenka, I remember everything."

26

1878-1881. Alexander II is murdered. Death of Nicholas Rubinstein

ON THE fourth of July, 1878, in full daylight on the streets of Petersburg, the Chief of Police, Mezentsev, was stabbed to death by an assassin. Anton Rubinstein was out at Peterhof that day, writing an opera about a tyrant, *Nero*.

A year later, Mezentsev's successor was driving in his coach along the Swan Canal when a horseman galloped up, fired through the carriage window, hit his mark and galloped off. The Nihilist movement that had begun in a vague, exalted idealism, had grown into something far short of idealism. Its members vied with one another to commit ever more daring, more spectacular murders. From Petersburg to Berlin to Zurich to Paris the plotters moved, avoiding arrest, quarreling among themselves, jealous, suspicious of one another. Bakunin, the restless, planless, intellectual anarchist, died and was succeeded by the fanatics who had as their Bible the bloodthirsty *Catechism of the Revolutionist*:

"The revolutionist is a doomed man. He is merciless toward the state—and in turn need expect no mercy. He must be ready to die at any minute, must train himself to stand torture. . . . All tender, softening sentiments of kinship, friendship, love, gratitude and even honor itself must be snuffed out in him by the one cold passion of the revolutionary cause. Day and night he must have one thought, one aim—inexorable destruction. The revolutionist enters the world of the State and of the educated and privileged classes and lives in it only for the purpose of its fullest and quickest destruction. He is not a revolutionist if he is attached to anything in this world, if he can stop before the annihilation of any situation, relation or person belonging to this world—everybody and everything must be equally hateful to him. All the worse for him if he has any relations of kinship, friendship or love; he is not a revolutionist if they can stop his hand."

For everyone—monarchist, Slavophile, liberal and revolutionary —it was a depressing time. In Petersburg the students rioted frequently, angry because of police interference with their schedules. Censorship was stupid, shortsighted to a degree. Even so loyal a monarchist as Tchaikovsky wrote anxiously to Nadejda Von Meck: "How Russia would revive if only the Emperor could finish his wonderful reign by giving us political rights! It is wrong for them to say we are not ready for constitutional reforms. . . . One meets Cossack patrols at every step, as though we were in a state of siege. These are terrible times, fearful times. On the one hand, an absolutely terrified government, so abandoned to fear that Aksakov is exiled for a brave, truthful word. On the other hand, unhappy, mad youth, exiled in thousands without trial—exiled where even the crow brings no bones."

Alexander II had been on the throne nearly a quarter century; only a year or two remained before the assassin's bomb would send him to a horrible death. Already he felt the net closing in upon him. The Paris Commune had been a dreadful shock; thrones once more were tottering. The Great Liberator who had championed the rights of all minority peoples, who had freed millions of slaves throughout his empire, now in the late 1870's began to view with alarm and after the fashion of aging Romanov emperors, proclaimed a frank conservatism. Even the women had gone over to the enemy and were demanding "rights," a university education, the chance to become doctors and lawyers. Alexander Nicholaievitch disliked the very sight of a girl-student on the streets in cropped hair and a Garibaldi cap. Everyone not frankly Imperialist and Orthodox began to be identified with the revolutionary movement.

It was in the midst of such a city, such a time, that Anton Rubinstein saw fit to stage an opera wherein the chief character, a respectable but defiant Moscow merchant, was hung by his Tsar, the tyrant, Ivan the Terrible. Anton Rubinstein was anything but rebellious, politically; in his *Merchant Kalasknikoos* he had been innocent of any *double entendre*, any criticism of the State. He had merely chosen to write a Russian opera. And how can a man choose a plot from Russian history without somebody being murdered on one side or the other? The opera was scheduled for performance in January, 1880. The morning of that very day, a Nihilist was executed in Petersburg and the city buzzed with underground whisperings.

It was too much for the authorities. They let Kalasknikoos sing upon his *papier mâché* scaffold for one evening—but one evening only. Next day the opera was withdrawn from the repertory and no explanation vouchsafed. Rubinstein proclaimed angrily that he saw no reason whatever for this procedure, and put the *Merchant* on the shelf for another nine years.

Patriotism was in the air, a narrower, noisier patriotism than Russia had known since Napoleonic days. Anton felt its excitement and, artistlike, responded emotionally to something his reason was later to reject. He sat down and wrote a symphony—his fifth—filled it with Russian melodies and called it the *Russian Symphony*. How often, in the old days, Helena Pavlovna had urged him to write a Russian symphony! It was good to be able to fulfill her wish even though she could not hear this music. He dedicated the symphony to his old friend, and in October of 1880, conducted it from manuscript at a big charity concert. Petersburg loved this music. Everywhere, the symphony proved popular; next to the *Ocean* and the *Dramatic*, this became the best known and best liked of Rubinstein's six symphonies.

In March, Anton was in Spain on tour when disturbing news reached him. Nicholas was ill and had left Moscow for the Riviera in search of health. This was ominous. Only gravest necessity would tear Nicholas from his beloved Moscow. As for health, how could a man who ate hugely, drank hugely and never took time for sleep expect anything but bad health and headaches? Anton, furiously busy with concerts, was relieved to know that Moscow friends were with Nicholas. They would watch over him well.

A day or two later, news arrived that sent Russian travelers, shocked and sorrowful, hurrying for the Eastern border. Alexander II had been assassinated, blown to a mangled mass as he drove through the streets of his capital in an open carriage. Reading of his sovereign's end, of how he had lain upon a sofa in the Winter Palace and bled to death, Anton remembered the very room, the very couch. How often he himself had walked through that arched and golden place on his way to play for the Imperial family! He felt no quick and personal grief such as he had suffered when Nicholas I had died; instead, foreboding moved him, a vague dread of the future. Alexander's son would mount the throne, that huge young man who could bend an iron horseshoe in his fingers and whose patriotism took the form of many hatreds. Year by year this young man had watched the death of all his father's hopes, had seen his father threatened by bomb and hidden dagger and had grown to manhood hating every word that hinted of liberalism. Autocracy was Russia's only hope, a central government absolute and unyielding, lawmakers swift, imperial, unafraid. Alexander Alexandrovitch intended to set his country's affairs in order and to do it by the old way of tsarism: absolutism, the ukase and the knout.

Anton longed to go home and see for himself the state of his country. But first he must fulfill his concert engagements. He played and practiced, practiced and played, homesick, worried. He was due in Ireland in May, then Scotland and London. Von Bülow would precede him to London, Bülow, whom the British loved. Grimly, Rubinstein set himself to perfect a repertory that would, once and forever, show these British what could be done with a pianoforte under Russian hands, under the hands of an artist.

During the second week of March, Anton had word that Nicholas was still in Paris, consulting with doctors. Since playing at the Exposition three years ago, Nicholas had been well known in Paris. Anton knew that he would have the best of care; Helen Tretiakov wrote that Dr. Potin was visiting him faithfully, that Nicholas Gregorovitch was suffering from pains in his abdomen but there was no danger. On the 23rd of March, Anton received a wire that his brother was desperately ill with tubercular enteritis. He caught the first train north—but he was too late. Arriving in Paris, Anton heard that his brother was dead.

Nicholas Gregorovitch had not expected to die. Two years ago in Moscow he had begun complaining of his health, grumbling because he could not work and eat and drink as much as he liked. Dr. Zacharin warned him to be careful. Nicholas did not trust Moscow doctors; next time he was in Petersburg he would, he told his friends, consult Dr. Botkin. In Petersburg Anton frowned and told his brother he looked pale, that his clothes seemed too big for him. Nicholas went to see Dr. Botkin. The two had a pleasant hour reminiscing, exchanging highly spiced Moscow and Petersburg gossip. "Your health?" said Botkin. "Oh, one can envy you your health, Nicholas Gregorovitch! The cramps are mere colic. Try hot wine at bedtime. A full glass, taken not too rapidly."

But even the largest tumbler of wine did not relieve these abdominal cramps. Nicholas could bear pain easily, but during the summer of 1880, something other than pain began to visit him, something he had never experienced, that bewildered and troubled him. He was tired—not sleepy as if he had been playing cards all night—but exhausted, drained as it were of blood, limp, dizzy, depressed. Moscow took note that his concert programs had changed. "Nicholas Gregorovitch conducted the *Eroica* last night. Did you see his face after the *Marche Funèbre*? He is always playing funeral pieces." In October, Nicholas dragged himself to Petersburg to help Anton with his annual charity concert. At the end Nicholas, white and shaken, had to be helped from the platform. But he had played with fire and precision; he had not missed a note. Looking at his brother, Anton remarked that Nicholas was the better player of the two. "I dropped more notes than usual," said Anton gloomily. Accustomed to after-concert scoldings from his brother, Nicholas looked up, astonished. "I would exchange all the notes I ever played, Tonia, for just one of your dropped ones."

That night on the train for Moscow it was cold. Wrapped in his rug on the narrow seat, Nicholas slept fitfully, racked by pain, shivering, feverish. In the early morning at Klin station he dragged himself from the train for a glass of tea. Klin—Peter Tchaikovsky had a house not far from here. What a confounded nuisance the man was, with his everlasting divorce that didn't come off, with his neuroticism and his rich widow who gave him money to seduce him from his post at the Conservatory! The best theory teacher the school ever had, he would still be in his classroom except for Nadejda Von Meck. Every time he thought of Frau Von Meck, Nicholas' blood rose. After all that he, Nicholas Gregorovitch, had done for Peter Ilyich! Playing his pieces all over Europe, producing *Onegin* when the experts had condemned it as nothing but a sketch, a pleasing bit of lyrical nonsense. There was no gainsaying the fact that the man wrote better music than anyone in Russia. Paris had gone quite wild over the *B Flat Minor* concerto when Nicholas played it at the Paris Exposition of '78. And how furious the Five had been at home, because Nicholas had played Tchaikovsky instead of Moussorgsky, Borodin *et al.*!

Shivering, with his blanket round his knees, Nicholas watched Klin station go by and grinned, recalling the welcoming dinner in Moscow when he came home from the Paris Exposition. There had been quail, sturgeon, champagne in rivers. Peter Ilyich had been there. Responding to the first toast, Nicholas had risen and pointed straight at Peter. "It was not I who brought honor to Russia abroad," said Nicholas. "There is the man. He wrote the music. I only played it."

Peter Ilyich had gotten to his feet, blushing like a girl, had stumbled over a few words and fled the hall like a madman. God knows, musicians were hard to deal with. Not one of them had a practical bone in his body. Who would carry on the business of the Conservatory if he, Nicholas Gregorovitch, fell ill? Klindworth? These confounded pains, this everlasting weakness, fatigue, fever. . . . Perhaps he had better go abroad and take a cure.

In Moscow, Dr. Zacharin advised the Riviera. Nicholas had strength for only one or two farewell calls; he went to see old Countess Tolstoi whom he dearly loved and Prince Dolgoroukov who dearly loved Nicholas. The Prince was more outrageous than ever in his brown wig and stays, his dyed moustache and brightly rouged cheeks. "The Grand Duke Serge thinks I am too old to govern Moscow," he told Nicholas. "He wants my job for himself. . . . Go and get well, Nicholas Gregorovitch, and come back soon. Moscow needs you."

No one believed that Nicholas Gregorovitch was seriously ill. Nicholas himself, however, put his papers in order, burning many. He left with the Tretiakovs at midnight. Moscow gave him a farewell party, trooping to the station to see him off. Agathon loved it. Standing behind his master he received the farewells through the car window. "Don't stay long! Be well, Nicholas Gregorovitch, and play for us again very soon."

On the train it was gay; the food was marvelous. Olivier himself was on board—the most famous chef in Moscow, which was fame indeed. Olivier owned the Hermitage Restaurant. "Do you remember the dinner for Dostoyevsky last May?" Nicholas asked him. "That turtle soup, Olivier! You surpassed yourself." Olivier smiled. The singers Nicholas Gregorovitch had brought in had nearly ruined him, he said. Two hundred of them. Oh, they had sung well enough. But how they had eaten! Enough fish to stock a lake, and they had crept behind the serving screens and stolen strawberries by the quart from under the very eyes of those half-witted Tartar waiters. . . .

At Vilna the party received news of Tsar Alexander's assassination. Tretiakov, who was mayor of Moscow, turned around and went home immediately. But Madame Tretiakov stayed with Nicholas; at Berlin, other friends met the train and took him to a hotel. Racking along over Berlin cobblestones, Nicholas groaned, gasping, his hands over his abdomen. "I thought no streets so bad as Moscow streets, but now I know better." The women were anxious and hurried him on to Paris, where were doctors who knew their business. They settled in the Grand Hôtel, next door to the *Opèra*; Nicholas went to bed and the two women nursed him. He was really ill now and the doctor came daily. "You must not eat so much," Potin told his patient, frowning at the loaded tray by the bedside. "Great men always eat a lot," Nicholas replied serenely. "Beethoven was a huge eater. Do you know what Schopenhauer said to somebody who was shocked to see him devour his dinner? 'I eat a great deal, sir, because I have a great mind.'"

With his left hand against the wall, Nicholas began to run imaginary scales, flexing his fingers. *"Je ne perdrai pas l'habitude du piano, n'est-ce pas, Docteur?"*

Potin smiled and shook his head. "In a week's time, I hope that Paris can hear you play."

In spite of his pain, Nicholas' room was gay with visitors. All the musicians in Paris visited him: Saint-Saëns, Colonne, Pasdeloup, Madame Viardot-Garcia. Turgenev, too, came often, more apprehensive than the doctors, fearing Nicholas' unnatural thinness, avoiding the sight of his hands from which the flesh had fallen, revealing enormous bones, wide transparent reaches at the base of the fingers. A Madame Ivanovska, admirer of Nicholas' playing, left her card, asking Nicholas Gregorovitch to visit her as soon as possible. Nicholas sent word that he would be around tomorrow. Next morning he got up and dressed for the occasion, but fell back on the bed exhausted.

Daily, Nicholas asked for Russian news. He was much shaken over the Tsar's death; he had not met Alexander II often, but he remembered well the few occasions. In '72, the day after the Moscow performance of *Orpheus*, the Tsar had invited Nicholas to lunch at the Neskuchny Palace. Nicholas had talked about music; afterward he wondered if he had said too much: Alexander II was not a man to be cozened or persuaded. But next morning Dolgoroukov informed Nicholas triumphantly that the Conservatory was to receive 20,000 roubles a year for the next five years, adding that conversation with Nicholas Gregorovitch was dangerous for a man with a full purse. When Nicholas began talking about the needs of musical Moscow, he was a man bewitched.

It was this grant of money that had enabled Nicholas to refuse the American offer. America urged him to make a tour in the wake of his famous brother. No money at all, Nicholas had replied, could seduce him six thousand miles from Moscow.

Lying sleepless and pain-racked on his bed in the Grand Hôtel through the Paris nights, Nicholas had time to remember. Strange scenes came back to him, faces he thought he had forgotten long ago. . . . The 'cello-playing postmaster at Tver when he was visiting Prince Obolensky. Invited to play sonatas with the great Nicholas Gregorovitch, the postmaster had become so excited that he only survived the tuning of his 'cello, then fell over dead as the first chord was struck.

How much of death a man saw by the time he was forty! Nicholas was forty-five now; he had no idea his own death was near, or at least he did not admit it. To his visitor he talked of plans for the coming Moscow Exposition. He would repeat the programs he had used in Paris—Tchaikovsky's *Tempest* especially, and the *B Flat Minor Concerto*. *Dieu!* did Turgenev remember the flat trumpet in the *Serenade* at the last Exposition concert in the Trocadèro? The final chord had been a nightmare. . . . All the same, Turgenev reminded him, the city of Paris gave you a silver crown that night.

As the pain grew worse, Nicholas' weakness increased. When he was alone with Helen Tretiakov he wept openly. "But when we get to Nice," he told her quickly, "I shall be better." He was very careful of his appearance, asking often for the hairbrush and mirror, wearing his silk dressing-gown with an air. Once only, he gave way to discouragement. Raising his hands against the light, he looked at them, spreading his thin fingers, moving them slowly. "Helen Andreyevna," he said quietly, "I believe my artistic career is ended forever."

Slowly, painfully, the days wore by. Through the window came the sounds of the city: horses' hooves, the rattle of wheels on cobblestones. In the late afternoon, children shouted, the heels of the *midinettes* tapped neatly against the pavement.

On Tuesday, March 22nd, Madame Tretiakov wired Anton in Madrid.

The night before, Nicholas' suffering had been terrible. Somehow, he had got through Tuesday and Tuesday night. On Wednesday morning he seemed better, and at ten o'clock demanded his dinner. "Oysters!" he said. "Nothing, Helen Andreyevna, will do me so much good as a dozen cold oysters. And an ice afterward."

Helen Tretiakov pulled the bell rope for the waiter. Sitting up, Nicholas ate his oysters and was instantly racked with pain and vomiting. Madame Bernhard hurried out for the doctor, but when he arrived Nicholas was unconscious. "It is all over with him," said Potin. Until afternoon, Nicholas lay without moving, his body growing slowly cold. The two women watched by his side; Turgenev was there and a boy student from the Moscow Conservatory who adored Nicholas and whom the women had not the heart to send away. Present also was Agathon, his customary sulky silence broken by sobs. Clumsy, stupid, he blundered about the room, beseeching the doctor, on his knees, to do something and when the doctor shook his head, stumbling to the ikon in the corner, lighting another candle, kneeling, his head bowed in his huge peasant hands.

At three in the afternoon on Wednesday, March 23rd, Nicholas died in Turgenev's arms.

It was dusk when Anton Rubinstein arrived in Paris. He walked into the Grand Hôtel, out of the noisy Paris streets, down a gaslighted corridor to Room 25, his black Homburg hat in his hand, his face stony, expressionless.

Beyond the candles, beyond the weeping, kneeling group about the bed, he saw a face incredibly wasted and gray. Stranger even than the strangeness of death was the terrible stillness of this figure. Nicholas who had never been still, whose very sin was restlessness, whom his brother had admonished so often to be quiet, to cease running after the world, to stop and think, stop and write music— Nicholas lay now in a quietude that tore at his brother as even the sight of yesterday's suffering would not have torn him. These candles, this priest with his smooth Latin words of comfort and absolution—what good were they to a Nicholas who would have laughed at them, a Nicholas who went to confession every year for the benefit

274

of the census taker, whose spirit no one had reached except *Maman* and, once or twice, himself?

It was a terrible thing that *Maman* could not be here, that Nicholas had died in a strange land, far from the Moscow he loved. Of her five children, Nicholas had been *Maman's* favorite—and with reason. Nicholas had responded to love. . . . Looking now upon his brother, Anton knew that Nicholas had loved him better than he had loved Nicholas, and the knowledge caused him bitter grief. Nicholas was more capable of affection; his nature was warm and quick. He had possessed a generosity natural and unassuming; where other people reached for things, Nicholas had given things away, had given his music, his money, his rich extraordinary talent for teaching. . . . How could he, Anton Rubinstein, go home and face *Maman*, tell her that he had been too late, had let Nicholas die alone? He had been on tour, under contract; he had not known that danger was so near. Always, *Maman* had cautioned the brothers to give up all else where contracts where concerned. Nothing must give way to professional engagements. Nothing? Not the death of a brother? . . .

Downstairs the hotel orchestra played dance music; next door at the *Opéra* they were preparing for a *Bal Masqué*; the coming and going was continuous. How Nicholas had loved noise, the bustle and confusion of rehearsal, the suppers that followed upon performance! If one could open the doors now and the shutters and let in this world that Nicholas loved! Sweep out these weeping women! Christian prayers, the telling of beads . . . Holy water . . . Anton's face hardened. He could not pretend to a faith he had never owned.

Peter Tchaikovsky, meeting Anton in the Old Slavonic Church whence the body was removed early on Thursday morning, professed himself shocked at this brother's impassiveness, disappointed when Anton answered tears with silence. "I am crushed with grief," Tchaikovsky wrote to Nadejda Von Meck. "My God, my God, how terrible are such moments in our lives!"

It is from Peter Ilyich that we have the story of those succeeding days in Paris. Anton himself said nothing, shared his grief with no one. The funeral was held in Paris on Friday, March 25th. The church was crowded with Russians and with Nicholas' French friends: Turgenev and Madame Viardot, Massenet, Lalo, Colonne the famous orchestra leader. Turgenev had made arrangements to send the body home to Russia. Just as the coffin was about to be closed and slipped into the leaden casket that would take it across the border, Madame Tretiakov stepped forward and laid a few roses on Nicholas' breast—roses that, fifty years later, would bear proof to a miraculous story.

Anton took his brother's body home to Moscow. At the Conservatory a memorial service had already been held; the halls were crowded, many wept openly. Nicholas' former students met a day or two later and founded a scholarship in their teacher's name for pianoforte students. The moment Moscow heard that the body was coming home for burial, the town began characteristically to gossip. A wild rumor spread that the coffin had been lost at the border and a box containing the body of an old woman sent on in its place. A baroness, she was, from the Baltic provinces. By the time the body actually arrived, Moscow had decided upon at least three different deaths that had been died by Nicholas Gregorovitch. Tubercular enteritis? said Moscow. What sort of ending is that? Nicholas Gregorovitch died fighting a duel; he died because one of the Polovtsev brothers broke three of his ribs to avenge their sister's honor. Colorful was the life of Nicholas Gregorovitch, said Moscow, and colorful must his death have been.

On the fourth of April, Nicholas Rubinstein's body arrived in Moscow and was taken to the University Church. The coffin, unopened, was visited by hundreds of mourners. From all over Russia they came—from Kharkov, Kiev and Yaroslavl with flowers, testimonials signed by students and friends. On the sixth of April the body was taken out to the Danilov Monastery, a long procession through ankle-deep mud under a gray cold sky. The pall-bearers were professors from the Conservatory—Taneiev, Klindworth, Albrecht, Kashkin—men who had loved Nicholas deeply. Whether Kaleria Rubinstein was there, we do not know. She was 78; the

Nicholas Rubinstein. *Photograph taken shortly before his death*

journey from Odessa was long. Upon all details of these days her son Anton retained silence; he wrote no letters, he made no notes. We know only that his face remained stony, impassive, so cold that his friends remarked upon it.

The long street of processional, that raw April day, was lighted with gas after the new Western fashion of mourning—the first time this custom was observed in Moscow. At the grave, one of Nicholas' old friends tried to deliver an address—"Nicholas Gregorovitch has come home," he said. "But it is not thus that Moscow would have welcomed her son"—and wept and fell upon the grave in confusion.

It was extraordinary how the memory of Nicholas Gregorovitch remained alive in Moscow. Returning from abroad, Tchaikovsky described Moscow without Rubinstein as a ship without a helmsman; even the man's enemies confessed it. Tchaikovsky was urged to accept the Directorship of the Conservatory but refused, recommending Serge Taneiev, the scholarly pianist-composer, Nicholas' pupil. Next winter in Rome, Tchaikovsky, who never ceased to mourn his friend and Chief, began to write the *Trio* that he afterward dedicated, as all the world knows, *"À la mèmoire d'un grand artiste"*—Nicholas Rubinstein.

More than forty years later, this *Trio* was played one evening at Tolstoi's country house, Yasnaya Polyana, for a group of Nicholas' old friends. Taneiev was at the piano; the windows of the great hall were opened onto the park. Bearded, grave, Tolstoi sat and listened. One of the guests left an account of the evening, remarking upon how vivid was this portrait written by a man so widely different in character from the man he depicted. The music is designedly elegiac, yet except for the second movement it is very gay, filled with dance tunes, waltzes and melody. And so was Nicholas Gregorovitch gay, in tune with the moment almost to frivolity except where music and teaching were concerned. The second movement— Adagio and variations—ending with a religious chant and solemn chords, impressed the company profoundly that night at Yasnaya

Polyana. This music, bringing afterward a deep sense of loss, evoked the very presence of their friend. Tolstoi's eyes were filled with tears.

Legend has never ceased to follow the name of Nicholas Rubinstein. His was one of those personalities to which the world clings, loath to relinquish the color, the contagion of vitality that was there. Under a cold gray sky of 1881 his body was consigned to dust. And on a summer morning, fifty-three years later, in a new Russia, a new generation that Nicholas Gregorovitch would scarcely have recognized as Russian, the coffin was opened. Inside it lay no skeleton but Nicholas Gregorovitch in an astounding state of preservation, his features clearly recognizable, his clothes in good condition, even the roses on his breast faintly pink, the petals scattered from the stem.

This was in October, 1934, when Moscow cemeteries were being dug under to make way for playgrounds and new buildings. The occasion was reported by Professor Popov, director of the Moscow Institute for Legal Medicine. The newspapers made much of the incident, their tone carefully skeptical as becomes a country conscientiously atheistic. The paper called *Bezbozhnik* (Godless) carried an especially detailed account. Workmen had been present when the coffin was opened—and the masses love to marvel. Bodies had been found before in Russia, in the chalk soil of Poltava and Kherson, preserved like this, and the people had invariably responded to the sight. "A saint!" they cried, "preserved by God's grace, that we may worship the relics." Or a sinner forever damned, his body repudiated by God, refused outright by Mother Earth.

And Nicholas Gregorovitch—which was he, saint or sinner? Those who had known him smiled; he was a little of each, they said. Scientists, examining the body, found it had never been embalmed and that the earth where it was buried contained no properties of antiputrefaction. The oaken coffin was lined thickly with cotton and sawdust, covered with silk; the leaden outer casket was perfectly soldered—"which," finished the newspaper, *Godless,* "should disprove forever any notion of the supernatural or miraculous."

278

The body of Nicholas Rubinstein, yellowing in the air like the relics of a true saint, was removed to the Novo Devitchy Cemetery. Nicholas, who in his lifetime never bothered to deny rumors and gossip, had in death been followed by a rumor that his body had been exchanged, before burial, with the body of a woman. Old Alexander Amphitheatrov, the exile, writing in a Paris newspaper, seized upon this: "To deny this last rumor of all, Nicholas Gregorovitch merely remained incorruptible in death as in life, so that old Muscovites, gazing upon his opened coffin, saw once more their Nicholas Gregorovitch, short, stocky, curly-haired, lacking only that feature so often described by Tchaikovsky—the pensive look of the powerful gray-blue eyes, closed more than fifty years ago."

27

*1881–1887. Il Demonio. Artiste je suis. Hermann
Wolff and the Historical Recitals*

AFTER his brother's death, Anton Rubinstein did not play in public
for nearly two months—perhaps the longest silence he had ever
maintained in the concert season. In May he went over to England.
London had heard about the opera, *The Demon,* and on a June day
of 1881, staged it under the title of *Il Demonio.* Anton conducted it
and *Punch* caricatured him with its usual acerbity. Clothed all in
dragon scales, Rubinstein sits at the piano, hair on end, a frightful
expression on his face, displaying a tail screwed upward like a treble
clef sign. The caption reads, "Il Demonio, Rubinstein-o. As this
accomplished but somewhat eccentric foreigner is said to have taken
away about ten thousand pounds English coin this season, he may
be considered as not only having composed *Demonio,* but having
made De-money-o."

London did not like *Il Demonio*; its fantastic story needed Russian listeners, credulous as children, who could accept a demon lover
on the stage. They did not like the *Tower of Babel* either, which
Anton conducted at the Crystal Palace. But they liked his recitals at
Saint James's Hall. "The hero of the season," Joseph Bennett called
him, "who snuffed out Hans Von Bülow."

Snuffing out Von Bülow was quite a feat; London had adored
Bülow for years. Traveling home to Peterhof, to the green Northern
sea and the nightingales in the woods, Anton thought of Bülow and
grinned. The two were friends of long standing, although Bülow
was pompous and as frankly anti-Semitic as Wagner. Bülow had
called on Anton in London, sending up a card on which was engraved the full list of his titles: *Doctor of Philosophy, Court Director
of Music for His Highness the Duke of Meiningen,* etc. Returning

IL DEMONIO, RUBINSTEIN-O

the visit, Anton delivered a card, blank except for his name, under which he had written the two words: *Slavischer Semit*.

At home in Russia Rubinstein found a new patriotism, intense and fanatical. He threw himself with gusto into this atmosphere, writing Russian compositions and playing them for the next five years all over Europe. Before he died, Nicholas had prevailed upon his brother to write music for the forthcoming Moscow Exhibition— a big piece for orchestra and chorus entitled *Russia*. Anton came down to Moscow and conducted it himself, performing also his *Russian Symphony*. Early that spring he played in Petersburg with the beautiful Essipova, his new and very attractive four-hand concert piece for piano, called *Bal Costumé*. Later it was orchestrated and used as a ballet all over Europe; today, young ladies play its lilting waltzes with their teachers at school commencements. . . .

Napravnik conducted the orchestra that night of 1882. Napravnik was a significant figure in Petersburg musical life. He was a Czech who had come up from Prague in 1861 to take charge of Prince Youssupov's private orchestra; Liadov soon recommended him as Balakirev's successor to lead the Musical Society's symphonic ensemble. Taking over the orchestra from Anton Rubinstein in 1867, Balakirev had antagonized every musician from trombone to piccolo by talking Russian at rehearsals. The men were nearly all Germans. What kind of a language was Russian, they grumbled, to talk music in? Let Balakirev's patriotism express itself some other way! Napravnik, succeeding him, was a welcome relief; he suited everyone, raising the orchestra to the level of any in Europe. Anton liked to play under his baton. Napravnik was not an inspired conductor but he was reliable—a quality somewhat rare in a Russia that boasted, in artistic circles, more inspiration than steadiness.

That summer of 1882, General Skobelev, hero of two Turkish wars, died suddenly in Moscow. Rubinstein sat down and wrote a *Heroic Fantasy* for piano and orchestra—wrote as fast as his pen could make the notes. It sounded very badly indeed, except when, as on the first night's performance, Rubinstein himself played the piano part. Down in the audience Moscow musicians looked at each other and grinned. Anton Gregorovitch was a wizard. He could make bad music sound inspired; he could make a wearisome succession of diminished sevenths melt into the tonic or crash into the tonic in such a way that one thought it was music by Beethoven . . .

To the powers at Court, the *Heroic Fantasy* was suitable and highly pleasing. The Court hated Jews, but there was no doubt that this Rubinstein gave what he had to his country. Petersburg desired to raise a monument to Glinka, whose name had become the very symbol of musical patriotism. Rubinstein gave a concert and raised 5000 roubles. The authorities accepted the money as they always accepted Anton's offerings—and when the monument was unveiled, did not invite Rubinstein to the ceremony. They could not forget, they said, the article Anton Gregorovitch had written twenty years ago in Berlin, criticizing Glinka's dilettantism.

From now until the end of his life, where Anton was concerned, the Court blew hot, then cold. In the spring of 1883 the Tsar gave Anton another decoration—the Cross of Saint Vladimir, Third Grade, "for special merit in the musical education of Russia." Anton took the medal out to Peterhof and told Vera to put it in the glass case with the illuminated albums. He wondered a trifle sardonically who had been busy this time in his behalf. It could not have been the Grand Duke Konstantin; the Sailor Prince was in high disfavor. His Imperial nephew had scarcely mounted the throne when he removed this too-liberal Uncle Konstantin from the honorary office of State Councillor, leaving him free to follow his ballet dancer to Paris and to grow his grapes in the Crimea. Alexander III, frightened, intensely pious, could not do other than hate the Jews, tainted as they were with Western culture, with internationalism. He had not been on the throne a month when all over Russia, anti-Jewish riots took place. The May laws interned the Jews once more in their villages; the terrible Pale was resurrected; Jews who in Alexander II's reign had moved outside the Pale were severely examined; many were expelled from their villages. Home, for Israel, became insecure once again. Outside of Russia, the civilized world spoke its horror, but the Tsar would not listen.

Pobyedonostsev, Procurator of the Holy Synod, once Alexander's tutor, was very close to the throne and Pobyedonostsev, although a dangerous reactionary, was a well-educated man who favored the arts. Called the "Second Torquemada," Pobyedonostsev, like the Inquisitors of Spain, could be propitiated by conversion to the faith— and Rubinstein was a baptized, Orthodox Christian. That he was a reluctant convert did not alter the facts. Rubinstein himself was well aware of these things and of their implications for the future. Just before he received the Vladimir Cross, he wrote in a friend's guest album a line that expressed succinctly his private idea of what constituted aristocracy. Looking down the list of names, Anton saw in the album many proud titles; across his mind flashed the arrogant motto of the Rohan family:

> *Roi ne deigne,*
> *Dieu ne puis,*
> *Rohan je suis* . . .

Anton took up his pen.

> *Roi ne deigne,*
> *Dieu ne puis,*
> *Artiste je suis.*

I am an artist. Always, this had been Anton Rubinstein's creed and title; always, it would remain so. What Anton truly desired was to give his whole dowry of talent to Russia. His mind began to hint that Russia would perhaps refuse this offer, but for a long time his heart refused to listen. Moreover, he was too busy, these years of the 1880's, to indulge in much speculation. Each year, the moment the European concert season was over he came home to Peterhof to write music. *Nero* was finished, a seventh movement added to the *Ocean Symphony*. Long ago in Vienna, Ambros, the musical historian, had championed the *Ocean*, comparing it to Beethoven's *Pastoral Symphony* and suggesting that a movement be added to express a storm. It would not, said Ambros, be easy to write. That was enough for Rubinstein; his professional pride rose, as always, to the challenge. Rubinstein himself recommended that no more than four movements be played at a concert, but orchestra leaders were tempted by such opportunity, and from Berlin to New York, audiences, bewildered but obedient, sat through all seven movements.

In Petersburg, a new generation of musicians was growing up; Anton watched its development with pride and delight. In the autumn of '82 young Glazunov's first string quartet was played in public. The boy was seventeen; Rubinstein took him by the hand and led him to the stage as Mendelssohn, long ago in London, had once taken Anton Rubinstein by the hand. Of all the brilliant Russians writing music during the 1880's, Rubinstein prophesied greatest things of this one.

Teaching, playing, conducting, writing for the musical papers defenses of his Biblical operas, Rubinstein scarcely saw the next two years go by. Time was marked by concert dates, by arrival and departure in Europe and Russia. And then, in the summer of 1885, Anton shut himself up at Peterhof to prepare for the biggest task he had undertaken in all his years of concert playing.

He had determined to give a series of recitals in every principal city of Europe—six concerts covering the whole range of piano music from Couperin to Tchaikovsky. It was to be a farewell tour. Rubinstein was fifty-six; his powers must soon begin to wane and he had a horror of artists who forced themselves on the public when their best days were gone. "Beautiful women can't grow old, artists can't leave the stage," he said. "This is wrong. For an artist, the worst fate is to outlive himself."

The tour was a gigantic project—the greatest feat of piano playing undertaken by anybody before or since. The business details would be managed by Hermann Wolff, the shrewd Berlin concert agent whom Anton had met in '72, when Wolff was a clerk at Breitkopf and Härtels. Rubinstein and Wieniawski had walked in, searching for someone to arrange the details of their coming American tour, Jacob Grau being ill and his nephew on the other side of the ocean. They wanted someone, said Anton, who could speak business English better than the Americans, who were reputed to be very sharp in contractual matters. With no hesitation, Wolff proclaimed himself the man. It was the beginning of a long and highly successful career as impresario. Anton liked Hermann Wolff; he knew he would enjoy this association during the Historical Recitals.

Beginning to practice, out at Peterhof, Rubinstein found it would require seven, not six recitals to cover the historical ground. In his turret room that summer of 1885, Anton practiced as he had not practiced in years—as he had been used to practice when he was young, hour after hour, oblivious to noon, to mealtime, heat or cold. Downstairs, the villa was gay with young people. Pretty Anna was engaged to marry a Guardsman, handsome, correct and penniless. Anton Gregorovitch, said Petersburg, was undertaking this giant *tournée* in order to dower his daughter. Anton adored her, liked her to fill the villa with her friends in the evening. Then he would sit at the piano and play waltzes for the girls to dance—as he had played, so long ago, in Helena Pavlovna's palace for the young Princesses. . . . The two Rubinstein boys were growing up; Alexander was twelve, a delicate, beautiful boy; Jacob was younger. None of the three was musical, or, if they were, their father did not encourage it. He had no ambition, he said, to see a child of his enter the professional artistic arena.

In October, Rubinstein was ready to start his tour. The shrewd Herr Wolff desired to open the series in Berlin. Fifteen years ago, it would have been Paris, but since the Franco-Prussian War there was no doubt as to which city dominated Europe in art as well as politics. Berlin was proving the observation often made by artists that the capital of that country which leads the world politically becomes the center for science and art.

In Berlin Rubinstein gave not seven concerts but seventeen, playing formally in the evening for the public and next morning repeating the program, free, for music students. "Morning and evening concerts," wrote Anton laconically, "were crowded. It was really a great undertaking."

Rubinstein Historical Concerts

FIRST CONCERT

WILLIAM BYRD
The Carman's Whistle.

JOHN BULL
The King's Hunting Jigg.

FRANÇOIS COUPERIN
La Ténébreuse. La Favorite. La Fleurie. Le Bavolet flottant. La Bandoline. Le Réveil-matin.

JEAN PHILIPPE RAMEAU
Le Rappel des oiseaux. La Poule. Gavotte et variations.

DOMENICO SCARLATTI
Fugue, G minor (Cat fugue). Sonata, A major.

JOHANN SEBASTIAN BACH
Fantasia Chromatica e Fuga, D minor. Gigue, B flat (from the first Partita). Sarabande and Gavotte, G minor (from the third English Suite). The Well-tempered Clavichord: Preludes and fugues: C minor, D major; Preludes: E flat minor, E flat major, B flat minor.

GEORGE FREDERICK HANDEL
Air et Variations (The Harmonious Blacksmith) from the Suite in E major. Fugue, from the Suite in E minor. Sarabande and Passacaille, from the Suite in G major. Gigue, from the Suite in A major. Aria con variazioni, D minor.

CARL PHILIPP EMANUEL BACH
Rondo, B minor. La Xénophone. Sibylle. Les Langueurs tendres. La Complaisante.

JOSEPH HAYDN
Theme and Variations, F minor.

WOLFGANG AMADEUS MOZART
Phantasie, C minor (K. 475). Gigue, G major (K. 574). Rondo, A minor (K. 511). Rondo alla turca, from Sonata in A major (K. 331).

SECOND CONCERT

LUDWIG VAN BEETHOVEN
Sonata, C sharp minor, Op. 27, no. 2. Sonata, D minor, Op. 31, no. 2. Sonata, C major, Op. 53 (Waldstein). Sonata, F minor, Op. 57 (Appassionata). Sonata, E minor, Op. 90. Sonata, A

major, Op. 101. Sonata, E major, Op. 109. Sonata, C minor, Op. 111.

THIRD CONCERT

FRANZ SCHUBERT
Fantaisie, C major, Op. 15 (The Wanderer). Six Momens Musicals, Op. 94. Menuetto, B minor, from Sonata in G major, Op. 78. Impromptu, C minor, Op. 90, no. 1. Impromptu, E flat major, Op. 90, no. 2.

CARL MARIA VON WEBER
Sonata, A flat major, Op. 39. Momento capriccioso, Op. 12. Aufforderung zum Tanze, Op. 65. Polacca brillante, Op. 72.

FELIX MENDELSSOHN-BARTHOLDY
Variations sérieuses, Op. 54. Caprice, E minor, Op. 16, no. 2. Lieder ohne Worte: E major, Op. 19b, no. 1. A minor, Op. 19b, no. 2. F sharp minor (Venezianisches Gondellied), Op. 30, no. 6. A major (Frühlingslied), Op. 62, no. 6. E flat major, Op. 38, no. 1. B minor, Op. 67, no. 5. E major, Op. 67, no. 6. A flat major, Op. 53, no. 1. E flat major, Op. 53, no. 2. F major, Op. 53, no. 4. A minor (Volkslied), Op. 53, no. 5. Presto à capriccio, F sharp minor.

FOURTH CONCERT

ROBERT SCHUMANN
Fantasie, C major, Op. 17. Kreisleriana, Op. 16. Etudes Symphoniques, Op. 13. Sonata, F sharp minor, Op. 11. Fantasiestücke, Op. 12: Des Abends; In der Nacht; Traumeswirren; Warum? Vogel als Prophet, Op. 82, no. 7. Romanze, D minor, Op. 32, no. 3. Carnaval, Op. 9.

FIFTH CONCERT

MUZIO CLEMENTI
Sonata, B flat major.

JOHN FIELD
Nocturne, E flat major. Nocturne, A major. Nocturne, B flat major.

JOHANN NEPOMUK HUMMEL
Rondo, B minor, Op. 109.

IGNAZ MOSCHELES
Etudes Charactéristiques, Op. 95: No. 2, Réconciliation; No. 4, Junon; No. 5, Conte d'enfant.

ADOLF VON HENSELT

Poème d'amour, Op. 3. Berceuse. Liebeslied, Op. 5, no. 11. La Fontaine, Op. 6, no. 1. Schmerz im Glück, Op. 6, no. 2. Si oiseau j'étais, Op. 2, no. 6.

SIGISMUND THALBERG

Thème original et étude, A minor, Op. 45. Grande Fantaisie et Variations—Don Juan, Op. 14.

FRANZ LISZT

Etude de concert No. 3, D flat major. Valse Caprice. Consolation, No. 3, D flat major. Consolation, No. 2, E major. Au bord d'une source. Rhapsodie hongroise No. 6, D flat major. Rhapsodie hongroise No. 12, C sharp minor. Soirées musicales de Rossini: No. 4, La gita in gondola; No. 2, La regata veneziana; No. 10, La serenata; No. 9, La danza. Auf dem Wasser zu singen (Schubert). Ständchen von Shakespeare (Schubert). Erlkönig (Schubert). Soirée de Vienne, A major (Schubert). Réminiscences de Robert le Diable de Meyerbeer.

SIXTH CONCERT

FRÉDÉRIC CHOPIN

Fantaisie, F minor, Op. 49. Préludes, Op. 28: E minor, A major, A flat major, B minor, D flat major, D minor. Mazurkas: B minor, F sharp minor, C major, B flat minor. Ballades: G minor, Op. 23; F major, Op. 38; A flat major, Op. 47; F minor, Op. 52. Impromptu, F sharp major, Op. 36. Impromptu, G flat major, Op. 51. Nocturne, D flat major, Op. 27, no. 2. Nocturne, G major, Op. 37, no. 2. Nocturne, C minor, Op. 48, no. 1. Barcarolle, F sharp major, Op. 60. Valses: A flat major, A minor, A flat major. Scherzo, B minor, Op. 20. Sonata, B flat minor, Op. 35. Berceuse, D flat major, Op. 57. Polonaise, F sharp minor, Op. 44. Polonaise, C minor, Op. 40, no. 2. Polonaise, A flat major, Op. 53.

SEVENTH CONCERT

FRÉDÉRIC CHOPIN

Eleven Etudes: A flat major, F minor, E major, C minor, E flat minor, E flat major, B minor, A flat major, A minor, C sharp minor, C minor.

MIKHAIL GLINKA

Tarantelle, A minor. Barcarolle. Souvenir d'une mazurka.

Mili Balakirev
Scherzo, B minor. Mazurka, A major. Islamey, Fantaisie orientale.

César Cui
Quasi scherzo, B flat major, Op. 22, no. 4. Polonaise, C major, Op. 22, no. 1.

Nicholas Rimsky-Korsakov
Etude. Novellette. Valse.

Anatol Liadov
Etude, A flat major. Intermezzo, D major.

Peter Ilyich Tchaikovsky
Chant sans paroles, Op. 2, no. 3. Valse Scherzo, A major, Op. 7. Romance, F minor, Op. 5. Scherzo à la russe, Op. 1, no. 1.

Anton Rubinstein
Sonata, F major, Op. 41. Theme and variations from C minor sonata, Op. 20. Scherzo from A Minor Sonata, Op. 100.

Nicholas Rubinstein
Feuillet d'album. Valse, A flat major, Op. 16.

The words sound apologetic, as though the fact needed evidence. It needed no evidence. Rubinstein played and Berlin responded as never before. All Europe responded. Rubinstein used a Bechstein piano from the famous Berlin factory. Young Hermann Wolff, in the wings, watched anxiously as the great hands flashed upward. Of all the virtuosi that Wolff would serve in fifty years of managership, this Russian was the most violent—and the best player. Wolff adored him, traveled over Europe with him, soothed and comforted him, and always stood up in Anton's presence. "Why should I not stand," asked round, fat little Hermann indignantly, "in the presence of genius?"

One night when the last piece, the last encore had been played and Anton came on to face a shouting, stamping audience, his collar was gone, the buttons had burst from his shirt front. His hair hung in matted strands, his shoulders sagged and from the wings Hermann Wolff saw him gasp, drawing his breath like a man who has run a race. It was not well when Rubinstein panted so; Anton called it nothing, a little asthma—but a little asthma does not rack a man's body as Rubinstein's was racked when he played too long. It was a pity Anton suffered so from nervousness before these concerts. Nothing could quiet him. He would pace the artist's room like a caged beast. The difficulty was, the man never played a piece the same way twice. If he had been like Bülow, for instance, who had everything calculated beforehand to a degree, the hazard would not have been so great. Rubinstein relied on his temperament, on the mood of the moment, and this was at the same time a danger and a very great strength. Anton's temperament never failed him; the variety of his performance was a continual inspiration not only to the audience but to the player. Pacing the artist's room before the concert, Anton, called to the stage by Wolff, would shoot as from a catapult toward the piano, head down, walking fast but dragging his feet, shuffling like a huge bear, never looking at the audience until he was quite done playing. The only thing that could wring a smile from him was when someone in the audience shouted a Russian greeting: "*Zdrastvooyte!*—Anton Gregorovitch—*Zdrastvooyte!*" Anton's face

287

would light up, he would raise his head, smile, nod, and running both hands through his hair, turn eagerly to the piano.

For *matinée* Rubinstein wore a black dress coat, called a frock coat in those days. His string tie was always awry; invariably, when he walked out on the stage, one shoe string dragged. On this tour, Rubinstein was far too prodigal with encores; Wolff saw that if this continued, Anton would be dead before the tour was half completed. The man seemed ready to play all night. "Let me repeat the last movement of the sonata," he would entreat Wolff, backstage. "I played too fast. I dropped too many notes. I did not do justice to the music." Shaking his head firmly, Wolff would send the janitor on the stage to lock the piano. All over Europe, this became the signal that Rubinstein would play no more that night.

No one knew "backstage" so thoroughly as Hermann Wolff or sensed with shrewder prophecy what the public wanted. His offices in Berlin, that at first had been one room on the Karlsbadstrasse, took up two floors now, and instead of *concert agent* he called himself Concert Director. He was a power to reckon with in the musical world, knowing everyone, fearing no one.

After the last concert in Berlin, Rubinstein's friends gave him a party at the Hotel Kaiserhof. Joachim was there, the beautiful Essipova, Désirée Artot the singer, whom Tchaikovsky had once loved, Klindworth, who used to teach at the Moscow Conservatory, Jules Rodenberg, friend since thirty years when in London he and Anton had begun to read the Old Testament together. Rodenberg was an important man now, publisher of the *Deutsche Rundschau*. He got up and proposed a toast to Anton: "We who have so often been his guests in the world of sound have dared invite him here tonight. He casts a light over our gathering and in his laurel crown are flowers of friendship. . . . We are pedestrian, but this man bears us aloft and along on a stormcloud."

Berlin, Hamburg, Leipzig, Dresden, Vienna. . . . All winter long, from October till June, playing, traveling, arriving, departing—and always, practicing. From the train, Anton gazed out at a flying scene that was not lake or forest or city roofs, but notes upon a black-lined page. Treble clef, bass clef, key signature. The turn of the page, the end of a movement. Pianissimo, crescendo. Louder, ever louder. *Fortissimo!* From his seat in the opposite corner of the carriage, Hermann Wolff saw Anton lean forward, hands raised. "Is it necessary," asked the little man softly, "to play concerts in railway cars, where no one has paid for a ticket?"

In Vienna, Wolff asked Rubinstein to take him out to Weimar to meet Franz Liszt, the only musician in Europe whom Wolff did not know. Liszt was white-haired now and venerable, living, when in Weimar, at the *Hofgartnerei* where he was fêted by the Grand Ducal family and visited by crowds of worshipful pupils who quoted the Master's word all over Europe. In Liszt's parlor, Wolff watched the two artists greet each other, watched them together by the piano, white mane and black, talking eagerly, recalling old times, old names. The small man was forgotten. Hearing sharp coughs from somewhere by the window, Rubinstein turned and with an exclamation, beckoned to Wolff and taking him by the hand, presented him to the Master. Liszt smiled, stroking his long white hair. "Ah," he said, "you are the owner of the menagerie that has so many lions."

"Jawohl, Meister!" replied Wolff quickly, softly. "But with one difference. Usually the owner feeds the lions. In this case the lions feed *me.*"

As for Anton Rubinstein, he took singularly little notice of the gate receipts that fed the lions' keeper. Wolff asked high prices for tickets and the world paid. If this was a farewell tour, argued Wolff, it would be well to make enough for Rubinstein to live on for the rest of his life. . . . A strange thing though, to manage an artist who would rather play for poor music students than for princes! Crazy things happened. In Vienna, one piano teacher required his pupils, sitting up front, to count the notes played by Rubinstein. There were sixty-two thousand, nine hundred and ninety-nine notes, the brightest pupil reported. . . .

Vienna, like Berlin, gave Rubinstein a wonderful party after the Historical Concerts. Scenes from his ballet, *The Vine,* were danced, poems read, toasts drunk in champagne. Even the professional critics, those gentlemen who took fright when a piece was played a little differently, a little off-schedule, even these wrote extravagant praise. The hardest-bitten, the most merciless of them all succumbed. Edouard Hanslick wrote a review that began cautiously and ended in a burst of enthusiasm: "Young virtuosi must beware of imitating the excesses of Rubinstein's playing, rather learning from him to play with expression, keeping strict watch over the tempo. . . . The merits of Rubinstein's playing are found principally in his elemental powers, and from this source spring also many of his faults. With years, his playing has become more equal. The bewitching beauty of his tones, the power and delicacy of his touch have now reached their climax. One seldom finds in contemporary pianists that genuine, spontaneous inward fervor which in the heat of passion dares all things, even to indiscretion, rather than pause to reason and reflect. Where reflection is absent, there may be heard the overwhelming voice of the passions and the heartstrings echoing in response. Rubinstein's temperament is of such compelling force that exhausted Europe yields submissive to his will."

28

A Holy Procurator intervenes for a baptized Jew.
Farewell London

You will have to get me home in time for Christmas," Rubinstein told Hermann Wolff. Wolff did, and kept his lion in Petersburg all through January and February to play the Historical Concerts for his countrymen—the hardest test of all. The schedule was cruel. Anton played in Moscow and Petersburg alternately, giving two concerts in each city until fourteen had been completed both north and south. Every Sunday he played in Petersburg, repeating the program next morning for Conservatory students free of charge. Monday evening he left for Moscow, going straight to his hotel. Tuesday evening he played in the Hall of the Nobility, Wednesday morning for students, taking the midnight train for Petersburg, which gave him three days at home to prepare for the next concert.

"I suffered no inconvenience," wrote Rubinstein, "either from fatigue of mind or body; my memory served me faithfully."

A hundred descriptions of these concerts have been written, giving every detail: How a piano string snapped with a singing noise, how in the intermission the tuner came on the stage to mend it. Anton's stiff shirt melted at the first sonata; backstage his valet, old Matvey, waited with a fresh one. The best of all these accounts comes from Serge Rachmaninov, then a boy of twelve studying at the Moscow Conservatory under the brilliant and erratic Sverev. Rachmaninov went to the concerts both evening and morning. "In this way," he wrote, "I was able every Wednesday morning to reexamine my impressions of the previous evening. I stored up wonderful memories, with which no others in my experience can compare.

"It was not so much Rubinstein's magnificent technique that held one spellbound as the profound, spiritually refined musicianship, which spoke from every note and bar he played, and singled him out as the most original and unequaled pianist in the world. Naturally I never missed a note, and I remember how deeply I was affected by his rendering of the *Appassionata* or Chopin's *Sonata in B Minor.*

"Once he repeated the whole finale of the *Sonata in B Minor*, perhaps because he had not succeeded in the short crescendo at the end as he would have wished. One listened entranced, and could have heard the passage over and over again, so unique was the beauty of the tone which his magic touch drew from the keys. I have never heard the virtuoso piece *Islamey*, by Balakirev, as Rubinstein played it, and his interpretation of Schumann's little fantasy, *The Bird as Prophet,* was inimitable in poetic refinement; to describe the diminuendo of the pianissimo at the end as the 'fluttering away of the little bird' would be hopelessly inadequate. Inimitable, too, was the soul-stirring imagery in the *Kreisleriana*, the last (G minor) passage of which I have never heard anyone play in the same manner. One of Rubinstein's great secrets was his use of the pedal. He himself has very happily expressed his ideas on the subject when he said, 'The pedal is the soul of the piano.' No pianist should ever forget this."

The last Moscow concert was held on March 2nd; the town planned a glorious celebration for the occasion. Petersburg prepared for like festivities a few days earlier. In Moscow all would be plain sailing; from Prince Dolgoroukov with his red wig to the humblest janitor of the Conservatory, everyone sought an invitation.

But Petersburg foresaw a hitch, and a bad one. What if the Tsar refused to come? The Little Father had decorated Rubinstein, it was true, but a star out of a box is one thing and the personal Presence quite another. An important party in the Tsar's city without the Tsar was a calamity; in this particular case it would amount to insult. Anton Rubinstein was a public character; he was one of the greatest assets his country boasted. Surely, in the interests of art, Majesty should forget, this once, all fear and hatred of Jews! Pobyedonostsev, Procurator of the Holy Synod, was worried. As tutor to Alexander III, he remembered well the value Alexander's

father had put upon Anton Rubinstein. Pobyedonostsev's influence
at Court was enormous, greater perhaps than any other man's. This
huge iron-bodied Romanov (Russia called him the Crowned Peasant) was difficult to handle; he was as stubborn as any ignorant Ivan
in his realm.

Pobyedonostsev sat down and wrote a long letter:

February 18, 1886
"Do not be angry, Your Imperial Majesty, for the present writing
with which I venture to disturb you.

"Next Saturday, in the Hall of the Nobility, Rubinstein's historical concerts will reach their conclusion. In the musical world of
all Europe these concerts are an event. They were given last autumn
and winter in Berlin and Vienna, arousing universal enthusiasm and
amazement. All classes of society, beginning with members of the
reigning family, took a vivid interest in the matter. In Vienna when
the concerts were over a festival for Rubinstein was arranged in
which royalty, including many of the Grand Dukes and Duchesses
of Cumberland, took part.

"Without doubt, Anton Rubinstein stands now as the first and
greatest authority in the musical world; since Wagner's death no one
has equaled him. In musical technique, in perfection of execution,
no one, it is generally conceded, has achieved such fulness and
power. It is pleasing to realize that this artist, the peer of all others
in his line, belongs to Russia. By birth, education, social relationships
and connections, by his habits and way of life—Anton Rubinstein is
a Russian, and, despite brilliant and repeated offers from abroad, has
remained in Russia.

"Moreover, he is a man of great education and noble heart; everyone acknowledges this. In all the big cities where he gave his concerts, regardless of the work required by this long and arduous
program, he won much sympathy by repeating his concerts, free,
for conservatory pupils and music students. He is doing the same
now, in Moscow and Petersburg. Anton Rubinstein's strength is
ebbing. Probably he will not live long; very likely these concerts are
his swan song.

"Rubinstein himself I see very rarely and by accident; I do not go
to his concerts (I have neither time nor strength) and I have never
solicited for him.

"But it seems to me that it would be right and just and consonant

with the dignity of the sovereign power as patron of art if Your Imperial Majesty and the Empress would honor with their presence
one of these concerts of Rubinstein, taking some notice of the name
of a Russian artist who is famous all over Europe. I know that many
for whom Russian art is dear will rejoice to the bottom of their
hearts at such a sign from you.

"Next Saturday the entire concert will be of Chopin's works,
which, as I believe, the Empress likes to hear. The concert following,
which is the last one, will be on Saturday evening, February 27th,
and will be dedicated to the music of Glinka, Tchaikovsky and
others.

"Konstantin Pobyedonostsev."

So wrote the Procurator from the depths of a troubled heart—and
read his letter and re-read it and shook his head and put the letter
in a desk drawer and left it there unsent.

The celebration took place without Tsar or Tsarina. But it was a
success none the less. All the intelligentsia of Petersburg were there:
scientists, writers, teachers. The ceremony was in a theatre; in the
right proscenium box sat Helena Pavlovna's daughter, the Grand
Duchess Catherine with her own daughter Helena, who already
sang so well. Across in the left-hand box were Vera Rubinstein and
the boys and pretty Anna with her blonde hair. The Grand Duke
Konstantin was out of town or he would most certainly have been
there in spite of his Imperial nephew's frown.

When Rubinstein entered the hall with Hermann Wolff, the Conservatory orchestra was playing its loudest, but applause drowned it
completely. Scenes from Anton's *Sulamith* were performed, poems
read, a huge album presented, containing drawings and cartoons of
Russian musicians. Then the prettiest pupils of the Conservatory
passed through the hall, dressed as heroes of Rubinstein's operas.
Nero, tall and shapely in toga and sandals, the Demon frowning in
a black cloak, the Merchant Kalashnikoff ready to face the scaffold.
Anton loved it; he was always touched when music students showed
him affectionate attention.

The Petersburg-Moscow concerts were completed by March 2nd,
bringing in 80,000 roubles. Then Rubinstein went to Germany to

294

present the series in Leipzig. He and Hans Von Bülow passed each other on the way—Bülow *en route* to Petersburg to conduct Rubinstein's *Russian Symphony* for the Musical Society. The Leipzig concerts took all of March. In April Rubinstein played his historical programs in Paris with enormous success, although the Chopin pupils, assembled in judgment, refused to accept this Russian as an authoritative Chopin interpreter. His tone was too big for Chopin, they said, too rich and full. This was matter for argument, and argument raged. James Huneker heard the recitals and said Rubinstein played Chopin inimitably.

The trouble was that when a piece was marked *presto*, Anton took it *prestissimo*. Over in Vienna, Hanslick grumbled at this, inquiring whether Rubinstein did it from nervousness or whether he simply could not resist the temptations of his virtuosity. ("I play as a musician, not as a virtuoso," Rubinstein growled in reply.) But audiences were funny things; in different countries one could expect certain very definite manifestations. Here in Paris, for instance, after a brilliant passage people—women especially—exclaimed, *"Charmant!"* One learned to anticipate it with dread, a hissing noise, *cha, cha, cha* all through the hall. Rubinstein, very tough-skinned where audiences were concerned, was not put off by such things. Paderewski and De Pachman hated it and said so. "No artist," wrote one critic during these concerts, "has ever shown his audience so merciless a front as Anton Rubinstein. His programs and his attitude are absolutely uncompromising. At first sight one is conscious of something stern, even inimical in his bearing toward his audience, as though a chasm were fixed between them, and he stood ready to plunge single-handed into the conflict. But gradually the sense of hostility vanishes, and the great artist conquers once and forever."

Here in Paris, people were more than cordial. From the amazingly beautiful Countess Potocki to the hard-working, highly companionable Saint-Saëns, the city sought out Rubinstein in the Hôtel du Helder. Anton, however, kept strictly to his routine, dismissing his guests always at eleven. Watching him, Hermann Wolff was worried. His breathing came too hard. Rising from the piano his chest moved with sharp, deep exertion. "You are sick," Wolff told him. "Why are you so stubborn about not seeing doctors? You should let someone listen to your heart."

Anton continued stubborn—and after the next concert, fainted. It was nothing, he told Wolff. He had often fainted; when he first came to Paris as a boy he had fainted in a tea room when a girl came in and cut her finger and he saw the blood. The trouble was, said Anton gravely, he had made this journey to Paris on a Friday. Bad luck! Moreover, driving to the concert hall he and Wolff had passed three lights and just as Anton was ready to go on stage, some fool of a Frenchman had wished him success. Everyone knew it was ruinous to be wished success before playing. Let Hermann see to it they drove around the block tonight and avoided the three lights.

Wolff sighed and shook his head. That night Anton fainted again, and this time he was not so easily revived. For the first time in his life he was really ill. Hermann put him to bed. "What is the matter with me?" Anton demanded irritably. "Is it old age? I must be in Dresden next week to play."

Rubinstein got out of bed and reached Dresden on schedule. His health returned. But something remained of this nameless sickness, a warning, an insistent premonition that could not be denied. When he got home he would, Anton told Wolff, see Dr. Vompe, his old friend. But they had done well to plan this tour now, and not wait. Europe must not see Anton Rubinstein slip downward, must not hear one faltering note, one diminuendo that came from weakness, not design.

Dresden, Brussels, then London for the last time. This was June, 1886, and Rubinstein broke through London's last defenses. "As Saul, the son of Kish, among the men of Israel, so is Anton Rubinstein among pianists," wrote Joseph Bennett. "Time was when Mr. Rubinstein appealed almost in vain to English amateurs. He piped unto them but they would not dance. At last he turned toward us his Boanergian side and roared as became a Son of Thunder. Surely the passionate Rubinstein is a phenomenon—a volcanic eruption attended by noises, fire and smoke. One thinks of the warhorse:

'He paweth in the valley and rejoiceth in his strength. He mocketh at fear and is not affrighted. He swalloweth the ground with fierceness and rage.'"

It was natural that critics, in describing Rubinstein, should have recourse to Biblical language. There was a largeness here, an Old Testament grimness that shouted from the mountain-top, that spoke its message from the burning bush. . . .

In London when he was not playing or practicing, Anton gave his time to whist and *Préférence* and piano pupils. He could not resist the hope that he would discover, in one of these girls or boys, a genius. One day a beautifully mannered, well-dressed young English girl was brought to him. She played and sang. Anton, who had been pacing the room restlessly, touched her on the shoulder. "Too much Belgrave Square," he said, shaking his head and smiling.

The gloomy silence that his friends were beginning to dread descended upon Rubinstein in London, engulfing him. Sir Arthur Sullivan called one evening and Rubinstein took him on the balcony for a smoke. They rolled their cigarettes and puffed away. After a long pause, Sir Arthur remarked, "You are, I presume, a great admirer of Beethoven?"

"Yes," said Anton.

"And of Wagner?"

"No."

Another long silence. The two musicians rocked their chairs and smoked. Then Sir Arthur said it was time to be going. "Stay a bit longer," Anton urged. "It is so nice to talk with you."

More cigarettes were rolled and consumed. Sir Arthur rose. "I really must be going. I think we have chatted long enough."

Rubinstein, taking out his watch, looked up astonished. "It's half after two. Impossible! How time flies with someone pleasant to talk to!"

The story went all over London, went up to Glasgow and was retold with embellishments and a different name for the visitor. But Rubinstein considered he had good cause for gloom. London rang with applause—and every bit of it was directed at Rubinstein the pianist. Rubinstein the composer was scarcely mentioned in this laudatory press, with its talk of steam-hammers and war-horses. Anton cut out the best clippings and sent them, as was his custom on tour, to his mother in Odessa. She would laugh at these wild descriptions of her son; no doubt she would greet her boy with them, satirically embellished, next time he came down to see her. Kaleria was over eighty; Anton regretted deeply that he could not see her more often. Every visitor to the south he charged with messages for *"ma vieille"* and the visitors, returning, reported themselves captivated by Kaleria Christoforovna, with her strong face and prim starched caps. She was so hearty, cried these returning visitors. And so simple and cordial in manner.

The thought of *Maman* made Anton homesick for his own country and his own people. It was a trifle ironic, the way everyone on the Continent called him Russian, and the minute he reached home he was called foreigner. "Russians call me German, Germans call me Russian, Jews call me a Christian, Christians a Jew. Pianists call me a composer, composers call me pianist. In this way I satisfy nobody," said Anton Rubinstein.

Hermann Wolff escorted Rubinstein across the Channel and for once, Rubinstein was not sick. Somebody had given him a remedy for seasickness; skeptically, Anton had swallowed it and the result seemed to him a simple miracle. All the way home to Russia he talked about it. "This medicine must be given to the world!" he cried. "Hermann, we must raise a fund . . ."

"Must we always have crusades?" Hermann replied. "*Nein,* we cannot have the first pianist of Europe playing for the benefit of seasick travelers . . ."

It was hard for Wolff to bid good-bye to Rubinstein. In the train the two talked of the musical response of these nations they had played to; a few years later, Anton wrote down his ideas on the subject:

"I believe that Germany is the most musical nation in the world, in spite of the peculiar brand of mystic patriotism existing there just now. All of Germany's strength—alas!—is at present concerned with bayonets and national unity, a condition that cleaves through the spirit of culture like a scalpel. Even so, dividing the thing mathematically, I would call Germany fifty per cent musical, France sixteen per cent and England—the most unmusical of all the nations—two per cent. Even the Americans understand and love music better than the English, although, if this is made public, the sons of Albion will be very angry with me. In France, music is advancing along one very specialized line. As for Russia, she stands apart in her wonderful folk music and I leave her out of the discussion, repeating that a true understanding of music exists only in Germany."

June, 1886. . . . The Germany that Rubinstein was leaving, the Germany he loved so well, had always, in spite of its Bismarck and its bayonets, appreciated not only music but Anton Rubinstein. He was returning to spend the rest of his days (or so he thought) in a country he loved even more passionately than Germany, a country which at the moment was enjoying a nationalism quite as virulent as anything sponsored by Bismarck. Russian patriotism had lately required the assistance, in its city streets, of mounted Cossacks with lead-tipped whips. Far from resenting this fanatic nationalism, Anton saw himself as part of it, saw his nation striding forward with himself at the musical helm. The Conservatory needed him; it was in a bad way under Carl Davidov who was too kind, too easygoing to withstand the intrigues and jealousies of Petersburg musical life. Anton knew that the moment he stepped into town he would be overwhelmed with private pupils, beseeching his help, and with the business of the Conservatory and the Musical Society. Belayev, the music publisher, had endowed a brand-new series of concerts; Petersburg teemed with talent, from young Gabrilowitsch and Glazunov to Liadov and Rimsky-Korsakov teaching their classes at the Conservatory. Ippolitov-Ivanov was down in Tiflis now, running the Conservatory there and doing a splendid job by all accounts. Young and old and middle-aged, Russians were writing music, talking music.

Rubinstein was glad that he was taking home a substantial fortune from these Historical Concerts. Enough to support his mother as long as she lived, enough to dower his daughter Anna. . . . This

Guardsman of Anna's was an empty-headed jackanapes, but if Anna wanted a handsome soldier, her father would buy her one. He would not, however, squander all this new fortune privately. Peterhof was expensive to run and Vera would never be anything but extravagant. It would be wise to give away a good big sum before the money crossed Vera's palm. As soon as he reached home he would announce his plan for the International Piano Competition, with an endowment of 25,000 roubles from his private purse. The prizes would be large enough to be scholarships, and it would be a healthy leaven for this intense nationalism that flourished all over Europe. Musicians needed a reminder that while patriotism is an excellent soil for creative art to root in, beauty is international, with no boundaries of flag or tongue. The very eclecticism of his own life and training made Anton Rubinstein a most suitable guardian for this deep growth that could be so easily warped. What was it Felix Mendelssohn had said? *Maman* had quoted it, long ago: "The inspiration of my career is to help the progress of art along the path that seems to me the right one."

Anton Rubinstein looked forward to devoting the remainder of his life to this cause.

29

*1886-1888. The Conservatory once more. Anton
becomes an Excellenz*

AT PETERHOF, Rubinstein received royal welcome. The whole town
came out to see him, pleased when he consented to conduct the
concerts of the Musical Society for the approaching winter season.
That summer he commenced another sacred opera, *Moses,* which he
had had in mind a long time and for which Mosenthal in Vienna
had written the libretto. When autumn came, the family remained
at Peterhof, but Anton moved back into the big apartment in the
Troitsky Pereulok and opened rehearsals for the symphony concerts. Crowds stood in line for tickets; on concert nights mounted
police regulated carriage traffic; the beautiful Hall of the Nobility
was filled to overflowing.

Yet from a technical point of view, Rubinstein's conducting left
much to be desired. His eyesight was beginning to fail; the players
were nervous. One never knew if Anton Gregorovitch would bring
in the trombones a measure too soon. He paid no slightest attention
to the orchestra; playing under Rubinstein, one of the men reported,
it was Rubinstein and the music—not Rubinstein and the musicians
that mattered. Unbridled temperament is all very well on the piano,
where a man has only his own fingers to control; when Rubinstein
found himself in the middle of music, he desired to let go and
roar—and nothing could stop him. In the orchestra, when Anton
commenced to conduct an *andante,* nobody knew if it would be a
presto before he got through.

At rehearsals he was merciless and would keep on for hours at a
stretch; when he finished he seemed as energetic as ever. The men
grumbled—and worshiped Anton and fought for places in the orchestra. Anton Gregorovitch, said they, truly loved music. More-

over, he possessed a quality, hard to define, for which each generation has its own euphonic slang. 1939 calls it by several names; the past has called it *zip, oomph*. In the 1880's it was *un*. One night at supper, Auer came up and begged Rubinstein to let him conduct the next symphonic concert. "Just one piece, Anton Gregorovitch. Please!"

"You? No!" said Anton promptly. "Leopold, you have no *un*."

Anton's frankness was terrifying; with years he became quite merciless where music was concerned. Prince Volkonsky, a rich amateur, wrote some music and at Madame Abaza's suggestion—the once beautiful Julie Stube—played it for Rubinstein who walked up and down, drummed on the window and replied vaguely to the Prince's questions. Afterward it was repeated to Volkonsky that Anton had said, "He has ability, but he is a prince. So nothing will come of it." Personal friendship did not spare the victim; even the Grand Duke Konstantin was a target. "Tonight I go to the Palace," Anton told a friend. "The Grand Duke will play a Mozart concerto from memory. That is something—for a Grand Duke."

Rubinstein loved to play *ensemble*. But the other players must possess ensemble sense, for which no amount of technique and temperament could substitute. Sarasate was in Petersburg giving a concert and was invited to one of Rubinstein's evening parties. The world has not held many better violinists than Pablo Sarasate—but for Rubinstein, Sarasate proved too much the soloist that night on the Troitsky Pereulok. The two sat down to the *Kreutzer Sonata* that Anton had played so gloriously in America with Wieniawski. Sarasate went roaring off on his own tempo. After a few lines, Anton stopped. "Oh," he said, "I do not feel well. I have a headache. Monsieur Sarasate, will you play for us alone?"

Sarasate played alone.

Boris Kamensky told this story. Kamensky was first violinist of the string quartet maintained by Helena Pavlovna's grandson, Duke George of Mecklenburg-Strelitz and Kamensky lived in the same apartment building as Rubinstein and had lessons from him in *ensemble* playing. Old Matvey, Anton's valet, guarded his master warily, never letting anyone near him, but he liked young Kamensky and came to him sometimes in the morning. "Anton Gregorovitch is practicing," he would pronounce solemnly, and would lead Kamensky downstairs to the Rubinstein kitchen. Here, ignoring the cook's protest, the young man sat for hours in the big warm room among the copper pots and kettles with the door propped open that led through the dining room into the music room. "To hear Anton Gregorovitch play scales," said Kamensky, "brought you to your feet."

Kamensky is exiled now; he lives in Paris, an old man full of memories. Walking up and down the room, frowning, his shoulders hunched, he can bring Anton Rubinstein to life in a flash. At Petersburg parties he used to be deputed as mimic; he remembers Anton's one and only funny story. Never the wit that Nicholas had been, Anton realized sometimes that he was too silent in company and his own silence began to bore him. Sometimes he would get up and leave the table abruptly and not return. But occasionally he would make a fearful effort and begin to tell his elephant story. Everyone was pleased, waiting respectfully, affectionately for a climax known to all of Petersburg.

"There was a circus manager," Anton would say, "who took his circus to tour the provinces. The first night, a grand success, a crowded tent, much applause. Everyone in town was there. 'How can I bring them back tomorrow night?' the manager asked himself—and got up and told the audience that tomorrow night the elephant, Georgette, would play the piano. 'A-a-h!' breathed the audience. 'But, marvelous!' Next evening the tent was again crowded. Impatiently one awaited the musical elephant, Georgette. She came onto the platform, sat down at the piano, gazed at the keyboard, and dropping her head to her shoulders, closed her eyes. 'A hoax!' cried the people, enraged. 'Why does not the elephant play as we have been promised?'

"The manager came out, grave, concerned. 'Alas!' he said. 'Georgette is too sad to play. She is broken-hearted. She looks at the keyboard and she sees—*Ah, Dieu!* she sees the teeth of her dead *Maman!*' "

Rubinstein had been in town only a few months when, in January of 1887, he was invited to assume once more the directorship of the Conservatory. The offer was not unexpected; since his arrival in Russia the previous spring, Anton had been much disturbed by reports from the school.

During the twenty years since Rubinstein had resigned his directorship, the Conservatory had had three leaders: Zaremba, Asantchevsky and Davidov, not one of whom had been strong enough to weather the intrigue and factionalism that seemed invariably to surround the school. Excellent professors had been added to the staff during this time, notably Rimsky-Korsakov, who was enrolled as early as 1871, when by his own confession he had never "written a single contrapuntal exercise, could not harmonize a chorale properly, did not know the names of the augmented and diminished intervals, had no real knowledge of the technique of strings and only a hazy grasp of musical form." Furiously he set to work, and within the title of professor became, he said, "perhaps the Conservatory's best pupil."

Rubinstein, taking up the directorship in the autumn of '87, found Rimsky-Korsakov the best teacher in the school—the best teacher of composition, perhaps excepting Moscow's Taneiev, that Russia ever had. Carl Davidov, exchanging his directorship for a post as 'cello teacher, handed Rubinstein a list of eight hundred students in all departments. Some of them did not play very well, said Davidov apologetically. But they were poor, they needed a diploma to help them earn a living.

No one in Russia, perhaps no one in Europe, had been more generous to needy music students than Anton Rubinstein. Yet now he showed himself merciless; the reputation of the Conservatory, the standards of musical education itself were at stake. Rubinstein held an examination for every one of the eight hundred students—and dismissed two hundred of them. Some among the lost souls had passed years at the Conservatory and were in despair. Controversy raged, but Anton would hear no appeal. If you were not a musician, said he, you had better make a living some other way. . . . The students were not the only ones who suffered. Professors were dismissed right and left. For the past few years, scandal had been rife concerning too much intimacy between pupils and teachers. Davidov himself, a married man with grown-up children, had fallen in love with a beautiful student, a Turkish girl named Maharina, and the affair had upset the entire school. Anton loved Davidov and tried to reason with him and ended by dismissing him from his professorship. Carl Yulievitch had better teach 'cello at home, Anton said grimly. He sent for a carpenter to put glass doors in every lesson room in the building.

All day long Rubinstein worked in his office, arriving as of old at nine o'clock and remaining until five. His punctuality was the more disturbing as no offices in Petersburg opened before ten and the more important government functionaries never appeared before noon. Russians hate to get up in the morning, particularly Petersburgers who face a short, dark winter day. "What is Anton Gregorovitch doing?" grumbled the professors. "We shall all have to be in bed by midnight. It is an outrage!"

Outside the house in the Troitsky Pereulok a line of cabmen waited each morning. "Come with me, Anton Gregorovitch! My horse is fastest. My sleigh is smoothest." Young Kamensky, watching from the window above, said the cabmen of Petersburg, like everyone else, adored Rubinstein. "Next time I shall go with you!" Anton would call to the disappointed one, and drive off with a flourish of whips.

On his office wall hung a clock. One morning when he arrived, it showed 9.20. Anton rang every bell available. "Am I late, or is the clock fast?" The clock was fast.

Even when he had no work to do, Rubinstein stayed until five, roaming the corridors, popping in and out of lesson rooms. Enemies were made daily. Dismissals continued; in Petersburg a cartoon was published showing Rubinstein in the garb of janitor, sweeping a medley of figures from the Conservatory steps. But the fact that the new Director took no money for his services was most certainly disarming; moreover, he never ceased collecting funds for the school and trying to raise the salaries of his professors. A music school, said he, must beware of becoming a music factory, beware of routine examinations where a pupil, who had been drilled to make a good showing in one or two pieces, received a diploma before he was ready for independent work. After much opposition Anton succeeded in arranging a series of double examinations, whereby each pupil was required to prepare alone, without a teacher, pieces representing various types of music: chamber music, solo concerti of the Lisztian, fireworks variety and the older classical sonatas of Scarlatti and Mozart. These the pupil played for Rubinstein and the other piano teachers—and no "cramming," no all-night practice could hide a lack of true musicianship here. Afterward the pupil played his exhibition pieces in public at the regular June graduation exercises.

Twice a week Anton held a piano class at the Conservatory, twice a week an orchestral class and twice a week played for the students, lecturing and explaining. He advised every would-be composer to learn to sing and to play the violin: "Otherwise you will think only in terms of percussion, of the piano." To his piano students he also recommended singing; at a false phrasing he would cry out, "*Sing* the melody! Sing it aloud! Then you will see for yourself how to phrase—where to breathe. That is the trouble with all of you. I tell you to enter the singing classes and learn to sing—and you come to me with certificates from the doctor that you cannot sing! That is why you cannot play even the simplest melody.

"And on the other hand, when it is time to play *fortissimo*, you are afraid of hurting your fingers. See, I am not afraid!" And striking the keys with all his force, Rubinstein made the keys scream with discord. "If it hurts, why, let it hurt. Blood!" he cried. "I will have blood!"

Anton Gregorovitch, morning after morning, tried to wring blood from what were too often stones. Yet he never despaired. "I love to

306

teach!" he said. "I, who to concert audiences am mad and impatient, I can sit for hours—so long as there is a spark to fan to life. I say to pupils, 'The problem is not so much how to execute these notes. . . . How does it *sound*? That is the question. Listen, listen to yourselves!' "

The magnetism and sympathy of Rubinstein's playing were so convincing as to bring, sometimes, a peculiar and rather amusing reaction. Members of his audience, amateurs whose love of music exceeded their technique, imagined the piece could be played no other way and that they themselves played it with exactly the same effect as Rubinstein. A young Moscow law student who played the piano quite badly was overheard describing one of the Historical Concerts. Without a suggestion of boasting, the young man, who truly loved music, said enthusiastically, "Just think, Anton Gregorovitch played everything on the program exactly as I play it myself!"

Rubinstein was a little puzzled by this reaction; he quoted a pupil who came to him after he had played a Beethoven sonata: "Why, Master, you play it exactly as I do!" What could the boy mean? In truth it was a kind of magic. Something elemental issued from Rubinstein at the piano, something that paralyzed the listener's will and opened the doors to some other, deeper realm of consciousness. When pupils asked if his tone, his caressing touch on the keys was natural or acquired, Rubinstein admitted that his heavy, padded finger tips had something to do with it, but he fiercely resented the notion that all this effect came down from heaven on the wings of a dove. "I have spent thousands of hours to find this tone and that," he said. "Ever since I can remember, I have been working at the problem. Genius is soon forgotten, but the worker, the true worker, can always make himself known to the world."

At the turn of the year—1888—Rubinstein received from his Tsar a new honor, the brightest star his buttonhole had held so far. He was made an *Excellenz*. "His Imperial Majesty"—so runs the document—"most graciously grants to the hereditary nobleman, Anton

Rubinstein, the grade of valid State Councillor (*Excellenz*) for his useful work in the progress of musical education in Russia."

The "hereditary nobleman" referred, of course, to the promotion of 1877. Petersburg laughed: Anton Gregorovitch, an *Excellenz*? Nevertheless, the town used the title freely, especially porters, janitors and cabmen. "Anton Gregorovitch—*Excellenz*—drive with me. *Excellenz,* let me open the door." Rubinstein enjoyed it; he could not help enjoying it. To be an *Excellenz* was no small business. For the rest of his life, as though in return for this honor from his government, he gave away every kopeck of his ticket money.

In February, the Tsar and Tsarina visited the Conservatory, choosing to come in the evening for a pupils' concert. Alexander III was an enormous man, not fat but very tall and broad; legend said he wore beneath his uniform a set of chain mail to protect him from the assassin's knife. This was the Romanov who as Tsarevitch, had played the trumpet in Haydn's *Toy Symphony* and surprised himself, upon squeezing his instrument zealously, to find it crumple in his fist. He loved noisy music and in his palace sometimes played trombone in a brass quartet, blowing out his huge chest to his heart's content.

So far, Alexander III did not actively dislike Anton Rubinstein or, if he did, tolerated him because of the Tsarina's outspoken liking and Pobyedonostsev's frank support. In Petersburg there had long been a saying, "We don't like Jews, but that doesn't mean Anton Gregorovitch." At first, Alexander III tacitly concurred. The trouble was that Anton himself could not tolerate being an exception to racial persecution. He did not approve the Tsar's anti-Jewish policies and did not like the man who initiated them. Rubinstein was not the man to conceal his dislikes. He began taking quite mad liberties with the Court. Invited one night to play at the palace at nine, he arrived, as was his custom, on time. Finding no one in the music room he sat down and played—and went home before Majesty so much as emerged from the dining room.

Again, a rich nobleman named Polovtsev gave an elaborate *soirée* to which the Tsar and Tsarina were invited. Rubinstein agreed to

Anton Rubinstein in the late 1880's

play for a fee of three thousand roubles which would be given to the poor students of the Conservatory. Polovstev was more snob than musician; a servant showed Rubinstein through a back door. Remembering London, Anton grinned and said nothing; after all, the students needed that three thousand roubles. He went upstairs and played long and generously; then he went home. The Tsar and Tsarina came late; the Tsarina asked immediately if she might have Rubinstein as a supper partner. Polovstev's chagrin was great; Rubinstein had left an hour ago.

At Easter, Anton went down to Odessa to see his mother, as was his custom every spring. At eighty-five, Kaleria was a sight any son might be proud of; she was one of those persons upon whom the scars of life sit gloriously. Her face, pink with health, bore its tale of battle proudly. "Free Artist, *Excellenz*—which is better?" she demanded slyly. Her son laughed. "I expected that, *Maman*. Both titles are good. I have a presentiment that I shall need this *Excellenz* some day against the very powers that gave it to me. For all your baptism at Berdichev, we are Jews, you and I and sister Sophie."

Kaleria said nothing; she was used to her son's reproaches concerning conversion. Anton had been only a baby. How could he know the terrors this baptism had saved him? She was eager, as always, for news of the Conservatory and advised her son to continue his ruthlessness where necessary. These classroom scandals were absurd. Carl Davidov was an old fool to have got himself mixed up with the Maharina. The women, replied Anton gloomily, certainly played havoc with music teachers. Did his mother remember Nicholas and the girl who shot herself in the Moscow *Salle de la Noblesse* with his portrait clutched to her bosom? "Give me credit," Anton said, "give me credit, at least, for never making love to pupils."

Scandals or no, the Conservatory was shaping up well. Anton told his mother he wished she could be in Petersburg next winter for his Historical Lectures. They were to last from September to May; nobody would be invited except graduate students of the

309

piano class. He would cover musical history from Rameau to the moderns. The whole thing would be very informal; it would be fun to talk as well as play.

"Good!" said Kaleria. "Work hard! But remember your manners at Court, Tonia. People have brought me tales. After all, this is your Tsar, this is the grandson of Nicholas Pavlovitch whom we loved. Will rudeness at Court benefit your Conservatoire?"

30

1888-1889. Anton talks to his pupils about music and is very rude to his Tsar

On Friday evening, September 28th, Rubinstein gave the first of the Historical Lectures. He had announced plainly that no one but piano students would be permitted entrance. Nevertheless, Petersburg crowded the streets before the Conservatory, begging for tickets. To hear Anton Gregorovitch talk as well as play—Anton the gruff, the silent, who never smiled at an audience, let alone spoke to them—how enchanting!

Observing the nature of the crowd, which had arrived in carriages, Rubinstein issued a limited number of tickets at a hundred roubles each, the money to go toward a new Conservatory building. Petersburg society fought for the tickets; moreover, when Anton announced that the lectures would begin exactly at eight, snow or hail, Petersburg ladies got there on time—homage seldom accorded to art in Russia in those days. In the end, even the stage was filled; Anton permitted his colleagues, the professors, to sit behind him.

Rubinstein was at his happiest on these evenings, playing with the music before him, pausing to illustrate and explain. He smiled, joked, told about his meetings with Chopin, Mendelssohn and Liszt, his manner like a father's with his children. He had always hated what he called the *tutti-frutti* arrangement of concert programs, believing that even orchestral evenings should be devoted to the works of one composer, or at least to a particular epoch in art. Now before him lay thirty-two Saturday evenings on which to present music as he thought it should be presented. Rubinstein had a strong historical sense, disliking intensely any separation of music from life. He felt the long continuity of art, believing music to be "the echo and re-echo of historical events." He told his students that he could trace for them, through music alone, the historical milestones of their own century, and proceeded to do so with the logical precision of a scholar.

Anton told his students that he had always been consumed with curiosity to know how the early classical compositions had really sounded. Time alters the tone of musical instruments; in the big room at Liszt's house in Weimar, Mozart's harpsichord was a gorgeous relic—but only a relic. However, though a perfect physical reproduction of eighteenth-century tone is impossible, still we know that a Mozart *forte* and a Beethoven *forte* are two different things and must have different pedal treatment. "I do not even like to hear the string quartets of Haydn and Mozart played with a large, broad bowing," said Rubinstein, "nor their symphonies with a big orchestra. Playing Handel and Bach, who belong to the organ epoch, I try to *register* on the piano: that is, to give the music an organ-like character by means of pedaling. Hummel, I try to play with scholastic, short, clear touch and very little pedal. Weber and Mendelssohn with very brilliant execution and pedal—expressing operatic, dramatic or lyric character as the case may be. For Beethoven, Schubert, Schumann, Chopin, I use all the resources of our modern pianoforte."

Down in the front row, his dark eyes wide, alert, sat little Ossip Gabrilowitsch, nine years old, a lace collar over his blouse suit. Young Glazunov was there, and Rimsky-Korsakov, tall and academic in his spectacles. Liadov, sitting erect as a soldier, Lavrovskaya, Malozemova, and the rest of the vocal staff. Leopold Auer, Boris Kamensky the violinist with his blue eyes and quick smile. The great Obolensky family, Prince Volkonsky and Anton's friends from Court and society. One and all could understand Rubinstein's words, which were simple—and if a child could not understand his words, his manner at the piano was illustration enough. Bach he played reverently, sitting quite still with no flourish of hands, no tossing back of hair. Humanity, said Anton, was too small for Sebastian Bach; heaven itself had lived in him while he was on earth. "You must study Bach very thoroughly, my children. He will be your best teacher. He will refresh you like cold water on a hot day."

And turning to play Handel, Rubinstein gave a great technical display, using *pianissimo*, playing the fast passages very fast and pausing to remark that compared with Sebastian Bach, Handel had been a *mondain* who lived in the world and was of the world. "All that is connected with Sebastian Bach must be dear and sacred to us; next week we shall concern ourselves with his sons and his nephews." And next week, true to promise, Anton played Emmanuel Bach for two hours, recommending that all the "moderns" in the audience study Emmanuel's book on the art of clavier playing.

The tenth lecture fell on Rubinstein's birthday; he was fifty-nine. On the piano he found a letter containing three hundred roubles, donated by the students toward the erection of a new Conservatory building.

"Dear Master," he read. "It is you who have put Russia on a level with the musical nations of Europe, you who have opened our country to music. Besides your great energy, you are very kind, and to us your kindness is wonderful. It was a happy fate that permitted us to live in your time and go along with you. We are sorry for the thousands who wanted to hear your lectures and could not because our hall is too small. So we ask you to accept our little donation, a cornerstone toward the realization of your dreams."

Anton was touched. He smiled, and played Haydn—four sonatas. "Listen!" he said. "In this music, someone is laughing. Did you notice, children, that I kept my left foot down all the time? Our modern instrument is too heavy for Haydn." He played Mozart, and sat silent a moment. "Singular," he said, "that in our time we give Mozart's music only to children of nine and ten! It takes grown-up children to play Mozart."

The twelfth lecture brought the series to Beethoven, who was Rubinstein's god, and everyone knew it. The next seven evenings he devoted to this master; at closing time neither he nor the audience wanted to go home. "It is ten o'clock, and I am sorry," Anton said. Finishing the first sonata in F minor, he looked at his audience.

313

"Have you, thus far, heard anything like this Finale? Here you feel our own century, our agitation and nervous excitement. I cannot get over my astonishment at this man of the eighteenth century who felt the modern spirit so far in advance. . . . And let me remind you, children, that in Handel and Bach, the repeat-signs may be disregarded, but in Haydn, Mozart and Beethoven they are an integral part of the structure. Omission is *lèse-majesté*."

The fifth Beethoven lecture fell on Christmas Eve. Not a seat was vacant. "Up to that evening," one of the students reported, "Rubinstein had tried to restrain his fiery nature and had striven to play in a clear, classical style. But Beethoven's music carried him away. The Finale of the *C sharp Sonata*, Opus 27 No. 2, he played with such force that the platform trembled. 'I do not know why this sonata should be called *The Moonlight Sonata*,' he said. 'Moonlight awakens a lyric feeling, while this music tells of a sky heavy with leaden colors. In the Finale the storm breaks; only the short middle movement is lyric. To call the whole work after this movement is absurd. Beethoven knew nothing of this title.'

"In all, he played eight sonatas that night. The Finale of the *Appassionata*, Opus 57, he took at such a dizzy pace that we fairly held our breath. Half the audience rose from its seats, so intense was the excitement, and at the end a deafening burst of applause greeted Rubinstein as he left the platform, apparently half dazed. Returning, he said, 'It is really barbarous to play one Beethoven sonata after another as I have done. Each one is a world of thought and feeling, enough to fill more than an evening. But what can we do, when we have so little time?' "

Often, while he played at these lectures, Rubinstein talked aloud, half to himself, half to the audience. "Wonderful music! Delicious music!" Once, playing Haydn, he made a mistake. "I beg your pardon," he muttered, as if to the composer. On New Year's Eve he began the lecture with Beethoven's charming sonata in F sharp Major, Opus 78, expressing his delight with the first movement, adjuring the students to note the conciseness of the second movement. "How much Beethoven tells in a few words! As Liszt says, 'It is the frugality of the rich.'"

He would not admit to the conventional three periods of Beethoven. "In my opinion there are only two; the period of health and the period of suffering, when Beethoven withdrew from the world and lost himself in the visions of an abstract universe." Reverently he spoke of the Master's deafness. "Unspeakable grief for him, unspeakable joy for us who play this music!" Playing the Sonata, *Les Adieux,* Opus 81, Anton explained that this was the first program music to express emotional feeling. "I myself have so lived in this sonata that I could give the meaning of every measure in words."

At the last Beethoven lecture, after playing the sonata in A flat, Opus 110, Rubinstein declared that for sheer expression, no aria from any opera could compare with it. "Can you not see, here, how instrumental music stands higher than vocal music? The deepest feeling, the greatest grief, the most exultant rapture can find expression only in tones, not words.

"How are we," he continued, "to explain Beethoven's following this deeply touching movement with a fugue—the coupling of such godlike melody with reason and science? It is cynicism, bitterness, as if the composer would say, 'See what I can do—suffer and weep— yet be so clever as to show my learning!' Beethoven had an astounding prophetic instinct for the future mechanism of the piano. In the fifth measure of the Adagio he felt that a time would come when the tone could be 'sung.' He desired a long-sustained tone—and now we can sustain it!"

Rubinstein might better have said, "Now *I* can sustain it." As Beethoven interpreter he was supreme. . . . What he said in these lectures is hardly musical news; yet he said it, somehow, with such force of sincerity, such depth of love that after fifty years the words live again as the words of platform lecturers seldom live. We are with Rubinstein on those winter evenings in the gas-lit hall with the snow driving fine and cold against the windows; we see the player, dark-haired, heavy-shouldered, turn from the keyboard to the rows

315

of eager young faces. "I have lived through this sonata," he says. "You ask me, was Beethoven the Alpha and Omega of music? Not quite. He has taken us with him in his flight to the stars. But from below, a song is heard, 'O come hither to earth, that is so beautiful!' This is Schubert, singing for our return from heaven."

And playing Schubert, Rubinstein remarked that students must always bear in mind the lyric character of this music. "Sometimes my pupils play Schubert to me and it sounds so terribly dry! I ask them, 'Has this theme really no meaning for you?' When I hear it, I want to embrace someone." Playing the melody exquisitely with his right hand, Rubinstein made a wide, sweeping gesture with the left as though pressing someone to his heart. "When you play the Finale to the Schubert *A flat Sonata*, then you must smile, not only with the lips, but with the fingers."

Schumann, Anton called the greatest of all the Romantic composers. But it was when he came to Chopin that Anton was able to let fly. He gave four evenings of Chopin. For Rubinstein, earth held no greater pleasure than to play the music of this man whom he called the "piano-bard, the piano-rhapsodist, the piano-mind, the piano-soul." . . . "Whether," said Anton, "the spirit of this instrument breathed upon Chopin or he upon it, I do not know. But only the complete transfer of one into the other could call such compositions to life."

The last lecture, on May 26th, was devoted to Liszt. Rubinstein gave no time to the modern school. "That," said he, "belongs to the future, and the future lies with us in Russia. The present is a period of transition; the moderns use excess of coloring at the expense of line, frame at the expense of picture. What the future will bring, I shall not live to see."

On this last evening the students presented Rubinstein with a silver plaque on which were engraved the names of the composers whose music he had played. Anton smiled and said he did not deserve a present. "I have only enjoyed myself playing the music I loved best. I have told you that, with the music of Chopin and Schumann, *finis musicae*. I am old and must go the way of the old.

Therefore I love the old composers rather than the new. But you are young; I do not wish to turn you from young composers. Love them and study them if you will. But do not forget the old ones, the great ones."

In Petersburg the lectures made a profound impression. This was more than Rubinstein the magician, the virtuoso; it was Rubinstein the scholar, the analyst and historian, come home to share his wisdom with Russia. The Tsarina seized upon this, talked of it to her spouse—and in the very midst of the lectures, under the influence of the Christmas season, persuaded him to give Rubinstein the old Bolshoi (Grand) Theatre for a Conservatory. . . . Did Alexander Alexandrovitch not see that the present hall was too small? Had he not, indeed, nearly got stuck in his chair for lack of room? Majesty smiled, and on New Year's Day, 1889, presented the Bolshoi Theatre to Anton Rubinstein's Conservatory.

The Bolshoi was an enormous affair, very dear to the citizens of Petersburg. Here Mario had sung, and Grisi; here the old beloved operas had been performed. The building stood on a fine square, one of the handsomest situations in town. From Petersburg's point of view, it was a munificent gesture for the Tsar to make.

But from Rubinstein's point of view the gesture was a little less than munificent. In spite of its lavish gilt-and-plush effect, the old theatre was anything but sound. It was, in fact, falling to pieces. The ceiling had been declared unsafe; a new one would cost a fortune. Strolling through the empty building with an architect friend, Anton looked at the gilt and the dusty chandeliers and shook his head sourly. Now, if the Tsar had presented an endowment with this handsome white elephant . . .

A *soirée* was planned to thank the Tsar publicly for his gift. Rubinstein, white-shirted and tailed, with his hair mussed, stood grimly in a corner. Affable, as is the nature of the patron, the Tsar approached and tapped Anton on the shoulder. "*Eh bien,* Rubinstein, you like my gift?"

Standing quite straight, without inclining his head as was the custom, Anton looked his sovereign steadily in the eye.

"*Non!*" he said.

Was the man mad? Bystanders listened in frightened silence. This was no way to receive Father Tsar's bounty.

"And why do you not like it?"

"Your Imperial Majesty," said Anton, "if I gave you a beautiful cannon, all mounted and embossed, with no ammunition—would you like it?"

Alexander's grandfather would have laughed at this; Alexander's grandfather understood artists. But the grandson of Nicholas I did not laugh. He was angry and showed it, and gave not one kopeck of endowment. Rubinstein began arranging concerts for the benefit of a new Conservatory building and kept them up until he died.

That summer of 1889, workmen arrived on Theatre Square and began to tear down the Bolshoi, which had been found hopelessly rickety. But in spite of unsoundness, the old building withstood the workmen's hammers; dynamite had to be used. Petersburg stood around gloomily while the charges went off. But Anton Rubinstein did not weep. Pencil in hand, he sat with the architect, planning classrooms, an auditorium, an operatic stage for pupils' performances—and then went out and played the piano to earn money for the realization of his dream. He persuaded Tchaikovsky to come up from Moscow and conduct the concerts of the Musical Society, and in turn he himself went down to Moscow and played for the benefit of Nicholas' Conservatory.

But he had chosen a bad moment to be rude to his Tsar. The very month of the Bolshoi gift—January, 1889—the *Merchant Kalashnikoff* was scheduled for performance at the Maryinsky Theatre. This was the fateful opera that had been withdrawn nine years ago after one performance which, unluckily, had taken place on the very day a Nihilist was hung in Petersburg—far too significant an analogy with the *Merchant* who also met his fate at the hands of a Tsar. Lately, however, Alexander III had commanded a revival of the opera which he had been told was truly Russian. It was his firm

318

policy to patronize Russian art. After all, no Nihilists had been hung lately. What this monarch considered the firm policies of his reign were succeeding admirably; the country was comparatively quiet.

Arrangements went forward and then, a few days before the dress rehearsal, Rubinstein received a letter from the directorship of the opera house, informing him the *Merchant* was again withdrawn "for political reasons." This, said Rubinstein grimly, was opera-house politics, not national politics. Indignant and powerful friends went straight to the Tsar. Faction ran high; Prince Obolensky was enthusiastic in the opera's defense, the Counts Lamsdorf and Hirz professed themselves "shocked" by the rehearsal they had seen. And then the Procurator himself, Professor Pobyedonostsev, took a hand. In all good faith he attended the dress rehearsal—and emerged, he reported to his sovereign, "as if stunned." Horrible vice, corruption and violence were depicted on a stage decorated like a church with ikons—even haloed ikons. Songs set to the words of the holy Psalms were sung to *motifs* recognizable as church music! Above all, Tsar Ivan, a monster of a creature, indulged in an orgy of drinking right there in the holy place. "I write these lines at night, after the theatre. Let Your Majesty believe me—coming out of the box I saw two people with tears in their eyes and heard them say: 'My God, why do they show us such a scene? Above all, why show it now, when Russia is just beginning to live again, when every eye is turned toward our Tsar and finds, at last, ideal traits that our people have so ardently, passionately desired in their ruler?' The first time *Kalashnikoff* was performed, in 1880, things were quite different in our country; it was a time of madness, irritation, of great sedition. But now! Even if the Tsar and Tsarina, in the simplicity and purity of their hearts, see no offense—we Russians, we the people, are offended by that scene which reviles all that we hold saintly."

But the Tsar, who had commanded this production over his own signature, refused to yield without a trial. He asked for a private performance and sat through it from beginning to end with his Tsarina by his side. Next day Rubinstein was curtly informed that the opera had been withdrawn from the repertory.

Had Anton been more the courtier, he might have healed this breach—the most serious he had opened so far between himself and the Court. His friends urged him to rewrite the opera, retaining all the music but re-decorating the scenes minus ikon and halo to please the Holy Synod. Rubinstein refused, blaming the opera directorship and not the Tsar for what had occurred. Who was actually to blame we do not know, but we do know that the Petersburg opera directorship, first and last, was hostile to Rubinstein. Anton loved battle, liked to meet a hostile audience, face it, conquer it and make it his. But he was not equipped for the kind of battle that Herman Wolff, for instance, rejoiced in: the bargaining and manipulation and cajolery and cool bullying that go on behind every theatre stage before a work can be produced. Whether the Tsar or the Theatre was hostile to his opera did not much matter. The point was that Rubinstein could not get his operas staged.

Once more, *Kalashnikoff* was laid upon the shelf. Anton finished his lectures and the school year and went out to Peterhof, grim, disillusioned, but looking eagerly forward to beginning a new composition.

3 *1*

The Jubilee

Jᴜʟʏ, 1889, marked the fiftieth anniversary of Rubinstein's début as a concert pianist. . . . Walking alone under his fruit trees at Peterhof or sitting by his tower window looking out over the forest to the blue summer sea, Anton remembered the night in Moscow long ago when, a little boy in frilled blouse and buttoned boots, he had played his first concert at Petrovsky Park. Ever since, for him, the world had been filled with stages and audiences and pianos—but especially with pianos. Looking back, the audiences were not, somehow, so important. It was the instrument itself that had become, as years rolled by, as much part of life as daylight and breathing. People tried to tell Anton that if his life had held no pianos he would still have made his name known to the world; he would have been painter, statesman—anything that gave outlet to that deep, restless energy. But Rubinstein knew it was not so; he knew that when his mother tied him to that hard chair to make him practice, she had done right. She had introduced him to the one instrument that could give perfect outlet to the strength within him.

Russia loves anniversaries. The Conservatory and the Musical Society were busy with plans. It would not do to have the festivities in summer with everyone away; celebration was postponed until autumn. Anton would be sixty in November; the Jubilee could be built around his birthday.

The villa at Peterhof was gay that summer. Both sons were at home and Anna with her baby daughter, born last January. Anton adored the baby, spoiled her in true grandfather style and took her picture with him everywhere; she was named Vera after her grandmother. On July 11th, the day of the first-concert anniversary, telegrams poured in from all over the world; the family sat around and watched their father open them. The most august message of all came from the Tsar's palace at Peterhof, only two miles away.

The Tsarina must have had a hand in this, thought Rubinstein, and, at his wife's insistence, drove over to thank his sovereign. It was a beautiful summer day; along the shore, birches leaned to the breeze; from the palace turrets, flags flew. The Imperial household was well disposed toward the world on that summer day and invited Rubinstein to lunch.

He returned home more than a little thoughtful. On his last visit to Odessa, Anton's mother had cautioned him concerning his manners at Court, but how could any musician feel easy in the presence of Alexander III? There was too much Holy Synod around the palace and too little art. No wonder the Grand Duke Konstantin spent his time in Paris with his wicked, warm-hearted old ballerina. Alexander III was the first Romanov to remain faithful to his wife. A bad sign; the Romanovs had always been bigamists of the most energetic kind. Romanovs were big and lusty; their whiskers grew long and thick. In spite of their German wives and their German generals, they were very close to the East. Apron-string government, domestic complacence sat ill upon them.

Opening his telegrams, reading letters of congratulation, hearing of plans for the Jubilee, Rubinstein was restless. There was something too valedictory about this. His health was good, his energy abounding. Much work remained to be done, much writing of music and above all, much teaching. His eyesight and failing memory interfered with his conducting orchestras and sometimes with his playing, but after all it was more an inconvenience to the orchestra than to Rubinstein! Lately, when his memory failed him at the piano, he had gone into visible rages. In Vienna, playing the Schumann Concerto he had got lost completely and when the conductor placed the music before him Anton had dashed it to the floor and finished the Concerto in a burst of tremendous passion. One evening in Petersburg, playing a Handel fugue, he could not get beyond a certain passage and played it over and over, searching a way out. Down in the audience Vera Rubinstein, sitting straight and tall with her feather boa round her neck and her lorgnette uneasily at her eye, turned to Leopold Auer. "A very long fugue, is it not?"

But after all, lack of memory was a minor disability; Anton knew that it only attacked him in public and that in spite of it his performance was as magnetic as ever. Moreover, he had been too busy to let these things depress him. After the fainting fits in Paris, Dr. Vompe at Peterhof had cautioned him to change his way of life; this girdle of pain around the chest after playing was nothing to be cavalier about, said the good doctor. Anton had merely laughed and forgotten all about it.

But these Jubilee congratulations made a man remember such things, made a man think of the future in terms of the past—something Anton Rubinstein, who lived furiously in the present, had never done. Reading telegrams about what one has accomplished in fifty years is not a healthy occupation; one begins to question this smug flattery. There was no doubt that Anton Rubinstein was the first pianist of Europe. But what kind of title, after all, was that? The continued failure of his big compositions wiped all pleasure from the laurels of *premier virtuoso*. Bitter memories visited Anton; the night in Berlin when he had played a whole concert to a crowded theatre that had applauded vigorously the first half of the program when he played Schumann and Chopin—and walked out almost to a man before the last half, which was all-Rubinstein. Like most artists, Anton tried to ignore newspaper criticism, but how those black phrases could stick in a man's mind! In Vienna the day after the production of *Nero*, all the funny men in the comic sheets were after the opera like a pack of laughing hyenas, caricaturing, making verses. Hanslick had flayed it, so had Speidel and Domke and Helm. As for London *Punch* after *Il Demonio*, it was best to forget those British puns: "There was a great demonstration in favor of *Il Demonio*; but the Opera was so heavy that we found it impossible to carry any of it away with us; so let us leave it as it is. . . . Dull music by Rubinstein, brilliant English translation of the libretto by our own Pittman."

In New York they had played the character-piece, *Ivan the Terrible*. A reporter had written that it was "like the black draught of our youth—good for us but we didn't like it. We'd rather have the black draught, though, than Ivan IV." Bülow had played Anton's *G Major Concerto* in Boston a few years ago; Anton had seen one of the criticisms. "The audience got so bemuddled as to take refuge in the delusion that they were all delighted. We cannot describe Rubinstein's music, if music it may be called. It makes the orchestra and pianoforte rave like inarticulate monsters in pain; its progress is by jerks and spasms, it is without form and void of sense—the gibberish of the Pythoness calling herself modern German Music."

How could anyone mistake the *G Major Concerto*, either in form or substance, for Wagnerian *Zukunftmusik*? When Anton tried to write a straight piano concerto, the critics called it "modern German"; when he wrote, in all reverence, musical scenes from the Bible, they said the form was theatrical or impossible. Thinking on these things, black depression settled upon Anton Rubinstein. Old Bartholf Senff, his Leipzig publisher, wrote him a letter of congratulation on his Jubilee. In a dark hour, Anton sat down and poured out his heart to his old friend:

"I confess that the net result of all my artistic activity is the completest disappointment. That upon which I have lavished all my hopes and all my study—my composition—is a failure. My whole existence is a mockery. I who am convinced that art is entirely dead, that no eight measures are written nowadays worth a penny, that even reproductive art—vocal and instrumental—is not fit to latch the shoestring of what has gone before—I, who believe this, spend my whole time educating pupils in composition and execution, knowing all the while that my efforts are love's labor lost. You can imagine therefore, the irony I shall have to summon on the occasion of my so-called Jubilee this autumn. *'Eitel, eitel ist des Menschen.'*

"But greetings to you, dear Herr Senff. Tear up this letter and think as well as before of your unfortunately not-yet-crazy, and no longer reproductive and creative

"Anton Rubinstein."

Rubinstein sent off this letter early in September. Perhaps it acted

324

Anton Rubinstein. *From the portrait by Repin*

as an emotional purge for one who was habitually so reticent. Anyway, Anton put his depression aside long enough to go up to his turret study and finished a *Concertstück* for piano and orchestra to play at the Jubilee. *All is vanity,* he had written to Herr Senff. And yet, one thing in his life had not been vain. The Conservatory stood firmly on its feet where Anton had planted it thirty-seven years ago, expanding, taking music to places and people where music was needed. "When I am dead," said Anton, "all that I care men shall remember me by is this Conservatory—that they should say it was Anton Rubinstein's work."

Consistency is a quality that belongs to no man; the pronouncements of discouraged artists must not be taken too literally. Rubinstein knew that the Jubilee would be trying. People would expect him to make speeches. If only Nicholas were here, if *Maman* could come for the celebration, it might hold an element of pleasure. Nicholas had been marvelous at speechmaking; as toastmaster he could make any banquet succeed. . . . Well, the affair would last an evening and then, Anton told himself, he could forget it and proceed with his work.

But Petersburg had no intention of the Jubilee's lasting a mere evening. The Conservatory opened in an air of pleasant excitement. Rehearsals of *tableaux vivants* from Rubinstein's operas, rehearsals of chorus and orchestra. Tchaikovsky had written a brand new *Intermezzo* for the occasion and was coming up from Moscow to conduct Anton's *Russian Symphony.* There was to be a huge ball in Nobility Hall, featuring one of Rubinstein's ballets. His new opera, *Gorusha,* would fill another gala evening. Whispers in the Conservatory halls when Anton Gregorovitch appeared. . . . Doors closing suddenly. . . . Pretty girls in costume fleeing laughingly around corners . . .

Rumors of this reached the Tsar. It was suitable for the Conservatory to honor its director; but what was all this talk about aristocratic society joining in—even Imperial society? Helena Pavlovna's daughter, the Grand Duchess Catherine, planned to return from abroad for the celebration. Surely, the Imperial luncheon last summer had been reward enough! Must Petersburg feast for five days because a pianist had played for fifty years?

"Will Jienshin be there too?" asked the Tsar. Jienshin was the Grand Duchess Catherine's very musical daughter Helena, named after her grandmother. Jienshin was indeed to be there. So was her brother the Grand Duke of Mecklenburg-Strelitz, who adored music and played the 'cello. The Imperial family was taking too prominent a part in this absurd affair, said the Tsar, and told his ministers to stay away. At one of the ceremonies, Rubinstein was to receive the promise of a lifetime governmental pension of 3000 roubles a year. Not a large sum, considering what the man had done for Russian education, but from an Imperial point of view, quite adequate for a musician to live upon. Surely, the man must have made a great deal of money, playing in concerts all over the world. . . .

Other people differed with Majesty on this question. The Grand Duke Konstantin's wife sent her son Konstantin to petition for increase of the pension. Alexander did not like the Konstantins, father or son. He did not like the way the young man worded his plea, either: "Rubinstein has given thousands of roubles to Russia." It was not for Jewish artists to patronize Russia; patronage belonged to Majesty. Frowning, Alexander III read the petition and tore it to shreds.

The opening celebration was planned for 1 a.m. in the Hall of the Nobility—an hour not at all extraordinary for Russian celebration. It would be the first hour of Rubinstein's sixtieth birthday. As a matter of fact, Anton himself had quoted his birthday two days wrong all his life; he declared now that he was too old to change, so let them celebrate it on the 26th as always, not on the 28th as the chronologists insisted. . . . Everyone went to dinner parties first and then on to the Hall of the Nobility to await Rubinstein's appearance on the stage.

In the Imperial box sat—not the Tsar—but the Grand Duchess Catherine with her daughter Helena and her nephew Konstantin, who had written a poem for the occasion. The Rubinstein family had the box opposite, Vera looking handsome and severe, her décolleté covered with the inevitable feather boa, Anna and the sons, straight and young and beautiful. Rubinstein's sons were extraordinarily handsome; Jacob especially. The big hall was jammed with artists, musicians and many figures from the fashionable world whose loyalty to Rubinstein dared Imperial displeasure. On the stage was a huge bust of Rubinstein done by Ober and two large statues of the Muses, behind which sat the orchestra and chorus of the Musical Society.

At one o'clock Rubinstein walked onto the stage with Helena Pavlovna's grandson, Duke George of Mecklenburg-Strelitz. The audience leaped to its feet, cheering and waving. Almost everyone knew Rubinstein personally; there was more affection than formality to this occasion. Prince George got up and talked about his grandmother, Helena Pavlovna, of her affection and admiration for Anton Gregorovitch, of the founding of the Musical Society and the Conservatory. Senator Markevitch made a speech, and then everyone sat back and listened to Tchaikovsky's choral *Intermezzo*. Becker, the Petersburg piano maker, presented Rubinstein with a dazzling white instrument decorated with Anton's portrait in bronze and silver bas-relief. The Musical Society presented a handsome gold medal. Anton came forward and bowed, his face impassive. The Mayor pronounced him an honorary citizen of Petersburg. Anton bowed again. Somebody came forward and made him an honorary member of the Petersburg University. Anton bowed, wishing grimly that Nicholas were here—Nicholas who had been so careful not to let his brother forget that only one of the Rubinstein musicians had a university degree.

Count Vorontsov-Dashkov, emissary of the Court, handed Rubinstein the Imperial order for the 3000-rouble pension and in the audience a slight restlessness was noticeable. Eyes turned toward the Imperial box. Many knew the story of the Grand Duchess' petition. What one Grand Duchess knew, another knew. No doubt Catherine Michailovna saw eye to eye with her sister-in-law over this matter. . . .

Then the out-of-town delegations began to be heard from. There were sixty-six of these, some from abroad, some from the Russian towns where Rubinstein had founded music schools. The Dutch representative received an especial ovation. "The country of Rembrandt comes to honor Anton Rubinstein," began the *Meinherr*— and the crowd roared approval; Anton had often been likened to Rembrandt. Then the grandchildren of Count Vielgorsky, Anton's old 'cello-playing friend who had helped him found the Musical Society in '59, walked onto the stage holding the famous Sokolov portrait of the Rubinstein brothers as boys. Vielgorsky himself had had it painted; it had been much reproduced and already was so familiar as a picture that many households where it hung had no idea who the boys were and told their children these were the little English princes in the tower. . . .

The Moscow delegates were Serge Taneiev, Nicholas' great pupil, and Safonov, Director of the Moscow Conservatory. Tchaikovsky was to arrive next day.

The only persons who stayed away were the Tsar and his immediate entourage, the directors of the Imperial theatres, and Mili Balakirev, one-time leader of the *Kutchka*. The theatre directors had always been hostile to Rubinstein and as for Balakirev, he had latterly become so morose that he frightened away even his dearest friends. His refusal to attend the Jubilee made a sensation in Petersburg. "Rubinstein has done nothing but harm to Russian music," Balakirev wrote in answer to his invitation.

Opposition only strengthened the zeal of Rubinstein's friends. Anton himself behaved like a man in a dream. He had had no idea the thing would assume such proportions and was possessed by the strange sensation that he was merely a witness to something intended for another man. Soon the hero would come forward and he, Rubinstein, would applaud with the rest. . . . When his friends poured into the box he greeted them, but spoke no word to the crowds below and kept his eyes turned to the stage. . . . The trophies were sent home to be boxed and carried out to Peterhof.

Next day there was a gala concert; Tchaikovsky conducted the

Russian Symphony—Tchaikovsky whom Anton Rubinstein had taught and then ignored and whom Nicholas had helped to make known to Europe—Tchaikovsky who, in spite of everything, to the very end could not resist the personality of Anton Gregorovitch— "This extraordinary man who has only to hold out his hand and smile to make you fall at his feet."

That night Anton played his new *Concertstück* for piano and orchestra, written for the occasion. He might be old, he might profess himself "no longer creative," but the professional artist in him would not permit him to palm off his old music on the public whether the occasion were his own or another man's. He believed in occasional music; Mozart had written to order; so had Beethoven and Liszt; so did Tchaikovsky and Anton Rubinstein. To write for occasion was a sign of artistic health, said Anton Rubinstein; it showed that a country's art was not degenerating into mere platform music.

After the concert that night there was a supper party. One hundred and fifty guests drank a toast to Anton Rubinstein, to Alexandre Villoing, lying now in the Nevsky churchyard—and lastly, a toast to Anton's "first teacher, his mother, Kaleria Rubinstein."

During every ceremony so far, Anton's face had remained blank, immovable. Now at last, expression came upon it. As the glasses were raised, Anton's face softened and he smiled. Everyone looked to him, awaiting a reply, but he shook his head, sitting silent, his eyes filled with tears.

Next evening, another big concert . . . Dances from *Feramors* . . . Two acts from the *Tower of Babel* . . . All Petersburg applauding . . . students . . . shopkeepers . . . porters . . . cab drivers who had driven Anton to and from the Conservatory. . . . A crowd so dense that people fainted and were carried out. . . .

In his palace the Tsar of all the Russias heard of this and frowned. A mere musician—and Russian men and women fought to do him honor, bribing ushers to let them stand for three hours in his presence. . . . How could a Tsar know that when this man made music, even stupid peasant-janitors stopped with their brooms outside his door, finger to lip. *"Anton Gregorovitch is playing!"*

On the fourth night, Rubinstein's new opera, *Gorusha,* was given its first and only performance. Sitting in his box, Rubinstein watched and listened and at the end, rose to face the crowd. His face showed great emotion. Speeches could not move him, but two things could. One was the gesture toward his mother last night, another was this staging of a new work. He hesitated. When he spoke his voice was low but everyone heard him. "I do not know how to express my gratitude. I did not expect this. Truly, I did not expect it at all. There is left for me to say only thank you, thank you." Anton sat down, his head bowed.

The Jubilee was nearly over. Only one celebration remained, a grand ball given next evening in Rubinstein's honor by his colleagues and fellow musicians for the benefit of the new Conservatory building. The Hall of the Nobility was bright with flowers and palms. A quadrille, waltzes, a cotillion . . . All the Conservatory students . . . Mammas of well-born daughters watchful . . . These Conservatory youths were endowed, obviously, with more talent than background. Why could not other musicians have the manner and bearing of a Rubinstein?

But the bearing of a Rubinstein did not derive, as the ladies may have thought, from fifty years of glory. It derived from fifty years of hard work. Fifty years of grinding necessity—necessity for money, for glory and for the release of something deep within, something hard, bright and uncomfortable with which the ladies themselves had never been troubled.

32

*Petersburg. Anton as teacher. He leaves the
Conservatory forever*

THE Jubilee was over. Anton Rubinstein, with half a century's applause, half a century's bitterness behind him, went back to his pupils and his Conservatory.

In Petersburg he moved with equal pleasure among three generations. He was a grandfather; the women who had loved him were old too. Julie Abaza lived in a palace with her white-haired military husband, gave musical *soirées* and took snuff behind her fan, confident that nobody noticed. When Anton sat down to play in her drawing room, with a wave of her hand she would call for silence, whispering loudly to the servant who came in with laden tray: "Efim, Efim, how many times must I tell you, 'No tea when there is music!'"

Anton only smiled. He was loyal to his old loves, to Malozemova, his pupil in the first class to graduate from the Conservatory, a professor now in the school and homely as a witch, to old Lavrovskaya the singer, once velvet-voiced and fêted. He called them his *Fidelky*, and when people asked why he had these old bores around, "They love me so," Anton said.

But if he was faithful to the old, Anton was still extraordinarily attractive to the young. His hair was black and thick as ever; he arrived as ever at the Conservatory on the stroke of nine, wrapped in his old fur *shuba* and stayed all day, sending out at noon for tea and sweet bread. Having such a Director brought extraordinary visitors to the Conservatory halls. The Grand Duke Konstantin came often when he was in town, always in uniform, always good-natured, looking for a chance to talk and gossip and perhaps to take part in a string quartet on a borrowed student 'cello.

When Anton went home at night to the Troitsky Pereulok, he was pursued by half of Petersburg. Up the two flights of stairs to his big rooms climbed poets, dramatists, musicians of all classes and degrees. Painters, journalists—this was the *rendezvous* for all the talent in or passing through town—salted by the prettiest and wittiest of Russian *grandes dames*. There were seldom less than twelve for dinner, often twenty or thirty. A place at this table was something to boast of; everything and everyone in the art world was discussed and dissected; the one forbidden topic was politics. The food was good; Anton liked to eat, liked to discuss the Italian dishes at which his Italian cook excelled. After dinner there were cards and then old Matvey brought in tea, Russian *tchai* in glasses with a silver holder, served smoking hot with lemon.

Now was the hour when everyone sat praying for Rubinstein to go to the piano; he did not like to be asked. A new pupil, a clever young Irish girl just arrived in Petersburg, did not know this rule and one evening, wickedly prompted by a fellow guest, innocently asked Rubinstein to give them some music. Anton scowled, there was a silence through the room and the girl, terrified, burst into tears. "Well, come now!" said Rubinstein. "Give me a kiss and I will play." Lillian shook her head, too shy to move. "So?" said Anton to the company. "Well, I shall play for her anyway because she is the first ever to refuse me." He played Chopin, a Nocturne, a Mazurka, ending with the *F sharp Minor Polonaise*. When he stopped his face was ashen, his breath came in gasps.

The disease he called asthma was slowly gaining way, but Anton refused to admit it was serious. He sat a moment, puffing at his cigarette, then stood up as a signal that it was nearly eleven and time for the company to go.

The girl who was victim that night, young Lillian Macarthur, was better able to take care of herself than the story would indicate. Her presence in Petersburg was the end of a long pilgrimage. Eight years ago, when she was a child of twelve, this girl had heard Rubinstein play in Dublin and had run away from home to hear him again in London. She had been introduced to him; he had ad-

332

mired her long red hair and had told her she might be his pupil after she had acquired the requisite technique. From that moment the girl lived only to see Rubinstein again. After years of study, topped by a winter with Von Bülow, she made her way alone to Petersburg and presented herself to the master. "*Nun,* Titian-head!" said Anton, kissing her hand. "So you have really come! I am very glad to see you and welcome you to Russia. But what have you done with your hair?"

She had cut it off, she said, to save the trouble of arranging it. "The police will be after you," Anton said. "You look like a Nihilist."

After the nightmare evening when she asked Rubinstein to play at his apartment, Lillian stayed in Russia several years, supporting herself by writing articles about Rubinstein for the English and American papers and acting as secretary to answer his English and German mail. Five nights out of seven she dined at his house. One evening among the guests she noticed a bearded, extraordinary-looking person and wondered who he might be. A new novel had lately been published, called *The Kreutzer Sonata.* It had been promptly prohibited by the censor but Rubinstein got hold of it and read parts of it aloud to his pupils—read indignantly, for he did not like the musical parts. Watching Rubinstein go up to the bearded man on the evening of the party, Lillian remembered *The Kreutzer Sonata.* "Count Tolstoi," said Anton bluntly, "in your book you missed entirely the meaning of Beethoven's music."

Tolstoi shrugged. "*Nitchevo!* One piece of music or another served my purpose for a romance."

Rubinstein's eyes flashed. "True," he said. "But no matter how great you may be in your own line, that does not give you the right to distort the work of another artist."

Tolstoi soon left the room. Rubinstein shook his fist at the closing door. "I never knew a novelist yet," he said, "who could write anything but trash about music."

It was now, in these last years of his life, that the great tradition

333

of Rubinstein's teaching was established—an extraordinary tradition, considering that, as teacher, Anton had no method whatever. Beyond his brochure on the use of the pedal and his *Conversation on Music*, he wrote nothing in the nature of a textbook. It was impossible for him to give specific answers to the troubled questions of students. "There are no rules," he said. "Your musical feeling must guide you. You must listen while you play. You must hear and hear and hear."

He taught only advanced students and was outraged if a new pupil came to him badly equipped, especially as to rhythm. "I am not here to teach pupils to count," he said. He distrusted modern editions of the classics, storming angrily when pupils brought to class the musical editions of Tausig, Bülow or Klindworth. "Do I want your rendering of Monsieur Bülow's Beethoven, Monsieur Czerny's Bach?" he would growl. Passages marked *forte*, Anton played *piano*, and vice versa. If a pupil showed surprise, Anton would say it mattered not at all if one played this passage loud, that one soft. "You are after contrast, dynamic color. Make it some way, any way—but make it."

He said often that he was only a practical musician. How therefore could he tell anyone how to play? "Go to Leschetizky. He is the most brilliant theorist I know." Leschetizky in his turn never tired of telling his pupils, over in Vienna, that they must learn to do things with simplicity, like Anton Rubinstein. "If you could only hear Rubinstein pedal! One seldom notices the pedal while he plays, but it is always there. He is sensible. Common sense—that is a great word."

It was a word Rubinstein himself used often to his pupils. Artistically, Anton liked the thing that *worked*. Especially he was cautious concerning anything that seemed a little fancy, or threatened to remove music from life. He disliked Wagner's idea of a hidden orchestra, desiring rather to see the fiddler's arms move and to be thoroughly conscious of the men who made this music. "Only in church," said Rubinstein, "where one looks within himself and not about him, is invisible music effective." Someone asked him why church music in Protestant countries was more earnest and serious than in Italy and France. Reminding the questioner of the influence of opera upon church music in Latin countries, Anton replied that it would be wrong to condemn Rossini's *Stabat Mater*, Verdi's *Mass* merely because the religious feeling differed from the Protestant ideal. "Heaven is different in Palermo than in Insterburg. A beautiful maiden of Palermo throws herself upon her knees at the street corner before an image of the Virgin Mary and prays, 'O Virgin Mary, help me to win Beppo for my husband, and I will offer thee my coral necklace!' Such a prayer, at such a shrine, I cannot imagine set to music other than an allegro melody in 6/8 time. But when a beautiful maiden of Insterburg turns to God with her heart's desires, then her humility, her earnestness and her contrition demand an adagio melody in 4/4, or perhaps 3/2 measure."

From his pupils, Rubinstein took no excuses. Red-haired Lillian Macarthur came to her lesson one morning with eyes swollen, confessing that she had cried all night from homesickness. "Good!" said Rubinstein. "Sit down and sing all your *Heimweh*, all your tears, into the piano. Then you will play like an artist, not like a student." When Lillian played badly, Anton would slam his hands on her shoulders with a jar that shook her from head to foot. It was by no means unusual for him to seize a student's arm and hurl him from the piano stool. "Go play billiards," he would roar. "Go play anything but music!"

"Why are my pupils afraid of me?" Anton asked plaintively one day. "All I do is stamp on their feet and scream at them. They should not fear a little screaming."

Villoing's birch rod across the shoulders in a Paris pension high above the street, *Maman's* ruler biting sharp against one's wrists, the cords across one's belly, binding one to the chair, hunger, homesickness, poverty . . . What were a few harsh words and stampings to frighten a boy or girl?

To new pupils, indeed to anyone, the first feel of Rubinstein's hand was a shock. A young man, just introduced, whose hand Anton clasped in both of his, exclaimed aloud at the size and extraordinary softness of the palms that enveloped him. Rubinstein chuckled. "I have no hands," he said, "I have paws." His sense of touch was abnormally sensitive; he seemed to caress rather than strike the piano keys. It was in hope of imitating this caress that students came to him from all over Europe. The "Rubinstein touch," the "Rubinstein pedal," were words to conjure with. With his great thick fingers, Anton would indicate on the back of a pupil's hand the touch he wanted for certain passages. "This—not this!" Lillian Macarthur said that when she succeeded in achieving the effect Rubinstein desired, she did it more by willing the tone than by hitting the note in a particular way. The trouble was that most students had not the imagination for willing a tone to weep or to laugh. Rubinstein thought he was being practical; what he really demanded was talent. One day, angry with a student for mistreating Schumann's *Carnaval*, Anton sat down and played it through until he struck a tone exactly as he wished. He held the note, pointing at it with the other hand. "Do you hear that tone?" he inquired of the trembling pupil. "Well, that tone is worth your life and more."

The vagueness and ruthlessness of this teaching succeeded with some pupils, with others it failed utterly. Young Alexander Siloti, once Nicholas' pupil (later to be one of the world's great pianists), came up to Petersburg for lessons with Anton—and after the first session left the room in despair, resolved never to touch the piano again. Young Joseph Lhevinne heard Rubinstein play, and for three days did not go near the piano. But not from discouragement. From reverence, as one who would not touch bread because he had feasted with the Master.

Rubinstein required his pupils to sit quietly at the piano—above all, to be relaxed. Rubinstein himself had amazing relaxation at the instrument. Leschetizky told his pupils that if they wanted to know how to relax at the piano, to watch Rubinstein. Watch him, at the beginning of a long phrase, draw deep breaths, watch his dramatic pauses when he sat motionless—and the listener felt there was more rhythm in silence than in sound. If a Rubinstein pupil dared mention the fact that in action the Master was anything but motionless, Anton replied that only bad habit made him throw his hands

336

around, and anyway, when he did it he never tensed a muscle; he was as easy as a fish swimming in the water.

He was very particular about the attack and would make a pupil begin a piece again and again until the character of the music had been established. It showed bad manners, he said, to make a careless beginning to a fine piece of music; it was like greeting royalty with covered head. One girl sat down to play Beethoven's sonata in E minor, Opus 90. Interrupting her, Rubinstein demanded to be told the character of the piece. "Sorrowful," the girl replied.

"So?" thundered Rubinstein. "But who suffers here? Not you, at all events. Every note must weep. Learn to weep, Fräulein. *Mein Gott!* I have to do everything with these young people—make them laugh, make them cry!"

"Play slowly, slowly, slowly!" Anton would cry. "Practice is not practice unless it is done slowly. And when an interesting passage lies ahead, you must prepare the hearer, so that when the passage arrives, he is waiting for it."

"Where," he asked angrily of a young lady pupil, "have you left the last note of that measure? You evidently associate with hussars. Do not look surprised. That is exactly how hussars play."

And pushing the girl from the stool, Rubinstein banged out a waltz with the bass notes hit or miss, the pedal down and much "expression." "So," he said when he was done. *"Le trop est l'ennemi du bien."*

"Ah, what a horror the piano is!" he told the class. "Come, children, show me that it is not a horror. Prove it to me. The piano is a lovely instrument. You must fall in love with it, with its sound, and then be tender with it to make it, in turn, be sweeter to you. Herein," and he laid his hand on the piano, "lies divine beauty, which can be evoked only by that player who is inspired by this divine beauty!"

"How do you practice, when you sit down to work in the mornings?" he asked a boy in class. "Do you know how John Field practiced? He cut a pile of paper clippings, placed them on the piano and played a passage as many times as there were bits of paper. He once played a passage three thousand times. That is the way you must practice." And at every uncertain place in the boy's playing, Rubinstein called out, "Three thousand times!"

It was when a pupil was careless or over-assured that Rubinstein showed real distress, as though the affront were against music itself. One boy remarked about Beethoven's sonata, Opus 53, that he knew it thoroughly; to practice it longer would be a waste of time. Rubinstein's face was grim. "You are eighteen and I am sixty. I have been half a century practicing that sonata, and I still need to practice it. I congratulate you!"

It was the end of his interest in that particular boy.

In class, Anton referred often to Nicholas' playing: "My brother, Nicholas, played it thus." Or, "My brother, Nicholas, used the pedal even under the impossible conditions I have shown you." In death as in life, Nicholas Gregorovitch was the exception that proved the rule—Nicholas who played so beautifully and never practiced after he was twenty. It was pleasant to quote Nicholas, to recall his playing whenever one could. Anton longed to find a Nicholas among his pupils, and, like all born teachers, never despaired of such a discovery. "Among forty pupils," he said, "I sometimes find one who can play."

Late in August of 1890, the first International Competition, announced by Anton three years before, was held in Petersburg. The prizes were high—the winners of the piano and composition awards received each five thousand francs. But the program was cruel; obviously, Rubinstein had decided the new generation was growing soft and needed stiffening. The pianists had to play:

A Bach prelude and fugue

A Beethoven sonata, either opus 78, 81, 90, 101, 106, 109, 110 or 111

A Chopin mazurka, nocturne and ballade

One or two pieces from Schumann's *Kreisleriana* or his *Phantasiestücke*

A Liszt étude.

A Rubinstein concerto for piano and orchestra.

It was a full concert program, one to tax the capacity of a seasoned

338

veteran. From all over Europe, young men came to compete. Girls were not included; Rubinstein still insisted that women's art belonged at home, not on the concert stage. The Tsar shed the luster of royal presence over the occasion. As long as Rubinstein remained in the teaching field, Majesty approved him; or if the Tsar did not approve, at least he was willing to patronize Rubinstein's efforts toward the musical education of Russia, willing to accept the gifts this man offered.

Moscow was represented by Safonov as one of the nine judges, scouting for talent and teachers for his Conservatory. He found both. A young Italian named Busoni won first prize for composition; Safonov carried him off to teach in Moscow. Busoni stayed a year, utterly miserable in a town where he said musicians sat up all night and came tipsy to lessons.

Once established, the International Competition became one of the most exciting musical events of Europe and was continued annually until the World War put an end to it.

And now, in the winter of 1890-'91, Rubinstein began to feel the real weight of that Imperial displeasure he had sensed for so long but had dismissed as a mere surface or personal antipathy. In youth, Anton's mother had taught him to accept tsardom, absolute monarchy, as a political conception. Moreover, while Helena Pavlovna lived, Anton had been very close to the Court. Even after she died, her nephew, Alexander II, was well disposed toward Rubinstein; the Empress Dowager had a real affection for him and so had the Grand Duke Konstantin. When Alexander II was killed, Rubinstein had hurried home, eager to help his country from its confusion, eager to give the benefit of his own very specialized services. The intense nationalism that had swept over Russia after the Tsar's assassination had seemed to Rubinstein only a healthy, natural reaction, part and parcel of a movement that was taking place all over Europe. Germany, it was true, had gone too far, making it plain that a nationalism which was maintained at the point of the bayonet left little time or spirit for art. But a Bismarck was one thing, a Father

339

Tsar another. Surely the son of Alexander II would desire peace and progress for his country. . . .

Year by year, as the 1880's wore on, Rubinstein observed uneasily the signs and portents. Nationalism was the watchword, and nationalism, it began to be plain, must have its scapegoat. Once more the minority peoples suffered. Stringent restriction laws limited Jewish university students to ten per cent within the Pale, three per cent in Moscow and Petersburg.

What had been called national policy was seen, very soon, to stem from the personal prejudices of the sovereign. This was nothing new; for two hundred years the daily life of Ivan had been affected by the personality and disposition of whatever Father Tsar occupied the throne. Alexander III hated Jews and when the herd discovered it, the herd began to follow. The campaign of "Russia for the Russians" directed its vengeance chiefly at three strains that had become mingled in the so-called Russian blood: German, Polish and Jewish. Anton Rubinstein was pure Jew, but all of these strains had long been associated with his name.

Petersburg, the Court City, was quick to mirror its sovereigns' moods. Petersburg had quite forgotten that Rubinstein was a Jew. Now, however, Petersburg began to whisper. The Slavophiles, knowing well that Rubinstein had never meddled in politics and that he had given thousands of roubles, hours of time, to Russia, spoke against the alien, the anti-patriot.

Anton had survived whispering campaigns before. But this was no mere personal intrigue; this was a movement that swept over Russia, inaugurating the worst two decades in the terrible history of Russian Jewry. Hordes of emigrants left for America; in 1891 alone, one hundred thousand Jews entered the United States. Down in Moscow, old Prince Dolgoroukov, Nicholas' friend, had been replaced by the Grand Duke Serge who declared openly that he desired to run every Jew out of town.

Far to the south, Kaleria Rubinstein heard talk she had not heard since Berdichev days, when grandfather Román had called the tribe together. The pogroms that were to usher in a new century had not yet begun, but any Jew who had lived through Nicholas I's reign could read the signs. Kaleria herself was in no danger. She and her daughter Sophie lived comfortably upon the money Anton sent south, supplemented by Sophie's earnings as a music teacher. Kaleria was eighty-five; the community knew and loved her. But, watching Israel herded once more into the Pale, hearing of cities crowded and hungry as Berdichev had once been hungry, Kaleria shook her head. There was no halting this evil spirit once it had been loosed. Certificate of Christian baptism does not stop a mob bent upon murder and bloodshed. "When I am gone," Kaleria told her daughter, "you must go north where Anton can watch over you and where they are slower to murder the people they hate."

Kaleria realized more quickly than her son what was going on. During his entire lifetime Anton had refused to take part in politics, refused even to discuss national affairs with his friends. His life, he said, was concerned with music. He had of course suffered scores of personal insults due to his name: at the Russian border with his passport, in Frankfort when he was refused entrance to the Library, long ago in Vienna when he had opened the Ambassador's letters. But these had been mere pinpricks, wounds to toughen a man's hide. None of it had halted Anton's progress or his conception of the progress of music. When his operas were outlawed from the Petersburg stage, Anton had blamed it on the theatrical management, not on the Tsar.

Now in the winter of 1890-'91 Rubinstein found his work balked at every turn. He desired to appoint Conservatory professors and to award student scholarships regardless of blood or creed. Was it his fault the world presented more good Jewish or German or Polish musicians than Orthodox Christian ones? Rebellion surged upward in Anton Rubinstein. Insult that he had been able to accept in his own name he could not accept for others—especially when it balked the progress of music. Moreover, there was no way to fight this thing. It never came to open battle; no uniformed officer arrived at the Conservatory floor with edict and command. It was a thing of whispers, an evil spirit, moving under cover, striking furtively. And when a man looked for his assailant, no one was there.

In March of 1891, Rubinstein resigned his post at the Conservatory. "Anybody can sign papers," he said.

At the Conservatory indignation was high. In two years Rubinstein had accomplished wonders for a school that was nearly moribund. A house that had been filled with rubbish was clear now and orderly, functioning smoothly, its honor and name increasing. Rubinstein was abandoning it. Who else in Petersburg would have courage to defy the Court, keeping the halls of art cleared for action?

From Liadov to the humblest pupil, the Conservatory mourned its loss. Liadov wrote some verses, caustic and bitter, which went from mouth to mouth. To translate them into verse is impossible; literally they said, "Now the king of kings is leaving us forever, and history will repeat itself. As before, scum will float to the top. Scum made of idiots for whom music is no more than a succession of sounds, note piled upon note."

The last time Anton had resigned from the Conservatory, in 1867, he had done so partly in anger because the Board would not let him keep standards high enough, and partly because he desired to be free to write music and to play in concerts all over Europe. Now he was sixty and his concert days were over. He still desired to write music and to teach it. But how could he write music, teach music in this atmosphere of hatred and narrow nationalism? Looking about him, Anton was undecided where to go. He knew only that he must go, that his dream of giving his last years to his country was shattered forever.

There was a sad farewell in the Michael Palace where Helena Pavlovna's daughter lived now, ailing, under displeasure of her Imperial cousin. She had made her will, leaving the palace to her family. The Tsar was furious. What right had commoners like the Mecklenburg-Strelitz to a Romanov palace? Pobyedonostsev intervened, writing soothingly to his one-time pupil, pleading with him to make friendly gesture toward the Grand Duchess:

"I trouble Your Majesty with this letter because the Grand Duchess is very weak and sad and anxious. If Your Majesty would write to her, it would calm her. She seems to think often of death, and this expressed itself very clearly last Sunday evening when for the first time since the death of the Grand Duchess Helena Pavlovna, she opened the rooms of the late Grand Duchess and invited there all persons alive who for so many years were guests at her mother's musical parties, including Rubinstein, who began his musical career in those very rooms and who now plans to abandon his career forever.

"Gathered there, we all felt quiet and sad; many of us are old and remembered our youth and the pleasant hours spent in those rooms. It seemed a solemn parting with a place and a hostess and people no longer there. Many could not hold back their tears. At the end, Rubinstein sat down and began to play. As if at a solemn farewell he finished with Chopin's *Funeral March*, playing with extraordinary feeling. We were all strongly affected. When he was done the Grand Duchess said good-bye to everyone with especial kindness and affection."

It was a lost cause; Pobyedonostsev might better have put his letter in the desk drawer as he had done before. The Tsar let Catherine's will stand; in certain matters, Alexander III was just. But the Rubinstein appeal left him cold.

Anton went out to Peterhof in the spring of 1891. From his hallway the statue of Helena Pavlovna looked down and gave him no solace. Here at home something had gone wrong too, something about which Anton was silent. Neither of his sons cared for music and shrugged their shoulders when Father went to the piano. "He is practicing again," they said, half scornfully. When he had been playing for money, they had not been so scornful, Anton remembered grimly. Jacob played the guitar and sang with an artlessly lovely tenor voice; he talked of going to Italy to study for the operatic stage. But guitar playing and artless tenor voices are not music to a Rubinstein. Daughter Anna still lived at Peterhof with her husband and baby. But her marriage had gone badly; she was silent, unhappy, irritable. There was gaiety in the drawing room no longer, with Anton playing waltzes for the young people to dance. . . . What part Vera played in all this strife we do not know nor do we know if Anton sought solace elsewhere. We know only that the forests above the pale Baltic, the flowering plum and budding lilac were poisoned by the spirit that lay over Russia in this reign of His Majesty, Alexander III.

In the midst of Rubinstein's distress, an invitation arrived that settled for the moment the question of where to go for escape. Down in the Caucasus in a fabulous palace lived the Grand Duke Michael, youngest son of Nicholas I. Michael was no anti-Semite, he was the brother of Anton's great friend Konstantin, the Sailor Prince, the liberal whom Alexander III had once banished from Petersburg. Perhaps it was the Grand Duke Konstantin who, hearing rumors of what was going on in Petersburg, had engineered this invitation. Anyway, Anton received urgent and friendly summons to spend the summer of 1891 at the paradise called "Pearl of the Caucasus."

Anton had always longed to see the Caucasus. Nicholas used to talk about it; Nicholas had played the piano in Tiflis. Around Tiflis the mountains are high and wild, the air clear of faction. Here, five thousand feet above the sea, men spoke a strange Eastern language and knew nothing of court intrigue.

In June, Anton began his journey, planning to go first to Odessa and see his mother. Sitting by the grimy car window he watched the slow hot miles unfold. Moscow, Kaluga, Bryansk, Starodub . . . How vast and endless the forest of Chernigov! Once he had taken this journey in the covered wagon with *Maman*. No actual memories remained, only a sensation, a sudden startling recognition as, passing swiftly over the plains below Kiev, the train came suddenly upon the Dnieper, and crossing its wide sandy depths, Anton saw on the cliff above, the golden spires of an ancient monastery.

Berdichev, Balta—the heat was intense. How could *Maman* bear this dry air, this blinding light? Anton kept his hand before his eyes. In Odessa one had the breeze from the sea, but it could not cool the blood of a northerner. *Maman* seemed well and surprisingly cheerful, but for once she was neither active nor sharp-tongued. While Anton and Sophie played duets, Kaleria sat on the sofa, hands folded, her blue eyes deep and quiet. Vaguely worried, vaguely rebellious that one who had lived so bravely must sit now

344

with hands folded, Anton watched his mother with troubled eyes, sensing that a soul was making ready for departure. When at last he left her and boarded the steamer for Batum, Anton could not dispel the fear that he might never see his mother again.

The "Pearl of the Caucasus" was a dream of paradise with gardens, vineyards, fountains, flaming peonies growing wild amid the high grasses and at every turn, servants to do one's bidding. But the estate lay low, near the sea, and it was very hot. Languor pursued Rubinstein, a feeling he did not enjoy. "I cannot work here," he told his host, and went up to Tiflis, enchanted, as he drove ever higher, by the rocky, barren hills, the clear invigorating air, the strange Eastern speech and ways of the people.

In Tiflis he stayed by himself in a hotel, quite happy. There was an excellent music school in the town, directed by Ippolitov-Ivanov from Anton's own Conservatory. On August 12th, Anton gave a concert for its benefit. Tiflis was sophisticated and very Eastern; there was money here and lots of it. Oil magnates from Baku lived in cool white houses, wore their dressing gowns to supper, swathed their heads in turbans against noontide and could afford more than one wife.

One Herr Pitoyev invited Rubinstein to Kadz-Hary, five thousand feet above the sea, and gave a fabulous dinner party in his garden, then prevailed upon his guest to stay on for a month. Anton lived in a carpeted pavilion furnished with divans and rugs—and a very good piano. Here he wrote music and practiced all day, rising at seven to have tea and a cigarette on his terrace, reading the European newspapers and then going in to work. His pavilion was on the edge of Herr Pitoyev's estate, separated from the public park only by a fence. One morning he was overheard practicing; before long the town of Kadz-Hary came to listen, bringing camp-stools, rugs, picnic food. The young people foreswore evening parties for fear they would oversleep. Before eight in the morning the crowd had collected; they bored holes in Herr Pitoyev's wall to watch Anton walk from the terrace to his pavilion.

And now the news reached Tiflis and the daily diligence to

Kadz-Hary was crowded; one had to reserve places a week ahead. People came in peasant carts and landaus; on holidays there would be a thousand in the park sitting on their camp stools, chin in hand, listening, their eyes bright with wonder.

Anton, utterly unaware of all this, played on hour after hour, absorbed, frowning. In a month he must leave here; Wolff had arranged an autumn concert tour that would take him all over Germany, the proceeds of which would be given to charity.

One night at dinner, someone told Rubinstein of the crowds in the park. Anton was displeased; to climb five thousand miles for privacy and then be peered at like a sideshow in a circus! The people must be sent away. Next morning Anton looked out from behind his shutters. Strange that he had not noticed these people, had not heard the sound of their carriage wheels! They sat very quiet now and respectful, settled on their camp chairs, waiting for him to begin. Anton was touched. He threw open the shutters of his pavilion. Shouts of joy reached him, but he did not show himself.

Thereafter, morning on morning in the fresh mountain air, Anton played for his hidden audience, then told his host that he must leave these hills of enchantment. "Your clothes are very shabby," Herr Pitoyev said. "You cannot go to Dresden looking like that." Rubinstein replied that he did not like new clothes. "From time to time, my tailor in Petersburg copies my old suits for me. A new tailor would make strange clothes in which I should be most unhappy."

The Pitoyevs had become very fond of Anton Gregorovitch. Seeing him off in the diligence for Tiflis they felt sad, uneasy. Anton announced that he was leaving Russia forever. Pitoyev had heard Russians say this before, and always they had come home again. Rubinstein would come home too.

But he looked so shabby and alone, setting off with his one suitcase, his battered black felt hat on his head, his eyes blinking against the sun. Lighting his cigarette in its amber holder as the bus-driver pulled at his horses, Anton took off his hat, waving gallant, grave farewell.

33

1891-1894. Dresden. Rubinstein comes home

Eᴀʀʟʏ in September, 1891, Rubinstein reached Dresden. Since his youth he had known and loved this old city. Many Russians lived here; Anton decided upon it as headquarters for the rest of his life.

He took a bedroom and sitting room in the Europaischerhof, placed one photograph upon his work-table—his little grand-daughter, Vera—installed a Bechstein grand piano in one corner and then went off to Berlin to play in concert. Hermann Wolff came down to Dresden to meet him, half-crazy with pleasure to have his lion on the leash once more. Anton was to play only for charity. Nevertheless he was to play, and the mechanics of the tour would be the same in spite of this grand gesture. He was to begin with three concerts in Berlin, for students and professional musicians only. "If I see in the audience one single person who is not a musician," he told Wolff ferociously, "I shall get up and leave the platform."

Wolff was besieged by eager ticket buyers. "Princes are begging to come," he told Rubinstein. "They will pay good money." Anton shook his head and played in the *Bechstein Saal* for a crowd of students who were gathered for the autumn opening of the Berlin conservatories. The old magic was there; the nervousness that had visited Anton lately on the concert stage disappeared in the presence of these eager young musicians.

Two concerts remained, when one morning, news from Odessa plunged Anton into profound sadness. It was not unexpected; when it came, Anton realized that he had been dreading it. Last summer his mother's stillness, her remoteness had hinted that a chapter was closing. A soul, with the resignation and dignity that belonged to it, was making ready for departure.

On September 29th, Kaleria had died quietly, wrote Sophie, of no

347

disease but the disease of old age. She was eighty-six. Without pain or outcry she had taken her departure. It was right for her to go. Things were threatening in Kherson that it would not have been well for *Maman* to see. She was to be buried in the Orthodox churchyard in Odessa. "Do not come home," Sophie advised. "The journey is long and you would be late for the funeral. Keep your engagements; play your concerts on schedule as *Maman* would have wished you to."

Villoing, Nicholas, *Maman*—for the third time the strings of Anton's life were cut. He had never been close to his sister Sophie but now he longed for her, longed to resurrect in her presence his mother's face and speech and ways. But he did not go home. He stayed in Berlin and kept faith with the students, playing twice more in the *Bechstein Saal*, and the students blessed him.

Down in the audience one boy especially sat very quiet, utterly entranced. Josef Hofmann was fifteen, but, like Rubinstein at that age, already a veteran of the concert stage. Eight years ago, Rubinstein had heard the boy play in Warsaw and had told Hermann Wolff he had better snap up this phenomenon before somebody else got hold of him. "I do not believe in *Wunderkinder*," Anton had said, "but I believe in this one." In 1888, Hofmann had "retired" from the concert stage to study musical theory with Heinrich Urban in Berlin. He greatly desired to be a Rubinstein pupil. "Next year," Anton told him, "in Dresden when I have more time."

After the student concerts, on October 6th, Rubinstein played in the *Bechstein Saal* for the public and the public came with rejoicing, princes and all. Afterward, Kaiser Wilhelm called Anton to the palace and pinned on his coat the decoration called *Pour le Mérite*. Rubinstein was pleased and said so. This was the highest Prussian order available for a commoner; it came now as a salve to pride wounded by the indifference and neglect of Anton's own country. What a Tsar ignored, a Kaiser, very apparently, delighted to honor. Ordinarily, Rubinstein was indifferent to orders and decorations; this time he desired the news to reach Petersburg before him.

348

For he knew he must go home. A man could not exile himself from ties that were lifelong; the moment he tried it, death itself called him back. Anton would go home to Petersburg; perhaps Sophie would go with him for a visit. As for permanent residence, neither conditions in Petersburg nor conditions in the Peterhof villa invited it. Anna was at Peterhof with her Guardsman husband and three small children. Anton's second boy, Alexander, was ready to graduate from the Lyceum; the cough they had always feared was becoming more pronounced. The boy was losing weight and his condition frightened his mother into a state of continual depression. "Jasha," the second boy, was there too; he was toying with the idea of becoming a professional singer. Vera encouraged him, encouraged also his guitar playing, an attitude that to Anton was characteristic of his wife. Why should a boy of mediocre talent be encouraged to make these mediocre noises around the house? Surely a woman who had lived a quarter century with Anton Rubinstein should be able to differentiate between good music and bad, or at least between talent and something less! Vera liked Jasha's music and she liked Tchaikovsky's quite to excess. Her husband harbored a deep suspicion that to all other musical production she was indifferent.

Going home by way of Odessa, Anton forgot Vera and her musical tastes at sight of his sister's distracted grief. Sophie had lived all of her forty-eight years with her mother; life stretched ahead quite useless but for the saving fact that she must make her living. Anton's own fortune had dwindled until he had only enough for his own family.

"There are more piano pupils in Petersburg than Odessa," Anton told Sophie. "Come north and be introduced to a cold and wicked city."

Brother and sister went north together, arriving in time for Christmas. Vera and her boys, Anna with her children were out at Peterhof; they could no longer afford a town apartment in winter. Sophie's presence softened the embarrassment, the rancor of old bitternesses. Moreover, the enchantment of this wintry countryside

349

left no spirit for rancor. Driving in an open sleigh from the railroad station at Peterhof, wrapped to the eyes in fur, Anton delighted to show his southern-bred sister a countryside white and silent, the trees snowladen, the broad Neva and the Gulf beyond frozen solid—flat and motionless save where the wind blew the snow aside, revealing black, shining pathways. At night, stepping from his door, Anton saw a world that glittered white and silver under a high moon, unearthly still, charged with a northern magic, with the secret promise of spring beneath the ice.

The day after Christmas, Anton went into town and gave a benefit concert for the poor of Petersburg. He repeated the gesture in Moscow, then late in January went abroad once more, this time to remain for more than a year.

He was as ambitious as ever to have his operas performed abroad, and prodded Wolff, telling him by word and writing that if he could not succeed in getting *The Maccabees* onto the Berlin stage, or at least one opera performed in Paris, then he, Anton Rubinstein, would retreat to Peterhof, not to emerge until the day of his funeral. "What is this about 25,000 pounds offered for an American tour?" roared Anton. "Let me hear no more such nonsense, Hermann!"

In May, 1892, *The Maccabees* was successfully performed in Berlin, and that summer *Moses* had its *première* in Prague. Perhaps no one but Wolff could have achieved it. Prague devoted two long morning performances to *Moses*, treating it as a sacred festival. Anton was enormously pleased and gave a concert for charity afterward, playing his best. Wolff sighed his relief; as long as Anton Gregorovitch consented now and then to play the piano, the world would put up with these tedious dramas of the Old Testament. Prague, that had known Anton Rubinstein for fifty years, gave a Rubinstein festival, with serenades, and pretty girls in *tableaux vivants* and much good-will and music. Anton's pupil, Sophie Poznansky, who had followed him from Russia, was to be married, Anton wrote Sophie Rubinstein. All the same, the girl desired him to arrange a concert tour for her. "Pozia plans to play in public all next winter, then in April will give herself quite to love. Oh, *les femmes*!!!" continued Anton with three exclamation points. "How close the word to *infame*!"

From city to city Rubinstein traveled, playing for any cause that appealed to him: for the restoration of Beethoven's house in Bonn, for music students and now and again a recital to help old friends who came to him, penniless and hungry. Berlin, Dresden, Leipzig, Prague, Vienna—it was the route he had covered fifty years ago with Villoing. Everywhere the concert dates seemed to fall as a fiftieth anniversary. Perhaps the shrewd Herr Wolff saw to this.

Even next winter these anniversary festivals continued—always to Anton's genuine surprise. At the Leipzig *Gewandhaus* when he stepped on the stage, the orchestra met him with a flourish of trumpets while the audience stood up and shouted, waving handkerchiefs. Anton played almost no music but his own now; it was the only music in which his memory never failed him. That night he played his *E flat Concerto* and a group of eight solos. These last he went through without stopping, improvising interludes with skilful modulations that entranced the *Gewandhaus* audience, raised in the old tradition of concert improvisation that knew a good modulation when it heard one. When Rubinstein lifted his hands for the alternating B and E flats in the *Valse Caprice*, the audience held its breath as audiences had done in Philadelphia twenty years ago, and in London, Dublin, Warsaw, Tiflis and to the ends of the musical earth. Old age had not brought caution to Anton Rubinstein. He could not see, light pained him, gloom had descended upon his disposition. "It looks as if I shall never attain true success in anything," he wrote to Sophie Rubinstein. "I am through composing and playing in public. But at least I do not blind myself to the truth." He was more taciturn than ever. Nevertheless, musical passion, musical energy had not deserted him, had not indeed, diminished one iota.

Months passed, and Russia missed Anton Gregorovitch. In Moscow, young Joseph Lhevinne the pianist went to his Conservatory Director, inquiring when Rubinstein would play again. Safonov replied that he did not know; it might be well for some of the Moscow pupils to go to Dresden and hear him now, while there was yet time. Safonov ended by going himself and taking Lhevinne with him. In Dresden the boy was told the tickets were all sold. Terrified but determined, young Joseph went to the Europaischerhof and knocked on Rubinstein's door. An old lady, one of Anton's faithful friends who followed him to watch over him, opened it a cautious crack. "You cannot see the Master," she said. "He does not like to be disturbed."

Rubinstein appeared suddenly in the hall, smoking his cigarette in its famous amber holder. (All Europe knew when Anton broke this holder. He said it was bad luck and mourned for months.) "What do you want?" Anton asked. Lhevinne lost his voice completely. "Sit down!" roared Anton.

They sat in silence, Lhevinne staring, fascinated. "What are you studying now?" Anton asked at last.

"Beethoven sonata, Opus 106."

"Oh, very hard to play," Rubinstein said, shaking his head.

Silence. At last young Lhevinne screwed up his courage and asked for a ticket. "You don't need a ticket," Anton replied. "I'll tell them to let you in."

He will forget, young Joseph thought in a panic. How can he remember one of a thousand boys who will be at the gate tonight? Timidly, Joseph asked for Rubinstein's card. "No, no!" Anton replied. "I'll tell them. You won't need a card."

Rubinstein did not forget. Joseph had a good seat and heard Anton play his *E flat Concerto* and went back to Moscow resolved to study this music until he could make it sound as the Master made it sound.

During these long tours of the early '90's, Rubinstein spent the spring months in Dresden. At the Europaischerhof, Herr Sendig was proud of his distinguished client. The servants ran at his bidding, called him *Excellenz* and enjoyed his lavish Russian tips. Every morning at eight the maid, a homely creature whom Anton addressed as *mein Engel*, brought his tea in a glass. Anton sat by the window and drank it while he read the Russian newspapers, read with his face in the page, peering, insatiable. The rooms were filled with books; Anton still read the Bible but he read also Renan, Tolstoi, Goethe, Zola, every novel he could lay hands on in any language, and much history. He was working now on *Christus*, his latest Biblical opera, "my musical dream now this long time," he wrote his sister, and showed himself profoundly interested in Eastern folklore, Eastern dialect and song. In Dresden were many old friends of Anton's youth who came often to call, bringing flowers for his work table by the big window that gave onto the Pragerstrasse. His rooms were as plain as Peterhof's were luxurious; everything was in order, the music manuscript on his table covered with a clean sheet of paper. At Easter, Anton sent people scurrying for Russian colored eggs and was unhappy until they were found and brought to him. He had always hated shopping; from now on he refused to enter a shop; his friends laughed and did his buying for him. On the first of May, hot or cold, snow or springtime, he shed his winter woolens and stepped trustfully into linen.

Rubinstein was not, from Herr Sendig's point of view, a troublesome client. One thing he did demand: when he was in the hotel, no one should play the piano. There came an occasion when for three days Anton greeted his host glumly. "Someone," he said, "is forever playing in the next room. It must be a lady; it sounds like a lady." Sendig knew well enough who she was—the wife of an ambassador who fancied herself a musician. Heroically, Sendig went to her door. The playing ceased; next day the lady left the hotel. Not long afterward the tables were turned. Anton had guests one evening; they prevailed upon him to play the piano. There was a knock at the door; a servant announced that his mistress, next door, desired to sleep! This was the first time in his sixty-two years that Anton Rubinstein had been asked to stop playing the piano. In much confusion, he wrote his excuses on his card, sent it to the lady who read the name—and packed up her belongings and fled the hotel.

Here in Dresden, Anton at his friends' insistence sat down to

353

write his memoirs. (The autobiographical notes published at the time of his Jubilee were far from complete as a record.) He wrote—and read what he had written and tore it up. "To write about myself and myself and myself—that is disgusting!" he told his friends. "The history of my life is in six words: *'Ich habe gelebt, geliebt und gespielt.'*"

In summer, Anton moved out to the village of Klein-Schachwitz where the Conservatory pupils who had followed him from Russia could play for him occasionally. But he accepted only one private pupil, young Josef Hofmann who during two winters came down from Berlin for his lessons. Music case in hand, the boy would knock and be admitted. With a wave of his hand, Rubinstein sent his pupil to the Bechstein in the corner, always shockingly out of tune, which Anton did not seem to mind a bit. Hofmann played from memory; Anton sat at his work table with the music spread before him. "Just play what is written," Rubinstein said. "If you have done full justice to the music and still feel like adding or changing anything, why, do so." Remembering how the Master played Chopin and the liberties he took with all the Romantic composers, young Josef dared one day to call attention to the discrepancy between Rubinstein's word and his act. "When you are as old as I," Anton replied, smiling, "you may do as I do—if you can."

Stickler though he was for the correct note, Rubinstein would tolerate no monotony in the way a passage was played. Once, in a sequence, Hofmann played the passage twice alike. Rubinstein shook his head. "In fine weather you may play it as you did. But when it rains, play it differently."

"Once," wrote Hofmann, "I played a Liszt rhapsody pretty badly. After a little of it, Rubinstein said, 'The way you play this piece would be all right for Auntie or Mamma.' Then rising and coming toward me, he said, 'Now let us see how *we* play such things.'

"I began again, but I had not played more than a few measures when Rubinstein said loudly, 'Have you begun?'

" 'Yes, Master, I certainly did.'

" 'Oh,' Rubinstein said vaguely, 'I didn't notice.' "

And Rubinstein went on to explain, as he had so often explained to pupils, that before his fingers touched the keys, the player must begin the piece mentally; he must settle in his mind the tempo, the manner of touch and above all, the attack of the first notes. Once Hofmann asked Rubinstein to finger a complex passage for him. "Oh, play it with your nose," Anton said roughly, "but make it sound well."

"Rubinstein did not so much instruct me. Merely he let me learn from him," wrote Hofmann. "He indicated an altitude offering a fine view, but how I was to get up there was my own affair; he did not bother about it. If a student, by his own study and mental force, reached the desired point which the musician's wizardry had made him see, he gained reliance in his own strength, knowing he would always find that point again even though he should lose his way once or twice, as everyone with an honest aspiration is liable to do."

From Dresden in January of 1893, Anton wrote to his sister: "Once more I must launch on a musical voyage, which means I stop my work" (the opera, *Christus*). "A frightful nuisance, but it is necessary to make money. Moreover, my publishers insist the public must not be permitted to forget me."

In April, 1893, Rubinstein went over to Petersburg by way of Kharkov. At home he found Alexander ill with tuberculosis. Peterhof was too damp; the family agreed that the boy must be moved. Vera, Anna and Jasha took him to Cadenabia on Lake Como. Anton went up to Berlin for a performance of his *Children of the Steppes*. In June he returned to Cadenabia and settled down, day by day watching his boy grow worse, day by day trying to think he was better—was at least holding his own. Work on the new opera, *Christus,* was like a prayer, an anodyne. Every moment when he was not with the boy, Anton sat at his work table.

Even here the world sought him out. Young Moritz Rosenthal the pianist was living across the lake; he looked eagerly for a steamer to take him over to meet Anton Rubinstein. There was no steamer, his landlord told him with a shrug, and no rowboat. Rosenthal plunged into the lake and swam across. It took him an hour and a half. "Why is your hair wet?" Anton asked. When he was ready to leave, Rosenthal handed Rubinstein his card. *"Léander à son hèro,"* Anton read.

From time to time, Anton fled the villa and the sight of his son's suffering. From Dresden on September 11th he wrote to Sophie Rubinstein in Odessa: "Sasha lingers on. Anenka and Jasha help to keep up his spirits, but Vera I fear will break down under her suffering. For five months she has not left Sasha's bedside. Hourly, all summer, we feared the end. Had it not been for music, I myself would have lost hope in everything."

Eleven days later (September 22, 1893) Alexander died, a boy of twenty, from this disease that was as native to Petersburg as the autumn cholera. Years ago it had been prophesied, Anton wrote his sister, that Sasha would die this death, and at this time. The body was taken home for burial. Anton remained in Germany, traveling, conducting, playing. He was lonely and wrote his sisters in Odessa regretting that he could not send them more money, suggesting warmly that they come over to live with him in Dresden. "You will murder me when I say I have no money to send. A 2000-rouble debt of Vera's has just turned up and I must pay my librettist. On what does M—— live in Petersburg? You write that her husband has nothing to offer but love. And this couple that is visiting you—how much love floats about, and how little money! Good-bye, my darling. Write oftener. Kiss Luba for me and do not forget your very devoted brother."

It was Sophie who sent the news of Tchaikovsky's sudden death from cholera on November 6th. "What is this about Tchaikovsky?" Anton replied instantly. "Is it possible that such is the will of God? What a loss for music in Russia! And in the very flower of life; he was only fifty. All because of a glass of water! What senseless business is life and all creation."

But when Christmas came he could not endure his homesickness and went home and stayed for two months. *Moses* was performed in Petersburg and there was much business concerning its production. Moreover, the new Conservatory building was going up at last on the ruins of the old Bolshoi Theatre. Almost daily, Anton went to watch the workmen, building inch by inch in the winter cold. Prowling one day through the foundations, the bits of wall and new masonry, Anton stood while a friend photographed him in his long fur coat and black bowler. He emerged in print looking disreputable, morose and very distinguished—a man without a country, sad, disillusioned yet filled with perennial vigor that must find an outlet in music until the day he died.

On the fourteenth of January, 1894, Rubinstein played in the Hall of the Nobility. He knew it was to be his last public appearance in Russia and announced it so. He played only his own music that night, looking gaunt and tired, breathing heavily. But he played as well as ever and at the end the audience, as ever, was on its feet begging for more. When he had played all he would, the janitor walked onto the stage and locked the piano.

It was a gesture familiar to every concert hall of Europe; this time it carried something deeply symbolic.

From all over Europe, concert offers continued to pour in. Rubinstein refused them. "I am old. My memory fails me. People must have their money's worth." To a London impresario who offered a superb engagement, he wired: "I play no more in public. Not for any sum whatever."

But he did play again, in Vienna that April of 1894. Leschetizky persuaded him, Leschetizky who had known and adored him for fifty years. The theatre was decorated as if for a *gala*; in the artist's room beforehand, Anton was nervous, very white and shaken. Afterward, receiving the congratulations of admirers, he was unhappy over his performance. "If a pupil during rehearsal played as many false notes as I did tonight, he would certainly deserve to be thrown out the window."

While he was in Vienna, Anton agreed to play at one of Leschetizky's famous Wednesday class lessons. Overjoyed, Leschetizky instructed his servant to place the prettiest girls in the front row. "Herr Rubinstein is esthetic. Little things disturb him. We must have flowers also."

At the hour appointed, one hundred and sixty pupils marched in, the girls all in white, their arms filled with red roses. With greatest interest, Rubinstein heard them perform. He himself was to play at the end. As the next to last pupil began, Leschetizky missed Rubinstein and hurrying upstairs, found him in a back room, pacing the floor. "The matter? It is quite simple," said Anton. "I am too nervous to play for those pupils. They are connoisseurs, and they are crowded so close to the piano that they will see my fingers on every note I play."

Leschetizky led him to the waiting pupils and Rubinstein sat down at the piano. Young Mark Hambourg, seated almost under Anton's arm, told himself, "If he misses a key, I am a dead boy."

"I suffered," wrote Mark years later, "an agony of apprehension every time the great pianist lifted his hands off the keys, for he was in the habit of attacking them from an astonishing height. When he did miss one he did not hit me at all, but turned round and said whimsically, 'That, young fellow, is how not to do it.'"

Anton himself was in high good humor, once the evening had really begun. How pleasant to see Leschetizky again, to talk over old times when the world was young and all the women were princesses! Leschetizky, after two divorces, was about to embark on a third marriage—again with a pupil. Anton told his friend that for a man of 64, he did pretty well. "Remember, however, that I nearly married your first wife before you did. Are you not afraid to have me around the house? After all, I am only 64 myself, as young a blade as you, Theodor."

"Only play for me," Leschetizky replied, "and you may have all my wives and all my sweethearts. . . . " Leschetizky became famous for championing his hero at all times and places. Brahms, in particular, had to be put in order—Brahms who insisted that Rubinstein's music was hastily written, without structure or depth. "Now let me tell you, Johannes," Leschetizky would scream furiously, "in your

358

music I can put my finger on this page and say it sounds like Schubert, and on that one and it sounds like Bach or Beethoven, and on a third and it sounds like Chopin or Wagner. But I'll be damned if you can put your finger on any page of Rubintein's music and say honestly that it sounds like anyone but Rubinstein."

In June of 1894, Rubinstein conducted for the last time, in Stuttgart, where *Christus* was given its *première*. Stuttgart, childhood home of Helena Pavlovna, was a musically discriminating town, the kind of German town that Anton loved. After *Christus*, as was his custom when a city had staged one of his operas, Rubinstein gave a free concert, playing for hours, delighting his audience with encores that nobody in the world played but himself—pieces by Moscheles, Kalkbrenner, Hummel, indifferent composers who had written one or two good things that Anton thought should be rescued from oblivion.

"I am going home to Russia to die," he told his friends.

"You are better appreciated in Germany," his friends replied. "Russia is no place for a creative artist. Look at Dostoyevsky. Stay with us, Anton Rubinstein, not to die but to live as an artist should, free of Court, free of intrigue."

Anton shook his head. It was not applause or "freedom" that caused a man to love his country. Petersburg was a cold and heartless city that took from its artists what it could, and then forgot them. But outside the Nicholas Station, bearded cabmen would scream with joy when he stepped into the square, calling him by name, begging him to ride with them. On the Nevsky Prospekt, little boys would ride in the open horse-cars, jumping on and off for a dare. In the streets by Apraksin's market the shaggy vendors would call their wares. The Neva was blue now in June; along the quays sailors walked, their caps on the back of their heads and out toward Peterhof at the Restaurant Augustus one could sit down to fish soup and *Tsarsky studen*—cold jellied sturgeon served with crawfish and fresh caviar. In Peterhof the lilac would still be blooming and below the turret window, nightingales would call.

359

In the train, moving swiftly across Germany into Bohemia, over the Elbe, through the foothills of the Carpathians, Breslau and across the Oder River, Anton sensed his country drawing near and was deeply moved. For three years he had tried his best to stay away, and except for flying visits, he had stayed away. At the Russian border he stepped from the train, removed his hat and drew long breaths. "Here she is—*Russia!*" he said.

34

Death of Anton Rubinstein

THE villa at Peterhof was gay with young Rubinsteins—Anna and Rebesov, her husband, their three children and the baby who had been born in Italy. He liked having the children around, Anton wrote to Sophie Rubinstein. Especially as they were still below the vexing age when education was necessary. "Vera is always ill; she broods over Sasha's death and nothing can console her." The weather was beautiful now in July but already the cholera was increasing and everyone was in a panic. It was agreeable to have Rebesov in the house; he looked well in his uniform and he was good at billiards and whist. Old Dr. Vompe often came for an evening at cards. "I love him," wrote Anton, "not as a physician but as a man."

Up in his turret room Anton practiced his piano, while downstairs Jasha sang his scales. "He works steadily," Anton wrote resignedly to Sophie, "and I am glad he busies himself at something."

The Tsar was not in Peterhof that summer of 1894; he was down in the Crimea, ill. Strange to think of that huge iron creature ailing! Would his fierce intolerance—always an essential sign of weakness—increase or diminish its fury? If he died, another Nicholas would mount the throne, a small man, narrow-bodied, who did not look like a Romanov Tsar. With Alexander III away, with the Conservatory closed for the summer, Rubinstein was very much the private citizen and rejoiced in it. "I am working a little," he wrote to Sophie. "Nothing important, more as a pastime." He was composing a new orchestral suite and his last, unfinished opera, *Cain,* after Byron's poem containing Lucifer's brave apologia. The shining one, the rebel who pitted himself against the most glorious of foes—was a grateful subject always for the pen of a Rubinstein. Moreover, it meant experimenting once more with the Eastern scale and Oriental

361

voice inflection. For Rubinstein, music had always been very close to speech; he liked the word "recital," and said the composer should never forget that his music would be *recited*. The Chinese Minister came out to Peterhof one summer afternoon, carrying his bamboo-reeded flute. In his flowing colored silks he sat for hours playing Oriental tunes that to all listeners but Rubinstein were not melody at all but a tuneless, wavering whine. Anton, however, appeared enchanted; when his visitor was gone he hummed the strange phrases, translating them into familiar musical intervals.

More than ever Anton leaned upon the strict routine of a lifetime, rising early and going to his turret. Concert impresarios still besieged him. "Playing so much in public," he wrote, "I soon observed that I played better on the stage than when alone. And when I found that I played better for myself than for the public, I left the platform forever."

A simple statement—one that few musicians have the honesty to make. Anton still played for himself and his friends, still practiced to train his muscles in an exercise that was as necessary to him as life itself.

As summer wore on his friends observed that Rubinstein was not looking well. His face was gaunt, his shoulders thin, the Tartar cheekbones ruggedly outlined. Only his hair was dark and thick as ever. Vera begged him to rest. Could he not, when the November fogs came on, go south again to his friends in the Crimea? Anton refused. Rest cures were prison, he said. He refused also to consult a doctor. "I have done without physicians all my life. Teeth and seasickness have been my only ills." Shortness of breath, cramps around his chest could no longer be attributed to asthma and Anton knew it. But what made his friends and Vera more anxious even than physical symptoms of illness was Anton's manner, which had become unnaturally quiet, almost acquiescent. He was actually polite to people; he did not frown, he said "Yes," instead of hurling negation. Old Malozemova and Lavrovskaya wept openly to see the hero thus tamed. Vasily Bessel, Auer, the Gabrilowitsches shook their heads. "If only he would roar again!" they sighed.

On the tenth of September a family service was held in memory of Anton's son Alexander, dead now a year. In the evening there was to be an anniversary party in town for a friend. "There will be music tonight," Anton said. "And most certainly I shall have to play." For how many years now, had he celebrated death in public places, upon a piano keyboard? In Berlin with the news of *Maman's* death still scorching his brain, in a hotel parlor at Lake Como after Alexander died. In the American city of Boston on a winter day when he heard that Helena Pavlovna was gone. Perhaps it was best so—to celebrate one's grief with music as one celebrated evening and twilight and morning and one's daily bread! "Instrumental music is man's best friend. Especially, one knows this when in suffering and grief. Above all other instruments the piano makes response. That is why the study of piano should be made obligatory in the schools."

So wrote Rubinstein the teacher, who because his own fingers could give utterance to great grief, great joy, believed quite simply that the fingers of other men needed only training to achieve like utterance.

On October 16th, Rubinstein gave his newly completed orchestral suite to Leopold Auer. "They want me to see a doctor," Anton told Vasily Bessel that evening. "Must I take medicine and live ten years longer? It would be a calamity!" He returned to Auer a few days later to hear what he thought of the *Suite*. Auer said he liked it and had arranged for its performance during the winter at a concert of the Musical Society. Anton shook his head, remarking quietly that he would not be there to hear it. Auer dared not ask what he meant. At Rubinstein's request an immediate correction rehearsal was arranged; Anton sat through it with pencil and score.

Next day he went out to Peterhof. Driving through Petersburg to the Baltic Station, Anton found the city good to look upon. He did not know that he would never enter Petersburg again. The golden dome of Saint Isaac's, the shabby statues that lined the roof of the Winter Palace, Tsar Peter prancing on his huge horse by the Admiralty building, the cobblestones and cabmen of Petersburg would see Anton Gregorovitch no more.

On November 1st the Tsar died, down in the Crimea. Grimly Anton read of his passing. Outwardly at least, this man had been every inch the Emperor. Three Romanovs, Nicholas I and two Alexanders, tall strong men who looked like Tsars and acted—for better or worse—the part. Anton Rubinstein had known them all, had made music in their palaces, had been admired by their Empresses and their daughters and their sisters. People whispered that with the death of the Crowned Peasant, perhaps things would improve, oppression and censorship would relax. This respectable, small Nicholas who wore his epaulettes too modestly and whose German wife towered a good inch above him—what would he do for Russia?

Anton Rubinstein, asking himself the question, shrugged his shoulders with a tired gesture. It was well he could not see ahead to the terrible end of Nicholas II. Already Rubinstein had outlived his time and said so. Liszt was gone and Von Bülow, Tausig and Wieniawski, Zaremba, Asantchevsky, Tchaikovsky. How few were left of the Old Guard! Work was Anton's last remaining pleasure— work, a little whist in the evenings and the daily sight of the countryside around his villa, the forest below his turret window, the pale autumnal Baltic below the tree tops.

Watching the birch leaves turn to gold, to brown, feeling the cold mist creep up from the long Finnish marshes, Vera Rubinstein observed her husband day by day and was frightened. Anton complained of a pain in his left arm and shoulder; twice, that first week in November, he fainted. She begged him to see a doctor but Anton, grinning, reminded her of Dr. Eichenwald in Petersburg who ten years ago had warned him to give up concert tours and change his way of life. "Just before my Historical Concerts in Europe, too! And what happened? I went on tour—and Eichenwald took to his bed and died. The warner is dead and the warned one flourishes!"

It was as though Anton did not care, thought Vera. As though life were not a thing to cherish, cozen, cling to. Devout Russian Orthodox that she was, this attitude seemed to Vera heathenish, more than a little defiant in its skepticism. If Anton died, would he die a Christian? Vera knew he had no love for the Orthodox Church. "There are two kinds of priests," he had remarked: "those who fool the people and those who fool themselves." More than once he had said flatly that had he been of age he would never have consented to Christian baptism.

Did Anton believe anything at all? Vera had never seen him pray, although sometimes, as on the day of their son's memorial service, she had caught upon her husband's face a look remote and beseeching, as though he groped for guidance. She dared not to question him. But someone else dared. Young Lillian Macarthur, his Irish pupil, one winter night a year ago had demanded bluntly if Anton Gregorovitch believed in immortality. "Yes," he had replied. "And after I am dead, small Lillian, I shall come and speak with you."

The girl had told Vera. But the older woman shook her head. This was too much optimism, too much romance for the man she had known so long. Men were always telling pretty women they would return to them—in death and in life. How often did they mean it? It seemed to Vera, these dark November weeks, that her husband's life was ebbing with the autumn sun that grew paler, briefer, day by day. In her heart she knew that Anton Rubinstein neither cared nor hoped for heaven.

On Monday, November 19th, the Tsar was buried in Peter Paul Fortress. The sound of the guns came shuddering down the river; in his turret room Anton heard them and raised his head, his pen hovering over the long sheets of music manuscript. All day he had worked on his opera, *Cain*. For the past week he had been troubled by insomnia, a new irritation to one who had always slept like a baby. Dr. Vompe had brought some sleeping medicine but Anton waved it away. Last night he had slept and today he felt better; the pain in his hands was gone.

In the late afternoon, Dr. Vompe climbed the turret staircase, stethoscope in hand. "Vera Alexandrovna says I must listen to your heart."

This was something Rubinstein had refused for ten years. He

365

opened the left side of his coat, holding it out. "Very well," he said. "Go on and listen."

Impossible, the doctor replied. An auscultation could not be effected through vest and shirt. Rubinstein rose, buttoned his coat and remarked heartily, "Good! Then let us go down and play whist. You can hear my heart some other time."

Covering the manuscript of *Cain* with an ink-stained cloth, he followed Dr. Vompe down the stairs.

The game that night was almost gay. Young Rebesov, the son-in-law who consoled himself for his wife's estrangement by spending most of his free time with his father and mother-in-law, joked with Dr. Vompe about his difficult patient. At eleven Rubinstein took his glass of Xeres wine as was his custom, bade the company good night and walked through the trophy room to his own airy chamber on the first floor, plainly furnished with a narrow student's bed, two tables, a few chairs and a couch.

Vera's room was on the other side of the trophy chamber. The doors were open; she heard Anton get into bed but noticed that his light remained burning. Uneasily she went to him and pointing at his candle, asked why it was not out. Anton consulted the watch on his bed-table. "It lacks five minutes to 11.30," he said.

Was ever man so meticulous about his routine? Going to her room, Vera undressed slowly and got into bed. The night was very still. Mist hung over the garden, obscuring the pallid outline of the birches, blotting out forest and river and every familiar, comfortable sight and sound. There was menace to this November stillness; by morning perhaps, snow would pad against the window, increasing as the wind increased, driving down across the Gulf from Finland, Lapland and the fierce long reaches of the icy Pole. In the morning there would be candles, lamps. Anton would complain as he always did on dark mornings. Matvey would give him his early tea by the window. With long familiarity Vera saw him sitting there, his eyes shaded, waiting for the sun to announce his working hours—his hours of life.

But this time, for Anton Rubinstein there would be no morning.

At one o'clock Vera, lying wide-eyed and restless, heard from her husband's room a single awful cry. She had barely time to light a candle when Anton appeared in the doorway, bedcovers trailing, one hand clutching his chest. "I am suffocating," he gasped. "A doctor! Quick! A doctor!"

Calling for help, Vera supported her husband to the bed. He was ghastly pale and suffered horribly, struggling for breath. By the time Dr. Vompe arrived, he was unconscious. Oxygen was administered; the heart still beat faintly but Anton's hands and feet were cold. Vera rubbed them but no warmth came.

At two o'clock Anton's head fell back and he was dead.

Anton Rubinstein was gone. Three hours ago he had laughed; that very afternoon before the sun went down his piano had sounded from the turret room, a remote, melodious thunder. Impossible to believe the world would not hear that sound again! Vera had complained of it once and had permitted the children to complain. Her husband had turned on his heel and left the house, left the city, left Russia. How she had feared his violence! How the world had feared it too—yet returned always, as Vera returned, to feed at this rich board. Violent this life and horribly violent this death. Anton Rubinstein had said he did not desire to live. Yet when death came he had fought furiously, struggling for breath, battling the enemy, defeated, yet somehow triumphant, as always.

No priest had been there, with bell and Book and incense to soften the departure and let a grieving wife believe his spirit had been ushered decently into heaven. Anton was gone. Only the world that remained—the bright world he had loved, the world of daytime and music, of hard work, struggle, injustice, triumph—must prove his immortality.

Early that morning Petersburg heard the news. Mass was said at the Conservatory, and some time after six a special train arrived at the little station of Stary Peterhof. Teachers and students descended into the pitch black country night. Carriages floundered in the muddy ruts; the villa, come upon suddenly through the trees, blazed

367

with light. In the big white hall lay Rubinstein; above his bier the figure of Helena Pavlovna, marble-white and faintly smiling, looked down. In gold-embroidered stole moved the priest, making the sign of the cross. Incense rose above the fronds of the potted palms, and from the dining room beyond, the voices of choir boys intoned the *Gospodi pomilui*, high, monotonous and clear.

On their knees, Rubinstein's pupils sang the ritual, then rising, walked slowly round the bier to take a last farewell of their master. How powerful this face in death, how tremendous the brow with the black hair swept back! At his feet on a black cushion lay all his medals and decorations. Weeping, the boys and girls left the hall and the lighted villa and took train for Petersburg and a school that would be stale, flat and empty, with no hope of the Master's return.

On Anton's birthday, November 28th, the public funeral was held. A crowd met the coffin at the Petersburg station. In the cold train-barn, boys from Anton's Conservatory raised their trombones and played a Bach chorale—greeting that would have pleased Anton Gregorovitch. Bearded priests, gorgeous in gold and purple, escorted the coffin to the Izmailov Cathedral. All day and far into the night the people came to pay their respects to this musician they had known and loved.

For the funeral, the Cathedral blazed with candles. The Archbishop raised a jeweled hand, the full choruses of the Imperial operas with the Archangelsky choir burst into majestic harmony for Anton Rubinstein who had loved the sound of many voices. On the casket lay wreaths from Tsar Nicholas II and his Tsarina whom Anton had never known, and from the Dowager Empress who had so often desired him as supper partner. When the procession started for the Alexander Nevsky Cemetery, four carriages were needed to carry the flowers that had come from all parts of Russia. The casket was quite hidden in living green. Spectators, asking whence came these laurels, were told, "From Germany."

But no one, that dark November day, called Anton Rubinstein a German. Now that he was gone, Russia claimed him for herself and was proud to give him burial in holy ground. Passing the Conservatory, the procession was met by a band of pupils with old Malozemova at their head. Her floral crown was the largest of all; Rubinstein would have smiled, seeing her raise her thin old arms to place it on the funeral coach.

Out the Nevsky Prospekt now, to the great Monastery gates—a long, slow procession. When the coffin had been lowered into the vault, friends spoke words of farewell over the grave. It was already dusk, a cold, miserable day. Most of the speeches, after the nature of funeral orations, were flat and formal. Of them all, the one that was simplest and most deeply felt came from a Moscow man, Safonov, who had known and loved Anton and Nicholas Rubinstein.

All over Europe Anton Rubinstein was mourned. How many cities claimed him as a son! Berlin, where Kaleria had brought him as a boy to study with Siegfried Dehn. Leipzig, where the *Gewandhaus* audience had welcomed him so often. Dresden, where he had spent his last years. Paris, where Saint-Saëns missed him like a brother. In Vienna, Leschetizky was grief-stricken and for many days could give no lessons. A boy brought a Rubinstein concerto to class and Leschetizky tried to accompany on the second piano. But at the opening chords his hands faltered; with great difficulty he finished the first movement. In the adagio his eyes were blinded by tears; he rose and left the room, weeping. Leschetizky, from now on, played and taught everything Rubinstein had written.

Teaching this music, Leschetizky would stop playing and ask the student to wait a moment. He would sit then with his bearded, handsome head in his hands and rising, walk about the room. Returning to the piano he played the piece again and again, explaining that at times Rubinstein played it so, at other times differently.

In England, young Josef Hofmann was on tour. Opening his newspaper on the train he read of Rubinstein's death. "To me the world appeared suddenly empty, devoid of any interest," Hofmann wrote. "My grief made me realize how my heart had worshiped not only the artist but the man. I loved him as if he were my father. My concert program next day happened to include Chopin's *B flat Minor Sonata*. As I struck the first notes of the Funeral March, the whole audience rose from their seats as if by command and remained standing with bowed heads throughout the piece, in honor of the great departed."

City after city arranged memorial concerts. Far to the west, America gave full programs in Rubinstein's honor, playing all seven movements of the *Ocean Symphony*. Against these opening arpeggios the chandeliers of Tremont Temple shook, and Boston remembered a big-shouldered man, shabby, black-haired, who had frowned and raised his hands—and when they fell they summoned thunder.

Hermann Wolff knew well the gesture that would have pleased the old lion most. Six months after Rubinstein's death, by threat or cajolery Wolff persuaded the operatic management in Bremen to stage *Christus*. From all over Europe, musicians flocked to hear it, discussed it—and forgot it forever.

Now that the charm of Rubinstein's presence in the conductor's box was gone, his operas died a natural death outside of Russia, although from time to time *The Demon* was revived. Paris, that had never staged a Rubinstein opera, produced *The Demon* in 1911 and liked it and said so in the public press. New York produced it in 1922 at the Metropolitan and again in 1928. Caruso made recordings from *Nero*.

But these were sporadic efforts, never very successful. It was Rubinstein's orchestral and piano works that kept his name alive as a composer. The *D Minor Concerto* remained in every musician's repertory. Josef Hofmann often plays it today, and the *G Major Concerto* also. The world that had wrongly called this music "modern German" soon learned to place it where it belonged, with Mendelssohn and the Romantics. The *B flat Piano Trio* remains popular with all who love melody. So does the *D Major 'Cello Sonata* and many of the songs, notably the Persian group with their haunting Eastern charm. Concert pianists, searching for encores, use

370

almost in spite of themselves the brief delectable *Barcarolles* in G major and F minor.

But there is no use pretending that a revival of Rubinstein's music will take place, or becoming optimistic concerning the unearthing of buried Rubinsteiniana. Before he died, Anton himself had intimations of this. "When I am gone," he wrote, "all that I care men shall remember me by is my Conservatory—that they should say it was Anton Rubinstein's work."

Anton's Conservatory is still alive, and so is his brother's. Moscow and Leningrad diplomas do not carry the words, "Free Artist"; there is no need now for these flaming titles of defense. The sons of Kaleria Rubinstein, if they could look upon their handiwork, would be very pleased.

Here were men in whom was a perfect welding of purpose and execution. Here were two who made their living by being, every minute of the day and night, themselves to the fullest. Whether or no they grew rich upon it does not matter; the world does not resent the riches that come sometimes to artists. Anton did grow rich—and gave away his money as fast as he made it. In Petersburg when his will was published, there was amazement at the meagerness of what remained. Newspapers recalled the fact that during his lifetime Rubinstein had given, on conservative estimate, at least three hundred thousand roubles to charity. His first concert in Moscow had been for the poor, his last in Petersburg for the blind.

Ask musicians if Anton Rubinstein's life was a success or a failure, and you will have many replies: *His music is dated; it sounds like Mendelssohn. He played the piano better than anyone alive. Better than Liszt. Not so well as Liszt. He founded a great Conservatory. Didn't he have a brother who played, too? His brother played better than he did.*

Boris Kamensky, the violinist who sat in Rubinstein's kitchen to hear him play scales—now old and exiled in Paris—has a simpler answer. "The world sought these Rubinsteins," he said, "because

371

they had so much to give. Their natures were rich, and the natures of most men are poor and timid and hungry."

These brothers were not saints, content to function quietly like a Sebastian Bach in organ loft unseen, praising his God. The Rubinsteins were actors who gloried in the stage. From platform to theatre door they walked when they had played, their shoulders hung with laurels—and enjoyed it. Weaker men they pushed aside; they were impatient, often ruthless. After failure they rebounded, angry, eager to meet the enemy once more. Nothing turned them from their purpose; they possessed an unalterable, unshakable and quite simple belief in what they were doing. Other men have believed in themselves, but other men have not been born to talent worthy of self-confidence. These brothers were born to it. Rich, abundant, it flowed full and inexhaustible until the day death stopped its source. *"Docteur,"* said Nicholas three days before he died, *"je ne perdrai pas l'habitude du piano, n'est-ce pas?"*

Call it talent or call it courage—faith—ambition—persistence. Men felt this in the brothers and hungered after it, longing to catch the meagerest breath of its contagion. It was for this Hermann Wolff stood up when Anton entered the room and it was this which caused men and women, young and old, to come silently into his presence, braving displeasure, rudeness, insult. *Give us of this bread for the spirit. Give us of this meat that makes the heart grow brave and fat!*

The world sought these brothers, said old Kamensky, because they had so much to give.

Appendix

Catalogue of Compositions
by Anton Rubinstein

Compiled by Otto E. Albrecht

WORKS WITH OPUS NUMBERS

YOUTHFUL COMPOSITIONS

After publishing ten works during his youth numbered Opus 1-10, Rubinstein began again with Opus 1.

Op. 1 Ondine. Etude pour piano. Berlin, Schlesinger.

Op. 2 Zuruf aus der Ferne von E. Weiden. Lied für eine Singstimme mit Pianoforte. Cöln, Schloss.

Op. 3 Romance, "Comment disait-il," de Victor Hugo pour chant avec piano. Moscou, Gresser.

Op. 4 Lied mit russischem Text. Gebet von Lermontoff. Moskau, Gresser.

Op. 5 Die Nachtigall. Moskau, Gresser.

Op. 6 Die Lerche. Moskva, Gresser.

Op. 7 Hommage à Jenny Lind. Airs suédois transcrits pour piano. Berlin, Schlesinger.

Op. 8 Voix intérieures pour piano. No. 1, Volkslied. No. 2, Rêverie. No. 3, Impromptu. Wien, Wessely.

Op. 9 Trois mélodies caractéristiques pour piano à quatre mains. No. 1, Chanson russe. No. 2, Nocturne sur l'eau. No. 3, La Cataracte. Wien, Haslinger.

Op. 10 Deux nocturnes pour piano. Wien, Haslinger.

MATURE WORKS. OPUS 1-121

Op. 1 Sechs kleine Lieder im Volksdialekt von Rud. Loewenstein, für eine Singstimme mit Pianoforte. Wien, Spina.
1. Unerklärlich: "Weiss nit, was mir g'scheh."
2. Beim Fenstergehn: "Schlafst scho mei Greterl."
3. Liebeshändel: "Mäderl mit dem goldnen Latz."
4. Das gebrochene Herz: "I sah mal a Blimle."
5. Abschied: "I hab gedacht, dass i allei."
6. Beruhigung: "I hat e schön's Schatzerl."

Op. 2 Deux fantaisies sur des chansons populaires russes pour piano (E minor, A minor). Wien, Spina.

Op. 3 Deux mélodies pour piano (F major, B major). Wien, Spina.

Op. 4 Mazourka-Fantaisie pour piano (G major). Wien, Spina.

Op. 5 No. 1. Polonaise pour piano (C minor)
No. 2 Cracovienne pour piano (E flat major)
No. 3. Mazurka pour piano (E major). Wien, Spina.

Op. 6 Tarantelle pour piano (B major). Wien, Spina.

Op. 7 Impromptu-Caprice pour piano (A minor). Wien, Spina.

Op. 8 Sechs Lieder aus dem Russischen von W. Osterwald für eine Singstimme mit Pianoforte. Leipzig, Senff.
No. 1. Der Traum: "Am Wiesenhügel schlummert' ich" (Zhukovski).
No. 2. Frühlingsgefühl: "O, du leichter, loser Wind" (Zhukovski).
No. 3. Das Blättchen: "Vom Freundeszweig getrennt" (Zhukovski).
No. 4. Die Blume: "O Blümlein, das den Wiesenrand einst zierte" (Zhukovski).
No. 5. Sehnsucht: "Gönnt mir goldne Tageshelle" (Lermontov).
No. 6. Der Schiffer: "Rauscht die See im Sturme springend" (Davidov).

Op. 9 Octetto in D pour piano, violon, alto, violoncelle, contrebasse, flûte, clarinette et cor. Leipzig, Peters.

Op. 10 Kamennoi-Ostrow. Album de 24 portraits pour piano. Mayence, Schott.

Op. 11 No. 1. Trois morceaux pour piano et violon
No. 2. Trois morceaux pour piano et violoncelle
No. 3. Trois morceaux de salon pour piano et alto. Leipzig, Schuberth.

Op. 12 Première sonate pour piano (E major). Leipzig, Peters.

Op. 13 Première sonate pour piano et violon (G major). Leipzig, Peters.

Op. 14 Le Bal. Fantaisie en 10 numéros pour piano. Berlin, Bote & Bock.
1. Impatience. 2. Polonaise. 3. Contredanse. 4. Valse. 5. Intermezzo. 6. Polka. 7. Polka-Mazurka. 8.

Mazurka. 9. Galop. 10. Le Rêve.

Op. 15 Deux trios pour piano, violon et violoncelle. Leipzig, Hofmeister.
No. 1. F major. No. 2. G minor.

Op. 16 Trois morceaux pour piano. Leipzig, Hofmeister.
No. 1. Impromptu (F major). No. 2. Berceuse (D major). No. 3. Sérénade (G minor).

Op. 17 Trois quatuors pour 2 violons, viola et violoncelle. Leipzig, Breitkopf & Härtel.
No. 1. G major. No. 2. C minor. No. 3. F major.

Op. 18 Sonate pour piano et violoncelle (D major). Leipzig, Breitkopf & Härtel.

Op. 19 Deuxième sonate pour piano et violon (A minor). Leipzig, Breitkopf & Härtel.

Op. 20 Deuxième sonate pour piano (C minor). Leipzig, Breitkopf & Härtel.

Op. 21 Trois caprices pour piano. Leipzig, Breitkopf & Härtel.
No. 1. F sharp major. No. 2. D major. No. 3. E flat major.

Op. 22 Trois sérénades pour piano. Leipzig, Breitkopf & Härtel.
No. 1. F major. No. 2. G minor. No. 3. E flat major.

Op. 23 Six études pour piano. Leipzig, Peters.
No. 1. F major. No. 2. C major. No. 3. C sharp minor. No. 4. E flat major. No. 5. F major. No. 6. G major.

Op. 24 Six préludes pour piano. Leipzig, Peters.
No. 1. A flat major. No. 2. F minor. No. 3. E major. No. 4. B minor. No. 5. G major. No. 6. C minor.

Op. 25 Premier concerto pour piano avec orchestre (E major). Leipzig, Peters.

Op. 26 No. 1. Romance pour piano (F major)

No. 2. Impromptu pour piano (A minor). Wien, Spina.

Op. 27 Neun Lieder von Kolzoff, aus dem Russischen von A. von Viedert, für eine Singstimme mit Pianoforte. Wien, Spina.
1. Singe, Nachtigall
2. Lebewohl
3. Gieb' o heil'ge Geisternacht
4. Es singt der Ros' in Liebesdrang
5. Liebes goldnes Ringelein
6. Kleine Wolke
7. Keine Frühlingsluft
8. Wenn ich kommen dich seh'
9. Sturmewinde

Op. 28 No. 1. Nocturne pour piano (G flat major)

No. 2. Caprice pour piano (E flat major). Leipzig, Kistner.

Op. 29 Deux marches funèbres pour piano. Leipzig, Kistner.
No. 1. Pour le convoi d'un artiste (F minor)
No. 2. Pour le convoi d'un héros (C minor)

Op. 30 No. 1. Barcarolle pour piano (F minor)

No. 2. Allegro appassionato pour piano (D minor). Leipzig, Kistner.

Op. 31 Sechs Gesänge für vier Männerstimmen. Leipzig, Kistner.
1. Lied: "Die schlanke Wasserlilie" (Heine).
2. Trinklied: "Wie die Nachtigallen" (Mirza-Schaffy).
3. Meeresstille und Glückliche Fahrt: "Tiefe Stille herrscht im Wasser."

"Die Nebel zerreissen" (Goethe).
4. Jagdlust: "Waldnacht, Jagdlust" (Tieck).
5. Die Rache: "Der Knecht hat erstochen" (Uhland).
6. Wiederhall: "In diesem grünen Wald."

Op. 32 Sechs Lieder von Heine für eine Singstimme mit Pianoforte. Leipzig, Kistner.
1. Frühlingslied: "Leise zieht durch mein Gemüthe."
2. Frühlingslied: "Die blauen Frühlingsaugen."
3. Frühlingslied: "In dem Walde spriesst's und grünt es."
4. Lied: "Es war ein alter König."
5. Lied: "Du bist wie eine Blume."
6. Der Asra: "Täglich ging die wunderschöne Sultanstochter."

Op. 33 Sechs Lieder für eine Singstimme mit Pianoforte. Leipzig, Kistner.
1. Morgenlied: "Noch ahnt man kaum" (Uhland).
2. Lied: "An der Rose Busen schmiegt" (Hoffmann von Fallersleben).
3. Die Lerche: "Lerche steiget im Gesang" (von Sacken).
4. Räthsel: "Es schmachtet eine Blume." (Anon.)
5. Lied: "Siehe, der Frühling währet" (Hoffmann von Fallersleben).
6. Nachhall: "Ich sah dich einmal" (Mosenthal).

Op. 34 Zwölf Lieder des Mirza-Schaffy, aus dem Persischen von F. Bodenstedt, für eine Singstimme mit Pianoforte. Leipzig, Kistner.
1. "Nicht mit Engeln im blauen Himmelszelt"

377

2. "Mein Herz schmückt sich mit dir"
3. "Seh' ich deine zarte Füsschen an"
4. "Es hat die Rose sich beklagt"
5. "Die Weise guter Zecher ist"
6. "Ich fühle deinen Odem"
7. "Schlag' die Tschadra zurück"
8. "Neigl, schöne Knospe, dich zu mir"
9. "Gelb rollt mir zu Füssen"
10. "Die helle Sonne leuchtet"
11. "Thu nicht so spröde, schönes Kind"
12. "Gott hiess die Sonne glühen"

Op. 35 Deuxième concerto pour piano avec orchestre (F major). Wien, Spina.

Op. 36 Zwölf Lieder aus dem Russischem von F. Bodenstedt für eine Singstimme mit Pianoforte. Wien, Spina.
1. Der Felsen
2. Wenn deine Stimme mir tönt
3. Das Schiff
4. Die Wolken
5. Der Dolch
6. O frage nicht
7. Vernehmet ihr
8. Auf dein Wohl trink' ich
9. Die Erde ruht
10. Sie singt ein Lied
11. Der falsche Stern
12. Weht es, heult es trüb

Op. 37 Akrostichon pour piano. Wien, Spina.

Op. 38 Suite pour piano. Mainz, Schott. No. 1. Prélude. No. 2. Menuett. No. 3. Gigue. No. 4. Sarabande. No. 5. Gavotte. No. 6. Passacaille. No. 7. Allemande. No. 8. Courante. No. 9. Passepied. No. 10. Bourrée.

Op. 39 Deuxième sonate pour piano et violoncelle (G major). Leipzig, Breitkopf & Härtel.

Op. 40 Symphonie No. 1 für Orchester (F major). Leipzig, Kahnt.

Op. 41 Troisième sonate pour piano (F major). Leipzig, Breitkopf & Härtel.

Op. 42 Océan. Deuxième symphonie pour orchestre (C major). Leipzig, Senff. (An Adagio and a Scherzo were later added to the original five movements.)

Op. 43 Ouverture triomphale pour orchestre. Mainz, Schott.

Op. 44 Soirées à St. Pétersbourg. Six morceaux pour piano. Leipzig, Kahnt. No. 1. Romance. No. 2. Scherzo. No. 3. Preghiera. No. 4. Impromptu. No. 5. Nocturne. No. 6. Appassionato.

Op. 45 Drittes Concert für Pianoforte und Orchester (G major). Berlin, Bote & Bock.

Op. 46 Concerto pour violon avec orchestre (G major). Leipzig, Peters.

Op. 47 Trois Quatuors pour 2 violons, viola et violoncelle. Leipzig, Breitkopf & Härtel. No. 1. E minor. No. 2. B flat major. No. 3. D minor.

Op. 48 Zwölf zweistimmige Lieder aus dem Russischen von F. Bodenstedt, mit Pianoforte. Leipzig, Senff.
1. Der Engel: "Es schwebte ein Engel dem Himmel entlang" (Lermontov).
2. Sang das Vögelein: "Sang wohl, sang das Vögelein" (Delvig).
3. Im heimischen Land: "Im heimischen Land steht ein

friedlicher Hain" (Alekse-
iev).

4. Volkslied: "Mägdlein auf
die Wiese gingen."
5. Wanderers Nachtlied:
"Aller Berge Gipfel ruhn"
(Lermontov, from Goe-
the).
6. Beim Scheiden: "Beredt
war die Zunge."
7. Die Nacht: "Des Tages
letztes Glühen" (Zhukov-
ski).
8. Die Wolke: "Vorbei ist der
Sturm" (Pushkin).
9. Das Vöglein: "Glücklich
lebt, vor Noth geborgen"
(Pushkin).
10. Die Turteltaube und der
Wanderer: ''Sprich,
warum sitzest du dort auf
dem Zweige" (Dmitriev).
11. Am Abend: "Der drü-
ckend schwüle Tag hat
ausgeglüht" (Davidov).
12. Volkslied: "Sonne scheint
noch" (Kolzov).

Op. 49 Sonate pour pianoforte und alto
(F minor). Leipzig, Breit-
kopf & Härtel.

Op. 50 Charakterbilder. Sechs Klavier-
stücke zu 4 Händen.
Leipzig, Kahnt.
No. 1. Nocturne. No. 2.
Scherzo. No. 3. Barcarolle.
No. 4. Capriccio. No. 5.
Berceuse. No. 6. Marche.

Op. 51 Six Morceaux pour piano.
Leipzig, Senff.
No. 1. Mélancolie (G minor).
No. 2. Enjouement (B flat
major).
No. 3. Rêverie (A minor).
No. 4. Caprice (D flat major).
No. 5. Passion (F major).
No. 6. Coquetterie (B flat
major).

Op. 52 Troisième trio pour piano, violon et violoncelle (B flat
major). Leipzig, Senff.

Op. 53 Six Fugues en style libre, in-

troduites de préludes, pour
piano. Leipzig, Peters.

Op. 54 Das verlorene Paradies (Paradise Lost). Geistliche Oper
in 3 Theilen. Text frei
nach J. Milton. Leipzig,
Senff.

Op. 55 Quintetto pour piano, flûte,
clarinette, cor et basson
(F major). Leipzig, Schu-
berth.

Op. 56 Troisième symphonie pour orchestre (A major). Leip-
zig, Schuberth.

Op. 57 Sechs Lieder fur eine Singstimme mit Pianoforte.
Leipzig, Senff.
1. Frühmorgens: "Ich weiss
nicht" (Geibel).
2. Lied: "Nun die Schatten
dunkeln" (Geibel).
3. Neue Liebe: "Hinaus in's
Weite" (Geibel).
4. Clärchens Lied: "Freud-
voll und leidvoll" (Goe-
the).
5. Freisinn: "Lasst mich nur
auf meinem Sattel gelten"
(Goethe).
6. Tragödie: "Entflieh mit
mir" (Heine).

Op. 58 Scena ed aria: "E dunque
vero?" per soprano con
accompagnamento di or-
chestra . . . sulle parole
di M. Pinto. Mayence,
Schott.

Op. 59 Quintetto pour 2 violons, 2
altos et violoncelle (F
major). Leipzig, Senff.

Op. 60 Ouverture de concert pour orchestre (B flat major).
Leipzig, Senff.

Op. 61 Sechs Lieder für Mannerstim-
men. Wien, Spina.
1. Kriegslied: "Und wenn
uns nicht mehr übrig
blieb" (Geibel).
2. Liebesfeier: "An ihren
Liedern klettert die
Lerche" (Lenau).

379

3. V i n u m hungaricum: "Nullum vinum nisi hungaricum" (Löwenstein).

Nos. 4, 5, and 6 were announced on the title-page as "Dem rettenden Genius," "Die Unbeständigen," and "Trinklied des Alten," but apparently were never published.

Op. 62 Sechs Gesänge für Sopran, Alt, Tenor und Bass. Wien, Spina.
1. Gondelfahrt: "Horch, Mitternacht vorüber" (Grün).
2. Durch Erd' und Himmel leise: "Leise hinfluthet eine Weise" (Geibel).
3. Ein Fichtenbaum: "Ein Fichtenbaum steht einsam" (Heine).
4. Um Mitternacht: "Bedächtig stieg die Nacht an's Land" (Mörike).
5. Die erwachte Rose: "Die Knospe träumte von Sonnenschein" (Salis).
6. D i e Heinzelmännchen: "Wie war zu Cöln es doch vordem" (Kopisch).

Op. 63 Die Nixe: "Die Nixe sich wiegte auf bläulicher Fluth." Gedicht von Lermontov, aus dem Russischem übersetzt von R. Sprato, für Frauenchor und Alt-Solo mit Begleitung des Orchesters oder des Pianoforte. Leipzig, Senff.

Op. 64 Fünf Fabeln von Kriloff, aus dem Russischen übersetzt von R. Sprato, für eine Singstimme mit Pianoforte. Leipzig, Senff.
1. Der Esel und die Nachtigall: "Ein Esel sah die Nachtigall."
2. Das Quartett: "Der Affe, Herr von Putzig."
3. Der Parnass: "Zur Zeit als

Griechenland der Götter satt."
4. Der Adler und der Kukuk: "Der Aar den Kukuk."
5. Die Ameise und die Libelle: "Der muntern Hüpferin Libell."

Op. 65 Concerto pour violoncelle avec accompagnement d'orchestre ou de piano (A minor). Leipzig, Senff.

Op. 66 Quatuor pour piano, violon, viola et violoncelle (C major). Leipzig, Senff.

Op. 67 Sechs zweistimmige Lieder mit Pianoforte. Leipzig, Senff.
1. Lied der Vögelein: "Von Zweig zu Zweige" (E. Schultze).
2. Waldlied: "Der Nachtwind hat in den Bäumen" (Lenau).
3. Frühlingsglaube: ''D i e linden Lüfte sind erwacht" (Uhland).
4. Vorüber: "Vorüber, wo die lichte Rose" (Kletke).
5. Meeresabend: "Sie hat den g a n z e n T a g getobt" (Strachwitz).
6. Lied: "Die Lotosblume ängstigt sich" (Heine).

Op. 68 Faust. Ein musikalisches Charakterbild für Orchester. Leipzig, Siegel.

Op. 69 Cinq Morceaux pour piano. Leipzig, Siegel.
1. Caprice (A flat major).
2. Nocturne (G major).
3. Scherzo (A minor).
4. Romance (B minor).
5. Toccata (D minor).

Op. 70 Quatrième concerto pour piano avec orchestre (D minor). Leipzig, Senff.

Op. 71 Trois morceaux pour piano. Leipzig, Siegel.
1. Nocturne (A flat major).
2. Mazurek (F minor).
3. Scherzo (D flat major).

Op. 72 Sechs Lieder für eine Singstimme mit Pianoforte
(Bariton oder Alt). Leip-
zig, Senff.

1. "Es blinkt der Thau" (G.
von Boddien).
2. "Wie eine Lerch' in blauer
Luft" (G. von Boddien).
3. Die Waldhexe: "Vorbei,
vorbei durch Feld und
Wald" (G. von Boddien).
4. Morgens: "Nun gieb ein
Morgenküsschen" (Theo-
dor Storm).
5. "Veilchen vom Berg,
woran mahnest du mich?"
(Lemcke).
6. Verlust: "Ich hatte eine
Nachtigall" (Lemcke).

Op. 73 Fantaisie pour 2 pianos (F
major). Leipzig, Senff.

Op. 74 Der Morgen. Gedicht von Po-
lonsky, aus dem Russi-
schen übersetzt von Jos.
Wenzig, für Männerchor
mit Orchester. Leipzig,
Senff.

Op. 75 Album de Peterhof. 12 Morceaux pour piano. Leipzig,
Senff.

1. Souvenir (C major).
2. Aubade (E flat major).
3. Marche funèbre (G
major).
4. Impromptu (E flat major).
5. Rêverie (D minor).
6. Caprice russe (F major).
7. Pensées (F sharp minor).
8. Nocturne (G major).
9. Prélude (D major).
10. Mazurka (D minor).
11. Romanze (B flat major).
12. Scherzo (F major).

Op. 76 Sechs Lieder für eine Singstimme mit Pianoforte.
Leipzig, Senff.

1. Waldeinsamkeit: "Wal-
deinsamkeit, du grünes
Revier" (Eichendorff).
2. Nachts: "Hörst du die
Gründe rufen" (Eichen-
dorff).

3. An den Frühling: "Noch
immer Frühling"
(Lenau).
4. Frühlingsblick: "Durch
den Wald, den dunkeln"
(Lenau).
5. "Bedeckt mich mit Blu-
men" (Geibel and Heyse).
6. "Klinge, klinge, mein
Pandero" (Geibel and
Heyse).

Op. 77 Fantaisie pour piano (E minor).
Leipzig, Senff.

Op. 78 Zwölf Lieder aus dem Russischen von W. Osterwald,
für eine Singstimme mit
Pianoforte. Leipzig, Senff.

1. Hebräische Melodie:
"Mein Geist ist trüb und
schwer" (Lermontov, from
Byron's "My soul is
dark").
2. Lied: "Könnt' ich doch
stets in deine blauen
Augen" (Benediktov).
3. Der Engel: "An Edens
Thor ein Engel" (Push-
kin).
4. Der Sturm: "Auf steilem
Felsen steht" (Pushkin).
5. Klage: "O wie schwer die
Pein" (Kolzov).
6. Der Gefangene: "Im Ker-
ker gefangen" (Pushkin).
7. Neugriechisches Lied:
"Liebchen, als wir Nachts
uns küssten (Mikhailov).
8. Elegie: "Wenn stets in
stiller Nacht" (Maikov).
9. Lied: "Wie der Quell ist
mein Lied" (Polonski).
10. Sinngedicht: "Zur Kirche
rufet ernst" (Polonski).
11. Lied: "Rab' zum Raben
fliegt daher" (Pushkin).
12. Scene: "Alter Mann, grim-
mer Mann" aus "Die
Zigeuner" (Pushkin).

Op. 79 Iwan IV (der Grausame) (Ivan
the Terrible). Musikal-
isches Charakterbild für

Orchester. Berlin, Bote &
Bock.

Op. 80 Der Thurm zu Babel (The
Tower of Babel). Geist-
liche Oper in einem Auf-
zuge. Gedicht von Julius
Rodenberg. Leipzig, Senff.

Op. 81 Six Etudes pour piano. Berlin,
Bote & Bock.

Op. 82 Album de danses populaires
des différentes nations
pour piano. Berlin, Bote
& Bock.
1. Lesghinka (Caucase).
2. Csárdás (Hongrie).
3. Tarentelle (Italie).
4. Mazurka (Pologne).
5. Valse (Allemagne).
6. Russkaya i Trepak (Russie).
7. Polka (Bohème).

Op. 83 Zehn Lieder aus dem Franzö-
sischen, Italienischen und
Englischen übersetzt von
N. Roda und A. von
Winterfeld, für eine Singstimme mit Pianoforte.
Berlin, Bote & Bock.
1. "Rappelle-toi quand l'au-
rore craintive" (Musset).
2. "A Saint-Blaize à la
Zuecca" (Musset).
3. Chanson de Barberine:
"Beau chevalier" (Mus-
set).
4. La prière de femme:
"Quand on se rencontre"
(Lamartine).
5. "Tanto gentile e tanto
onesta" (Dante).
6. "Rondinella pelegrina"
(Grossi).
7. La prima viola: "Odorosa
foriera d'aprile" (Maffei).
8. The Tear: "On beds of
snow the moonbeam
slept" (Thomas Moore).
9. Good Night!: "Good
night! good night! and is
it so? (Thomas Moore).
10. A Dream: "I thought

this heart enkindled lay"
(Thomas Moore).

Op. 84 Fantaisie pour piano avec orchestre (C major). Leip-
zig, Senff.

Op. 85 Quatrième trio pour piano, violon et violoncelle (A
major). Wien, Lewy.

Op. 86 Romance et Caprice pour violon avec orchestre. Leip-
zig, Senff.

Op. 87 Don Quixote. Musikalisches
Charakterbild. Humoreske
für Orchester. Leipzig,
Senff.

Op. 88 Thème et variations pour piano
(G major). Leipzig, Senff.

Op. 89 Sonate pour piano à 4 mains
(D major). Leipzig, Senff.

Op. 90 Deux quatuors pour deux violons, alto et violoncelle.
Leipzig, Senff.
No. 1, G minor. No. 2, E
minor.

Op. 91 Die Gedichte und das Requiem
für Mignon aus Goethe's
"Wilhelm Meister's Lehr-
jahre" mit Pianoforte.
Leipzig, Senff.
1. Der Harfner: "Was hör'
ich draussen vor dem
Thor?"
2. Der Harfner: "Wer nie
sein Brod mit Thränen
ass."
3. Der Harfner: "Wer sich
der Einsamkeit ergiebt."
4. Mignon: "Kennst du das
Land?"
5. "Ich armer Teufel, Herr
Baron."
6. Der Harfner: "Ihm färbt
der Morgensonne Licht."
7. Mignon und der Harf-
ner: "Nur wer die Sehn-
sucht kennt."
8. Philine: "Singet nicht in
Trauertönen."
9. Der Harfner: "An die
Thüren will ich schlei-
chen."

10. Mignon: "Heiss mich nicht reden."
11. Aurelie: "Ich hat ihn einzig mir erkoren."
12. Mignon: "So lasst mich scheinen bis ich werde."
13. Requiem für Mignon: "Wen bringt ihr uns zur stillen Gesellschaft?"
14. Friedrich: "O ihr werdet Wunder sehen."

Op. 92 No. 1 Hecuba. Arie für eine Altstimme mit Orchester. Gedicht von L. Goldhann.
No. 2 Hagar in der Wüste. Dramatische Scene für eine Altstimme mit Orchester. Gedicht von Ferdinand von Saar. Leipzig, Senff.

Op. 93 Miscellanées pour piano. Leipzig, Senff.
Book 1. Ballade. Léonore de Bürger.
Book 2. Deux grandes études.
Book 3. Doumka et Polonaise.
Book 4. Cinquième Barcarolle.
Book 5. Scherzo.
Book 6. Deux sérénades russes.
Book 7. Nouvelle mélodie et Impromptu.
Book 8. Variations sur l'air "Yankee Doodle."
Book 9. Miniatures. 12 Morceaux. (1. Près du ruisseau. 2. Menuet. 3. Berceuse. 4. Hallali. 5. Sérénade. 6. L'Hermite. 7. El Dachtarawan. Marche orientale. 8. Valse. 9. Chevalier et Payse. 10. A la fenêtre. 11. Revoir. 12. Le Cortège.)

Op. 94 Cinquième concerto pour le piano avec accompagnement d'orchestre (E flat major). Leipzig, Senff.

Op. 95 Symphonie dramatique pour orchestre. No. 4. (D minor). Leipzig, Senff.

Op. 96 Deuxième concerto pour violoncelle avec accompagnement d'orchestre ou de piano (D minor). Leipzig, Senff.

Op. 97 Sextuor pour 2 violons, 2 altos et 2 violoncelles (D major). Leipzig, Senff.

Op. 98 Troisième sonate pour piano et violon (B minor). Leipzig, Senff.

Op. 99 Quintetto pour piano, 2 violons, alto et violoncelle (G minor). Leipzig, Senff.

Op. 100 Sonate No. 4 pour piano (A minor). Leipzig, Senff.

Op. 101 Zwölf Lieder und Gesänge aus dem Russischen des Grafen Alexis K. Tolstoi übersetzt von Caroline von Pawloff, für eine Singstimme mit Pianoforte. Leipzig, Senff.
1. Wie es sein muss: "Wer da liebt, lieb' überm Maasse."
2. Nebel und Gram: "Es wallt und woget schwer."
3. Am Meeresstrand: "Es brandet die Welle."
4. In stiller Nacht: "Es glitten nach rauschendem Regen."
5. Frühling: "Lerche wiegt sich im Gesange."
6. Die Wölfe. Ballade: "Wenn kein Lied mehr erschallet."
7. Sanftes Walten: "Wie bei des Zephyrs leisem Hauch."
8. Vergängliches: ''Hoch bäumen sich auf in die Lüfte."
9. Schlaf' ein: "Schlaf' ein, mein trauernd Lieb."
10. "Hätt' ich das gewusst, hätt' ich das geahnt."
11. Fürst Rostislav. Ballade:

"Im fremden Land, im Bett des Stroms."

12. Des Baches Geplauder: "Weithin dehnt sich ein Forst."

Op. 102 Caprice russe pour piano avec accompagnement d'orchestre. Leipzig, Senff.

Op. 103 Bal costumé. Suite de morceaux caractéristiques pour piano à quatre mains. Berlin, Bote & Bock.
1. Introduction.
2. Astrologue et Bohémienne.
3. Berger et Bergère.
4. Marquis et Marquise.
5. Pêcheur napolitain et Napolitaine.
6. Chevalier et Châtelaine.
7. Toréador et Andalouse.
8. Pélerin et Fantaisie (Etoile du soir).
9. Polonais et Polonaise.
10. Bojar et Bojarine.
11. Cosaque et Petite-Russienne.
12. Pacha et Almée.
13. Seigneur et Dame.
14. Sauvage et Indienne.
15. Patricien allemand et Demoiselle.
16. Chevalier et Soubrette.
17. Corsaire et femme grecque.
18. Royal Tambour et Vivandière.
19. Troubadour et Dame souveraine.
20. Danses.

Op. 104 Morceaux pour piano. Berlin, Bote & Bock.
No. 1. Elegie. No. 2. Variations. No. 3. Etude. No. 4. 6me. Barcarolle. No. 5. Impromptu. No. 6. Ballade.

Op. 105 Zehn serbische Lieder in deutscher Uebersetzung von Th. Hauptner für eine Singstimme mit Pianoforte. Berlin, Bote & Bock.

1. Wie wart ihr fröhlich, gold'ne Mädchentage.
2. Warum musst du welken, schöne Rose.
3. Rosendufte füllen rings die Lüfte.
4. Schüchtern brach der Mond durch Wolkenschatten.
5. Weithin rief die Mutter nach der Tochter.
6. Einen Bruder hatt' ich, einen Geliebten.
7. O Gott, wo ist mein Auserwählter.
8. Wie so launisch bist du, o Sonnenschein.
9. Willst du einen Ehemann erkennen.
10. Geh' bei Tagesanbruch auf die Strasse.

Op. 106 2 Quatuors pour deux violons, alto et violoncelle. Leipzig, Senff.
No. 1. A flat major. No. 2. F minor.

Op. 107 5ième Symphonie pour orchestre (G minor. Russian). Leipzig, Senff.

Op. 108 Trio pour piano, violon et violoncelle (C minor). Leipzig, Senff.

Op. 109 Soirées musicales. 9 Morceaux pour piano. Leipzig, Senff.
No. 1. Prélude. No. 2. Valse. No. 3. Nocturne. No. 4. Scherzo. No. 5. Impromptu. No. 6. Rêverie-Caprice. No. 7. Badinages. No. 8. Thème varié. No. 9. Etude.

Op. 110 Eroica. Fantaisie pour orchestre. Leipzig, Senff.

Op. 111 6ième Symphonie pour orchestre (A minor). Leipzig, Senff.

Op. 112 Moses. Geistliche Oper in acht Bildern. Text von Heinrich Mosenthal. Leipzig, Senff.

Op. 113 Concertstück pour le piano avec accompagnement d'orches-

Op. 114 tre (A flat major). Leipzig, Senff.
Op. 114 Deuxième Akrostichon pour piano. Leipzig, Senff.
Op. 115 Zehn Lieder für eine Singstimme mit Pianoforte. Leipzig, Senff.

1. Das erste Sommergras; Vor der Ernte: "Ich weiss es nicht" (Greif).
2. Was tut's: "O lass mich die trunkenen Blicke erheben" (Lipiner).
3. Am Strande: "Ich sass am Strand" (Scherer).
4. Seefahrt: "Hör auf deinen Fahrgesellen" (Baumbach).
5. An die Vögel: "Zwitschert nicht vor meinem Fenster" (Hamerling).
6. Liebeslied: "Und bist du auch ferne" (Leixner).
7. Der einsame See: "Wo Gletscherhöhen starren (Kalbeck).
8. Lass mich deine Augen: "Ob mein Mund auch dürfte" (Cornelius).
9. Gebet: "O Geist der heil'gen Liebe" (Kunze).
10. Der Dichter: "Du merkst nicht, wie so flüchtig" (Sturm).

Op. 116 Ouverture zu "Antonius und Kleopatra" von Shakespeare für Orchester. Leipzig, Senff.
Op. 117 Christus. Geistliche Oper in 7 Vorgängen mit Prolog und Epilog, von Bulthaupt. Leipzig, Senff.
Op. 118 Souvenir de Dresde. Six Morceaux pour piano. Berlin, Bote & Bock.
No. 1. Simplicitas. No. 2. Appassionata. No. 3. Novellette. No. 4. Caprice. No. 5. Nocturne. No. 6. Polonaise.
Op. 119 Suite pour orchestre (E flat major). Leipzig, Senff.

Op. 120 Ouverture solennelle pour grand orchestre. Leipzig et Moscou, Jurgenson.
Op. 121 Polka pour piano (C major). Moscou, Jurgenson.

COMPOSITIONS WITHOUT OPUS NUMBER

STAGE WORKS
(Place and date of first performance are given in parentheses)

Der Dämon (The Demon). Phantastische Oper in 3 Acten. Nach dem Russischen von Lermontov, übersetzt von Alfred Offermann. Leipzig, Senff. (St. Petersburg, 1875)

Feramors (Lalla Roukh). Lyrische Oper in 3 Aufzügen nach Thomas Moore's Gedicht von Julius Rodenberg. Leipzig, Senff. (Dresden, 1863)

Dmitri Donskoy (Dmitri of the Don, or the Battle of Kulikovo). Opera in three acts, libretto by Solugub and Zotov. Unpublished except for the overture (Berlin, Bote & Bock). (St. Petersburg, 1852)

Foma Durachok (Thomas the Fool). Opera in one act, libretto by Mikhail. Unpublished. (St. Petersburg, 1853)

Goriusha (Die Kummervolle). Opera. (Libretto by Averkiev.) Moscou, Jurgenson. (St. Petersburg, 1889)

Hadji-Abrek. Opera in one act after Lermontov.

Kalaschnikoff, der Kaufmann von Moskau (Kalashnikov, the Merchant of Moscow). Oper in drei Acten, nach einer Dichtung von Lermontov bearbeitet von N. Kulikoff. Deutsch von Hermann Wolff. Leipzig, Senff. (St. Petersburg, 1880)

Die Kinder der Haide (The Children of the Steppes). Oper in 4 Aufzügen. Text frei nach Carl Beck's poetischer Erzählung "Janko" von H. Mosenthal. Leipzig, Senff. (Vienna, 1861)

Die Maccabäer (The Maccabees). Oper in drei Aufzügen nach Otto Ludwig's gleichnamigen Drama von H. S. von

Mosenthal. Berlin, Bote & Bock. (Berlin, 1875)

Mest (Vengeance). Unpublished. (St. Petersburg, 1858)

Nero. Grosse Oper in 4 Acten. Dichtung von J. Barbier. Leipzig, Senff. (Hamburg, 1875)

Der Papagei (The Parrot). Komische Oper in 1 Act. Nach einem persischen Märchen von H. Wittmann. Leipzig, Senff. (Hamburg, 1884)

Die Rebe (The Vine). Ballet in 3 Acten (5 Bildern) von Taglioni, Grandmougin und Hansen. Leipzig, Senff.

Die sibirischen Jäger (The Siberian Hunters). Oper in 1 Act. Text nach dem Russischen des Jerebtzoff von Peter Cornelius. Leipzig, Senff. (St. Petersburg, 1852)

Sulamith. Ein biblisches Bühnenspiel in fünf Bildern, nach dem Hohen Liede Salomonis von Julius Rodenberg. Berlin, Bote & Bock. (Hamburg, 1883)

Unter Räubern. (Among Thieves) Komische Oper in 1 Act. von Ernst Wichert. Berlin, Bote & Bock. (Hamburg, 1883)

Orchestral, Vocal and Piano Works

Bacchisches Lied: "Was schweigt unser fröhlicher Chor," für eine Bassstimme mit Männerchor. Leipzig, Senff.

Barcarolle No. 2 pour piano (A minor). Wien, Spina.

4me Barcarolle pour piano (G major). Berlin, Bote & Bock.

Das begrabene Lied: "Hell schimmert das alte Königsschloss" (Baumbach). Ballade für Tenor mit Pianoforte. Leipzig, Senff.

Bluette pour piano. Berlin, Bote & Bock.

Etude No. 1 für Pianoforte (auf falsche Noten) (C major). Leipzig, Senff.

Etude No. 2 für Pianoforte (C major). Leipzig, Senff.

Etude No. 3 pour le piano (E flat major). Leipzig, Senff.

Euphemie-Polka für Pianoforte. St. Petersburg, Bernard.

Fantaisie sur des mélodies hongroises pour piano. Pesth, Rozsavölgyi.

Fatme: "Schlanke Fatme, hohe Palme," Gedicht von Felix Dahn, für eine Singstimme mit Begleitung des Pianoforte. Leipzig, Senff.

Glück: "Was rauscht vor der Thüre" (Pachler). Duett für Sopran und Tenor mit Pianoforte. Leipzig, Senff.

Grand Duo sur le Prophète de Meyerbeer pour piano et violon, par A. Rubinstein et H. Vieuxtemps. Mayence, Schott.

Herbstgedanken: "Wenn die Stürme schaurig tosen," für eine Singstimme mit Pianoforte. Hamburg, Schuberth.

Liebeswunder: "A quoi bon entendre les oiseaux des bois?" Gedicht von Victor Hugo, für eine Singstimme mit Begleitung des Pianoforte. Leipzig, Senff.

Vier Lieder für eine Singstimme mit Begleitung des Pianoforte. Berlin, Bote & Bock.

  1. Mitternacht: "Um Mitternacht hab' ich gewacht" (Rückert).

  2. Die Blume der Ergebenheit: "Ich bin die Blume im Garten" (Rückert).

  3. Hüte dich: "Nachtigall, hüte dich."

  4. "Wem ich dieses klage."

Sechs Lieder für eine Singstimme mit Begleitung des Pianoforte. Leipzig, Senff.

  1. Wir Drei: "Es steht ein Blümchen dort im Thal" (Backody).

  2. Bitte: "Weil auf mir, du dunkles Auge" (Lenau).

  3. Mein Herzensschatz: "Wie bist du nur" (Oelschläger).

  4. Verschiedene Wege: "Mein Verstand und armes Herz" (Bodenstedt).

  5. Die drei Zigeuner: "Drei Zigeuner fand ich einmal" (Lenau).

  6. Die Heimath meiner Lieder: "Wenn ich des Donners Stimme höre" (Boddien).

Mädchens Abendgedanken: "Wer der Meine wohl wird werden," für eine Singstimme mit Pianoforte. Berlin, Bote & Bock.

"Marche à la turque" des Ruines d'Athéne (sic) de L. Beethoven, transcrite pour le piano par A. Rubinstein. Pesth, Rozsavölgyi.

Points d'orgue pour piano. (Cadenzas to piano concertos). Mayence, Schott.

1. (To Beethoven's 1st concerto, Op. 15, C major)
2. (To Beethoven's 2nd concerto, Op. 19, B flat major)
3. (To Beethoven's 3rd concerto, Op. 37, C minor)
4. (To Beethoven's 4th concerto, Op. 58, G major)
5. (To Mozart's concerto in D minor, K. 466)

Quatre polkas pour piano. Moscou, Gresser.

Romance: "Dors pendant que je veille" de Musset pour chant avec piano. St. Petersburg, Bernard.

La Russie, morceau symphonique pour grand orchestre. Moscou, Jurgenson.

Sérénade russe pour piano, composée pour l'Album Bellini. Leipzig, Senff.

Ständchen: "Durch die laue Nacht," für eine Singstimme mit Pianoforte. Hamburg, Schuberth.

Trot de cavalerie pour piano. Moscou, Gresser.

Valse pour piano (A flat major). Leipzig, Senff.

Valse-Caprice pour piano (E flat major). Leipzig, Senff.

Wo? "Wo wird einst des Wandermüden" für eine Singstimme mit Pianoforte. Leipzig, Senff.

Systematic List of Rubinstein's Compositions

OPERAS

Among Thieves (Unter Räubern)
The Children of the Steppes (Die Kinder der Haide)
The Demon (Der Dämon)
Dmitri Donskoy
Feramors (Lalla Roukh)
Goriusha
Hadji-Abrek
Kalashnikov, the merchant of Moscow
Nero
The Parrot
The Siberian Hunters
Thomas the Fool (Foma Durachok)
Vengeance (Mest)

BIBLICAL OPERAS (Oratorios)

Christus, Op. 117
The Maccabees (Die Maccabäer)
Moses, Op. 112
Paradise Lost (Das verlorene Paradies), Op. 54
Sulamith
The Tower of Babel (Der Thurm zu Babel), Op. 80

BALLET

The Vine (Die Rebe)

ORCHESTRA

SYMPHONIES

Op. 40. No. 1, F major
Op. 42. No. 2, C major (Ocean)
Op. 56. No. 3, A major
Op. 95. No. 4, D minor (Dramatic)
Op. 107. No. 5, G minor
Op. 111. No. 6, A minor

MISCELLANEOUS

Op. 43. Ouverture triomphale
Op. 60. Ouverture de concert

Op. 68. Faust, Musikalisches Charakterbild
Op. 79. Ivan the Terrible, Musikalisches Charakterbild
Op. 87. Don Quixote, Musikalisches Charakterbild
Op. 110. Eroica. Fantaisie
La Russie, morceau symphonique

ORCHESTRA AND SOLO INSTRUMENTS

PIANO

Op. 25. Concerto No. 1 (E major)
Op. 35. Concerto No. 2 (F major)
Op. 45. Concerto No. 3 (G major)
Op. 70. Concerto No. 4 (D minor)
Op. 84. Fantaisie (C major)
Op. 94. Concerto No. 5 (E flat major)
Op. 102. Caprice russe
Op. 113. Concertstück (A flat major)

VIOLIN

Op. 46. Concerto (G major)
Op. 86. Romance et Caprice

VIOLONCELLO

Op. 65. Concerto No. 1 (A minor)
Op. 96. Concerto No. 2 (D minor)
See also: *Vocal Works with Orchestra.*

CHAMBER MUSIC

Op. 9. Octet (Piano, violin, viola, 'cello, bass, flute, clarinet, horn), D major
Op. 97. Sextet (2 violins, 2 violas, 2 'cellos), D major
Op. 55. Quintet (Piano, flute, clarinet, horn, bassoon), F major
Op. 59. Quintet (2 violins, 2 violas, 'cello), F major

Op. 99. Quintet (Piano, 2 violins, viola, 'cello), G minor

STRING QUARTETS

Op. 17. Three quartets (G major, C minor, F major)
Op. 47. Three quartets (E minor, B flat major, D minor)
Op. 90. Two quartets (G minor, E minor)
Op. 106. Two quartets (A flat major, F minor)

PIANO QUARTETS

Op. 66. Quartet, C major

PIANO TRIOS

Op. 15. Two trios (F major, G minor)
Op. 52. Third trio (B flat major)
Op. 85. Fourth trio (A major)
Op. 108. Trio (C minor)

VIOLIN AND PIANO

Op. 11, No. 1. Trois morceaux
Op. 13. First sonata (G major)
Op. 19. Second sonata (A minor)
Op. 98. Third sonata (B minor)
Grand duo sur "Le Prophète"

VIOLA AND PIANO

Op. 11, No. 3. Trois morceaux de salon
Op. 49. Sonata (F minor)

VIOLONCELLO AND PIANO

Op. 11, No. 2. Trois morceaux
Op. 18. First sonata (D major)
Op. 39. Second sonata (G major)

PIANO MUSIC
PIANO SOLO

Op. 1. Ondine
Op. 2. Deux fantaisies
Op. 3. Two melodies
Op. 4. Mazourka-Fantaisie

Op. 5. Polonaise, Cracovienne and Mazurka
Op. 6. Tarantelle
Op. 7. Impromptu-Caprice
Op. 7. Hommage à Jenny Lind
Op. 8. Voix intérieures
Op. 10. Two nocturnes
Op. 10. Kamennoi-Ostrow
Op. 12. First sonata (E major)
Op. 14. Le Bal
Op. 16. Trois morceaux
Op. 20. Second sonata (C minor)
Op. 21. Three caprices
Op. 22. Three serenades
Op. 23. Six études
Op. 24. Six preludes
Op. 26. Romance and Impromptu
Op. 28. Nocturne and Caprice
Op. 29. Two funeral marches
Op. 30. Barcarolle and Allegro appassionato
Op. 37. Akrostichon
Op. 38. Suite
Op. 41. Third sonata (F major)
Op. 44. Soirées à St. Pétersbourg
Op. 50. Charakterbilder
Op. 51. Six morceaux
Op. 53. Six fugues
Op. 69. Cinq morceaux
Op. 71. Trois morceaux
Op. 75. Album de Péterhof
Op. 77. Fantaisie
Op. 81. Six études
Op. 82. Album de danses populaires
Op. 88. Theme and variations
Op. 93. Miscellanées
Op. 100. Fourth sonata (A minor)
Op. 104. Morceaux
Op. 109. Soirées musicales
Op. 114. Second Akrostichon
Op. 118. Six morceaux
Op. 121. Polka
Barcarolle No. 2 (A minor)
Barcarolle No. 4 (G major)
Barcarolle No. 6 (C minor)
Bluette
Three Etudes
Euphémie-Polka
Fantaisie sur des mélodies hongroises
Points d'orgue (cadenzas)

Four polkas
Sérénade russe
Trot de cavalerie
Valse (A flat)
Valse-Caprice (E flat)

Piano Four Hands

Op. 9. Trois mélodies caracteristiques
Op. 50. Charakterbilder
Op. 89. Sonata (D major)
Op. 103. Bal costumé

Two Pianos

Op. 73. Fantaisie (F major)

VOCAL MUSIC
With Orchestra

Op. 58. Scena ed aria: "E dunque ver?" (Soprano solo)
Op. 63. Die Nixe (Women's chorus and alto solo)
Op. 74. Der Morgen (Male chorus)
Op. 92, No. 1. Hecuba (Alto solo)
Op. 92, No. 2. Hagar in der Wüste (Alto solo)

Choruses

Op. 31. Six songs for four men's voices
Op. 61. Six songs for men's chorus
Op. 62. Six songs for mixed chorus
Op. 91, No. 13. Requiem für Mignon
Bacchisches Lied (Bass solo and men's chorus)

Songs for Solo Voice and Piano

Op. 1. Six little songs in folk dialect

Op. 2. Zuruf aus der Ferne
Op. 3. Romance
Op. 4. Gebet
Op. 5. Die Nachtigall
Op. 6. Die Lerche
Op. 8. Six songs from the Russian
Op. 27. Nine songs of Kolzoff
Op. 32. Six songs of Heine
Op. 33. Six songs
Op. 34. Twelve songs of Mirza-Schaffy
Op. 36. Twelve songs from the Russian
Op. 57. Six songs
Op. 64. Five fables of Kriloff
Op. 72. Six songs
Op. 76. Six songs
Op. 78. Twelve songs from the Russian
Op. 83. Ten songs from the French, Italian and English
Op. 91. Poems from Goethe's "Wilhelm Meister's Lehrjahre"
Op. 101. Twelve songs of Tolstoi
Op. 105. Ten Serbian songs
Op. 115. Ten songs
Das begrabene Lied
Fatme
Glück
Herbstgedanken
Liebeswunder
Four Lieder
Six Lieder
Mädchens Abendgedanken
Romance
Ständchen
Wo?

Songs for Two Voices and Piano

Op. 48. Twelve two-part songs from the Russian
Op. 67. Six two-part songs

Bibliography

A separate list of Russian works consulted in the preparation of this book is given at the end of this bibliography. No attempt has been made to include all the many short articles inspired by Rubinstein's historical concerts, his jubilee, death or centenary.

ANTON RUBINSTEIN

Abell, A. M. "Impressions of Anton Rubinstein." *Musical Courier,* vol. 99 (1929), p. 26, 39.

Abert, Hermann. "Ungedruckte Briefe von Franz Liszt, Anton Rubinstein und Charlotte Buch-Pfeiffer." *Zeitschrift der Internationalen Musikgesellschaft,* vol. 4 (1903), p. 251-257.

Ambros, A. W. Bunte Blätter. Skizzen und Studien fur Freunde der Musik und der bildenden Kunst. 2v. Leipzig, Leuckart, 1872-74.

Anton Rubinstein, a sketch. New York, Koppel, 1872.

Aronson, Maurice. "Lest we forget Anton Rubinstein." *Musical Courier,* vol. 109 (Nov. 17, 1934), p. 6, 19.

Bagby, A. M. "How Rubinstein played the piano." *The Etude,* vol. 25 (1907), p. 646-647.

Bagby, A. M. How Ruby Played. Philadelphia, Penn Publishing Co., n.d.

Baskin, V. S. Episodes de la vie d'A. Rubinstein d'après M. Wladimir Baskine, par Ivan Martinoff. Bruxelles, Lombaerts, 1895.

Bennigsen, Olga. "The brothers Rubinstein and their times." *Musical Quarterly,* vol. 25 (1939), p. 407-419.

Berger, Francesco. "Retrospects (IV)." *Monthly Musical Record,* vol. 60 (1930), p. 106-107.

Bernstein, N. D. Anton Rubinstein. Leipzig, Reclam, 1911.

Bessmertny, Marie. "Anton Rubinstein über Mendelssohn." *Neue Musikzeitung,* vol. 30 (1909), p. 201.

Bobillier, Marie. "Rubinstein et l'opéra sacré," par Michel Brenet (pseud.) *Courrier musical,* vol. 15 (1912), p. 222-225.

Bowen, Catherine D. "Music comes to America." *Atlantic Monthly,* vol. 163 (1939), p. 591-602.

Busoni, Ferruccio. "Rubinstein in Wien." *Zeitschrift für Musik,* vol. 101 (1934), p. 1118-1121.

Catalog der im Druck erschienen Compositionen von Anton Rubinstein. Jubiläums-Ausgabe. Leipzig, Senff, 1889.

Chop, Max. Zeitgenössische Tondichter. Studien und Skizzen, von M. Charles (pseud.) Leipzig, Rossberg, 1888.

Droucker, Sandra. Erinnerungen an Anton Rubinstein. Bemerkungen, Andeutungen und Besprechungen in seiner Klasse im St. Petersburger Konservatorium. Leipzig, Senff, 1904.

Draeseke, Felix. "Anton Rubinstein." *Rivista musicale italiana,* vol. 2 (1895), p. 138.

Ehrlich, Heinrich. Aus allen Tonarten. Studien über Musik. Berlin, Brachvogel, 1888.

Ehrlich, Heinrich. Schlaglichter und Schlagschatten aus der Musikwelt. Berlin, Guttentag, 1872.

Ernest, Gustav. "Anton Rubinstein zum Gedächtnis." *Allgemeine Musikzeitung,* vol. 56 (1929), p. 1177-1178.

Ferris, G. T. Great violinists and pianists, Corelli to Paderewski. New York, Appleton, 1895.

Finck, H. T. Famous composers and their music, 16v. Boston, Millet, 1901. Vol. 5, p. 791-802.

Finck, H. T. Songs and song writers. New York, Scribner, 1900.

Finck, H. T. "Rubinstein's fate and future." The Music of the modern world. New York, 1895. Vol. 1, p. 68-70.

Geiringer, Karl. "Anton Rubinstein zu seinem 100. Geburtstag." *Die Musik,* vol. 22 (1929), p. 116-119.

Geiringer, Karl. "Pictorial biography of Anton Rubinstein." *Musical Courier,* vol. 99, no. 21 (1929), p. 27-34.

Graf, Emil. "Anton Rubinstein." *Zeitschrift für Musik,* vol. 96 (1929), p. 706-707.

Grau, Maurice. "Memories of musicians—Rubinstein and Wieniawski." *Music,* vol. 15 (1910), p. 442.

Halten, A. van. Anton Rubinstein. Utrecht, Leeflaug, 1886.

Hervey, Arthur. Rubinstein. London, Murdoch, n.d.

Hippius, Adelaide. "Anton Rubinstein in his class-room." *The Etude,* vol. 25 (1907), p. 230, 354, 436.

Hofmann, Josef. "What Rubinstein taught and told me." *Ladies Home Journal,* vol. 36 (1919), p. 39.

Huschke, Konrad. "Anton Rubinstein über Franz Liszt." *Signale für die musikalische Welt,* vol. 89 (1931), p. 337-340.

Huschke, Konrad. "Anton Rubinstein und Hans von Bülow." *Allgemeine Musikzeitung,* vol. 53 (1926), p. 741-745.

Huschke, Konrad. "Liszt—Rubinstein—H. v. Bülow im Lichte Clara Schumanns." *Allgemeine Musikzeitung,* vol. 58 (1931), p. 375-378.

Imbert, Hugues. Profils d'artistes contemporains. Paris, Fischbacher, 1897.

Isaacson, C. D. Face to face with great musicians. Second group. New York, Appleton, 1921.

Johnston, V. "In old Peterhof." *Era,* vol. 11 (1903), p. 374-380.

Keeton, A. E. "Anton Rubinstein." *Fortnightly Review,* vol. 83 (1905), p. 111-123.

Kinsky, Georg. Musikhistorisches Musuem von Wilhelm Heyer in Cöln. Katalog. vols. 1, 2 and 4. Cöln, Heyer, 1910-1916. Vol. 4, p. 570-632.

Kitchener, Frederick. "A neglected colossus: Anton Rubinstein." *Musical Standard,* vol. 29 (1908), p. 39.

Knorring, Marie von. "Anton Rubinstein über die russischen Verhältnisse seiner Zeit." *Signale für die musikalische Welt,* vol. 85 (1927), p. 1413-1416.

Kolff, J. van S. Muzikale en novellistiesche Schetsen. 's Gravenhage, Nijhoff, 1875.

Lahee, H. C. Famous pianists of to-day and yesterday. Boston, Page, 1901.

Lanier, Sidney. Music and poetry; essays upon some aspects and interrelations of the two arts. New York, Scribner, 1898.

Leschetizky, E. "Personal recollections of Anton Rubinstein." *Musician,* vol. 17 (1910), p. 442.

Lewinsky, Joseph. "Rubinstein als Umstürzler. Russische Reminiszenzen." *Neue Musikzeitung,* vol. 27 (1905-06), p. 154.

Liebling, Leonard. "Variations." *Musical Courier,* vol. 99, no. 21 (1929), p. 37-38, and no. 23, p. 31-32.

Lipsius, Ida M. Anton Rubinstein, von La Mara (pseud.). 8th ed., reprinted from her "Musikalische Studienköpfe." Leipzig, Breitkopf & Härtel, 1911.

Maclean, Charles. "Rubinstein as composer for the pianoforte." *Proceedings of the Musical Association,* vol. 39 (1913), p. 129-151. Reprinted in the *Sammelbände der Internationalen Musikgesellschaft,* vol. 15 (1914), p. 360-374.

Marmontel, A. F. Virtuoses contemporains. Paris, Heugel, 1882.

Martens, F. H. Anton Rubinstein. (Little biographies.) New York, Breitkopf & Härtel, 1922.

Mason, William. "Dr. Mason on Rubinstein's touch." *Music,* vol. 7 (1894-95), p. 390-392.

Mathews, W. S. B. "Antoine Rubinstein." *Music,* vol. 7 (1894-95), p. 384-389.

Mathews, W. S. B. The masters and their music. Philadelphia, Presser, 1898.

McArthur, Lillian. Anton Rubinstein, a biographical sketch, by Alexander M'Arthur (pseud.). Edinburgh, Black, 1889.

McArthur, Lillian. "A girl's recollections of Rubinstein," by Lillian Nichia. *Harper's Monthly*, vol. 126 (1912), p. 39-47.

McArthur, Lillian. "Rubinstein as a teacher," by Alexander McArthur (pseud.). *Music*, vol. 13 (1897-98), p. 365-369.

McCormick, W. H. "Anton Rubinstein." *Monthly Musical Record*, vol. 38 (1908), p. 198-200.

Moore, A. W. "Rubinstein's meteoric tour of America. Personal recollections of the great Russian master." *The Etude*, Vol. 29 (1911), p. 731-732.

Narodny, Ivan. "What Rubinstein did for Russia." *Musical America*, vol. 16, no. 5 (1912), p. 27.

Newmarch, Rosa. The Russian opera. London, Jenkins, 1923.

Norman, Ludvig. Musikaliska uppsatser och kritiker. Stockholm, Bagge, 1888.

Parsons, Albert R. "Rubinstein as pianist and how he composed his Ocean Symphony." *Musical Courier*, vol. 99, no. 21 (1929), p. 39.

Payne, Albert. Celebrated pianists of the past and present. By A. Ehrlich (pseud.). Philadelphia, Presser, 1894.

Philipp, Isidor. "Personal recollections of Anton Rubinstein." *The Etude*, vol. 56 (1938), p. 493-494.

Riemann, Hugo. "Anton Rubinstein." Century Library of Music, 1901. Vol. 7, p. 222-227.

Ritter, Hermann. "Personal recollections of Anton Rubinstein." *Music*, vol. 19 (1900-1901), p. 577-581.

Rodenberg, Julius. "My personal recollections of Antoine Rubinstein, together with letters." *Music*, vol. 8 (1895), p. 437-465.

Romain, Louis de. Essais de critique musicale. Paris, Lemerre, 1890.

Rubinstein, Anton. Anton Rubinstein's Gedankenkorb. Leipzig, Senff, 1897.

Rubinstein, Anton. Autobiography of Anton Rubinstein. 1829-1889. Tr. from the Russian by Aline Delano. Boston, Little, Brown, 1890.

Rubinstein, Anton. A conversation on music. Tr. by Mrs. John P. Morgan. New York, Tretbar, 1892. Also published with the title: "Music and its Masters."

Rubinstein, Anton. Die Meister des Klaviers. Tr. by M. Bessmertny. Berlin, Harmonie-Verlag, 1899.

Ryan, Thomas. "Personal recollections of Anton Rubinstein and Henri Wieniawski." *Musical Observer*, vol. 1, no. 12 (1907), p. 25.

Sabaneev, Leonid. "Anton Rubinstein." *Musical Times,* vol. 71 (1929), p. 977-980.

Saint-Saëns, Camille. Portraits et souvenirs. Paris, Société d'édition artistique, 1900.

Saint-Saëns, Camille. "Recollections of Antoine Rubinstein." *Music,* vol. 8 (1895), p. 423-430.

Saunders, C. E. "Rubinstein's Songs." *Music,* vol. 10 (1896), p. 112-116.

Schliepe, Ernst. "Anton Rubinstein." *Signale für die musikalische Welt,* vol. 87 (1892), p. 1453-1456.

Schnapp, Friedrich. "Busoni's persönliche Beziehungen zu Anton Rubinstein." *Zeitschrift für Musik,* vol. 99 (1932), p. 1053-1057.

Siloti, Alexander. "Memories of Rubinstein and Liszt." *The Etude,* vol. 38 (1920), p. 523-524.

Siloti, Alexander. My memories of Liszt. Edinburgh, Methven, Simpson, n.d.

Sohn, Joseph. "The centenary of Rubinstein." *The Etude,* vol. 47 (1929), p. 647-648.

Soubies, Albert. Antoine Rubinstein. Paris, Fischbacher, 1894.

Stanislavsky, C. "Rubinstein and Tolstoi." *The Forum,* vol. 71 (1924), p. 437-447.

Steinway, William. Correspondence with Rubinstein. MS.

Steinway, William. Diary. MS.

Steinway, William. "Reminiscences of Rubinstein." *Music,* vol. 7 (1894-95), p. 394-400.

Stevenson, Edward I. Prime-. Long-haired Iopas. Old chapters from twenty-five years of music-criticism. Florence, privately printed, 1927.

Tidebohl, Ellen von. "With Rubinstein in the class room." *The Etude,* vol. 26 (1908), p. 765.

Vogel, Bernhard. Anton Rubinstein. Biographischer Abriss nebst Characteristik seiner Werke. Leipzig, Hesse, 1888.

Vogt-Sudarskaja, Raissa. "Rubinstein-Erinnerungen." *Allgemeine Musikzeitung,* vol. 56 (1929), p. 1178-1179.

Walker, Bettina. My musical experiences. London, Bentley, 1892.

Walter, Victor. "Reminiscences of Anton Rubinstein." *Musical Quarterly,* vol. 5 (1919), p. 10-19.

Zabel, Eugen. Anton Rubinstein, ein Künstlerleben. Leipzig, Senff, 1892.

GENERAL WORKS ON MUSIC

Abraham, Gerald. A hundred years of music. New York, Knopf, 1938.

Abraham, Gerald. On Russian music. London, Reeves, 1939.

Abraham, Gerald. Studies in Russian music. New York, Scribner, 1936.

Auer, Leopold. My long life in music. New York, Stokes, 1923.

Bennett, Joseph. Forty years of music, 1865-1905. London, Methuen, 1908.

Berlioz, Hector. Memoirs of Hector Berlioz from 1803 to 1865. Ed. by Ernest Newman, New York, Knopf, 1932.

Bowen, Catherine D., and B. von Meck. Beloved friend, the story of Tchaikowsky and N. von Meck. New York, Random House, 1937.

Brandeis, Alice G. Notes from the life of a Viennese composer (Karl Goldmark), New York, Boni, 1927.

Calvocoressi, M. D. "Mily Balakirev, on the centenary of his birth." *Musical Quarterly,* vol. 23 (1937), p. 45-55.

Calvocoressi, M. D., and Gerald Abraham. Masters of Russian music. New York, Knopf, 1936.

Chopin, Frederic. Letters, collected by H. Opienski, tr. by E. L. Voynich. New York, Knopf, 1931.

Chorley, Henry F. Music and manners in France and Germany, 3v. London, Longmans, 1844.

Damrosch, Walter. My musical life. New York, Scribner, 1923.

Dent, Edward J. Ferruccio Busoni, a biography. London, Oxford, 1933.

Finck, Henry T. My adventures in the golden age of music. New York & London, Funk & Wagnalls, 1926.

Fuller-Maitland, J. A. Masters of German music. London, Osgood, McIlvaine, 1894.

Ganz, Wilhelm. Memories of a musician. London, Murray, 1913.

Geiringer, Karl. Brahms, his life and work. Boston, Houghton, 1936.

Gottschalk, Louis M. Notes of a pianist. Philadelphia, Lippincott, 1881.

Graves, C. L. The life and letters of Sir George Grove. London & New York, Macmillan, 1903.

Hambourg, Mark. From piano to forte. London, Cassell, 1931.

Henschel, Sir George. Musings and memories of a musician. New York, Macmillan, 1919.

Herz, Henri. Mes voyages en Amérique. Paris, Faure, 1866.

Huneker, J. G. Chopin, the man and his music. New York, Scribner, 1900.

Huneker, J. G. Franz Liszt. New York, Scribner, 1911.

Huneker, J. G. Preface to Chopin, Nocturnes, ed. by R. Joseffy. New York, Schirmer, 1915.

Indy, Vincent d'. César Franck, a study. Tr. by Rosa Newmarch, London & New York, Lane, 1910.

Landau, Rom. Ignace Paderewski, musician and statesman. New York, Crowell, 1934.

Lenz, Wilhelm von. Great piano virtuosos of our time. Tr. by M. R. Baker. New York, Schirmer, 1899.

Liszt, Franz. Life of Chopin. London, Reeves, 1877.

Mason, William. Memories of a musical life. New York, Century, 1901.

Mason, William. "Reminiscences." *Century,* vol. 60 (1900), p. 858-861.

Massenet, Jules. My recollections, tr. by H. V. Barnett. Boston, Small, Maynard, 1919.

Newcomb, Ethel. Leschetizky as I knew him. New York, Appleton, 1921.

Newmarch, Rosa. Tchaikovsky, his life and works. New York, Scribner, 1902.

Nohl, Ludwig, ed. Letters of distinguished musicians, tr. by Lady Wallace. London, Longmans, 1867.

Pougin, Arthur. Short history of Russian music. London, Chatto & Windus, 1915.

Rachmaninoff, Serge. Recollections, told to Oskar von Riesemann. New York, Macmillan, 1934.

Riesemann, Oskar von. Moussorgsky, tr. by Paul England. New York, Knopf, 1929.

Rimsky-Korsakoff, N. A. My musical life, tr. by Judah A. Joffe, ed. by C. Van Vechten. New York, Knopf, 1923.

Saint-Saëns, Camille. Musical memories, tr. by E. G. Rich. Boston, Small, Maynard, 1919.

Sitwell, Sacheverell. Liszt. Boston, Houghton Mifflin, 1934.

Soubies, Albert. Histoire de la musique en Russie. Paris, Flammarion, 1898.

Spohr, Ludwig. Louis Spohr's Autobiography. London, Longmans, 1885.

Stanford, Sir Charles V. Pages from an unwritten diary. London, Longmans, 1914.

Tajan-Rogé, D. Memoires d'un piano. Paris, 1876.

Thomas, Rose F. Memoirs of Theodore Thomas. New York, Moffatt, 1911.

Thomas, Theodore. Theodore Thomas, a musical autobiography. Ed. by G. P. Upton. 2v. Chicago, McClurg, 1905.

Toye, Francis. Giuseppe Verdi, his life and works. London, Heinemann, 1931.

Toye, Francis. Rossini, a study in tragi-comedy. New York, Knopf, 1934.

Turner, W. J. Berlioz, the man and his work. London, Dent, 1934.

Upton, G. P. Musical memories. Chicago, McClurg, 1908.

Wagner, Richard. Correspondence of Wagner and Liszt, 1841-1861, ed. by F. Hueffer. 2v. London, Grevel, 1888.

Baring, Maurice. The Russian people. London, Methuen, 1911.

Barry, Herbert. Ivan at home, or pictures of Russian life. London, The Publishing Co., 1872.

Clark, Charles U. Russia and Roumania on the Black Sea. New York, Dodd, Mead, 1927.

Comettant, Oscar. Trois ans aux Etats-Unis. Etude des moeurs et coutumes américains. Paris, Pagnerre, 1857.

Conders, J. Popular description of Russia, geographical, historical and topographical. London, J. Duncan, 1826.

Eckardt, J. W. A. Distinguished persons in Russian society, tr. by F. E. Bennett. London, Smith, 1873.

Fletcher, John G. The two frontiers, a study in historical psychology. New York, Coward-McCann, 1930.

Friedlander, Israel. The Jews in Russia and Poland; a bird's eye view of their history and culture. New York, Putnam, 1915.

Gilbert, L. Russia illustrated. London, the author, 1844.

Goldsmith, J. General view of the manners, customs and curiosities of nations. 2v. Phillipson, 1822.

Graham, S. Undiscovered Russia. New York, Lane, 1912.

Green, G. An original journal from London to St. Petersburg. London, Boosey & Hatchard, 1913.

Guthrie, K. B. Through Russia, from St. Petersburg to Astrakhan and the Crimea. London, Hurst and Blackett, 1874.

Hand-book for travellers in Russia, Poland and Finland. London, J. Murray, 1868.

Hodgetts, E. A. Brayley-. The court of Russia in the 19th century, 2v. New York, Scribner, 1908.

Kluchevsky, V. O. A history of Russia, tr. by C. J. Hogarth. 5v. New York, Dutton, 1911-31.

Kohl, J. G. Russia and the Russians in 1842. London, Colburn, 1842.

Malte-Brun, Conrad. Universal geography. 6v. Philadelphia, Finley, 1827-29.

Martonne, E. de. "Choses vues en Bessarabie." *Revue de Paris,* vol. 26 (1919), part 5, p. 499-534.

Mirsky, D. S. Russia, a social history. London, Cresset Press, 1931.

Morley, Henry, ed. Sketches of Russian life, before and during the emancipation of the serfs. London, Chapman, 1866.

Murray, Hugh. Encyclopedia of geography. Philadelphia, Carey, Lea & Blanchard, 1837.

Pelivan, I. G. Bessarabia under the Russian rule. Paris, Charpentier, 1920.

Perkins, Samuel. The world as it is. 2nd ed. New Haven, Belknap, 1841.

Platonov, S. F. History of Russia, tr. by E. Aronsberg. New York, Macmillan, 1925.

Podolsky, M. Apostles of Revolution, by Max Nomad (pseud.). Boston, Little, Brown, 1939.

Sachar, A. L. A history of the Jews. New York, Knopf, 1930.

Sears, Robert. An illustrated description of the Russian Empire. New York, Sears, 1855.

Slade, Sir Adolphus. Travels in Germany and Russia. London, Longmans, 1840.

Trotsky, L. My life, an attempt at an autobiography. New York, Scribner, 1930.

Urusov, S. D. Memoirs of a Russian governor, tr. by Herman Rosenthal. London & New York, Harper, 1908.

Vogüe, E. M. de, ed. The Tsar and his people, or social life in Russia. New York, Harper, 1891.

Volkonski, S. M. My reminiscences, by Prince Serge Volkonski. Tr. by A. E. Chamot. 2v. London, Hutchinson, 1925.

IN RUSSIAN

Aksakova, A. F. Pri dvore dykh imperatorov; vospominaniya—dnevnik. 2v. Moskva, Sabashnikovykh, 1928-29.

Amfiteatrov, A. V. "Netlennyĭ." *Novoye russkoye slovo,* May 9, 1937.

Asaf'yev, B. V. (Igor' Glebov, pseud.) A. G. Rubinstein. Moskva, Gos. Izdat., muzykal'nyi sektor, 1929.

Asaf'yev, B. V. (Igor' Glebov, pseud.) Russkaya muzyka ot nachala 19 veka. Moskva, Academia, 1930.

Baskin, V. S. "Biograficheski ocherk." *Russkaya mysl',* vol. 6 (1885), part 1, p. 259; part 9, p. 118.

Baskin, V. S. Sulamif'. Ocherk. Vasil'ki, St. Petersburg, 1901, p. 351-360.

Bessel', V. "Moi vospominaniya ob A. G. Rubinsteine." *Russkaya Starina,* vol. 100, no. 5 (May, 1898), p. 351-374.

Borodin, A. P. Pisma A. P. Borodina. 2v. Moskva, Gos. Izdat., 1927-1936.

Chaĭkovski, M. I. Zhizn' P. I. Chaĭkovskavo. 3v. Moskva, Jurgenson, 1902-03.

Chaĭkovski, P. I. Dnevnik. Moskva, Gos. Izdat., 1923.

Chaĭkovski, P. I. Perepiska s N. F. von Mekk. 3v. Moskva, Academia, 1934-36.

Chaĭkovski, P. I. Perepiska s Taneyevym.

Chaĭkovski, P. I. Perepiska s Yurgensonom. Moskva, Muzgiz, 1938.

Davidova, M. A. "Vospominaniya ob A. G. Rubinsteine." *Istoricheski vestnik,* vol. 76 (April, 1899), p. 76-95.

Davydov, N. Vospominaniya.

Dekhtereva-Kavos, S. T. A. G. Rubinstein. St. Petersburg, Stasyulevich, 1895.

Deyatelei revolyutzionnavo dvizheniya v Rossii; bio-bibliograficheski slovar'. 3v. Moskva, Vses. obshch. politich. katorzhan i ss.-posel, 1927-35.

Dostoyevsky, F. M. Perepiska. Leningrad, Academia, 1928.

Entziklopedicheski slovar'. 41v. Moskva, Brockhaus i Efron, 1890-1904.

Findeĭzen, N. F. A. G. Rubinstein. Moskva, Yurgenson, 1907.

Glebov, Igor', pseud. *See* Asaf'yev, B. V.

Goldenweiser. "Velikiye brat'ya." *Sovetskoye iskusstvo,* March 30, 1938.

Grechaninov. A. T. Vospominaniya.

Ivanov, M. M. "A. G. Rubinstein o muzyke." *Trud,* vol. 1 (1892), p. 180-195.

Karatygin, M. Vospominaniya.

Kashkin, N. D. "A. G. Rubinstein." *Russkoye obozreniye,* vol. 12 (1894), p. 971-986.

Kashkin, N. D. "Dve muzykal'nya pamyatki. N. G. Rubinstein i Musorgski." *Russkaya mysl',* vol. 4 (April, 1906), p. 16-42.

Kashkin, N. D. "Vospominaniye o N. G. Rubinsteine." *Russkoye obozreniye,* vol. 47 (Sept. 1897), p. 151-169; vol. 49 (Jan. 1898), p. 328-338.

Kolosova, Ye. M. Ostrovski i russkiye kompozitory. Moskva, Gos. Izdat., Iskusstvo, 1937.

Koni. Na zhiznennom puti. 5v. Moskva, 1914-29.

"Kontzert Imperatorskavo muzykal'navo obshchestva v pamyat' A. G. Rubinsteina." *Russkaya muzykal'naya gazeta,* vol. 2 (1895), p. 56.

"Kontzerty v pamyat' A. G. Rubinsteina." *Russkaya muzykal'naya gazeta,* vol. 2 (1895), p. 56.

Koptyayev, A. P. "A. G. Rubinstein v svoikh dukhovnykh operakh." *Russkaya muzykal'naya gazeta,* vol. 3 (1896), p. 961-976, 1189-1206.

Korganov, V. D. "Khristos. Dukhovnaya opera A. G. Rubinstein." *Russkaya muzykal'naya gazeta,* vol. 2 (1895), p. 404-408.

Kremlev. Leningradskaya gosudarstvennaya konservatoriya.

Lamsdorff, V. N. Dnevnik. 2v. Moskva, Academia, 1934.

Larosh, G. A. "A. G. Rubinstein." *Russkaya starina,* vol. 64, no. 11 (Nov. 1889), p. 589-600.

Larosh, G. A. "Pamyati A. G. Rubinsteina." *Yezhegodnik imperatorskikh teatrov,* vol. 1 (1893-94), p. 436-446.

Liskovski, N. M. "Letopis' sobytiĭ v zhizni i deyatel'nosti A. G. Rubinsteina." *Russkaya starina*, vol. 64, no. 11 (Nov. 1889), p. 601-635.

Lokhvitzki, I. V. "A. G. Rubinstein, vstrecha s nim v 1839 g." *Russkaya starina*, vol. 50, no. 5 (May, 1886), p. 440-441.

Meshcherski, V. P. Moi vospominaniya. 3v. St. Peterburg, Meshcherski, 1897-1912.

"Netlennoye telo N. G. Rubinsteina." *Novoye russkoye slovo*, November 14, 1938.

Neustroyev, A. A. "Villuan i pervoye kontzertnoye puteshestviye po Yevrope A. G. Rubinsteina." *Russkaya starina*, vol. 65, no. 1 (Jan. 1890), p. 247-280.

"Novyya vospominaniya o A. G. Rubinsteine." *Russkaya muzykal'naya gazeta*, vol. 6 (1899), p. 579-580.

Ossovski, A. "A. G. Rubinstein." *Russkaya muzykal'naya gazeta*, vol. 1 (1894), p. 249-258.

"Pamyati A. G. Rubinsteina." *Russkaya muzykal'naya gazeta*, vol. 6 (1899), p. 1166-1168.

"Perepiska Lista s A. G. Rubinsteinom." *Russkaya muzykal'naya gazeta*, vol. 3 (1896), p. 829-866.

"Pisma A. G. Rubinsteina k sestre." *Muzykalnoye obrazovanye*. 1930.

"Pisma N. G. Rubinsteina Dargomyzhskomu." *Russkaya muzykal'naya gazeta*, vol. 1 (1894), p. 151-152.

"Pogrebeniye tela A. G. Rubinsteina." *Russkaya muzykal'naya gazeta*, vol. 1 (1894), p. 257.

Polonski, ya. P. "A. G. Rubinstein." *Russkaya starina*, vol. 57, no. 3 (March, 1888), p. 811-812.

Rappaport, V. "N. G. Rubinstein." *Biblioteka teatra i iskusstva*, 1912, no. 4, p. 3-20.

Rozenberg, M. B. "A. G. Rubinstein." *Russkaya starina*, vol. 64, no. 11 (November, 1889), p. 579-587.

Rubinstein, A. G. "Avtobiografiya." *Russkaya starina*, vol. 64, no. 11 (November, 1889), p. 517-578.

Semevski, M. "A. G. Rubinstein." *Russkaya starina*, vol. 64, no. 11 (November, 1889), p. 514-516.

Shchegolev, P. Y. Alekseyevski ravelin. Moskva, Federatziya, 1929.

Sokolova, A. I. "Vstrechi i znakomstva." *Istoricheski vestnik*, vol. 127 (Feb. 1912), p. 532-542; vol. 135 (March, 1914), p. 849-865.

Storozhev, V. N. "Brat'ya Rubinsteiny." *Golos minuvshavo*, vol. 4 (Sept. 1916), p. 246-251.

V. A. "N. G. Rubinstein." *Russki arkhiv*, vol. 35 (Nov. 1897), p. 441-472.

Vaksel', P. "A. G. Rubinstein." *Russkaya starina,* vol. 65, no. 1 (Jan. 1890), p. 242.

Val'ter, V. "A. G. Rubinstein." *Vestnik Yevropy,* vol. 290 (Dec. 1914), p. 294-304.

Val'ter, V. "A. G. Rubinstein o muzyke." *Russkaya muzykal'naya gazeta,* vol. 11 (1904), p. 976-981.

Val'ter, V. Gorodetzki, and Vitol'. Lyadov.

Velikiĭ Knyaz' Konstantin Nikolayevich. Dnevnik. Krasnyi arkhiv.

Villuan, A. I. "Nekrolog." *Russkaya muzkal'naya gazeta,* vol. 3 (1896).

Viskovatov, P. A. "Moio znakomstvo s A. G. Rubinsteinom." *Russki vestnik,* vol. 243 (1896), p. 231-242.

Index

A Flat Sonata, Schubert, 316
A Minor Violin Sonata, A. Rubinstein, 109
Abaza, Madame (Julie Stube), 251, 253, 302, 325-326, 331
Academy of Music, New York City, 243
Adieu à Villoing, N. Rubinstein, 56
Adlerberg, Count, 260
Agathon, 195, 198, 201, 216, 271, 274
Aksakov, Ivan, 159
Aksakov, Madame, 157-158
Alard, Jean, 143, 241
Albrecht, Carl, 211, 276
Albrechtsberger, 19
Alexander I, 7, 85, 135-140
Alexander II, 135, 136-139, 168, 170-171, 183, 192, 266, 271, 272, 283, 339, 364
Alexander III, 268, 283, 292-294, 308-309, 317-320, 322, 340, 342-344, 361, 364, 365
Alexander Nevsky Cemetery, 263, 368
Alexandra Feodorovna, Tsarina, 52, 53, 58, 65, 86, 88, 110, 140, 157
Alexandra, Grand Duchess, 94
A Life for the Tsar, Glinka, 86, 130
Altenburg Castle, 115 *et seq.*
Ambros, August Wilhelm, 284
Amphitheatrov, Alexander, 279
Anenkova, Olga, 202
Anna Pavlovna, Queen of Holland, 36-37, 45
Appassionata, Beethoven, 241, 292
Apraksin, 140
Apsley House, London, 41
Arensky, Antony, 186
Arnim, Frau Von, 32
Artot, Désirée, 288
Atlantic Monthly, 237
Auber, Daniel, 29-30, 142
Auer, Leopold, 206-207, 219, 220, 235, 260, 302, 312, 323, 362, 363
Auerbach, Berthold, 111
Augusta, Empress, 111
Ayrton, William, 42
Azantchevsky, 221, 254, 304, 364

B Flat Minor Concerto, Tchaikovsky, 257, 270, 273
B Flat Minor Sonata, Chopin, 370
B Flat Piano Trio, A. Rubinstein, 370
Bach, Emanuel, 313
Bach, Friedemann, 228
Bach, John Christian, 147
Bach, Sebastian, 19, 43, 48, 62, 64, 90, 91, 92, 109, 120, 124, 182, 183, 198, 245, 312-314, 334, 338, 359, 368, 372
Bakunin, Mikhail, 77, 221, 265
Bal Costumé, A. Rubinstein, 282
Balakirev, Mili, 179, 180 *et seq.,* 218, 282, 292, 328
Barcarolle in G, A. Rubinstein, 235, 371
Bärmann, Karl, 232
Barnum, P. T., 227-228, 229, 231
Barthold, Herr, 130
Bashilov, Count, 20-22, 29
Bechstein, 287; —piano, 347; —*Saal,* 348
Becker, Dr., 37
Beecher, Henry Ward, 240
Beethoven, Ludwig van, 24, 42, 61, 66, 71, 98, 120, 122-123, 124, 128, 129, 143, 150, 165, 174, 215, 220, 228, 229, 232, 235, 243, 245, 250, 256, 261, 272, 284, 312-315, 329, 334, 337, 338, 351, 359
Begichev family, 190
Belayev, Mitrofan, 299
Belgiojoso, Princess, 29
Bennett, James Gordon, 230
Bennett, Joseph, 220, 280, 296
Bennett, Sterndale, 147, 152
Berceuse, Chopin, 241
Berdichev, 3 *et seq.,* 16, 80, 82, 309, 340-341
Bergmann, Carl, 235
Bériot, Charles Auguste de, 241
Berlioz, Hector, 26, 29, 30, 60, 77, 120, 121, 129, 142, 160, 175
Bernard's music shop, 82
Bernhard, Madame, 274
Bessel, Vasily, 177-178, 362, 363
Bezbozhnik, 278
Biebrich, 122-123

Biographie Universelle des Musiciens, 118
Bird as Prophet, The, Schumann, 292
Bismarck, Otto von, 220, 299, 339
Blessington, Lady, 41
Bludov, Countess, 251
Bogorodskoe, 196
Bohrer, Caspar, 38
Bohrer, Sophie, 38, 82
Bolshaya Morskaya, 83
Bolshoi Orchestra, Moscow, 198
Bolshoi Theatre, 317-318, 357
Borodin, Alexander, 182-183, 185, 270
Bortniansky, Dimitri, 87, 160
Bösendorfersaal, the, Vienna, 74
Boston Globe, 239
Botkin, Dr., 269
Brahms, Johannes, 90, 131-133, 220, 224, 225, 232, 233, 358
Breitkopf and Hartels, 285
Broadwood, Henry, 261
Broadwood, John, 39, 196
Browning, Robert, 261
Brüll, Ignaz, 225
Bull, Ole, 230, 233, 241
Busoni, Ferruccio, 339
Byron, Lord, 32, 361

Cain, A. Rubinstein, 361
Campan, Madame, 102
Carnaval, Schumann, 336
Carnaval de Venise, Paganini, 241
Carnaval de Venise, A. Thomas, 143
Caruso, Enrico, 370
Catechism of the Revolution, 265
Catherine, Duchess of Mecklenburg-Strelitz, 104, 251, 253, 294, 325-326, 342-343
Catherine II, the Great, 86, 160
Catherine, or the Brigand's Daughter, 53
Cavour, Count di, 141
Central Park Garden, 248
Chaconne, Bach, 245
Charlotte Mary, Princess. *See* Helena Pavlovna
Chaucer, 86
Chekuanov, Princess Vera. *See* Rubinstein, Vera
Chernigov, forests of, 13
Chernishev, Count, 18
Cherubini, Maria Luigi, 27-29, 39, 120, 142

Chesnokov, 81
Children of the Steppes, A. Rubinstein, 164, 167, 218, 355
Chopin, Frédéric, 28, 29, 30 *et seq.,* 51, 61-62, 64, 91, 124, 127, 131, 142, 143, 146, 150-151, 228, 232, 235, 241, 243, 256, 261, 262, 292, 294, 295, 311, 312, 316, 323, 332, 338, 343, 354, 359, 370
Choral Union, Chicago, 231
Christus, A. Rubinstein, 152, 353, 355, 359, 370
Christy's Minstrel Rooms, 261
Circourt, Madame de, 32
Citizens' Club, St. Petersburg, 89
Clarendon Hotel, New York City, 234
Clementi, Muzio, 17, 39, 48, 89, 91, 244
Clinton Hall, 229
Colonne, Edouard, 272, 276
Concerto in D Minor, Wieniawski, 241
Concerto in F Major, A. Rubinstein, 93
Concerto in G, A. Rubinstein, 147
Concertstück, A. Rubinstein, 329
Conservatoire, Paris, 28-29, 39
Contrast, Moscheles, 94
Conversation on Music, A. Rubinstein, 334
Cornelius, Peter, 117, 130
Cossmann, 209
Couperin, François, 228, 285
Cramer, Johann, 18, 28
Crimean War, 110, 112, 114, 139, 141, 146, 154
Cromwell, Oliver, 149
Cruikshank, George, 40
Cui, Cesar, 187
Cumberland, Grand Duke of, 293
Cuvier, Georges, 102
Czerny, Carl, 17, 48, 173, 244, 334

D Major 'Cello Sonata, A. Rubinstein, 370
D Minor Concerto, A. Rubinstein, 220, 235, 236, 240-241, 370
D Minor Sonata, Beethoven, 174
d'Agoult, Madame, 41
Dahl, Olga, 202
Daily Examiner, London, 146
Damrosch, Leopold, 247
Damrosch, Walter, 247

Damske, 92, 93, 94
Dargomizhky, Alexander, 181
Darmstadt, Grand Duke of, 65
Darwin, Charles, 221
David, Ferdinand, 148, 170, 220, 241
Davidov, Carl, 170-171, 260, 299, 304-305, 309
Deacon of Kazan Cathedral, 98-99
Dehn, Siegfried, 51, 63-65, 70, 71, 75-76, 78, 84, 86, 92, 134, 171, 369
Delacroix, Eugene, 29
Demidov family, 169; —mansion, 172
Demon, The, A. Rubinstein, 225, 257-258, 280-281, 323, 370
De Pachman, Vladimir, 295
Deutsche Rundschau, 288
Diabelli, Antonio, 17, 48, 244
Disraeli, Benjamin, 115, 128
Ditson's Music Store, 232
Dmitri Donskoy, A. Rubinstein, 105-106, 107, 131, 233
Dohler, Théodor, 143
Dohr, 209
Dolgoroukov, 192, 197, 198, 216, 271, 272, 292, 340
Domke, 323
Don Juan Fantasia, Liszt, 68
Don Quixote, A. Rubinstein, 221, 233
Donskoi Monastery, 14
Dormidont, Father, 65
Dostoyevsky, Feodor, 83, 203-204, 271, 359
Dramatic Symphony, A. Rubinstein, 254, 257, 267
Dreyschock, Alexander, 169, 176
Dubuc, 209
Dumas, Alexandre, 29
Duse, Eleanora, 127

E Flat Concerto, A. Rubinstein, 259, 351, 352
Eastbrook, Lady, 223
Edipus, Moussorgsky, 184
Ehrlich, Heinrich, 74
Eichenwald, Dr., 364
Eliot, Charles, 237
Ella, John, 147, 150, 196, 205, 219, 260-261
Emancipation, 137 *et seq.*
Emerson, Ralph Waldo, 237
Empress Dowager of Prussia, 117

Erard, Pierre, 29
Erard, Sebastian, 29, 39
Erlking, Schubert, 235, 237, 262
Ernst, Heinrich Wilhelm, 241
Eroica, Beethoven, 269
Essipov, Madame, 251, 288
Esterhazys, the, 109
Etude, Cramer, 18
Etude in D, A. Rubinstein, 44
Eugénie, Empress, 143
Europaischerhof Hotel, 347, 352-354

F Major 'cello Sonata, A. Rubinstein, 109
F Major Symphony, A. Rubinstein, 111
F Major Trio, A. Rubinstein, 109
F Sharp Minor Polonaise, Chopin, 332
Fantasia for Two Pianos, A. Rubinstein, 259
Faust, A. Rubinstein, 116, 130
Fenella, 53
Feramors, A. Rubinstein, 151, 219, 223-224, 255, 329
Fétis, 118
Fichte, Johann Gottlieb, 60
Fidelio, Beethoven, 142
Field, John, 20, 21, 33, 89, 90, 91, 160, 209, 250, 337
Fifth Symphony, Beethoven, 235
Finck, Henry, 232-233, 237
Fitch, the brothers, 38
Fitztum, 96
"Five, The," 181-187, 257, 270
Flying Dutchman, The, Wagner, 115
Fool's Scherzo, Gussakovsky, 180-181
Franck, César, 77, 143, 232
Franco-Prussian War, 221, 286
Free School, Petersburg, 180, 184 *et seq.*
Freischütz, Weber, 24, 29, 128
Frevil, 80
Frey, foreman, 15
Fries, Wulf, 237
Froude, James, 128
Fuhl, Baron, 75-76
Funeral March, Chopin, 343

G Major Concerto, Number 3, A. Rubinstein, 111, 324, 370
G Minor Nocturne, Chopin, 127
G Minor Symphony, Mozart, 220
Gabrilowitsch, Ossip, 299, 312, 362
Galakhov, General, 80-81

Galatea, The, 22-23, 53
Galitzin Hospital, 18
Galop Chromatique, Liszt, 19, 20, 21
Gedeonov, 105-106
George, Duke of Mecklenburg-Strelitz, 302, 326, 327
George III, 147
Gerke, Herr, 172, 176
Glazunov, Alexander, 285, 299, 312
Glinka, Mikhail, 12, 86, 87, 97, 104, 130, 160, 283, 294
Goebel, Franz, 19
Goethe, Wolfgang von, 32, 117, 128, 225, 353
Goldmark, Carl, 77, 164-165, 225
Golovnin, 159
Gorusha, A. Rubinstein, 325
Gottschalk, Louis, 143, 231
Gradus ad Parnassum, Clementi, 48
Grau, Jacob, 227, 285
Grau, Maurice, 226 *et seq.,* 253, 285
Greeley, Horace, 230
Grimm, Herman, 131-133
Grisi, Madame, 96, 233, 317
Grove, Sir George, 235
Grünberg, Barbara, 18
Gussakovsky, 180

Habeneck, François Antoine, 30
Halévy, Jacques, 29
Hall of the Nobility. See *Salle de la Noblesse*
Hallé, Charles, 261
Hambourg, Mark, 358
Handel, George Frederick, 41, 43, 235, 245, 312, 313-314, 322
Hanslick, Edouard, 149, 290, 295, 323
Harsher, Madame, 177
Harsher, Maria, 177
Harsher, Nadejda, 177
Harvard College, 232
Haslinger, 113
Haydn, Joseph, 24, 32, 71, 101, 109, 121, 156, 308, 312-314
Hegel, Georg, 60
Heindle, 74-76
Heine, Heinrich, 62-63, 73, 76
Helena, daughter of Grand Duchess Catherine, 326
Helena Pavlovna, Grand Duchess (Princess Charlotte Mary), 101-112, 114,

131, 134, 135, 137-142, 154-155, 157
et seq., 167 *et seq.,* 176, 180 *et seq.,*
221, 251, 253-254, 286, 302, 325, 327,
339, 342, 359, 362
Helm, 323
Henschel, George, 260
Hensel, Fanny Mendelssohn, 65. *See also* Mendelssohn, Fanny
Henselt, Adolf von, 20, 21, 44, 90, 91, 92, 160
Heroic Fantasy, A. Rubinstein, 282-283
Herz, Henri, 17, 39, 43, 61, 75, 227, 230, 235
Hirz, Count, 319
Historical Concerts, 285-290, 291-299, 307, 362
Historical Lectures, 309, 311-317
Hodinka Field, Moscow, 137
Hofmann, Josef, 111, 126, 348, 354-355, 369, 370
Hoforchester, Leipzig, 61 *et seq.*
Holmes, Oliver Wendell, 237
Hommage à Washington, Herz, 230
Honoré, Leo, 190, 209
How Ruby Played, 248
Howells, William Dean, 237
Hugo, Victor, 29
Hummel, Johann Nepomuk, 17, 20, 21, 33, 48, 61, 312, 359
Huneker, James, 124-125, 127, 295
Hungarian March, Liszt, 58

Il Demonio. See *Demon, The*
Intermezzo, Tchaikovsky, 327
International Piano Competition, 300, 338-339
Ippolitov-Ivanov, Michael, 299
Irving Hall, New York City, 232
Islamey, Balakirev, 292
"Island of Stone, The," 107
Ivan the Terrible, A. Rubinstein, 324
Ivan IV, 324
Ivanovska, Madame, 272
Izmailov Cathedral, 368

Jaell, Alfred, 235
"Janitor of Music," 108, 112, 135 *et seq.,* 156
Janko, A. Rubinstein, 161
Jardin des Plantes, 102

406

Joachim, Joseph, 117, 131-133, 148, 241, 288
Judaism in Music, Wagner, 152

Kalkbrenner, Friedrich Wilhelm, 17, 28, 31, 61, 142, 359
Kamensky, Boris, 302, 305, 312, 371-372
Kammenoy Island, 107, 112, 226
Kammenoy Ostrov, A. Rubinstein, 108, 115
Kanshin, 159
Karamzin, Nicholai, 86, 102
Kashkin, 212, 276
Kavelin, 159
Kazan Cathedral, 98-99
Keyserling, Count, 159
Kiel, Friedrich, 63
Kisilev, 192, 198
Klindworth, Carl, 117, 212, 270, 276, 288, 334
Kologrivov, 159, 188
Konstantin, Grand Duke, 36-37, 52, 97, 104, 107, 140, 159, 180, 254, 262, 283, 294, 302, 322, 326, 331, 339
Konstantin, son of Grand Duke Konstantin, 326
Kreisleriana, Schumann, 292, 338
Kremlin, the, 14, 16
Kreutzer Sonata, Beethoven, 241, 302
Kreutzer Sonata, The, Tolstoi, 333
Kronstadt, 101, 107, 114, 167, 252
Krushev, T. D., 192-193
Krusheva, 191-195, 262
Krylov, Ivan, 86
Kullak, Theodor, 63
Kutchka, Mogutchaya, 181-187, 201, 218, 257, 328
Kutuzov, Mikhail, 24

Lablache, Luigi, 41
Lalo, Edouard, 276
Lamsdorf, Count, 319
Langer, 209
Laroche, Herman, 169, 172 *et seq.,* 208, 212, 213
Laub, 209
Lavrovskaya, 312, 331, 362
Legende, Wieniawski, 241
Les Adieux, Beethoven, 315

Leschetizky, Theodor, 112, 134, 169, 176, 207, 215, 225, 334, 336, 357-359, 369
Levy, Carl, 80, 96
Lhevinne, Joseph, 336, 351-352
Liadov, Anatol, 282, 299, 312, 342
Lind, Jenny, 228, 229, 233, 235
Lipinski, 241
Liszt, Franz, 21, 28, 29, 30-35, 39, 43, 44, 47, 50-51, 58, 61-62, 71, 104, 115-126, 129, 131, 134, 145, 146, 155, 217, 224, 228, 232, 239, 243, 251, 263, 289, 306, 311, 312, 316, 329, 354, 364, 371
Lohengrin, Wagner, 115, 134
Lokhvitsky, 24
Longfellow, Henry W., 237
Louis Napoleon, 143
Louis Phillipe, King of France, "the Citizen King," 29, 143
Lower Rhine Festival, 224
Lvov, Prince, 80, 87
Lvov, General, 97, 160, 180

Macarthur, Lillian, 332-333, 335-336, 365
Maccabees, The, A. Rubinstein, 152, 254, 255, 258-259, 260, 350
MacMahon, Marshal, 263
Mad Week, 164
Maharina, 305, 309
Malakhov Hill, 112
Malozemova, 312, 331, 362, 369
Männergesangverein, 231
Margaret Street, London, 151-152
Maria Alexandrovna, Tsarina, 136
Maria Nicholaevna, Grand Duchess, 57-58, 109-110
Mario, Marchese di Candia, 87, 96, 233, 317
Markevitch, Senator, 327
Marx, Adolf, 134
Maryinsky Theatre, 257
Mashenka, niece of Dostoyevsky, 203-204
Mason, Lowell, 231
Mason, William, 116, 123, 231, 244
Massenet, Jules, 276; — family, 77
Matinée d'Adieu, 243
Matthew Passion, Bach, 62
Matvey, 302, 332, 366
Maurer, Louis, 161
Mayer, Carl, 91

Mecklenburg-Strelitz, Duke of, 105
Mecklenburg-Strelitz, Grand Duke of, 326
Mehlig, Anna, 235
Meine Laura, A. Rubinstein, 17
Melody in F, A. Rubinstein, 108, 235
Mendelssohn, Abraham, 60, 73
Mendelssohn, Fanny, 61, 62-63. *See also* Hensel, Fanny Mendelssohn
Mendelssohn, Felix, 41-42, 43, 51, 60-66, 71, 75, 120, 131, 132, 147, 165, 182, 183, 224, 250, 256, 289, 311, 312
Mendelssohn, Frau, mother of Felix, 47
Merchant Kalashnikoff, A. Rubinstein, 267, 318-320
Metsdorf, Richard, 172
Meyer, Leopold, 31, 231
Meyerbeer, Giacomo, 29, 31, 60 *et seq.,* 71, 87, 142, 175, 234
Mezentsev, Chief of Police, 265
Michael, Grand Duke, 344 *et seq.*
Michael Palace, 101 *et seq.,* 157 *et seq.,* 167 *et seq.,* 184, 342
Michael Pavlovitch, Grand Duke, 102 *et seq.,* 140, 251
Michelangelo, 117
Milanello, Maria, 39
Milanello, Theresa, 39
Milioutin, 138
Milton, John, 149-150
Moscheles, Ignaz, 17, 42 *et seq.,* 77, 94, 250, 359
Moscheles, son of Ignaz, 77
Moscow Conservatory, 117, 291, 318, 328; formally opened, 209; staff, 209-214
Moscow Musical Society, 197, 200 *et seq.,* 214, 218
Mosenthal, Dr. Von, 152, 161, 223, 252
Moses, A. Rubinstein, 152, 301, 350, 357
Moses Fantasia, Thalberg, 20
Moussorgsky, Modeste, 182, 183, 185-186, 270
Mozart Society, Chicago, 231
Mozart, Wolfgang Amadeus, 21, 32, 39, 71, 89, 101, 124, 147, 165, 175, 182, 183, 198, 220, 228, 235, 245, 261, 302, 306, 312-314, 329
Music Festival, Rotterdam, 118

Musical Society of Amsterdam, 36
Musical Union, London, 147, 150, 196, 205, 219
Musik Zeitung, 44

Napoleon I, 7, 24, 34
Napoleon III, 221
Napravnik, Edward, 282
Naumann, 58
Nernst, Herr, 27
Nero, A. Rubinstein, 265, 284, 323, 370
Neskuchny Palace, 272
Nevsky Prospekt, 83, 84, 85, 88, 95, 189, 359, 369
New York Oratorio Society, 247
New York *Tribune,* 246
Nibelungen, Wagner, 151
Nicholas, Grand Duke, 140
Nicholas I, Tsar, 3, 7, 23, 25, 36, 53, 55, 57-58, 77, 85-88, 91, 100, 101, 105 *et seq.,* 134, 136, 139, 160, 193, 318, 344, 364
Nicholas II, 361, 364, 368
Nightingale, Florence, 154
Nijinsky, Vaslav, 127
Nissen-Salomon, Madame, 169
Nocturne, N. Rubinstein, 58
Nocturnes, Chopin, 127, 233, 261, 262

Obolensky, Prince Yuri, 192, 197, 198, 200, 273, 319; — family, 312
Obolensky, Princess, 192, 201
Ocean Symphony, A. Rubinstein, 116, 129, 144, 148, 164, 220, 245, 248, 261, 267, 284, 370
Odoevsky, Prince, 29, 97, 192, 197, 198, 209, 216
Offenbach, Jacques, 28, 98, 143
Old Settlers Harmonic Union, Chicago, 231
Olga, Grand Duchess, 57
Olivier, 271
Ondine, A. Rubinstein, 44-45, 132
Onegin, Tchaikovsky, 257, 270
Opéra, Paris, 30, 93
Ormeny, 237
Orphée aux Enfers, Offenbach, 143
Orpheus, Gluck, 272

Paderewski, Ignace, 295

Paganini, Nicolò, 39, 40, 125, 143, 230, 241
Palen, Count, 19
Paradise Lost, A. Rubinstein, 116, 123, 124, 131, 133, 134, 149, 151, 184, 256, 260
Paris Commune, 266
Parsifal, Wagner, 119
Pasdeloup, Jules Étienne, 272
Pasteur, Louis, 221
Pastoral Symphony, Beethoven, 284
Paul, Tsar, 7, 85
Peabody, George, 248
Peter the Great, 161
Peter and Paul Fortress, 47, 83, 253
Peter I, Tsar, 89
Peterhof, 226, 252 *et seq.*, 280, 283, 285, 300, 301 *et seq.*, 320, 321, 328, 349, 361 *et seq.*
Petersburg Conservatory, founded, 168; staff and students, 168-179, 220, 299; Rubinstein resumes directorship, 304-307, 327, 367
Petrashevsky, Michael, 83-84
Petrovsky Palace, 25
Petrovsky Park, 20, 321
Phantasiestücke, Schumann, 338
Piatti, Alfredo, 205, 219
Pirogov, Dr., 154
Pitoyev, Herr, 345-346
Pittman, 323
Pleyel, Camille, 29, 39
Pobyedonostsev, M., 284, 292-294, 308, 319, 343
Pokrovsky Church, 82
Polacca Brillante, Weber, 129
Polonaise in A Flat, Chopin, 131
Popov, Prof., 278
Popper, David, 225
Portraits, A. Rubinstein, 108
Potemkin, Prince, 89
Potin, Dr., 268 *et seq.*
Potocki, Countess, 295
Pouchet, Dr., 221
Poznansky, Sophie, 350
Pozniakov, Madame, 14
Preobrazhensky Guard, 182
Prophète, Meyerbeer, 87
Pruckner, Dionys, 116
Punch Magazine, 280-281, 323
Pushkin, Alexander, 86

Raff, Joseph, 117, 207, 233
Rameau, Jean Philippe, 310
Ravina, 143
Rebesov, 361, 366
Red Cross, Russian, 114, 154
Rembrandt, 328
Remenyi, Eduard, 131
Renan, Ernest, 353
Revolution of 1848, 76-78
Rienzi Overture, Wagner, 235
Rietz, Julius, 148, 219
Rimsky-Korsakov, Nicholas, 182, 186, 299, 304, 312
Ring, The, Wagner, 175
Rode, Jacques, 160
Rodenberg, Jules, 151-152, 161, 218-219, 223, 288
Rondo, Mozart, 261
Rondo Brilliant, Hummel, 48
Rosenberg, Dr., uncle of Barbara Grünberg, 18, 20, 49, 93-94, 96
Rosenthal, Moritz, 108, 355
Rossini, Gioachino, 29, 77, 141-142, 335
Rozhdestvensky Boulevard, 213
Royal Academy of Music, Leipzig, 61
Rubini, Giovanni, 30, 33, 91, 93, 148, 170
Rubinstein, Abraham, 4
Rubinstein, Alexander, son of Anton, 286, 327, 349, 355-356, 361, 363
Rubinstein, Anna, 294, 327, 343, 349, 355-356, 361
Rubinstein, Anton Gregorovitch, birth and baptism, 5-10; childhood in Moscow, 11-24; first concert, 20-23; in Paris with Villoing, 35; first tour, 36-46; alone in Berlin, 60-71; first Petersburg concert, 52-53; second Petersburg concert, 57-59; poverty in Vienna, 71-75; revolution, 76-78; passport trouble, 79-82; Petersburg, 92-100; "Janitor of Music" for Helena Pavlovna, 107-111, 140-142; four-year European tour, 113-135; friendship with Liszt, 31, 71, 115-126; London, 40-44, 146-148, 150-152, 260-262, 280-281, 296-298; Russian Musical Society and Petersburg Conservatory, 141, 159-163, 168, 176-179, 182-188, 304-342; marriage, 207-208; first resignation, 217; European fame, 218-225; Ameri-

can tour, 226-227, 234-250; Peterhof, 251-259, 285-286, 361-365; "hereditary nobleman," 262; *Kalashnikoff*, 267-268, 318-320; Historical Concerts, 285-299; "Excellency," 307; Historical Lectures, 309-317; Jubilee, 321-330; flight to the South, 344-346; playing for charity, 347-351; memoirs, 354; last concerts, 357-358; death, 361-368; — as composer, 17, 44-45, 64, 73, 82, 105 *et seq.*, 129, 131, 133, 149, 224-225, 257-258, 355, 361-363

Rubinstein, Emmanuel, 4-5, 9, 69

Rubinstein, Gregor, 4-10, 11, 14-17, 22-24, 37, 45, 49, 53-54, 55-56, 66-67

Rubinstein, Jacob, 5-11, 15-17, 27, 45, 49, 56, 67, 68, 136, 190

Rubinstein, Jacob, son of Anton, 286, 327, 343, 349, 355-356, 361

Rubinstein, Kaleria Levenstein, 44, 45, 46, 53, 72, 92, 136, 177, 335; baptism, 5-10; removal to Moscow, 11-25; as teacher of Anton, 17-18; as teacher of Nicholas, 47-51; plans for Berlin, 53-56; Petersburg triumph, 57-59; Berlin, 60-67, 369; return to Moscow, 67-69; as governess, 94-95; in Anton's home, 157, 167, 208; teaching, 190; Nicholas' marriage, 191-195; old age, 213-214, 254-255, 262-263, 275, 298, 309-310, 322, 340-341; honored in Jubilee, 329; death, 347-348, 349

Rubinstein, Konstantin, 4

Rubinstein, Lubov (Luba), 11, 15, 45, 49, 54, 55, 67, 136, 356

Rubinstein, Nicholas Gregorovitch (Nicholenka), 25, 45, 94, 154, 158, 167, 328, 329, 336, 348; childhood, 47-51, 54-55; Berlin, 60-67; concert tours, 67-68; youth, 95, 136-137; marriage, 191-195, 263; degree, 193-194; founds Moscow Musical Society, 188, 189-199; founds Moscow Conservatory, 200-216; illness and death, 268-279, 372

Rubinstein, Román, 4-10, 73, 340

Rubinstein, Sophie, 54, 136, 167, 214, 341, 347, 356, 361

Rubinstein Troupe, 237 *et seq.*

Rubinstein, Vera, 207-208, 225, 226, 283, 294, 300, 322-323, 343, 349, 355-356, 361 *et seq.*

Rubinstein, Vera, granddaughter of Anton, 347

Ruins of Athens, Beethoven, 235

Rumiantsov Museum, 209

Russia, A. Rubinstein, 282

Russian Musical Society, 141, 159-164, 175, 179, 180, 187-188, 196-197, 254, 260, 291, 301, 327, 363

Russian Symphony, A. Rubinstein, 267, 282, 295, 325, 329

Sacred Music Society, Chicago, 231

Safonov, Vassily, Director of Moscow Conservatory, 328, 339, 351, 369

Saint Isaac's Cathedral, 252, 256, 363

Saint Nicholas' Church, Berdichev, 3-10

Saint-Saëns, Camille, 143-145, 221, 272, 295, 369

Salamon, Madame, 96

Salle de la Noblesse (Hall of the Nobility), 91, 96, 203, 214, 291, 293, 301, 309, 325 *et seq.*, 330, 357

Salle Erard, 30

Salle Herz, 144, 221

Sand, George, 29

Sarasate, Pablo de, 241, 302

Sauer, Emil, 216

Scarlatti, Domenico, 245, 250, 306

Scheffer, Ary, 29

Schelling, Friedrich von, 60

Schlesinger, Max, 261

Schloss Altenburg, 115 *et seq.*, 134, 149

Schopenhauer, Arthur, 272

Schubert, Carl, 96-97, 171

Schubert, Franz, 44, 71, 165, 215, 232, 312, 316

Schumann, Clara, 32, 132, 147, 240, 245, 261

Schumann, Robert, 44, 61, 97, 132, 223, 228, 232, 235, 245, 261, 292, 312, 316, 322, 323, 336, 338

Scottish Symphony, Mendelssohn, 41

Sendig, Herr, 352-353

Senff, Bartholf, 257, 324

Serenade, Brahms, 220

Serge, Grand Duke, 340

Serov, Alexander, 183-184, 209

Shulgin, Governor-general, 81

Siberian Hunters, The, A. Rubinstein, 109, 128 *et seq.*

Siloti, Alexander, 216
Simonovski Monastery, 14
Sivori, Ernesto, 143, 241
Skobelev, General, 282
Sokolov portrait, 68, 328
Solugub, Count, 97, 100, 105
Sonata Duet, A. Rubinstein, 221
Sonata in B Minor, Chopin, 292
Sonata Opus 106, Beethoven, 261
Sparrow Hills, 11, 14
Spectre de la Rose, Weber, 127
Spirit of the Times, 259
Spohr, Louis, 26, 40-41, 61, 76, 88, 89, 90, 241
Staatsbibliothek, Berlin, 45
Stabat Mater, Rossini, 335
Stanislavsky, Konstantin, 214
Stassov, Dmitri, 159, 257
Steinway Hall, 225, 235, 244
Steinway, William, 126, 226-227, 234 *et seq.*, 252
Stern, Herr, 134
Stone Guest, The, Dargomizhky, 181
Strogonov, Count, 80
Struve, Friedrich, 103
Stube, Julie (Madame Abaza), 157, 251, 253, 302, 325-326, 331
Sue, Eugène, 29
Sulamith, A. Rubinstein, 151-152, 294
Sullivan, Sir Arthur, 297
Sverev, 212, 216, 291
Swiss Concerto, Romberg, 170-171
Symphonic Society, New York, 247

Tajan-Rogét, D., 229
Tamburini, 96
Tamburlick, 96
Taneiev, Serge, 216, 276, 277, 304, 328
Tannhäuser, Wagner, 115, 142
Tausig, Carl, 117, 131, 334, 362
Tchaikovsky, Peter Ilyich, 88, 113, 114, 120, 133, 156, 172-174, 186, 209-211, 212, 213, 215, 216, 257, 266, 270, 273, 275, 277, 279, 285, 288, 294, 318, 325, 327, 328, 329, 349, 356, 364
Tempest, Tchaikovsky, 273
Tepleff, 20
Thalberg, Sigismund, 20, 21, 41 *et seq.*, 143, 227, 235

Third Symphony in A, A. Rubinstein, 164
Thomas, Ambroise, 143
Thomas, Theodore, 116, 231 *et seq.*
Tiflis Conservatory, 299
Tolstoi, Count Leo, 197, 271, 277, 333, 353
Tolstoi, Theophil, 183
Tom the Fool, A. Rubinstein, 109
Tomaschek, Johann, 169
Torch Dance, Meyerbeer, 234
Totleben, General, 187
Touchkov, Governor-General, 192, 198
Tower of Babel, The, A. Rubinstein, 152, 219, 224, 280, 329
Toy Symphony, Haydn, 308
Tremont House, Boston, 237, 370
Tretiakov, Helen, 268, 271 *et seq.*
Trio, Beethoven, 220
Triumphal Overture, A. Rubinstein, 118
Troubetskoy, Princess, 201
Turgenev, Ivan, 88, 272, 273 *et seq.*

Ullmann, 227
Urban, Heinrich, 348

Vaux, Countess de, 29
Valse Caprice, A. Rubinstein, 235, 241, 351
Vek, 167
Verdi, Giuseppe, 334
Viardot-Garcia, Madame, 142, 272, 276
Viazemsky, Prince, 97
Vichvatinetz, 6, 11, 15
Victor Emmanuel, King of Sardinia, 141
Victoria, Queen, 41, 43, 45, 53, 261-262
Vielgorsky, Count Matthew, 159-160, 170-171
Vielgorsky, Count Michael, 80, 97-98, 104, 140-141, 159, 160, 328
Vieuxtemps, Henri, 30, 92, 94, 96, 143
Villa Abigore, 141
Villa Bermin, 141
Villoing, Alexandre, 47, 70, 72, 74, 90, 95, 146, 149, 335, 348; takes Anton as pupil, 18-20; Anton's first concert, 20-22; Paris, 23-35; Grand Tournée, 36-46; Moscow, 51-56, 67; Petersburg: diploma, marriage, authorship, 176-

411

177; death, 263; honored in Jubilee, 329

Vine, The (ballet), A. Rubinstein, 289

Vogler, Abbé, 19

Volkmann, 232

Volkonsky, Prince, 302, 312

Volovski, 230

Vompe, Dr., 296, 323, 361, 365-367

Von Bülow, Hans, 60, 113, 116 *et seq.*, 134, 135, 207-208, 217, 245, 251, 268, 280, 287, 295, 324, 333, 334, 364

Von Meck, Nadejda, 213, 257, 266, 270, 275

Von Oettingen, 159

Von Reutern, 159

Vorontsov-Dashkov, Count, 327

Vosnesensky Prospekt, 92, 95, 98, 107

Wagner, Richard, 78, 114, 115, 119, 120, 132, 142, 147, 151, 152, 175, 224, 235, 251, 280, 293, 334, 359

Walter, Herr, 223

Weber, Carl Maria von, 24, 109, 128-129

Weimar, Duke of, 117

Wieniawski, Henri, 96, 169, 170, 196, 205-207, 218, 227, 234 *et seq.*, 285, 302, 364

Wilhelm II, 348

Wilhelm Meister, Goethe, 225

Winter Palace, 55, 89-90, 159, 363

Witgenstein, Princess, 51, 115, 118-119, 155

Wolff, Hermann, 39, 113, 285 *et seq.*, 291, 294 *et seq.*, 320, 346 *et seq.*, 370, 372

Yankee Doodle Fantasia, A. Rubinstein, 244, 246

Yasnaya Polyana, 277-278

Youssupov, Prince, 282

Zacharin, Dr., 269, 270

Zaremba, Nicholas, 171 *et seq.*, 183, 185, 218, 221, 254, 304, 364

Zimmerman, 28, 30

Zola, Emile, 353

Zukunftmusik, 115, 116, 119, 324

DATE DUE

GAYLORD   PRINTED IN U.S.A.